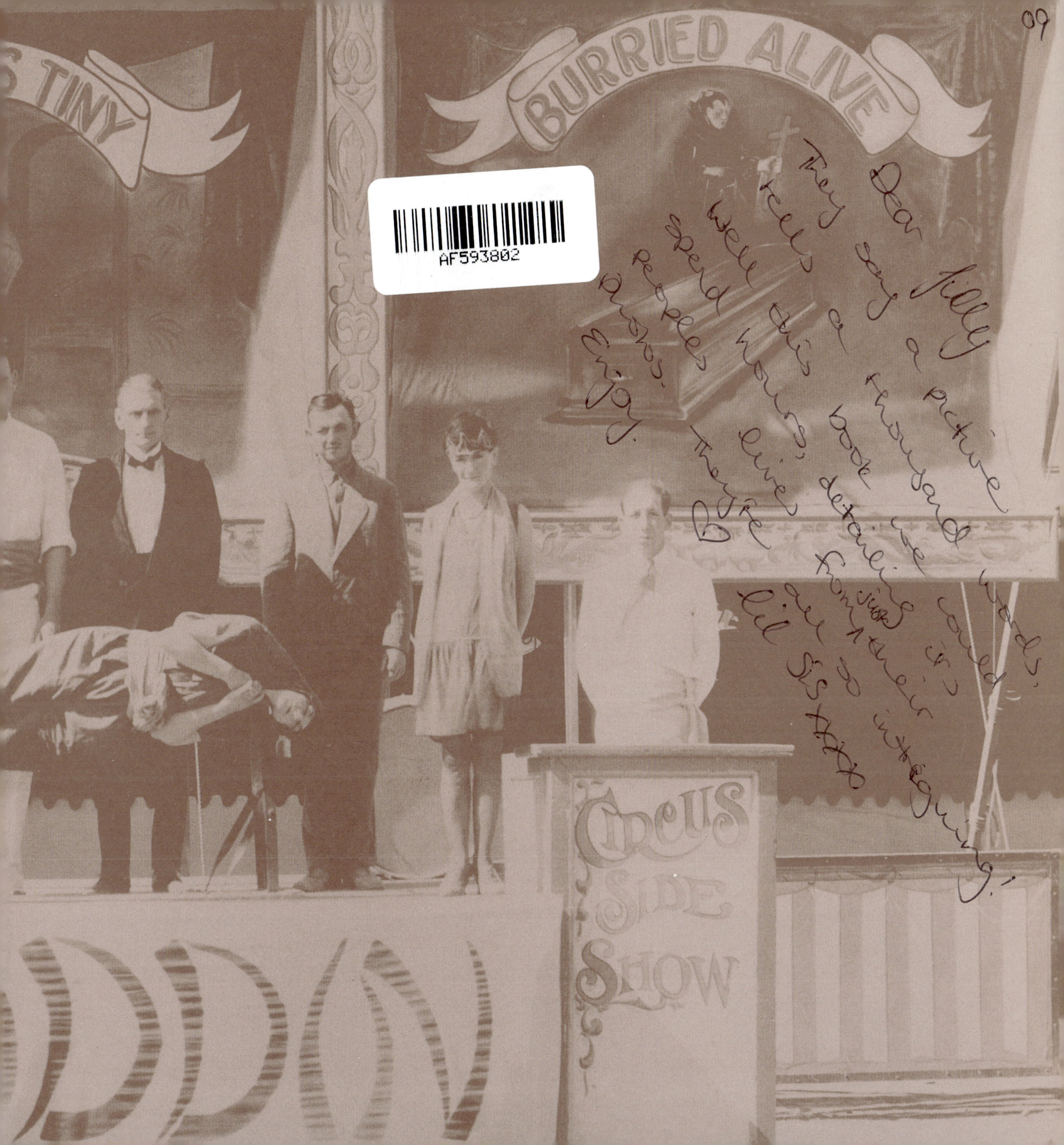
S TINY
BURRIED ALIVE
CIRCUS
SIDE
SHOW

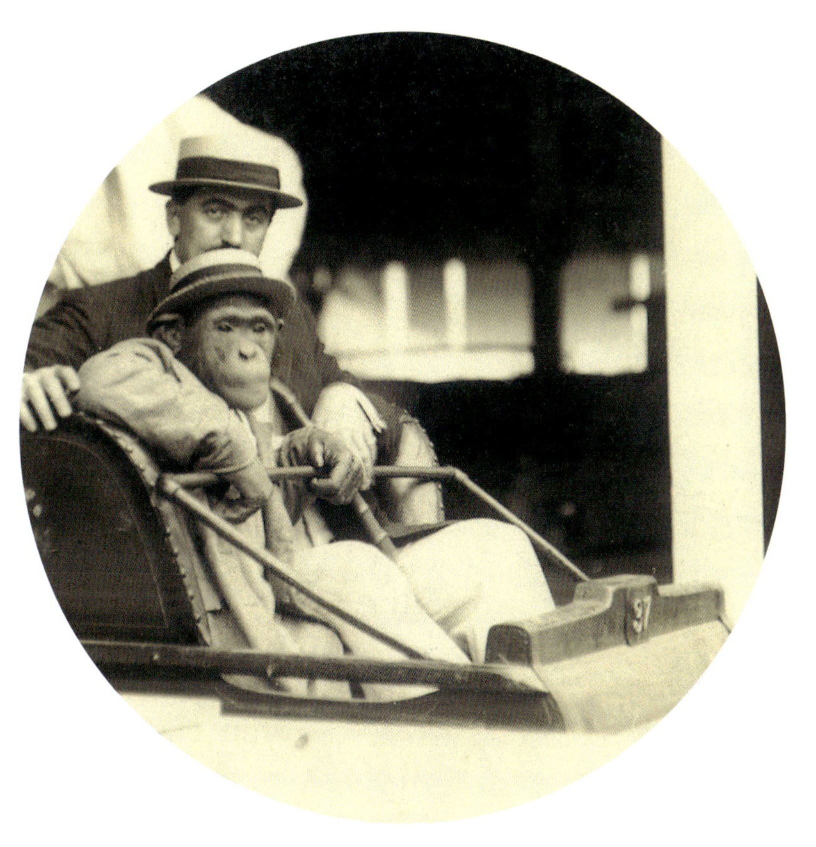

# Being Human

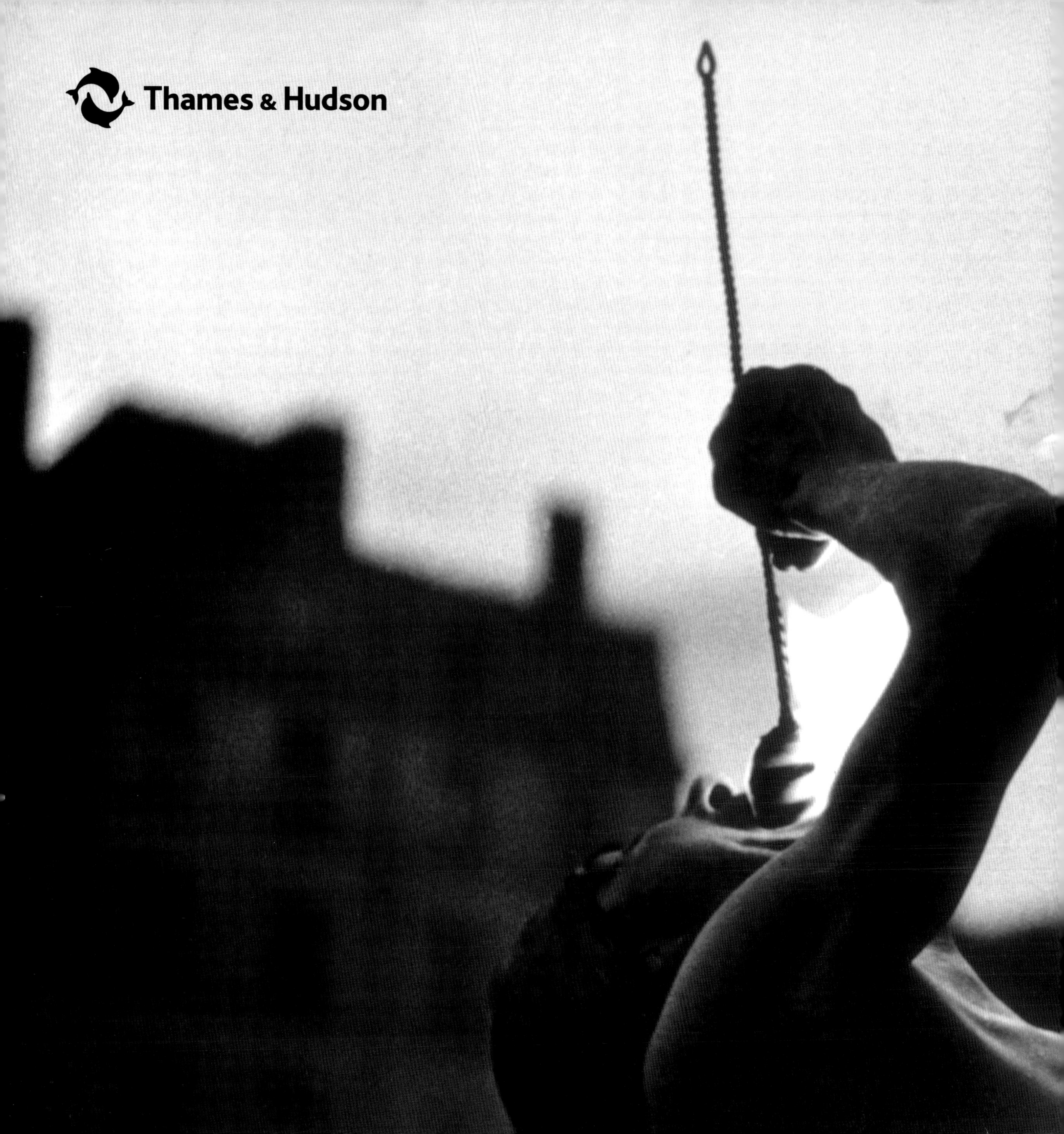
Thames & Hudson

# Being Human

## Enigmatic images of people by unknown photographers

Robert Flynn Johnson
with an introduction by Alexander McCall Smith

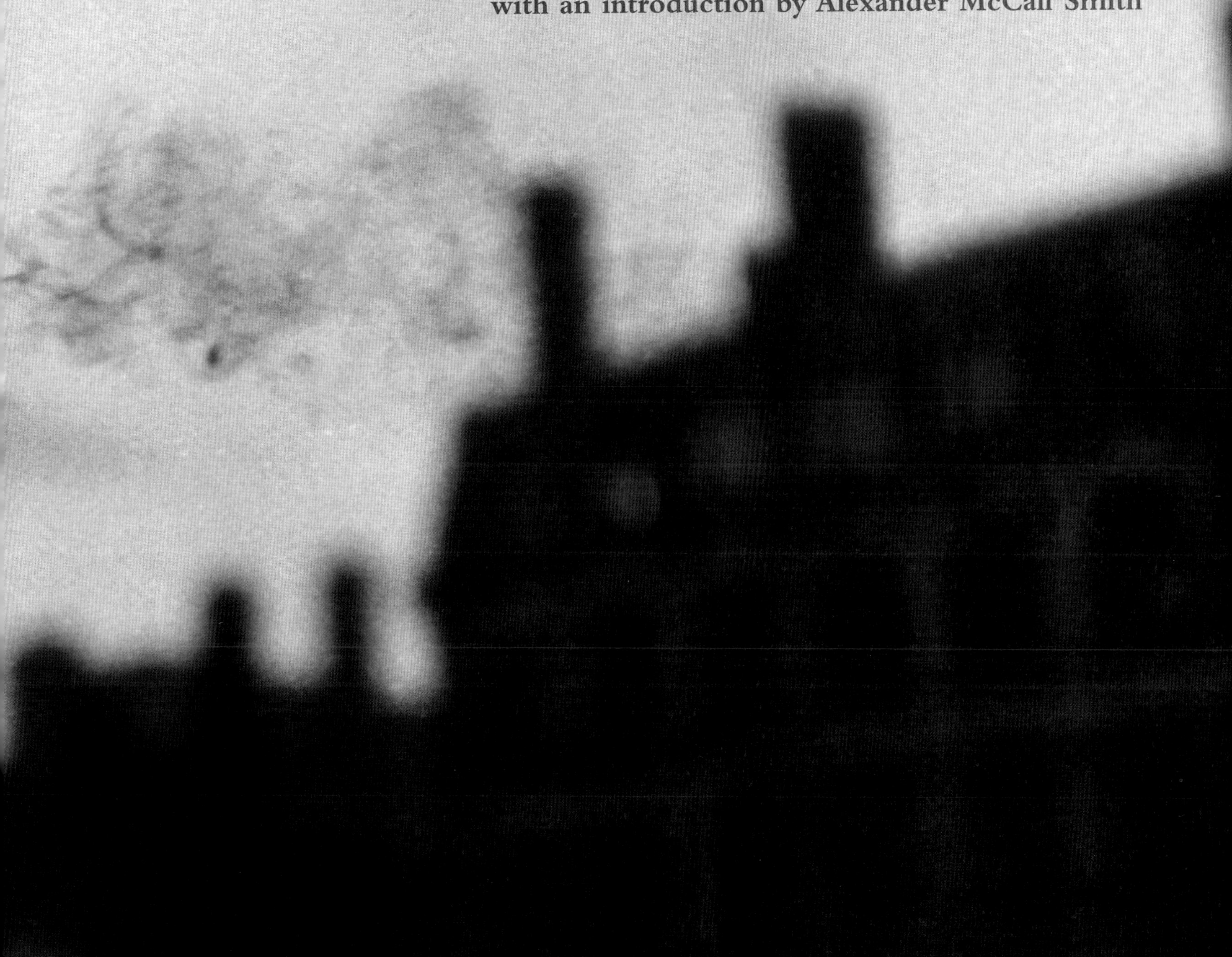

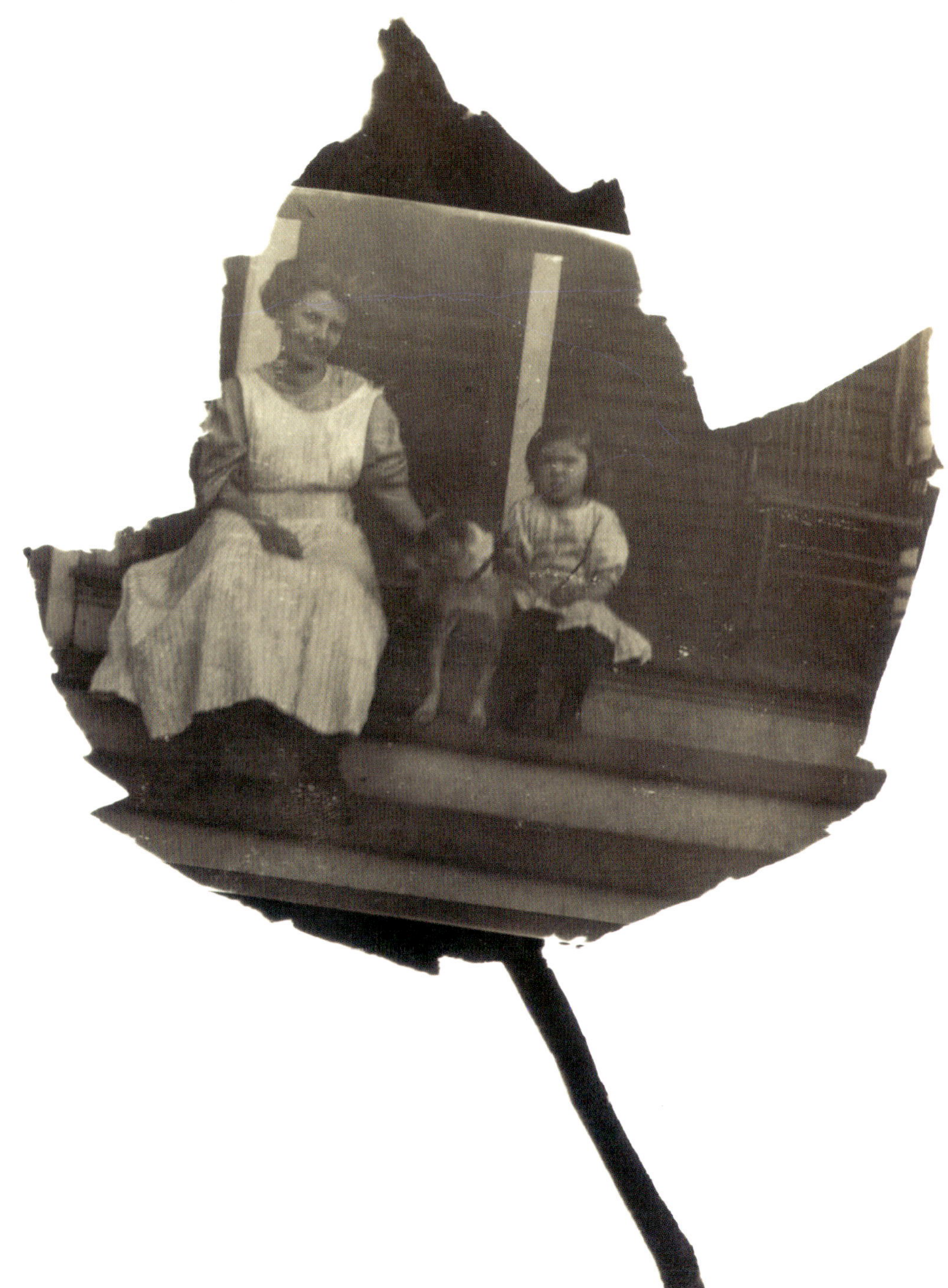

Design by Design Holborn



First published in the United Kingdom in 2009 by
Thames & Hudson Ltd, 181A High Holborn,
London WC1V 7QX

www.thamesandhudson.com



British Library Cataloguing-in-Publication Data
A catalogue record for this book is available from the British Library

ISBN 978-0-500-54372-6 hardback
ISBN 978-0-500-54376-4 hardback (limited edition with unique vintage photograph)

Printed and bound in China by C&C Offset Printing Co. Ltd

# Contents

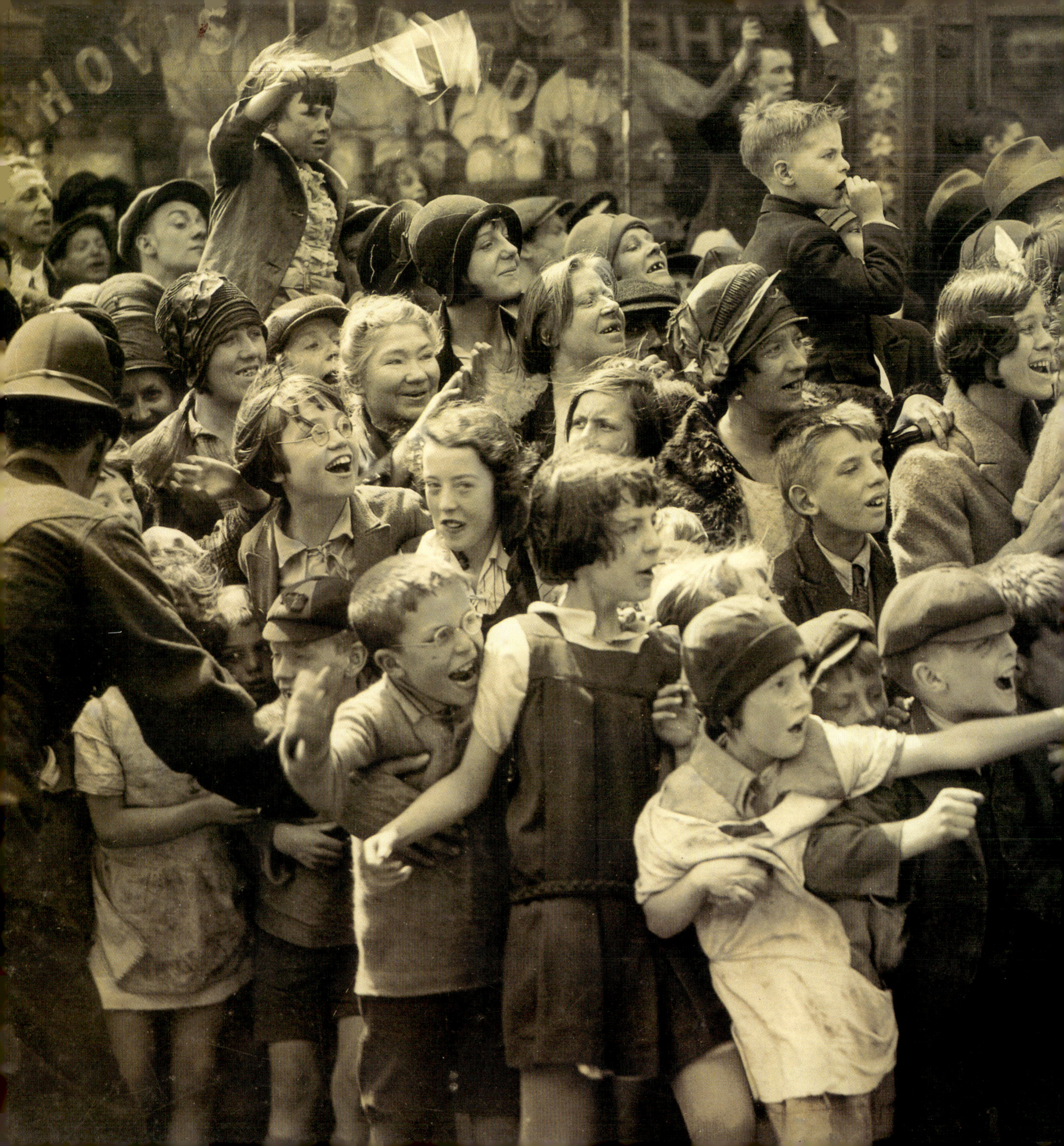

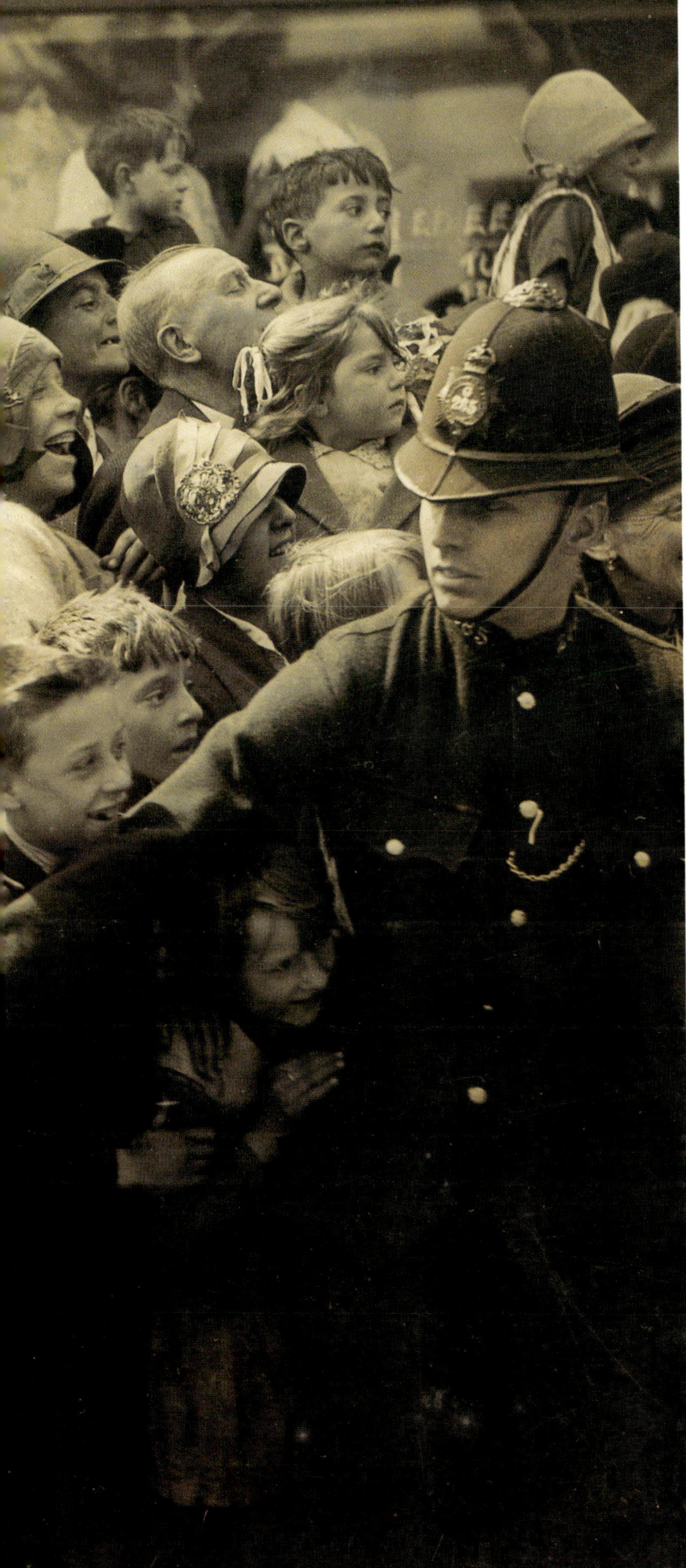

## Being Human
## Alexander McCall Smith

Photographs came in tins when I was a boy – large biscuit tins with sentimental pictures painted on them. There were families, perhaps, who kept their photographs in albums, but ours were kept in these tins, possibly because there were so many of them and they were in such a jumble; all black and white, snapped with simple box cameras, and all revealing a strong belief that the world revolved around one group of four children and their doings. When I look at these photographs now, taken in a world which has all but passed away, I still recognize the places, the incidents, the dogs in the background, the trees we used to climb. That is what family photographs are about: the capturing of intimate memory, the preservation of a sense of who we are and where we come from.

But what about the photographs of others, of people whose identity we do not know? Because we do not know the subjects we are not distracted by memories of the particular, and are drawn, instead, to what the photograph says about people and their ways, about the human condition. It is this that explains the poignancy of old anonymous photographs: they show us in all our human vulnerability. Our aspirations, our beliefs, our sense of ourselves are all revealed – but all of this is shown to be transient, impermanent. One thought that must come to mind here is this: the people in these photographs have probably all gone; an old photograph is a powerful *memento mori*. And another very strong impression is that we know their future. Look at a photograph of J. F. Kennedy starting his ride through Dallas. Look at the photographs of the Tsar enjoying himself on his estates. We now know what lay ahead. And even the crowds of the past have a collective future which we know but which they did not: the excited Londoners seen here, cheering on royalty, had no idea that the Blitz was coming their way.

Of course those are the photographs in which the story is apparent. In most of the photographs in this collection the story is not evident: we know nothing about the people or the context in which the photograph was taken. In these circumstances, the imagination can take over. Let us read something into the photograph; let the photograph be a trigger of a narrative. Here are rich pickings indeed for the novelist, who is susceptible to precisely this form of daydreaming, but we can all do it; we can all make up the story.

Take Helen and Walter McLaughlin, for example (p. 25). This is unusual in this collection because an unknown hand has thoughtfully annotated the photograph, so at least we know who they were and that they were aged six and eight respectively. Their four aunts are shown below, each placed on the leaf of a four-leaf clover. They were showered with love, those children – the apples of the auntly eyes – and their expressions show it. Helen wears a large satin bow which was given her for her sixth birthday by one of the aunts; Walter wears a strange jacket which another aunt copied from a picture of the outfit worn by provincial French *avocats*. He was greatly embarrassed by this present; he would have preferred his aunt to have made him a cowboy outfit or a guardsman's tunic. But he was a loving boy, used to humouring his doting relatives, and you can see this in his expression. His smile is a tolerant, affectionate one. Certainly his two years' advantage over his sister shows; she is impatient, and her smile is somewhat fixed. Trouble lies ahead. 'The aunts,' she later said, 'always preferred you. They did. I saw it.'

Walter McLaughlin was to lead something of a charmed life. How contrasting was the fate of poor young Clayton Brack, pictured with his miniature repeating rifle (p. 27). Clayton's problem was that of having parents with a different vision of how boys should be brought up. The Bracks lived in Fence, a small town in Iowa, a place of wide horizons but limited possibilities. Kathy Brack always longed for something else; she had been born in Fence and married the only boy she ever danced with at high-school dances. She had read of New York and Chicago, but had never been there. But she knew how people in such places lived. She read of towns where men engaged in conversation about the finer things of life; places where men were artistic in their interests, read poetry, enjoyed music. It was quite unlike Fence, where men drove trucks and went duck shooting.

Clayton would not be brought up to be one of those typical Fence boys. No, he was going to be brought up to appreciate those finer things of life, to be sensitive. And so he was dressed appropriately, like the boys in the pictures she had seen of Europe. His father, Tom Brack, did not see things quite that way. 'You're going to spoil that boy, Kathy,' he warned. 'A boy's got to be brought up to like boys' things.' This photograph embodies the clash between the two parental visions. It was taken by Clayton's grandmother, who had placed Clayton in the yard, in his best outfit which his mother had made for him, ready for the camera. 'Something's missing,' shouted Tom, running out to place the right masculine prop in his son's arms.

The photograph on the page opposite this one is unusual in that the subject does not know that she is being photographed: most of the photographs here involve a willing subject and a willing creator. The sleeping subject is a tender one: repose resolves conflicts and tensions. The sleeping figure is vulnerable; innocent, too.

The photographer here was seated on the opposing seat in a railway compartment. The journey had been a long one and unrelieved by conversation. The photographer, a young man in his first year of art college, had at first been puzzled by the woman's curt nod when he made an innocent remark about the weather. She did not want to talk to him, that much was obvious, and he had taken the hint. But then she had taken a magazine out of her bag and had started to read it. By craning his neck slightly, he had seen that the magazine was in some Slavic language, and he had concluded that she could not speak English. So her taciturnity was explained by an inability to sustain a conversation; it was nothing personal to him. He felt relieved.

The journey wore on. It was hot, and she had not drawn the curtain that can be seen immediately behind her head. He wished she had, but he could not ask her now; he felt too shy. And then she fell asleep, her head resting against her arm. He watched now, his artist's eye noting the high cheekbones, the fine line of her nose. He fumbled in his bag and took out his camera. The light on her face was strong; the shadows deep, delineating the jaw, the lower part of the wrist. The light and shadow seemed so charged, so full of possibility; they said so much, without speaking. That is what he

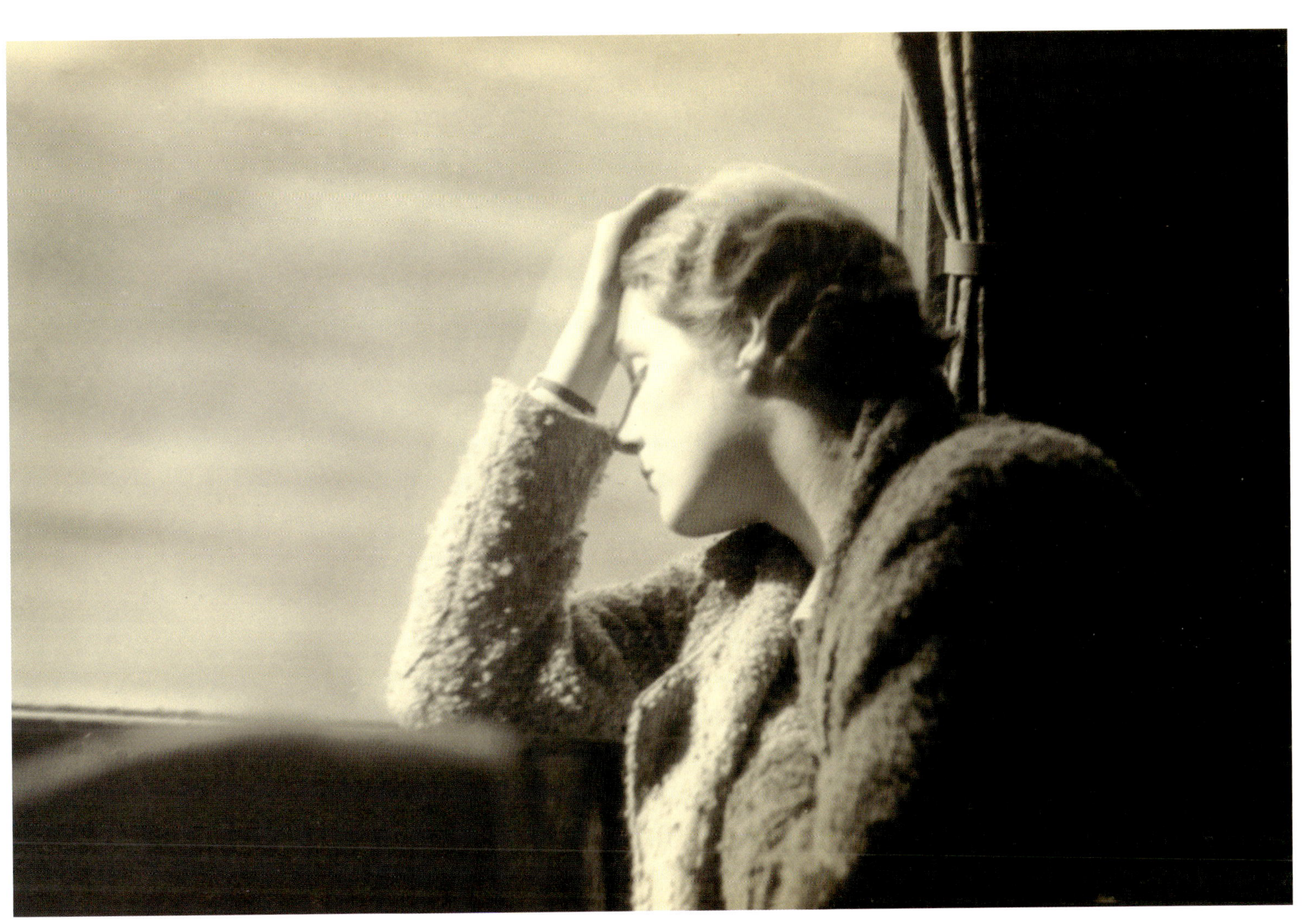

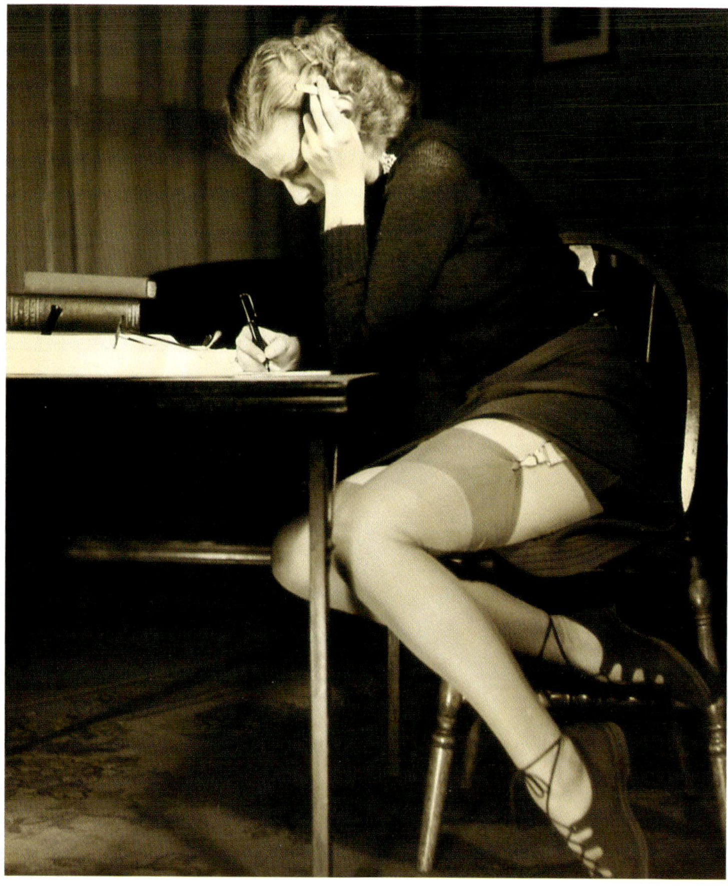

thought about light: that it revealed the *loneliness* of things. He would like to paint that one day; he would like to say something about how we are so lonely in places where we would expect there to be people. Bars at night. Streets. Hotel rooms. A railway carriage like this, with a curtain.

The camera shook in his hands. Would the sound of the shutter wake her, he wondered. And if it did, what should he say? Perhaps he should just be direct and introduce himself, so that he should no longer be an anonymous young man with a camera, caught like some peeping Tom, a voyeur, but a person with a name, Edward Hopper.

Many photographs of people are suggestive of loneliness because they single figures out, detach them. Many of these photographs, however, show people in the process of reaching out to others, hoping to use charms to attract the friend, the lover, that we all need. Mary, the convent educated girl pictured in the photograph on page 81, had been a compliant girl as far as the nuns were concerned. She came from a respectable family, worked hard, and never caused any trouble. There was something about her, though, that made Sister Perpetua worry. 'That girl, I fear for her. I can't put my finger on it. She's a dark horse, I think.' The nun to whom Sister Perpetua addressed this remark did not agree; she had never seen anything to suggest that Mary would be anything but a good Catholic girl who would, in due course, marry some decent boy and raise a fine Catholic family. Had she been in the Underground, though, on the morning of Mary's last day at school, she would have seen what Sister Perpetua meant.

And on the subject of shamelessness, the photograph on this page shows a young woman who was both intelligent enough to secure a place to study law at Cambridge – in days when women law students were a rarity – and at the same time astute enough to realize that her years at Cambridge provided her with the best possible opportunity of meeting an eligible young man. Though not quite as shameless as Mary, supra, Estelle succeeded in irritating and embarrassing the bachelor professors who would come across her at her studies in the law library in such circumstances as to suggest that while the law might be an engaging subject, so was the business of attracting a suitable young man. As it happens, she succeeded in finding a slightly raffish undergraduate to whom she soon became engaged; she never practised law.

People like that go through life without despair: an uncomplicated sex life is a blessing that an earlier age of repression and disapproval must have denied to so many. How many of the people in these photographs must have been disappointed or unfulfilled in that part of their lives. Auden's great poem on Sigmund Freud reminds us of the misery that comes from repression, of the world where 'the injured lead the ugly life of the rejected'; Freud, Auden said, changed all that. But for many in these photographs, the disapproving governess was still there. That was the only photograph that Jim had of himself with his friend (p. 92). He had wanted to face the camera, but his friend had said that was not a good idea; he had a job to keep. There were blackmailers. They could make your life hell, he said. It was easier for women. 'I love two things in this world,' said Eva to her friend (opposite). 'You and trees.'

A single photograph may show very little on the face of it, but can be a complete biography. Thomas Alfred Wilson, pictured here balancing a chair on his chin, led a life in which there were few saliences. He belonged to the generation that did National Service, a period of great boredom for many of those who were obliged to perform it. He was at least lucky in that there were no small wars to which he could be dispatched, but that meant long, tedious stretches in various military camps. The evening hours spent in soulless Nissen huts were relieved in his case by learning the trick of balancing chairs, taught him by a thick-set young man from Northern Ireland, who had been taught it in his turn by a simple uncle. By the time he left the army, Thomas was adept at the trick, which he would perform at the socials that followed sales conferences at the firm for which he worked. He was presented with this framed picture of him performing the trick. What the photograph cannot show is the laughter, the applause. That was like a drug to him.

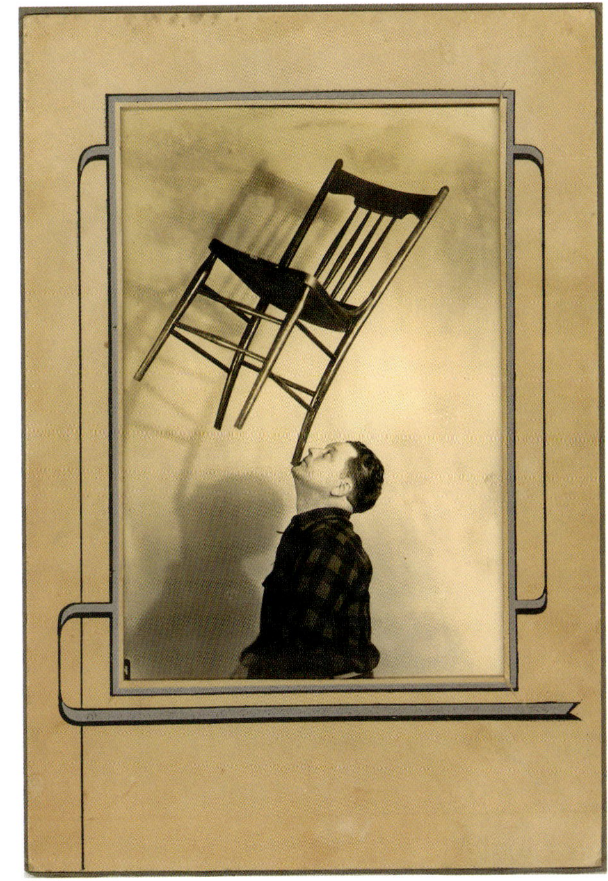

Was it pointless, this balancing of a chair on one's chin? No more, perhaps, than so many other things that we do because we have always done them, or because somebody has told us to do them. Photographs of children doing as they are told say a lot about compliance, and about how children learn to be like us. In the photograph on pages 154–55 the children run round in a ring; one child stands in the centre. The game is simple: the children on the circumference run round clockwise until the marker child – called the leader – has passed the same point ten times. Then the child in the centre calls out *sky about* and direction is reversed, with all the children running the other way, for ten complete turns. The child in the centre is replaced by the child on the right of the leader, and the entire process begins again.

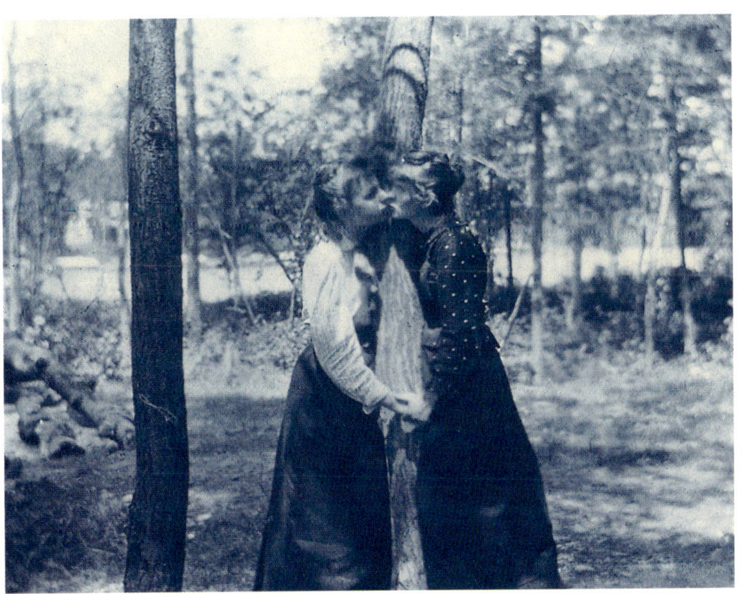

This unusual game was played only in this small Normandy town we see in the photograph. It was invented by the school's head teacher, a man of some eccentric learning, and one with a distaste for disorder and noise. It exhausted all the children who played it, as it could last for forty minutes, or indeed indefinitely. The children would then be quiet during their history lesson, which usually followed the game. We see them in the photograph on page 154, wearing the hat which the same head teacher designed.

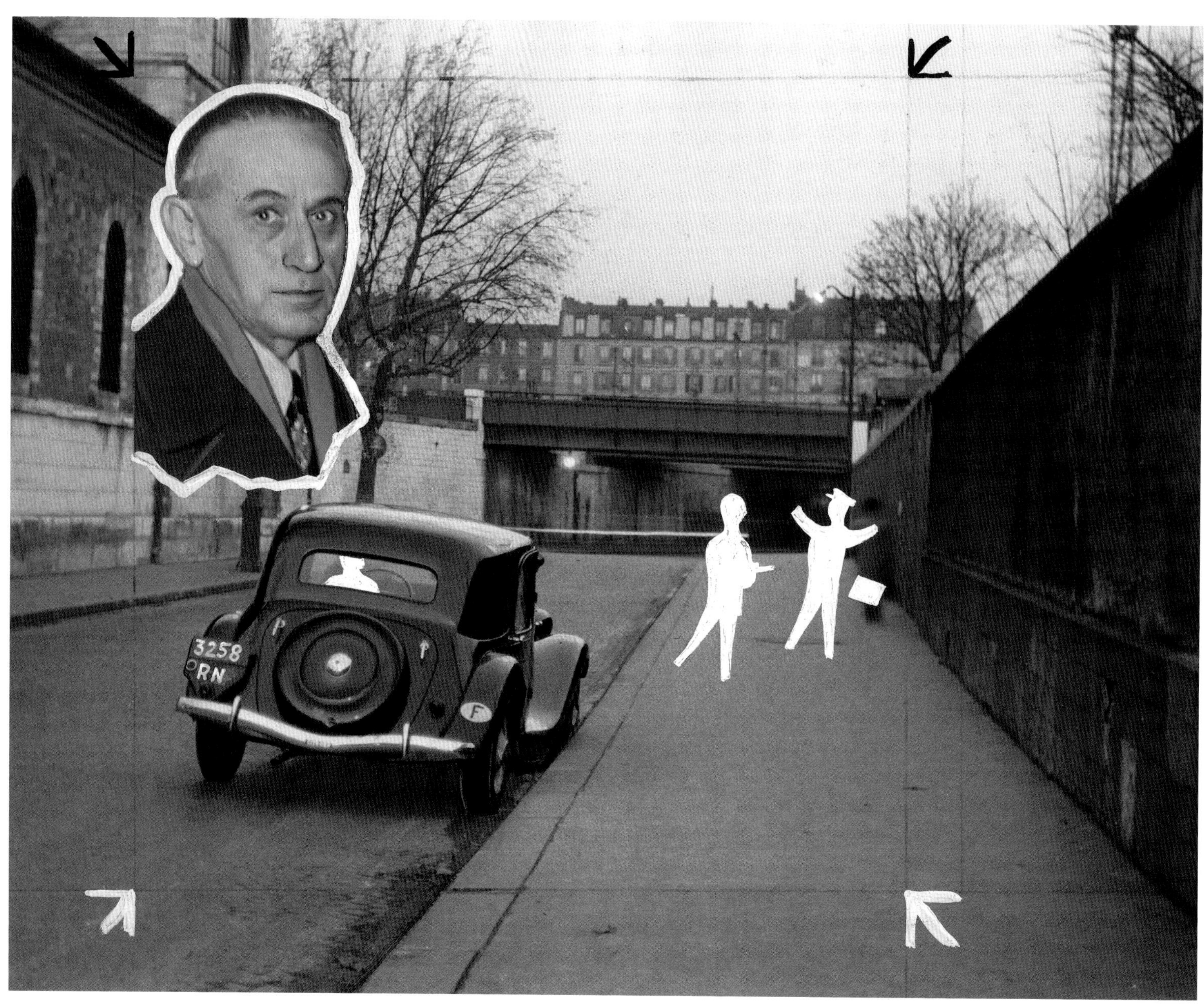
3258
RN

All of these stories are flights of pure fantasy, of course, *jeux d'esprit* which may not be appropriate for some of the photographs here. Being human involves laughter and levity, but also usually includes an element of tragedy. A photograph of misfortune most commonly engages us in thoughts of what it is like to be the *other* there depicted. Photographs of those in captivity can do this quite strikingly. I recall seeing a chilling photograph of a man being led into a prison building in California. The legend on the building said something like 'Death Row' (those were not the exact words, but 'death' was certainly in the title). I thought: two humans, distinguished only by their outer clothing, but so different in their fortunes. Curiously, the prisoner looked unconcerned. Perhaps he had lived on Death Row for years, as happens in such prisons. Perhaps it was an ordinary day for him; he had been taken to the dentist or the doctor. Yet how strange that the State should concern itself with the health of one whom it will later coldly destroy.

That thought arises with the photograph on page 186, where two men are armed and the others have their hands upon their heads. Again there is common humanity, but misfortune is visited on one and not the other: we know who in the picture we would like to be. Of course, in this photograph the caps reveal the rights and wrongs, and yet some of the men with hands on their heads are just boys, and did not ask for any of this. The photograph underneath, of prisoners in old-fashioned prisoners' garb, makes one think of why it is that they are there. What did they do? is the obvious question. But there can be no thought of just retribution when faced with a photograph like this; only sorrow, and pity for people who have been brought to this. It is America, one assumes, and some of them may be serving those absurdly long sentences that are handed down by American courts. Nine hundred and ninety nine years. The man in the white hat, in the centre, weeps; the others seem accustomed to their suffering. But he is innocent.

There is no room for levity when confronted with such images. But fantasy reasserts itself with the photograph opposite, an image used by Scotland Yard in its detection course for new recruits. The scene of the crime is clear, and there is a cut-out picture of the criminal intelligence behind it. Two hoodlums were involved; one drove the car, the other stepped out into a London street and shot the victim. But there is a clue, the noticing of which determined whether or not a would-be detective was successful. There is evidence that these criminals are foreign, but not everyone will spot it.

The book ends with images of the end that awaits us all. Being human involves accepting this end but living our lives as if it is never going to happen. This explains why the medical student in the photograph below was so well-suited for her occupation. She is shown at the Barts medical students' dance with her chosen partner for the evening. 'I've always liked thin men,' she joked to her fellow students – who all thought it highly amusing. She lived a contented life, married a thin man, but not one quite so thin, and died at the age of eighty-seven, after a long career of service to others. She left her own skeleton to the medical school that had given her so much. Which is not an entirely unlikely story.

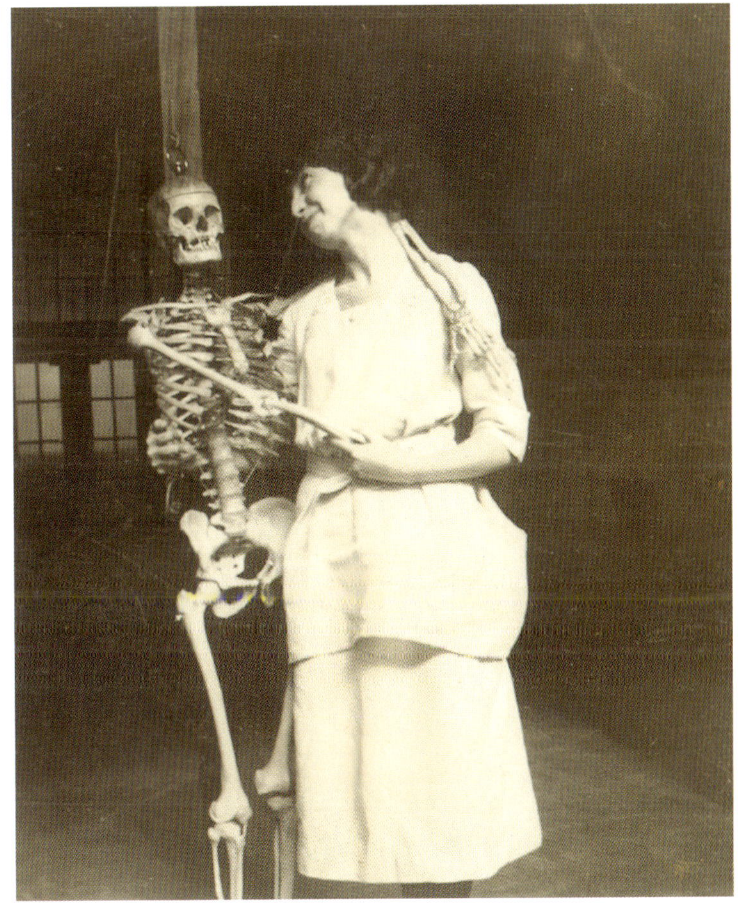

# Whole in One

Robert Flynn Johnson

*'Photographs. Many are overexposed, light-blasted, with a faded quality beyond their age, suggesting things barely glimpsed despite the simple nature of the objects.... There they are. The picture shows no more or less.... Why do these photographs have the power to disturb him, make him sad? Flat, pale, washed in time, suspended outside the particularized gist of this or that era, arguing nothing, clarifying nothing, lonely. Can a photograph be lonely?'*
**Don DeLillo, *Libra*, 1988**[1]

What is it about photography, with its unending flood of imagery flowing past our eyes every day, that makes us immune to truly caring about the nobility, futility or absurdity of our fellow man in pictures? Has our emotional attention span been narrowed to a point of near-extinction? W. H. Auden perceptively wrote, 'The ear tends to be lazy, crave the familiar, and is shocked by the unexpected; the eye, on the other hand, tends to be impatient, craves the novel, and is bored by repetition.'[2] The result is that in our fast-paced existence, simple recognition is mostly all that we have time for. Thoughtful reflection is not a luxury we can afford: only something visually extraordinary will slow down our restless eyes.

There are, of course, rare occasions on which some seemingly innocuous image will suddenly elicit an unexpected and deeply personal response. Like the scent of a food or a perfume that instinctively triggers some fond memory of a long-dead loved one, certain photographs strike deep into our subconscious. Unlike ephemeral sound or smell, those photographs, with their power to induce memory and feeling, are tangible.

By definition, a photograph is a discernible marker of what has been. It becomes part of history the moment it is taken. The world changes and we change, yet photographs remain as static visual clues to the past. The semblance of truth in these images, however, is illusory, especially now in our digital age. What stimulates the imagination is that every photograph contains an interweaving of obvious facts and subtle fictions. A weekend golfer of slight skill places a ball upon the tee of a par-three hole and swings away. Instead of the usual hook that would send the ball wildly off mark, on this particular day its trajectory is unexpectedly high, straight and true, as it softly lands on the green, bounces twice and rolls into the cup ... a hole in one. The same golfer could hit three hundred more tee shots that day and not even reach the green, but for that one improbable shot the aim was perfect.

In most human endeavours, whether athletic, creative or intellectual, high achievement comes only through the gradual accumulation of knowledge and insight that evolves with experience to a point at which an individual is equipped to put those hard-earned skills to work. In the case of photography, however, the mechanics of the camera throw the nature of earned excellence into question. George Bernard Shaw, a somewhat exasperated practitioner of the medium, wrote in 1901, 'The photographer is like the cod, which lays a million eggs in order that one may be hatched.'[3] By simply clicking a shutter, there is always the potential for even a rank amateur lacking imagination, perceptiveness or technical skill to create something magical. Through desire or by accident, an image of heartbreaking sensitivity and stunning visual power can occur ... the photographic equivalent of a hole in one.

Photography as a craft is built on technical expertise and consistency of execution. Photography as an art allows for creative vision and a personal style that makes the resulting photographs identifiable and gives them context within an established corpus of work. Many compelling anonymous photographs come out of this tradition – they are not just the lucky accidents of amateurs – but their lack of identification denies them context. Without a reassuring narrative, these photographic orphans must stand in splendid isolation, ultimately to be evaluated solely on their individual merits.

Photography has always been something of a stepchild in the family of fine art. Unlike the traditional activities of painting,

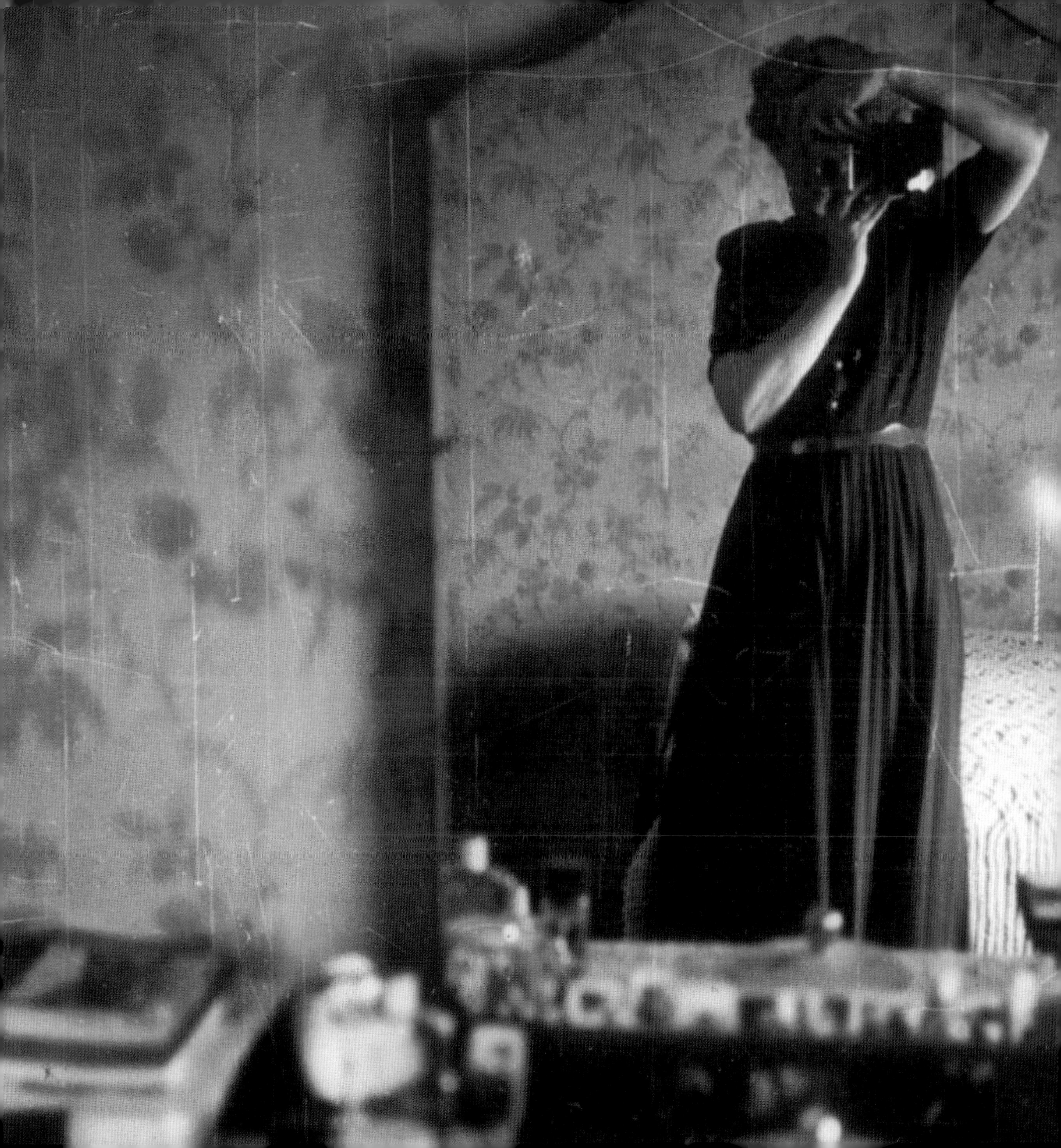

drawing and sculpture, the vast unwieldy body of photography defies easy classification. Since its earliest beginnings, there have been photographers who have sought to use the medium as a vehicle for aesthetic ends. Over the generations, their achievements have answered the question posed in a *Newsweek* cover article of the 1970s: 'Is Photography Really Art?' By the end of the twentieth century, the status of fine art photography as a medium of creativity – exploited by early practitioners from William Henry Fox Talbot and Gustave Le Gray to contemporary masters such as Irving Penn and Lee Friedlander – was indelibly fixed. It is not the established masters that have caused confusion. Like fine artists in other mediums, aesthetic photographers are judged on the merits of their creative output, pure and simple. There is now a vast network of museums, galleries, auction houses, publishers, magazines, curators, scholars and collectors who are deeply involved in the study and advancement of this area of photography.

There is also, however, a small but growing movement within the photographic community that sees photography as a broader, more complex medium, divorced from the fashionable area of the practice emphasizing reputation, influence and commercial success which many photographers have achieved, and still others aspire to. In this movement, the dilemma and delight of photography is in the aesthetic and judicial evaluation of the immense body of non-fine art photography that exists as a decidedly unwelcome guest at the table of art.

Let us be clear, the raw material contained in most photographs is of interest only to specific persons at specific times for specific purposes known only to them. For the rest of us, most of these images are an unending flow of numbing banality. As Jean Cocteau wrote of photography, 'Its cowlike eye stupidly registers everything that our own eye has to correct and distribute according to the needs of the case.'[4] The evaluation of these photographic images must be rigorous because there are no lofty names or reputations to lift the ordinary into the seemingly memorable by power of association. The truth is that the majority of photographs in the world are by unknown practitioners, or ones of such slight reputation as to be of negligible value. The sheer size and randomness of this pool of images, however, invests the individual who has the ability to make sense out of this visual chaos with a greater power of originality and creativity than one who simply reaffirms that which is already established and famous.

The most popular photographic exhibition of all time opened in 1955 at the Museum of Modern Art in New York. *The Family of Man* consisted of 503 photographs selected from over two million images taken by 273 photographers in 68 countries. The accompanying catalogue eventually sold over four million copies. The curator of the exhibition, photographer Edward Steichen, loftily wrote, 'It was conceived as a mirror of the universal elements and emotions in the everydayness of life – as a mirror of the essential oneness of mankind throughout the world.' A number of the photographs included were masterful works by significant artists. In hindsight, however, the whole idea of the exhibition was cynical and inauthentic. As portrayed in *The Family of Man*, mankind consisted exclusively of cute children, handsome men, pretty women and wise elders. It might have been the 'feel-good' exhibition of all time but its concept was emotionally manipulative and patently false.

An unintended form of rebuttal occurred eighteen years later with the 1973 publication of *Wisconsin Death Trip*. Conceived by Michael Lesy, it consisted of straightforward, often grim photographs taken between 1890 and 1910 by Charles Van Schaick, the town photographer of Black River Falls, Wisconsin, paired with news items from the local press of the day recounting crime, suicide and madness amongst the population. As Susan Sontag wrote of this book in her essay 'Melancholy Objects', 'The quotations have nothing to do with the photographs but are correlated with them in an aleatoric intuitive way, as words and sounds by John Cage are matched at the time of performance with the dance movements already choreographed by Merce Cunningham.'[5] The point of Lesy's provocative exercise was to destroy the nostalgic notion that the world was sunnier and people happier in 'the good old days'. *Wisconsin Death Trip* revelled in the assertion that the base and venial nature of man was ever thus. The extreme positions of optimism and pessimism contained in Steichen's and Lesy's two viewpoints are challenging, but serve ultimately as self-fulfilling prophecies.

It is hoped, however, that a more tempered view of mankind will emerge in the photographs contained in this volume. The full range of human states and activities are present, from absurdity to nobility and back again. The vast majority of these guileless photographs were never meant to be seen by anyone beyond the immediate circle of the person taking the picture. Simple documentation of events rather than careful aesthetic composition was the intent. This obvious lack of premeditation heightens the sense of emotional veracity that the photographs evidence.

When the picture on the right was taken is unknown, but the date that it was processed is stamped on the verso: December 5, 1946. It is one of the saddest photographs imaginable of someone assuming a role that they have no enthusiasm for or interest in projecting to the world. The circumstances of the photograph's creation and the identities of the sitter and photographer remain a mystery. It could be speculated, however, that the photographer was the boy's father. The lad, equipped with helmet and shoulder pads, reluctantly clutches a football with both hands in what appears to be the backyard of his home. This image of an introverted youth is as powerful in its display of adolescent melancholy as the 1962 Diane Arbus photograph, *Child with a Toy Hand Grenade in Central Park*, in its recording of manic behaviour.

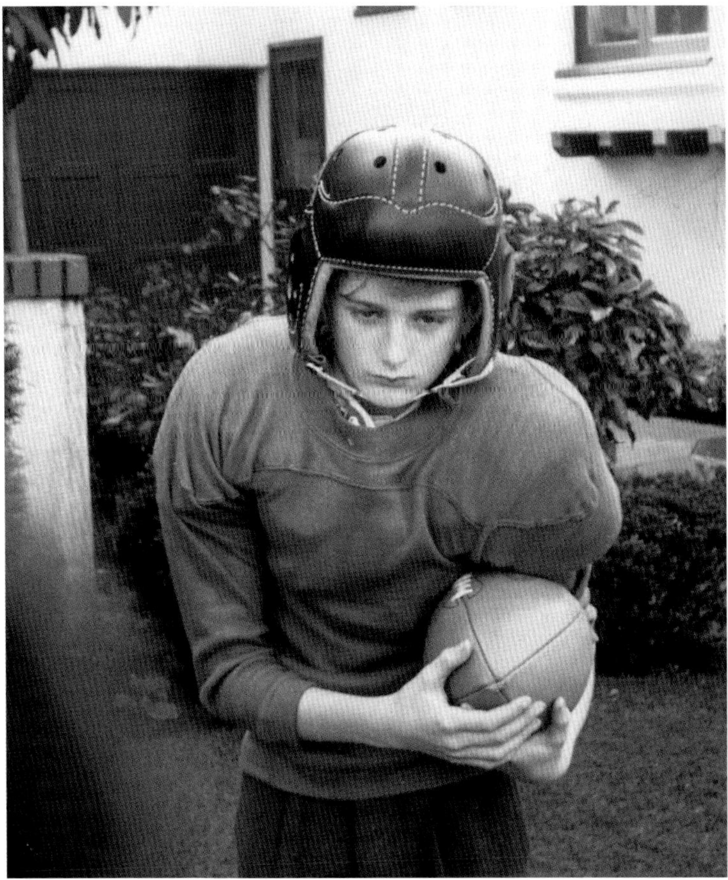

Mary McGrory, the late Washington newspaper columnist, once analogized about America that baseball was what we were and football was what we have become. It appears that this youth was being forced to live out someone else's athletic aspirations. Over sixty years after the photograph was taken, the discomfort in the boy's eyes and his body language is all too apparent, but was it to the person taking the picture? The question that always needs to be asked in confronting a photograph is we may look, but do we really see?

The theatre director Andre Gregory, in the 1981 movie *My Dinner with Andre*, articulated this inability to comprehend when talking about his wife: 'I have this picture of Chicquita that was taken ... I always carry it with me ... it was taken when she was about twenty-six or something, and it's in the summer and she's stretched out on a terrace in a sort of old-fashioned long skirt that is kind of pulled up, and she's slim and sensual and beautiful, and I've always looked at that picture and just thought about just how sexy she looks, and then last year in Israel, I looked at the picture and I realized that that face in the picture was the saddest face in the world, that girl at that time was just lost, so sad and so alone.... You know, I have been carrying this picture for years and not ever really seeing what it is, you know, I just never really looked at the picture.'[6]

The ability to register the facts of a photograph while maintaining an inability to comprehend the impact of what we are seeing is a common occurrence. Intimacy with photographs we know makes us visually lazy. Apathy is our usual response to the familiar.

There is a poignant anonymous photograph of around 1917 that portrays my own mother as a little girl posing with her two brothers and one of her sisters on a veranda in Manchester, New Hampshire. She is the youngest one present, leaning on the hood of a toy car. Because of its beautiful composition and evocation of era, I would have been attracted to this image even if I knew nothing of

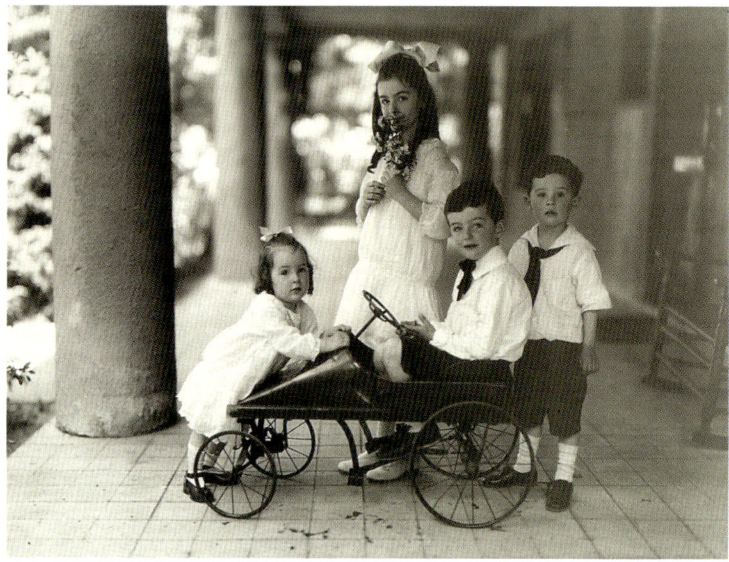

its subjects. The fact, however, is that I do know a great deal about the four people in it and what their futures would be. They are all gone now. Their lives were filled with normalcy punctuated by occasional triumphs and sombre tragedies. The depth of my knowledge of this photograph was also experienced by other people at other times regarding every photograph in this volume until time and fate intervened to separate memory from image. In truth, my mother's photograph is only one accident or act of carelessness or moment of apathy away from joining the ranks of the unknown.

Human beings have always acted in ways noble, normal and notorious. The ability to capture those actions visually has only been possible since Daguerre took the first photograph of a human being in 1839, depicting a man having his shoes shined on the Boulevard du Temple in Paris. We know the people in this volume existed or exist, but except for celebrities we have no knowledge of their backgrounds or fates. For example, was it a midget, a dwarf or even a child that was forced to wear a diminutive penguin suit to advertise Kool cigarettes on a city street sometime in the 1960s? As amusing as the photograph is, one cannot help but wonder what brought the person inside that outfit to the point of such desperation that they would accept such a demeaning occupation.

In the end, these photographs are evidence. They attest to and record aspects of human existence. Mostly they keep their secrets intact, as the majority of us do in our own lives. We will never know the circumstances that came together for three young girls to leap exuberantly into the air and be captured on film in a Japanese photograph of the 1930s. It is also a mystery how over the decades this fragile image travelled thousands of miles to turn up eventually in a pile of photographs in a dealer's stall at an open-air book fair at Place Saint-Sulpice in Paris several years ago.

Mark Twain wrote, 'You can't depend on your eyes if your imagination is out of focus.'[7] The evaluation, study and appreciation of anonymous photographs of human beings is an often intriguing and meaningful activity. The experience enhances both our clarity of vision in seeing others and in knowing ourselves.

1 Don DeLillo, *Libra* (New York: Viking, 1988), pp. 182–83.
2 W. H. Auden, *The Dyer's Hand* (New York: Random House, 1962), foreword.
3 George Bernard Shaw, cited in Helmut Gernsheim, *A Concise History of Photography* (New York: Dover, 1986), p. 186.
4 Jean Cocteau, cited in Ian Crofton, ed., *A Dictionary of Art Quotations* (New York: Schirmer, 1988), pp. 141–42.
5 Susan Sontag, *On Photography* (New York: Farrar, Straus, and Giroux), p. 73.
6 *My Dinner with Andre* (1981), written by Andre Gregory and Wallace Shawn; directed by Louis Malle.
7 Mark Twain, *Mark Twain's Notebook* (New York: Harper & Brothers, 1935), p. 344.

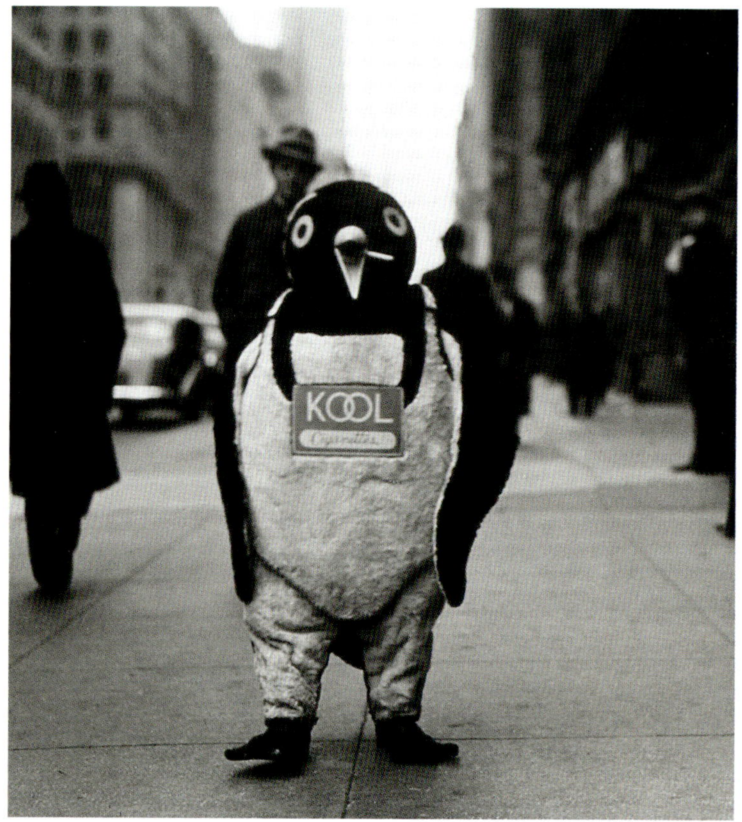

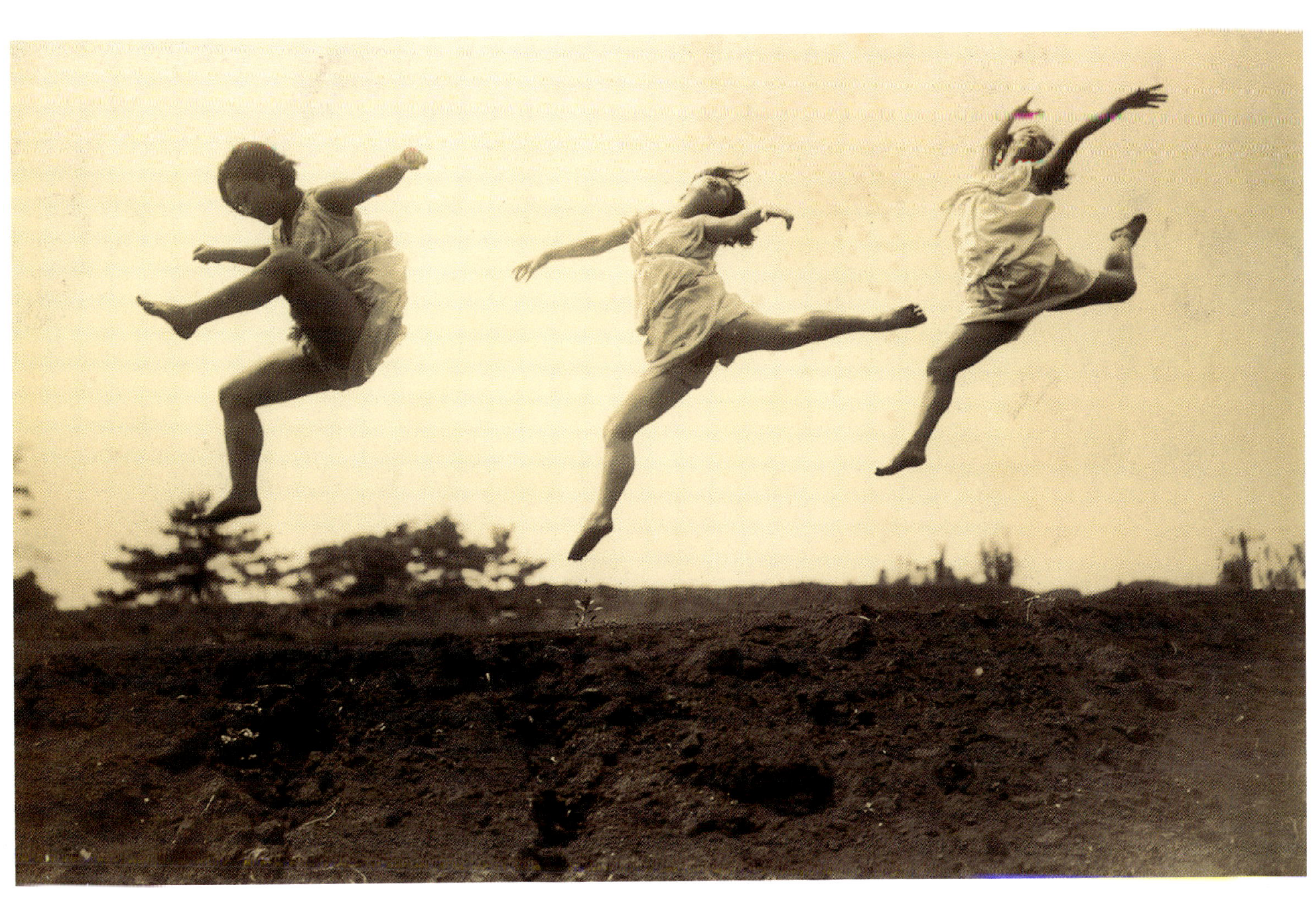

# Immaturity

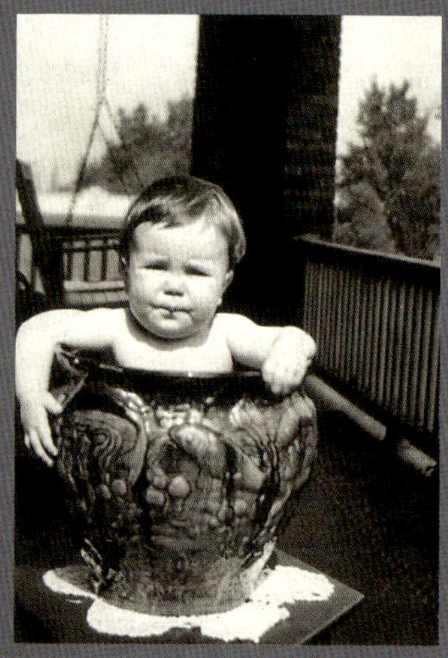

*'Before I got married I had six theories about bringing up children; now I have six children and no theories.'*
John Wilmot,
Earl of Rochester
(1647–1680)

In *On Photography* (1977) Susan Sontag wrote, 'Cameras go with family life. According to a sociological study done in France, most households have a camera, but a household with children is twice as likely to have at least one camera as a household in which there are no children. Not to take pictures of one's children, particularly when they are small, is a sign of parental indifference....' Despite this, photographs of infants tend to look somewhat generalized: aspects of individuality have not yet had a chance to emerge. Yet there do exist photographs in which children, through facial attitude and body language, can appear startlingly defined, displaying young personalities.

By the beginning of the twentieth century, low-cost cameras were in principle available to children to photograph each other, but there is the distinct sense that an adult – usually a parent or a relative – is the invisible presence pressing the shutter. Although children, by nature, are creatures of near-constant activity, the majority of the photographs taken of them are static and posed. Often the child is dressed in their Sunday best – to be worn only on special occasions, or to be buried in if some childhood disease has proved fatal. The unseen photographer becomes the director of a photographic drama, with the child assuming the uneasy role of actor. This is especially apparent in formal photography of earlier eras.

Inexpensive cameras and film later created a hobby mentality, with the result that the sheer number of photographs taken of children constitutes an indiscriminate visual chronicle. The appearance of a camera was so common as to elicit childhood indifference. On occasion, however, images of surprising candour appear out of this activity of obligatory documentation.

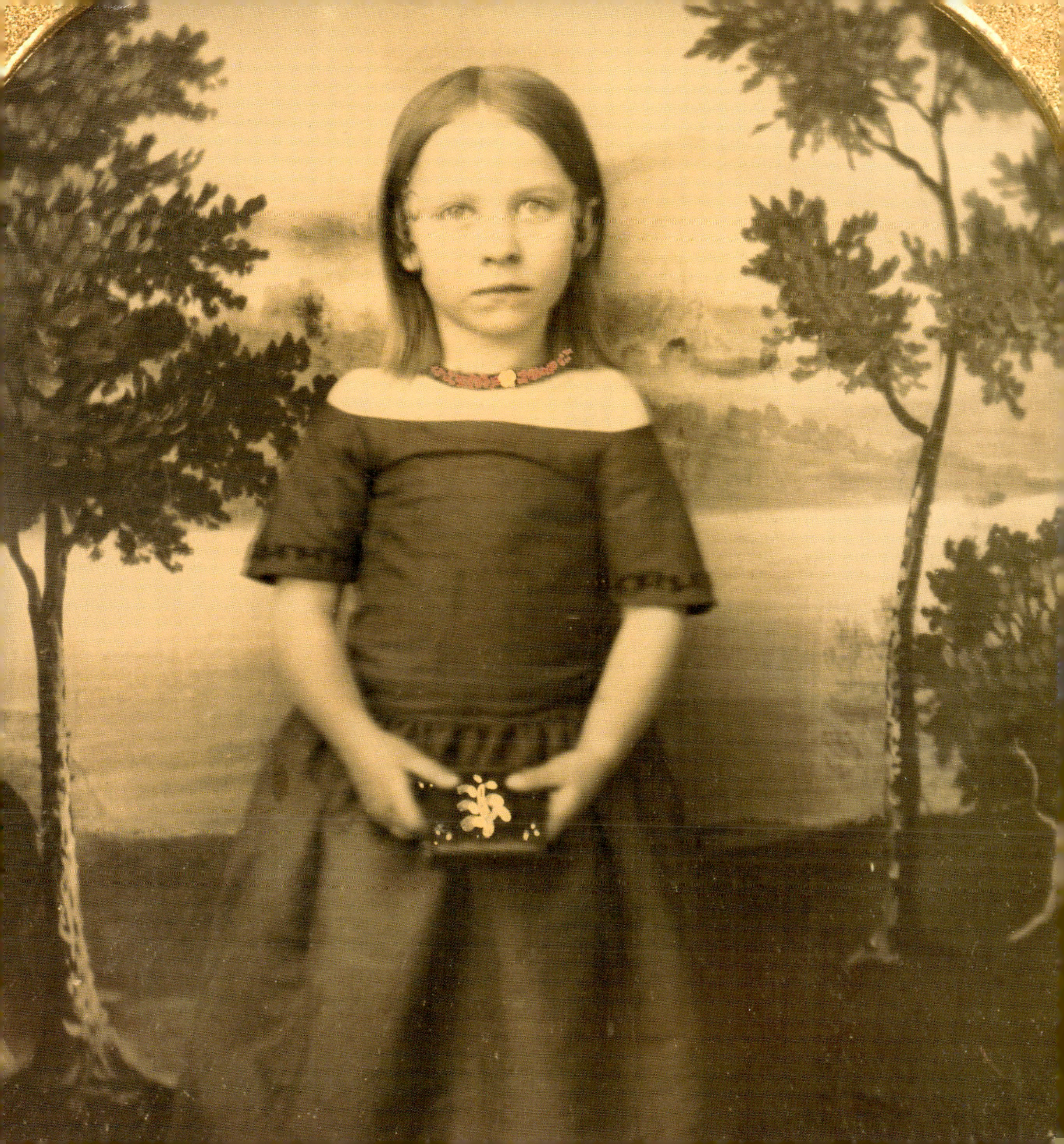

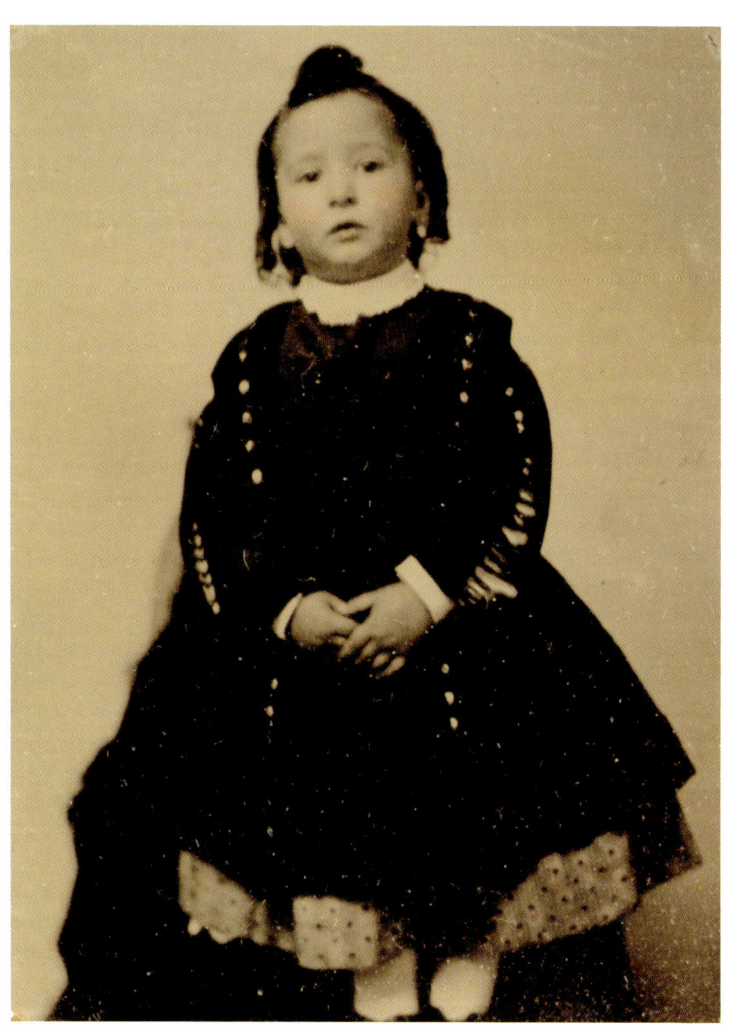

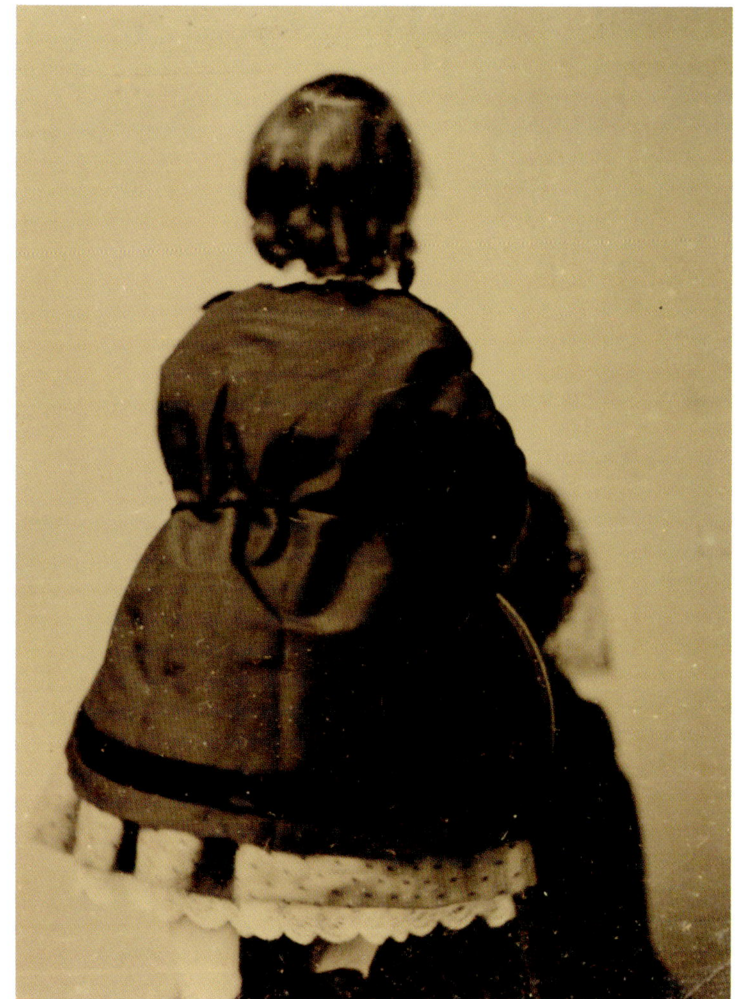

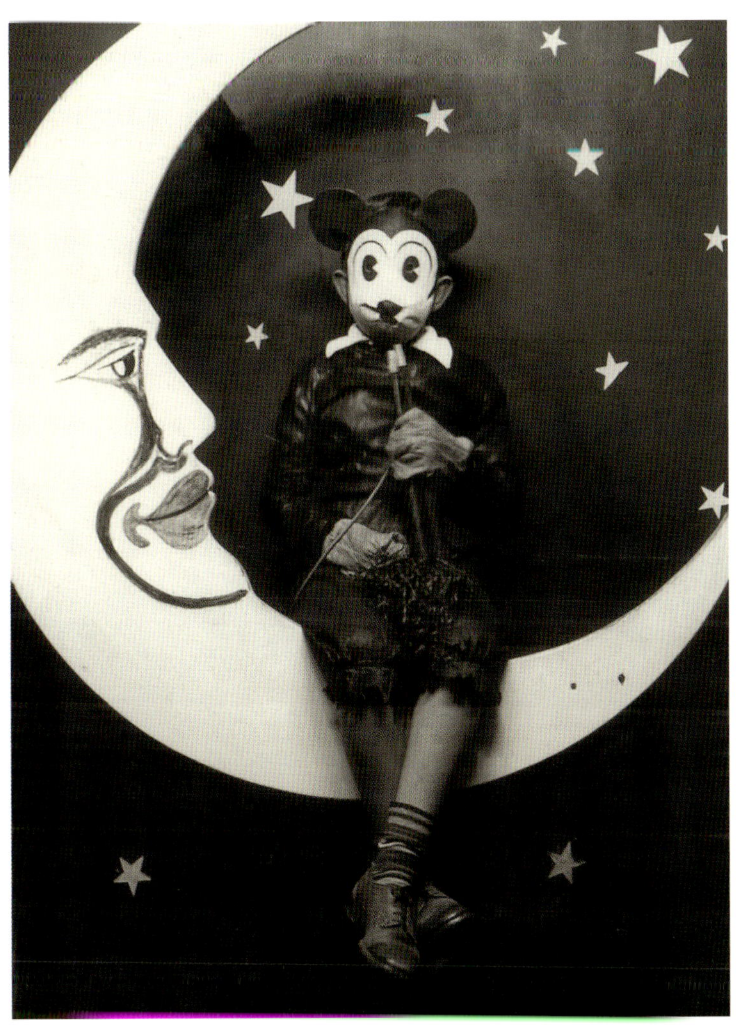

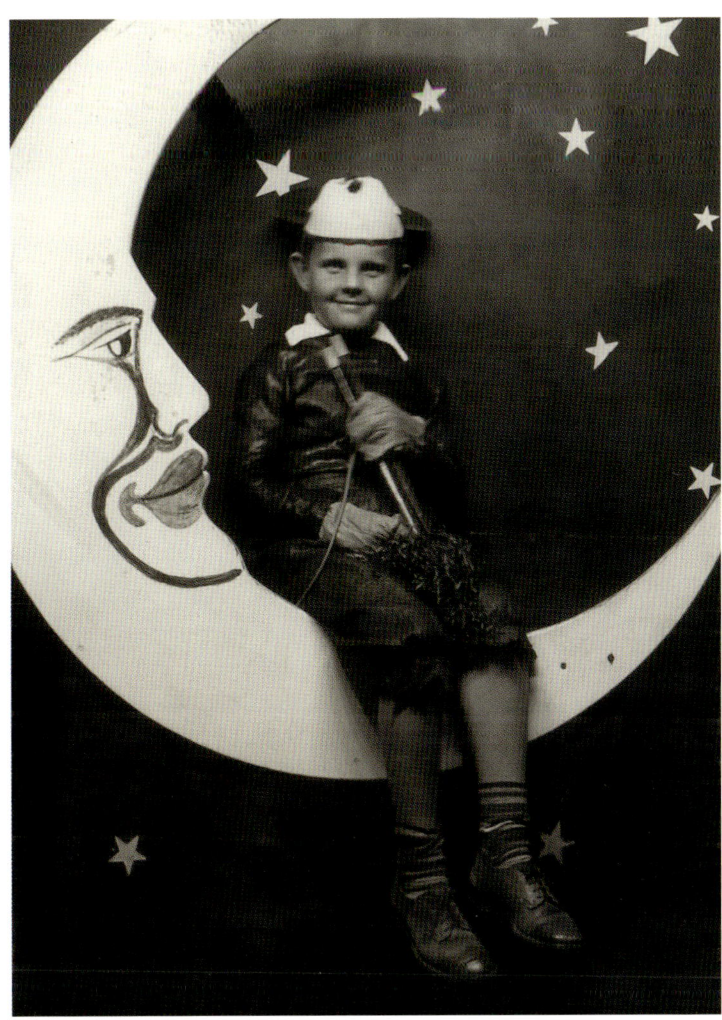

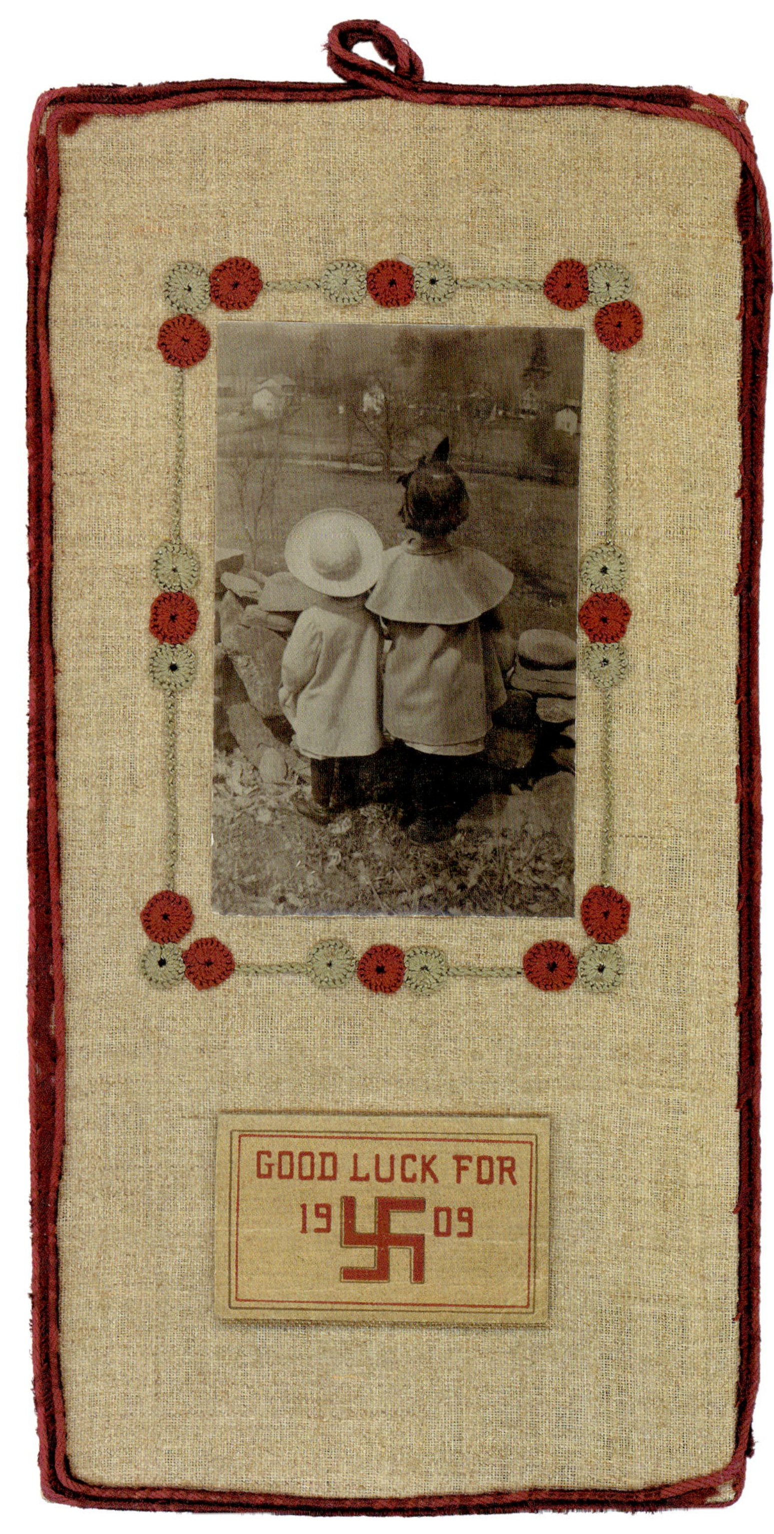
GOOD LUCK FOR
19 09

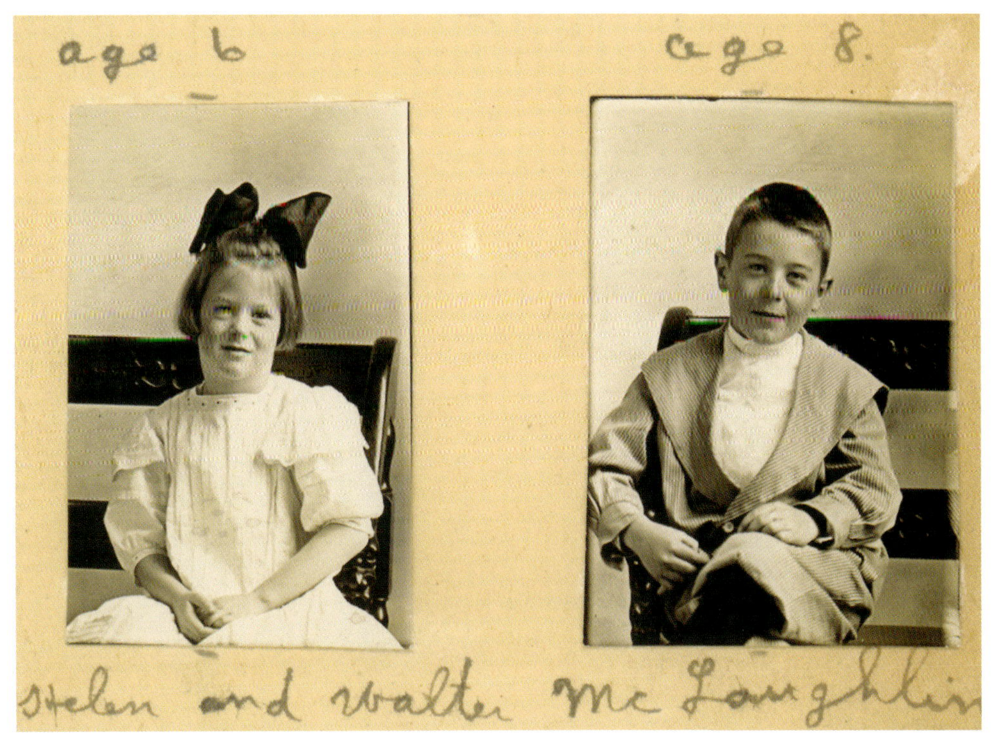
age 6
age 8.
Helen and Walter McLaughlin

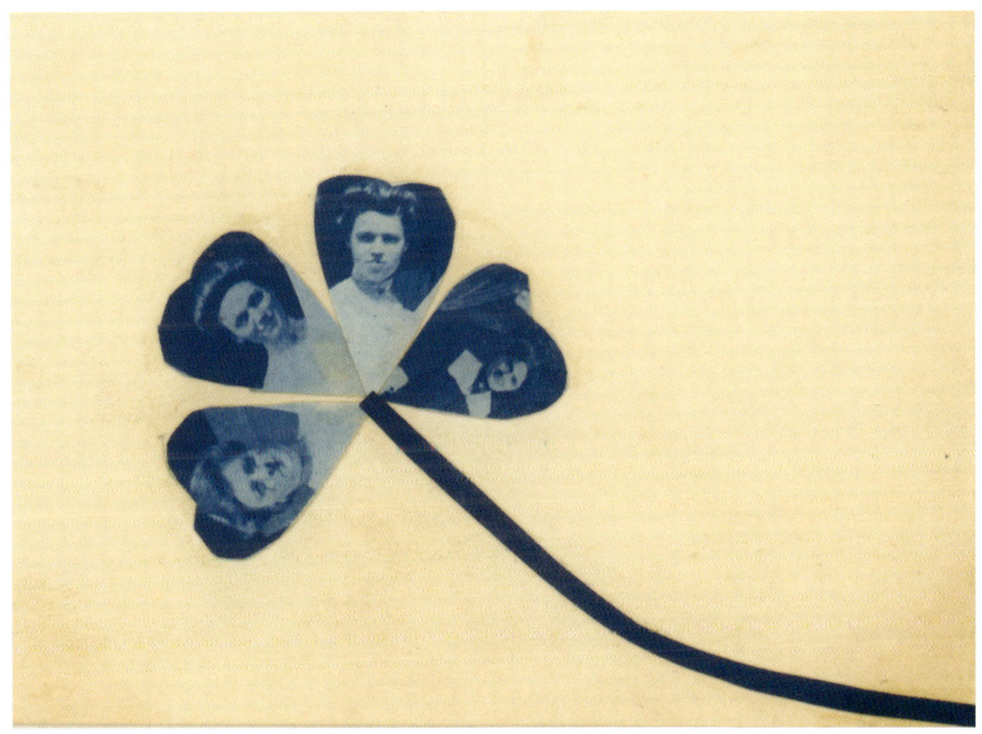

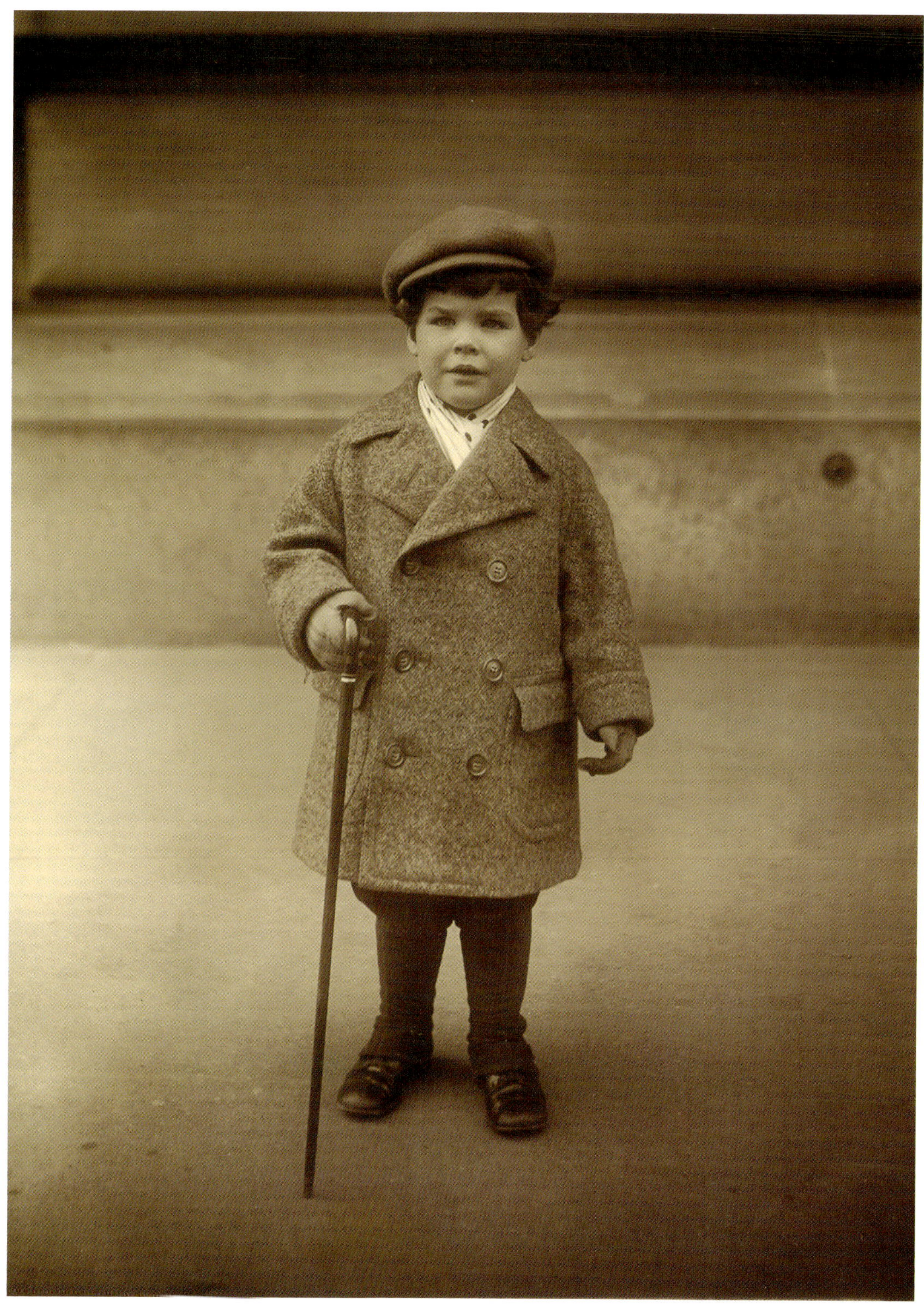

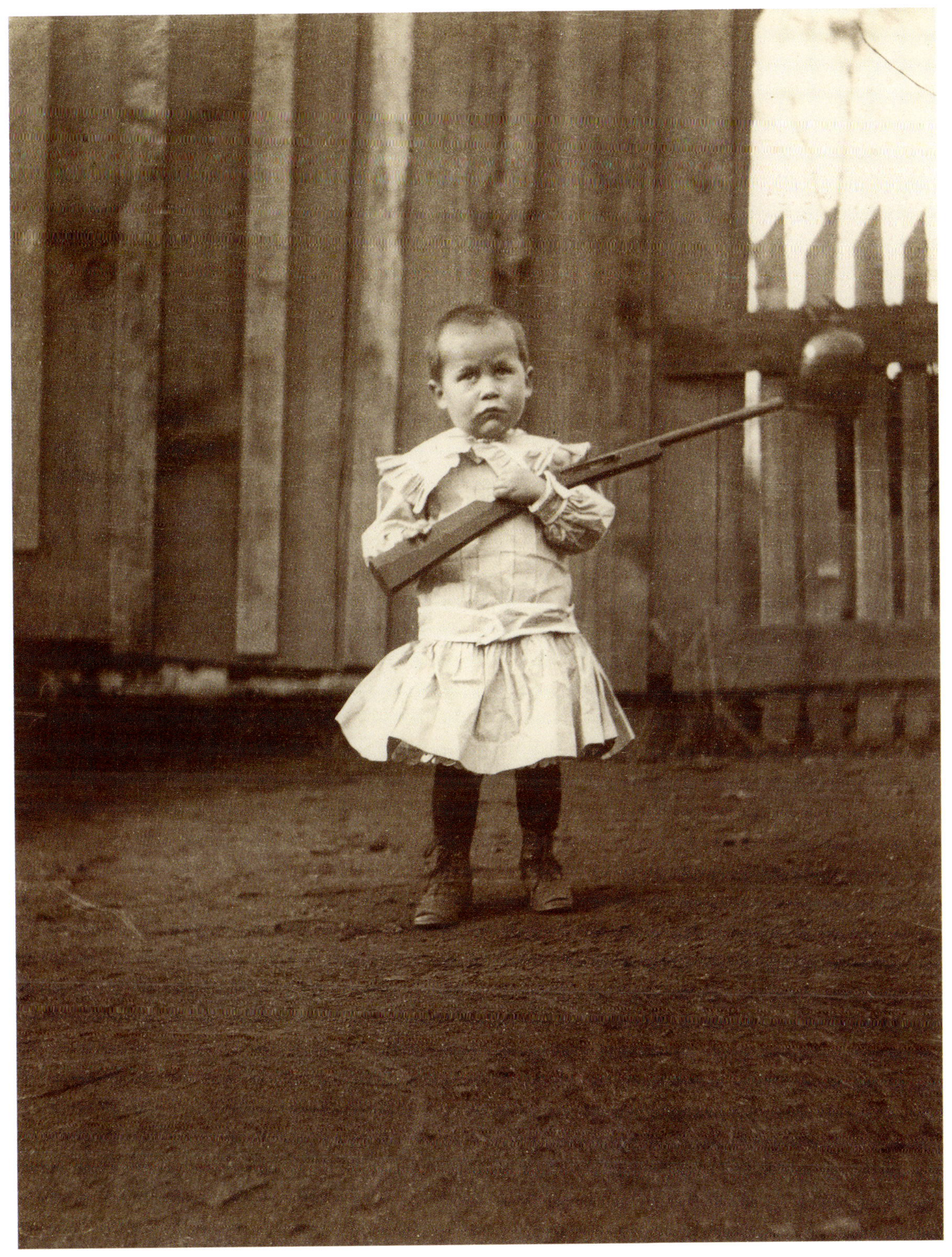

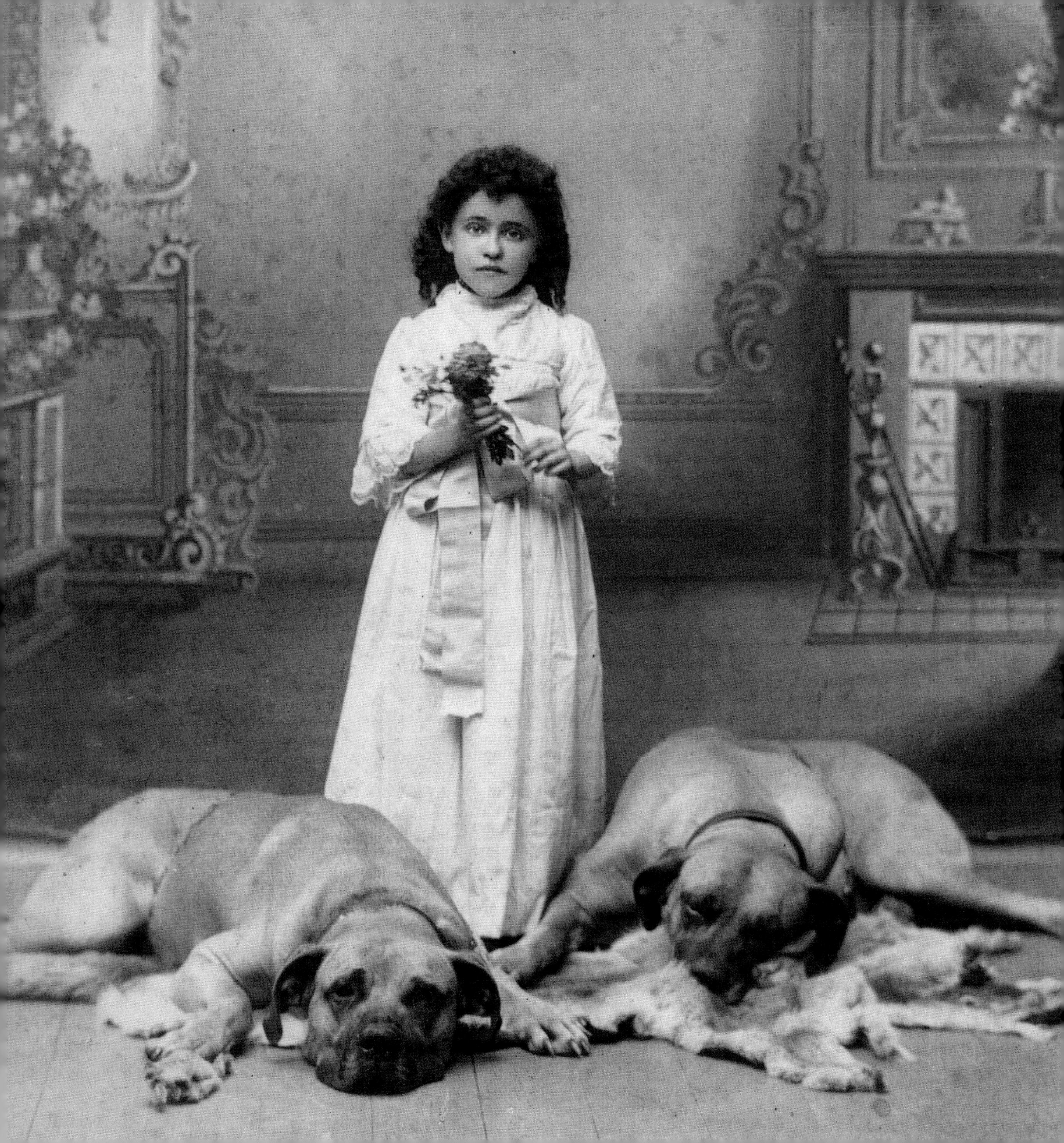

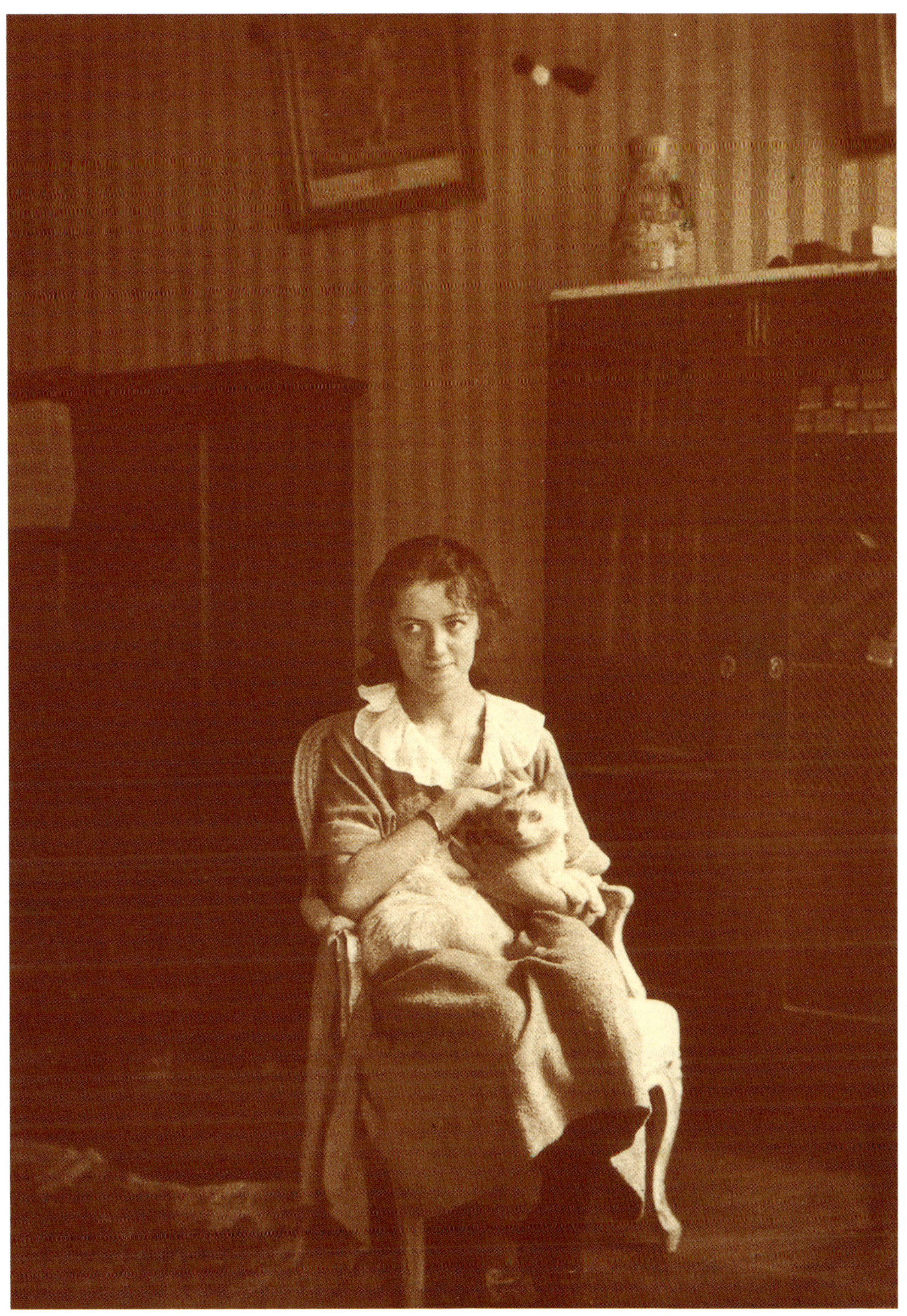

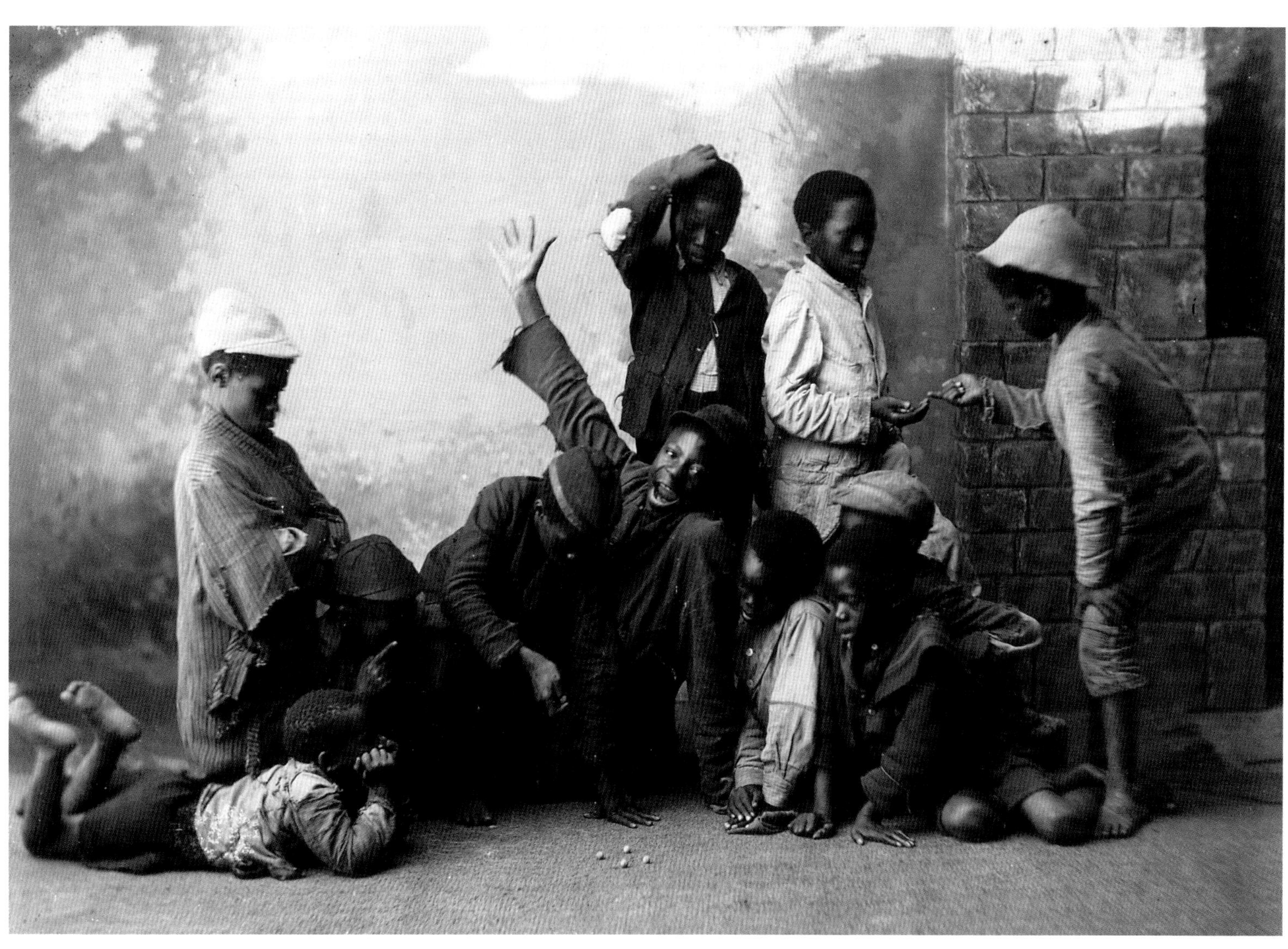

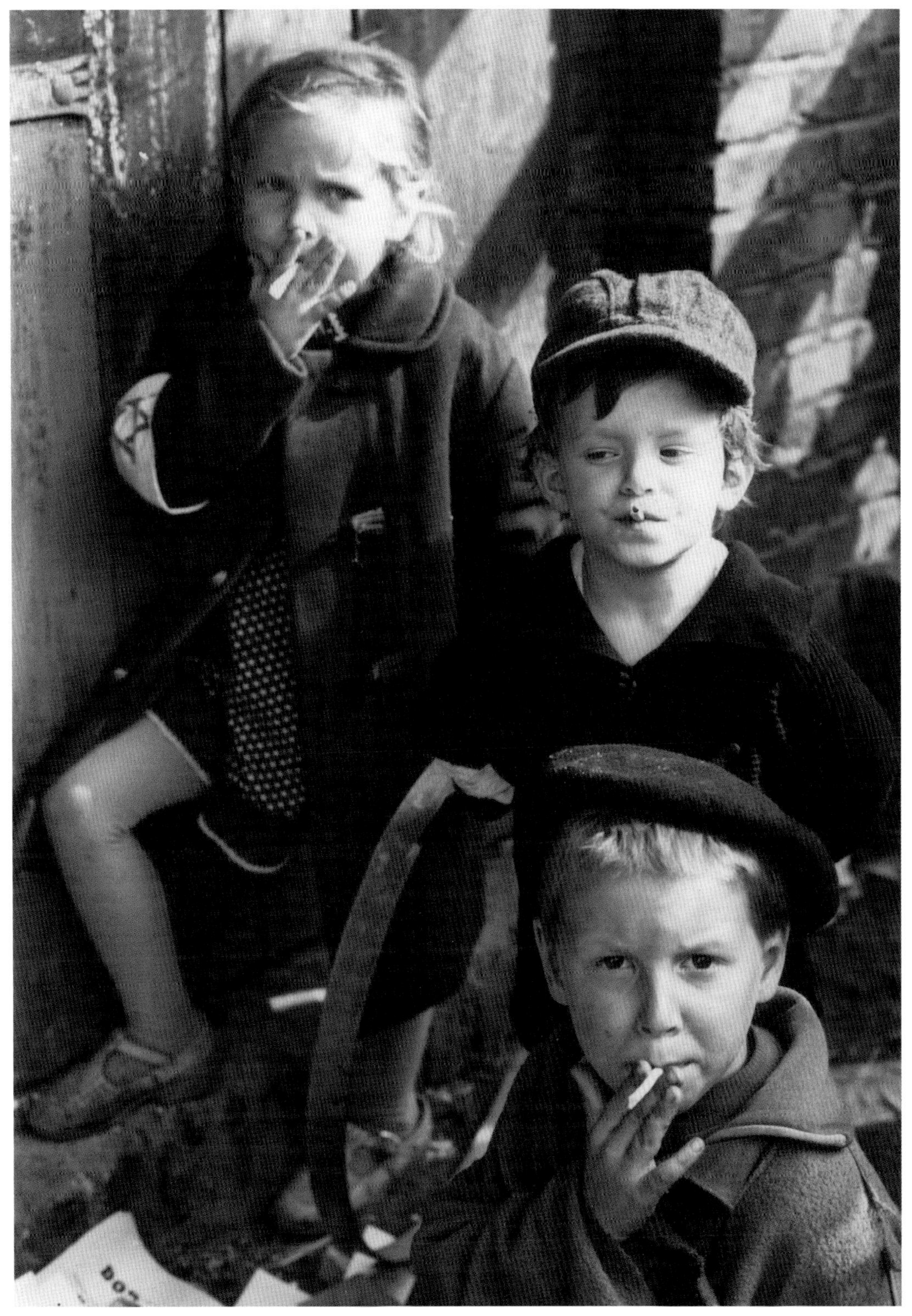

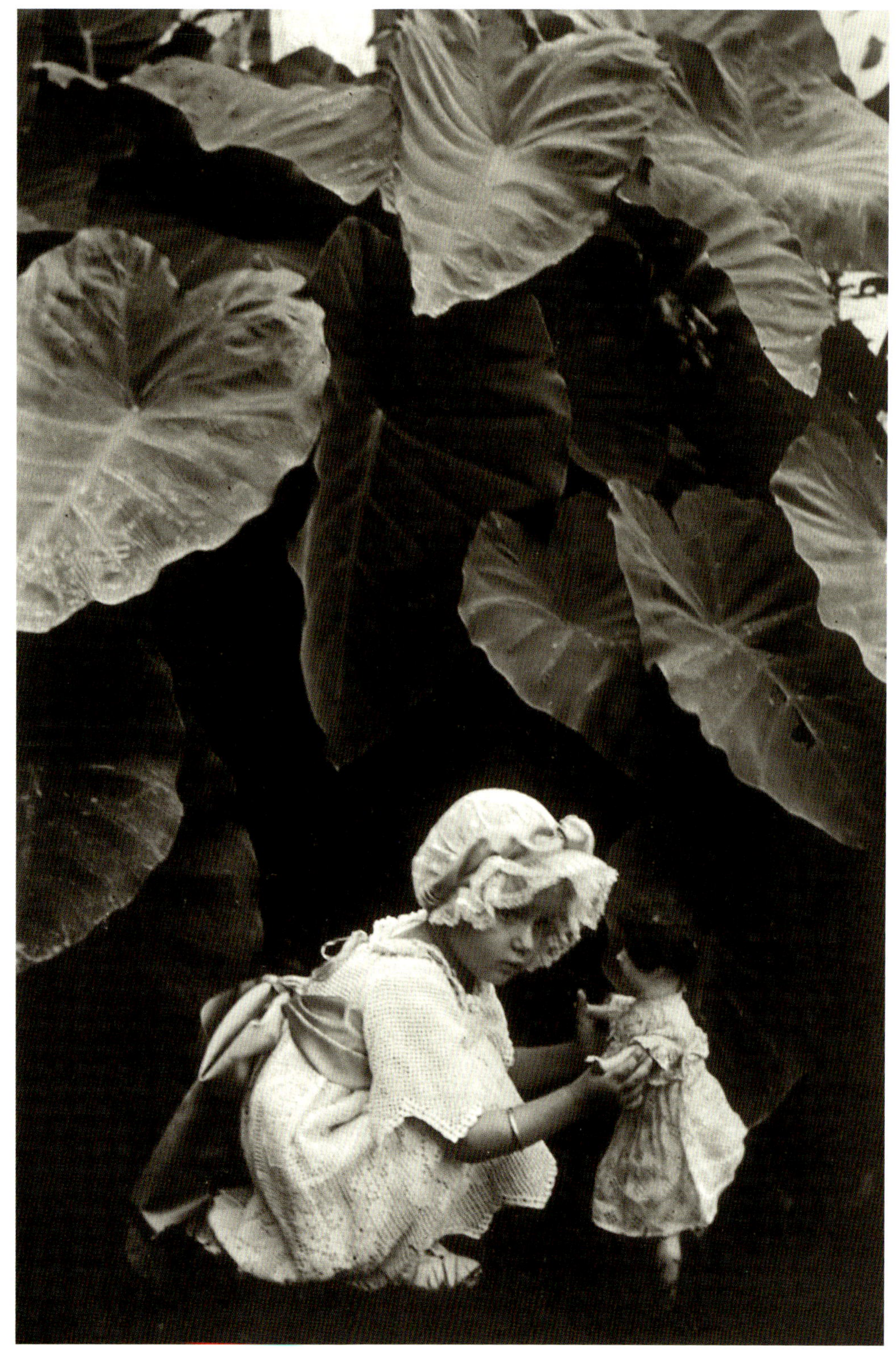

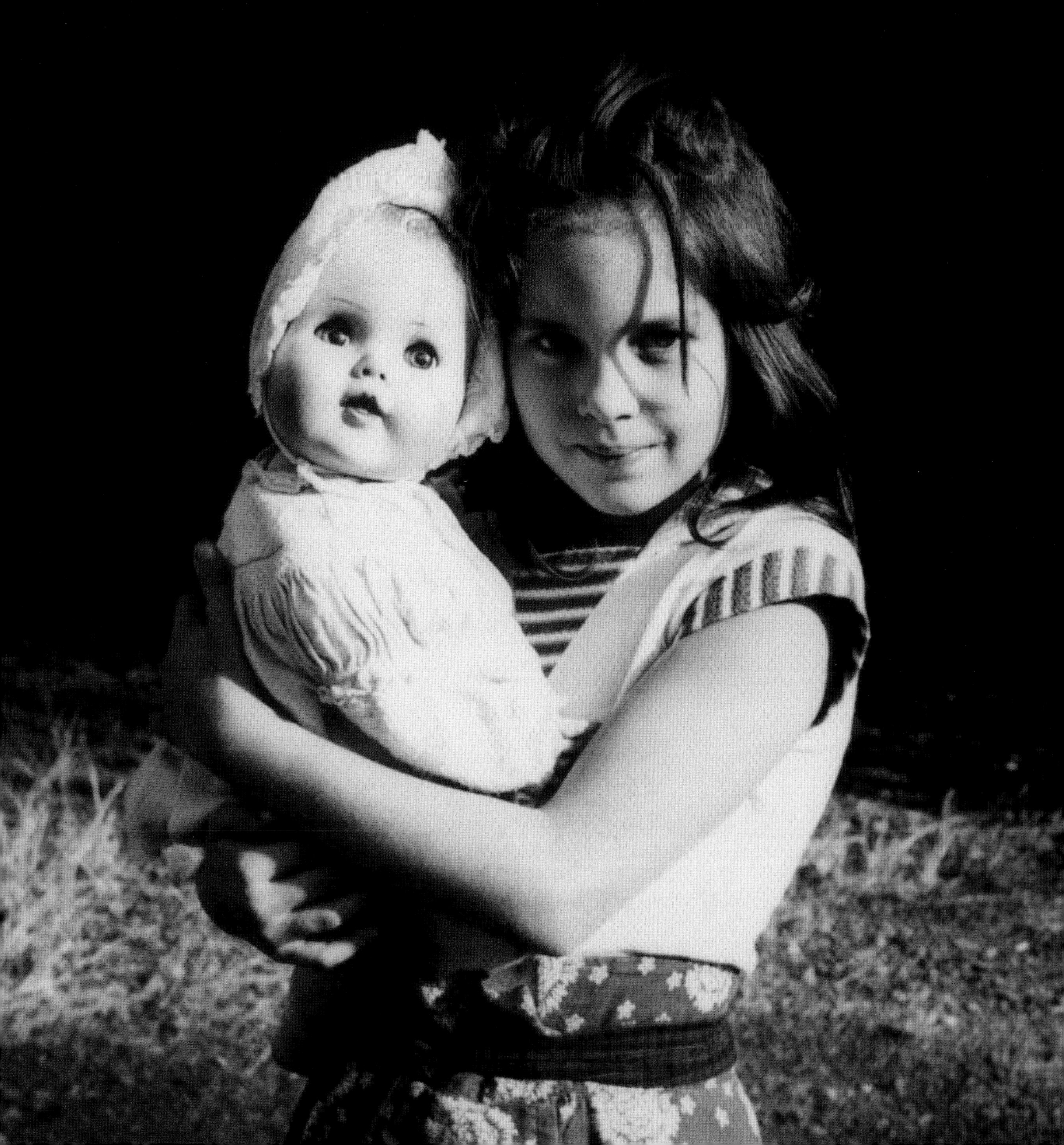

# Masculinity

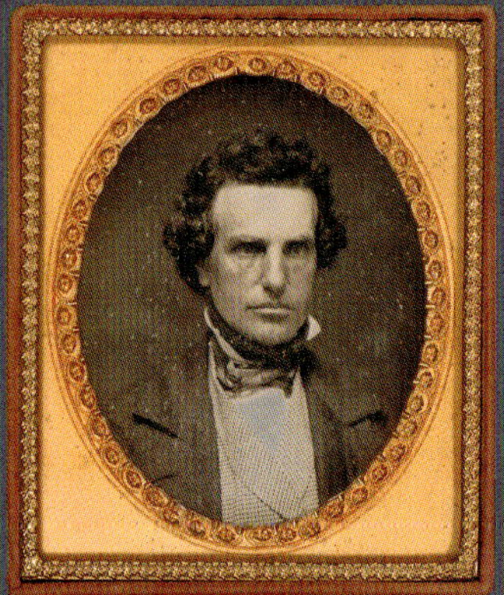

*'Every man has three characters - that which he exhibits, that which he has, and that which he thinks he has.'*
Alphonse Karr
(1808-1890)

There are two predictable attitudes that the majority of men assume when confronted with a camera. The first is to take the implications of the picture seriously, supposing that what the world will see is how the individual will be perceived and remembered. Such men have a natural tendency – usually through the bluff of pose, costume or accessories – to manufacture, by bravado, an heroic image of self. The second attitude, either out of disdain, suspicion or stupidity, is to dismiss the importance of photography, assuming that nobody will take the resulting image seriously. This abdication of responsibility takes the form of humour. What results is usually self-conscious, sophomoric and forced.

Portraits of disarming innocence and humanity do occur, but only rarely. The collective male psychology, in preserving an aura of manliness, discourages conscious revelation of vulnerability or emotion.

One of the most enduring photographic images of man is that of the hunter/gatherer. The proud farmer poses in his field of wheat, or beside his prize pumpkin. Even more common is that of the angler/sportsman, who elaborately displays before us an impressive arrangement of dead fish, birds or animals. These photographs somewhat defensively record the desire of men to parade their potency in controlling and shaping their environment. If the camera had been invented thousands of years ago, it is a foregone conclusion that there would exist numerous photographs of cavemen posing triumphantly beside recently slain mastodons or sabre-tooth tigers.

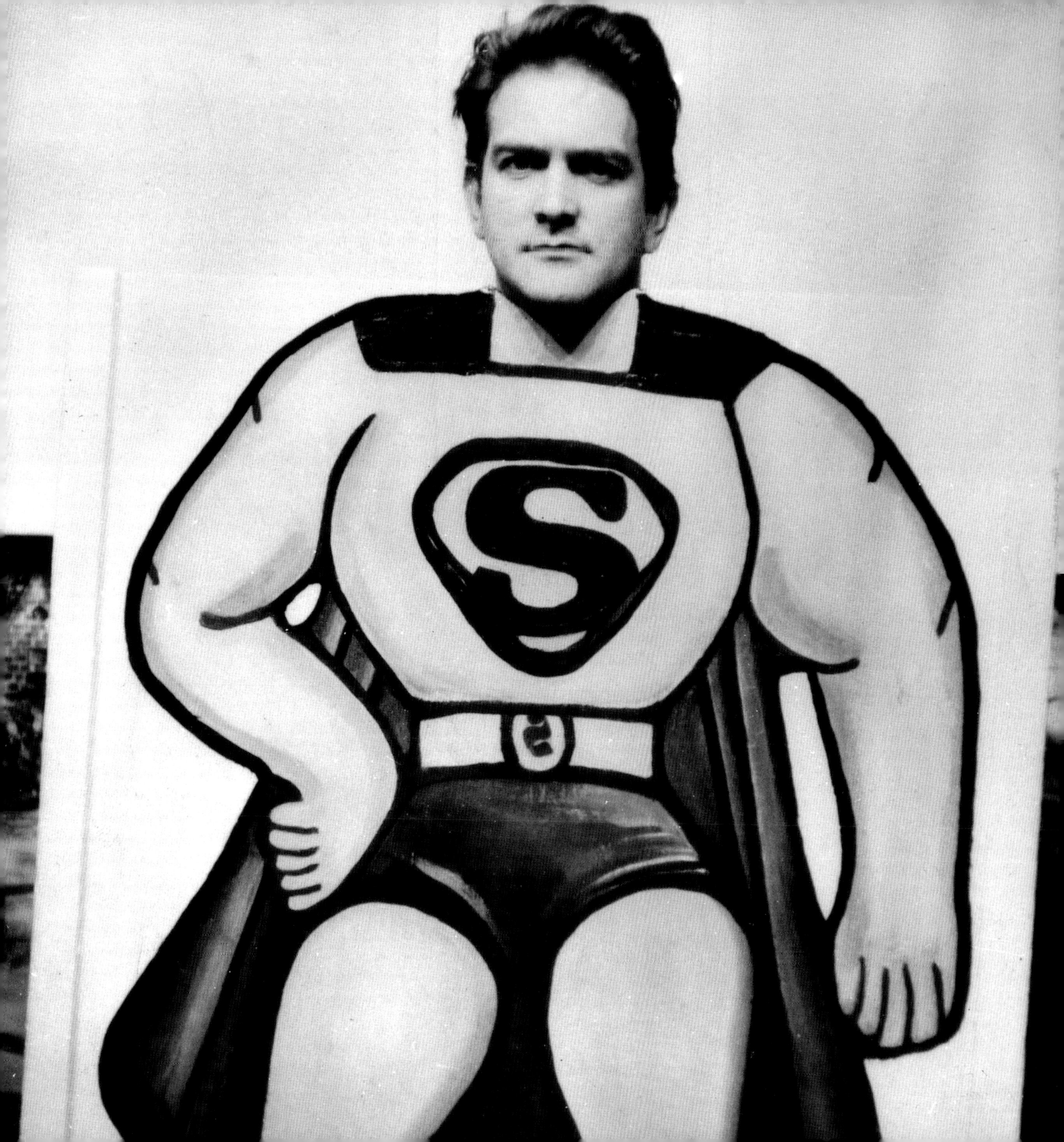

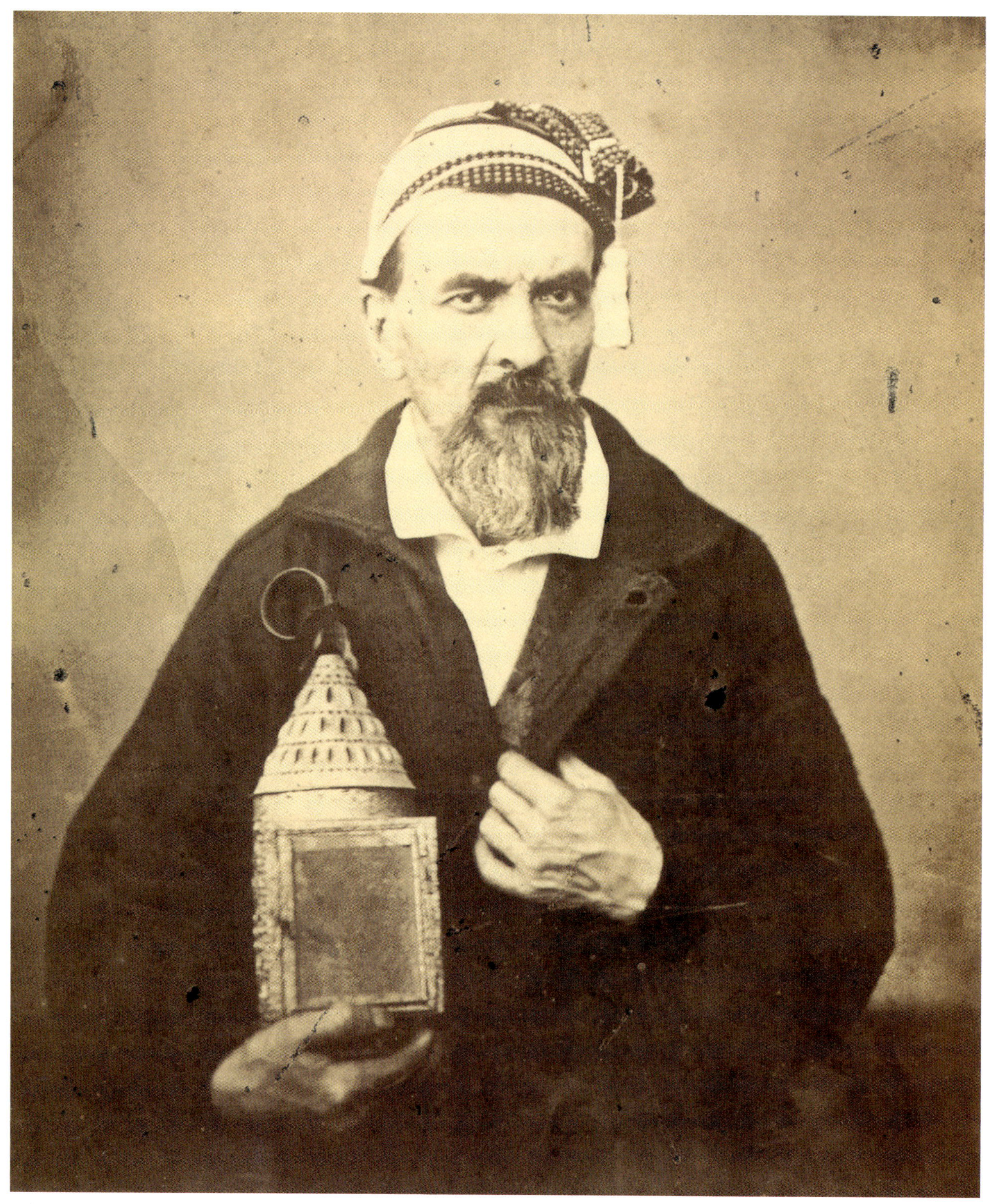

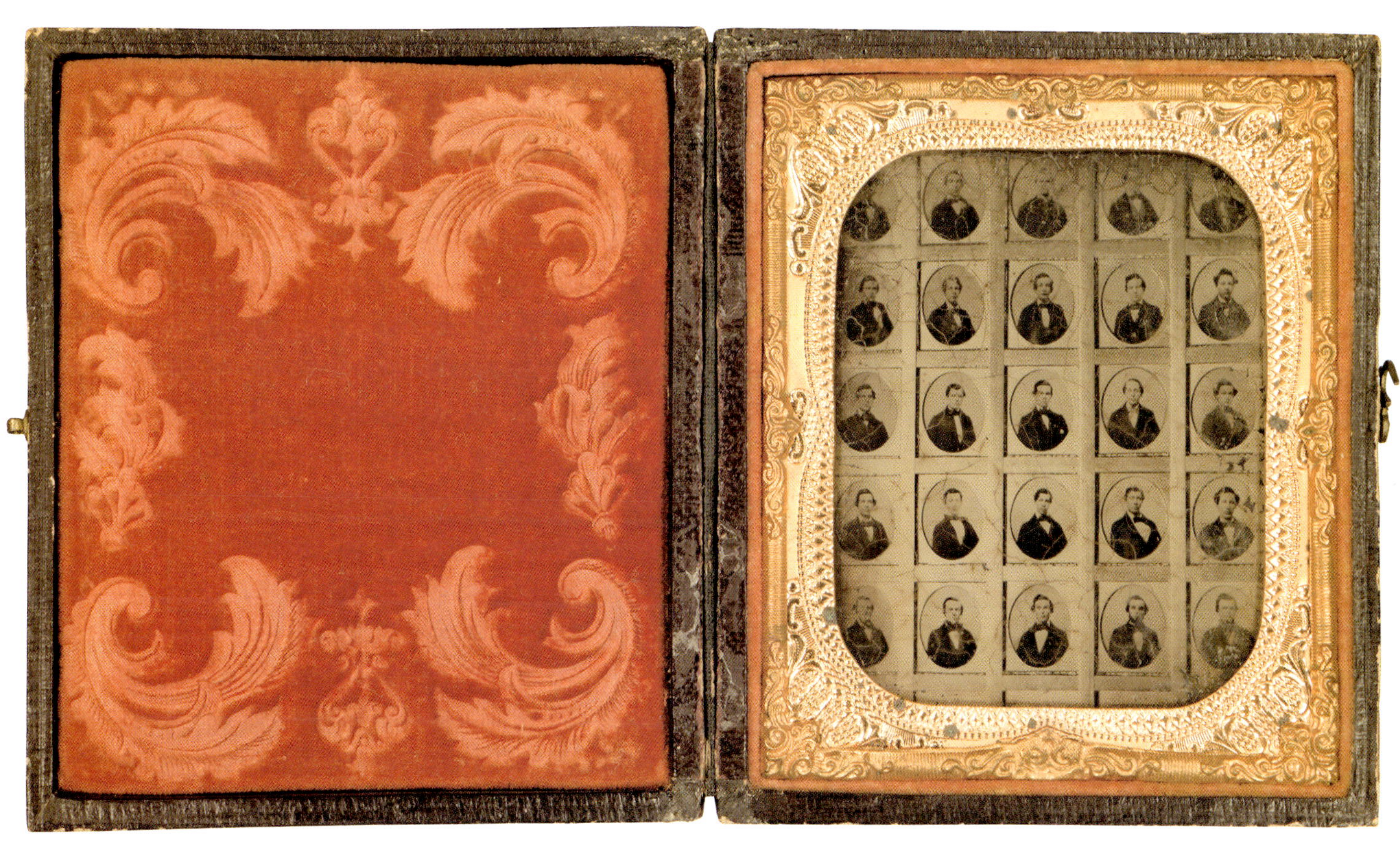

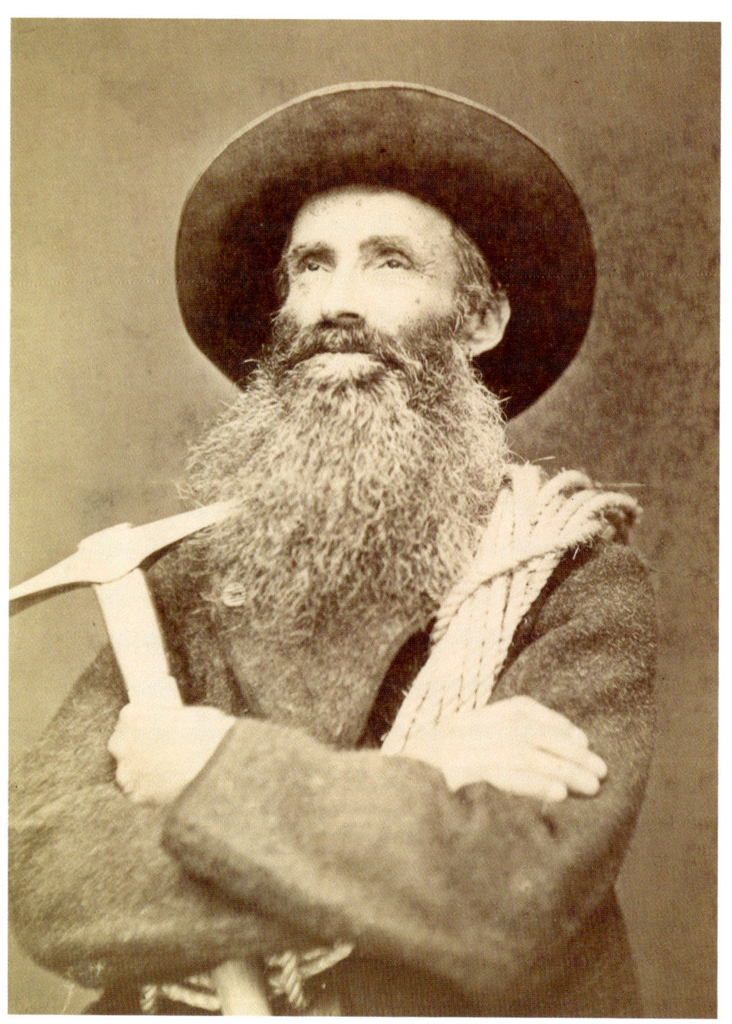

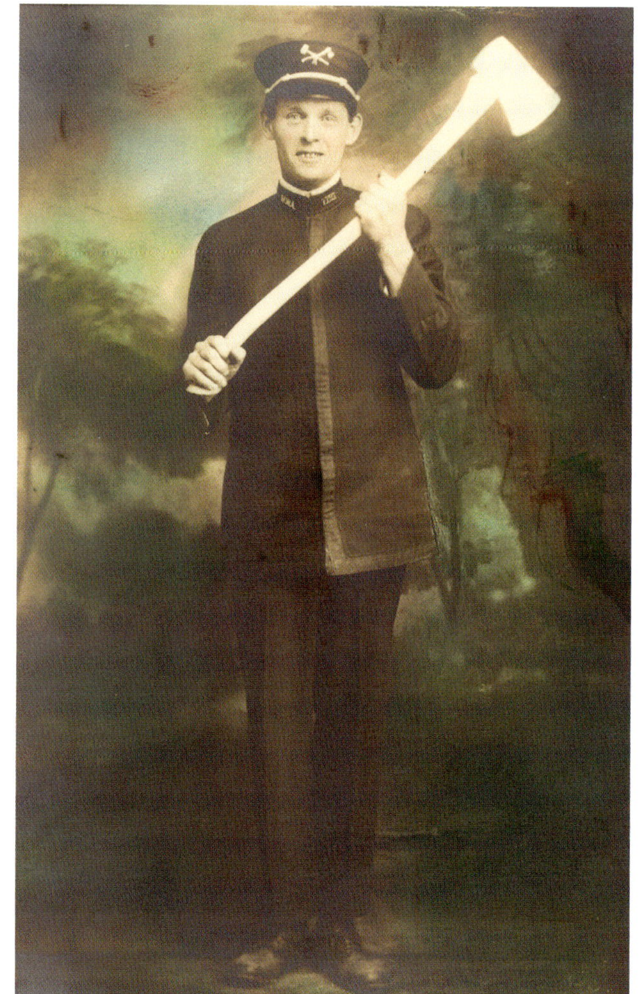

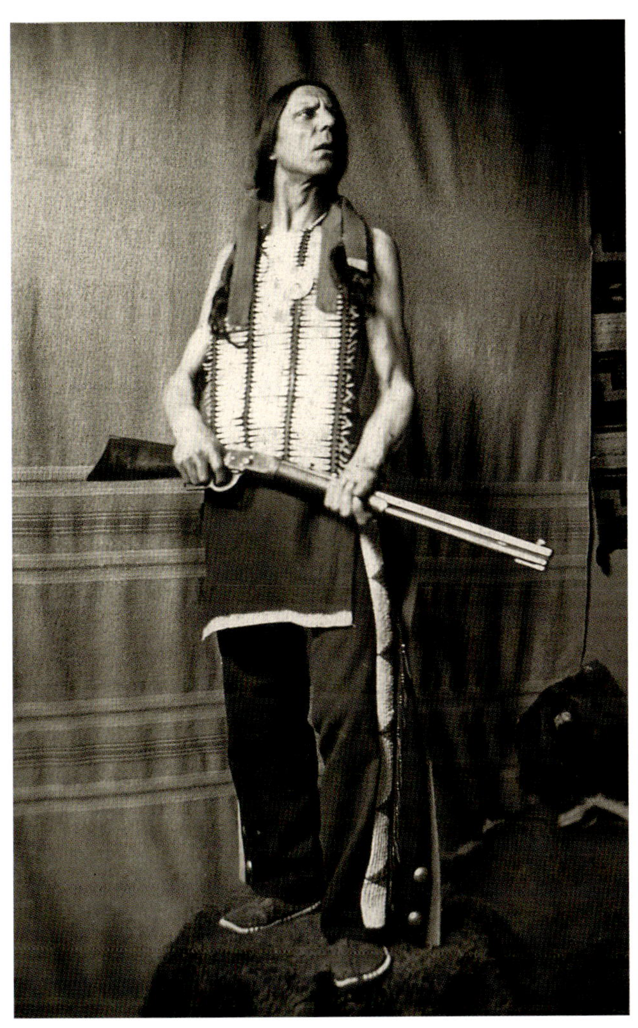

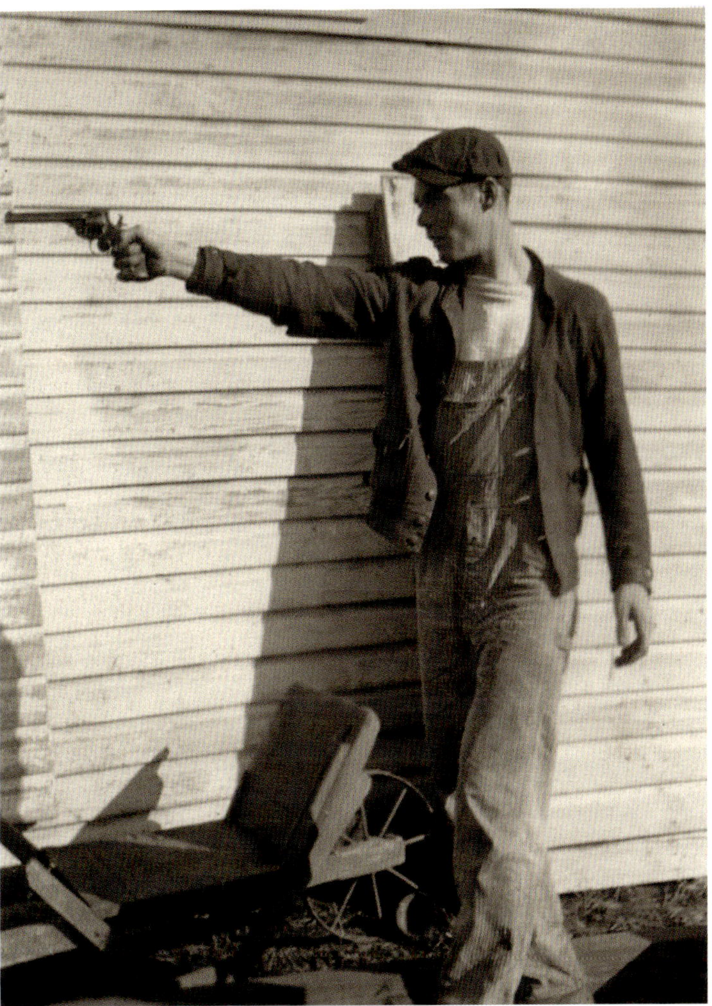

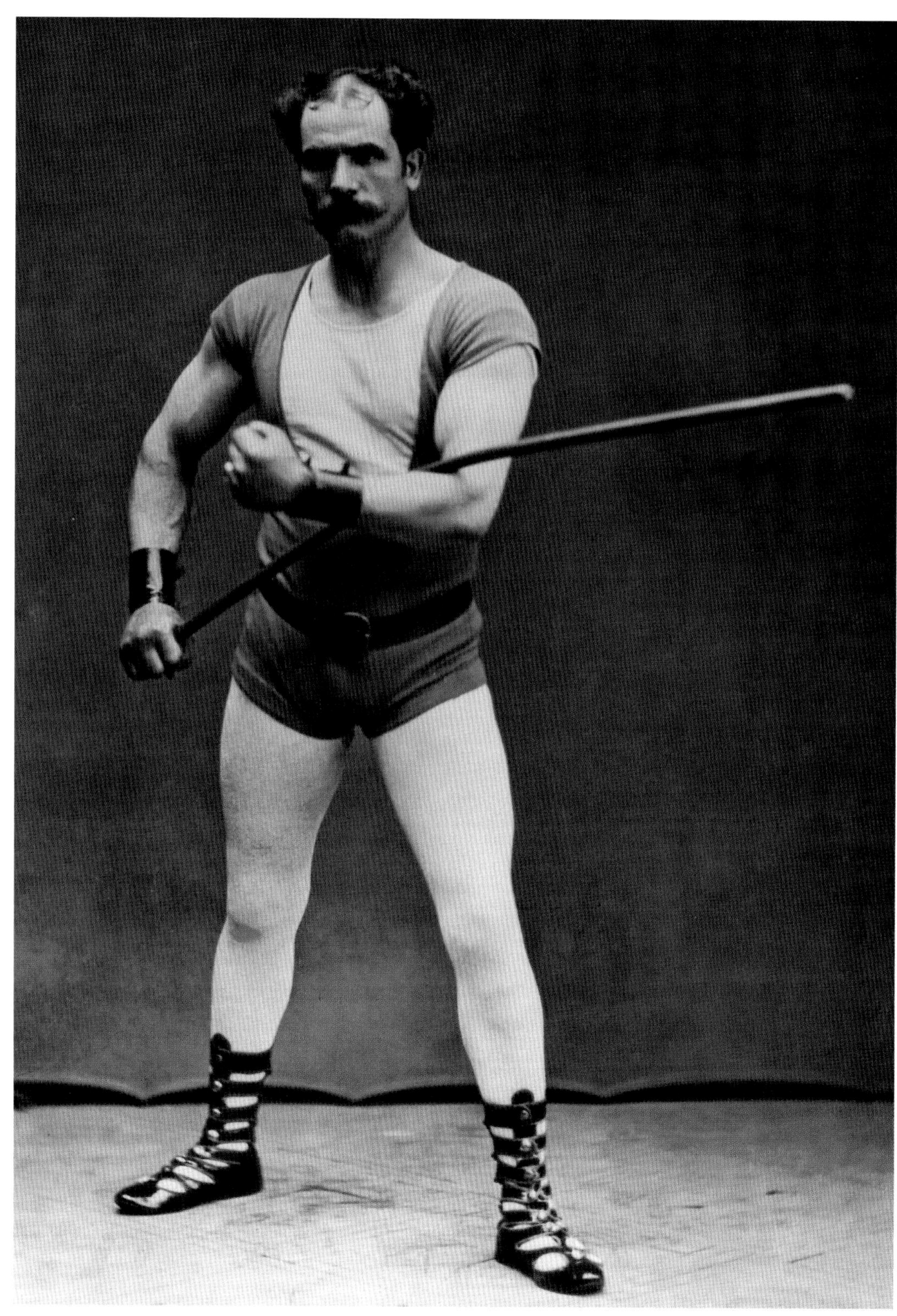

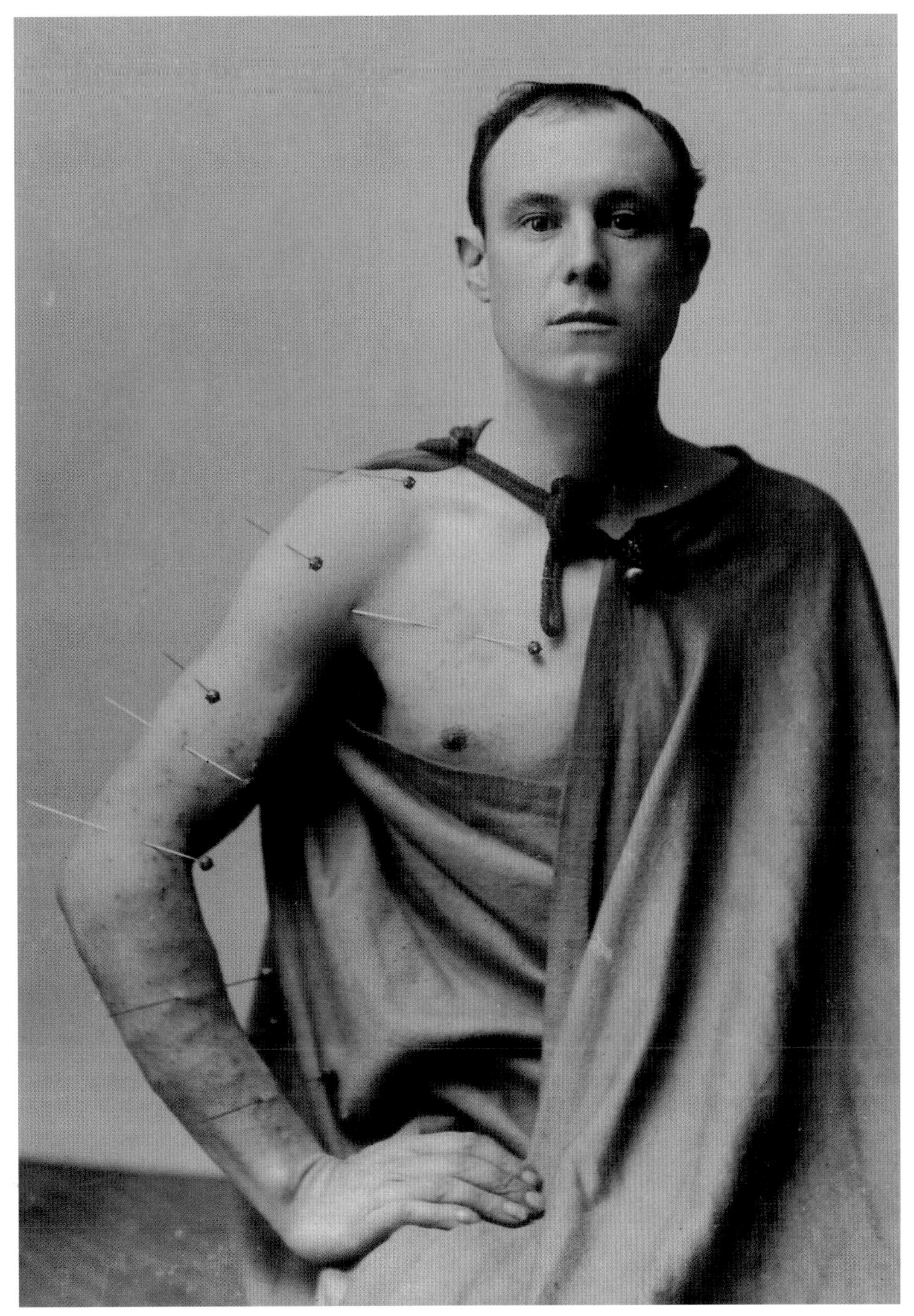

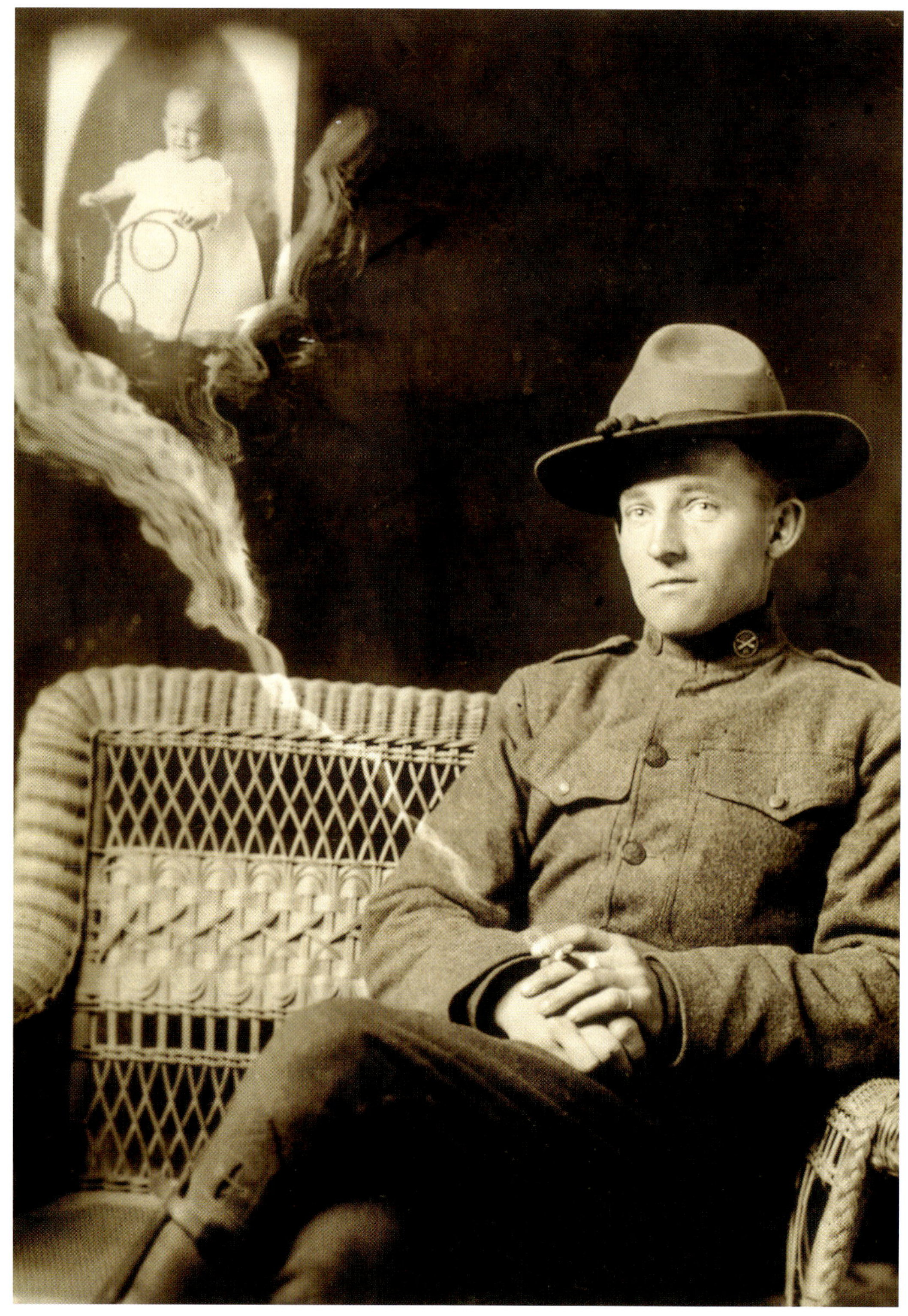

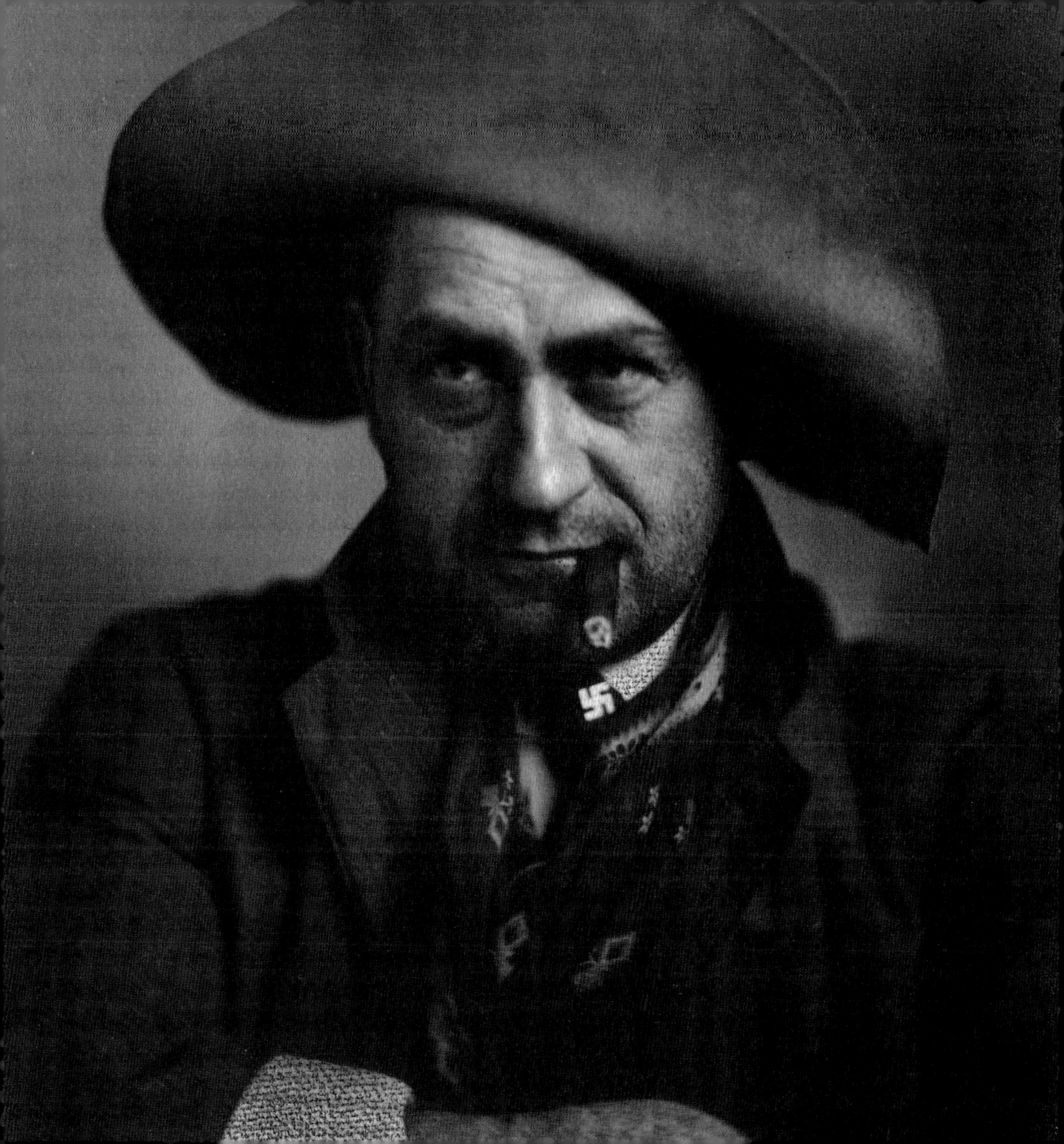

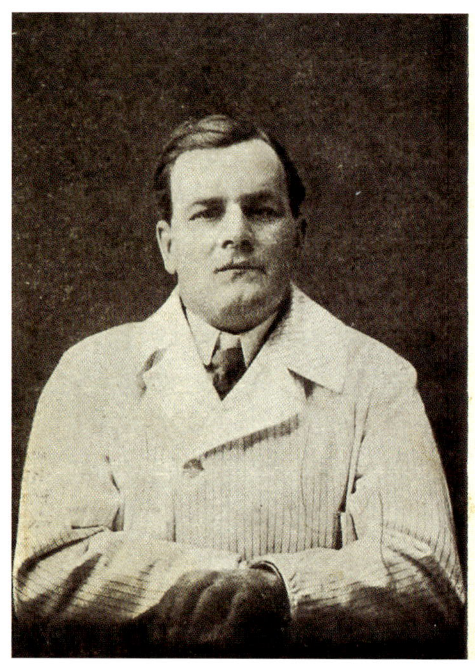

Good mixed tea
28 cents per lb
4 lbs 1 oz
822
15
41 10
822
1233 1146

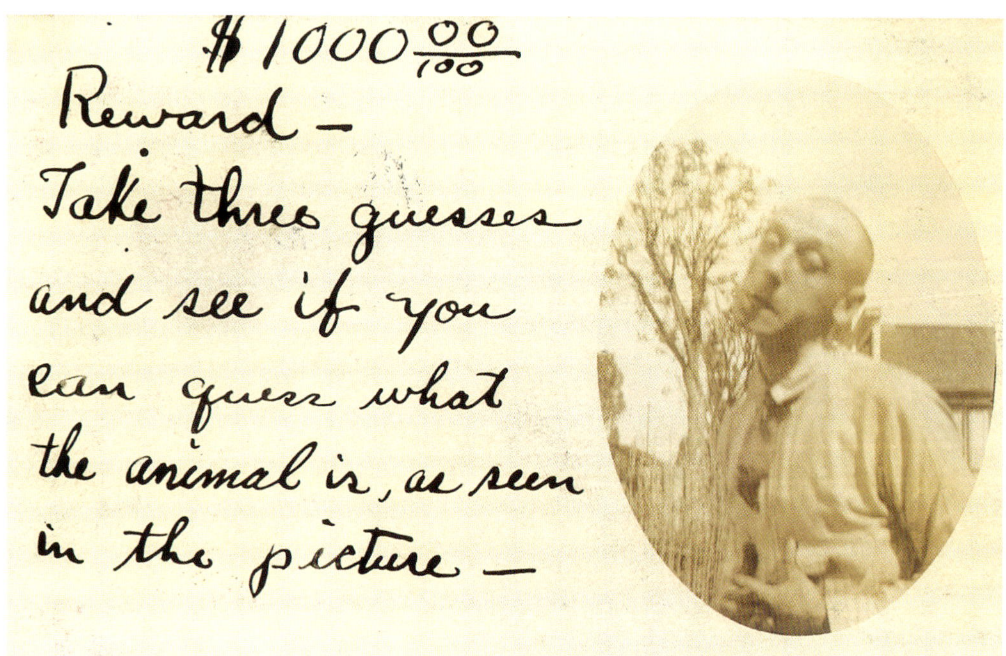

Hello Miss Bessie how
is this this is the leatiest
dont you think so
how do you think
you will like this I
gess you will like it
like a dog likes hick
ery Remmber well
Remmber true Remmber
me and I will you

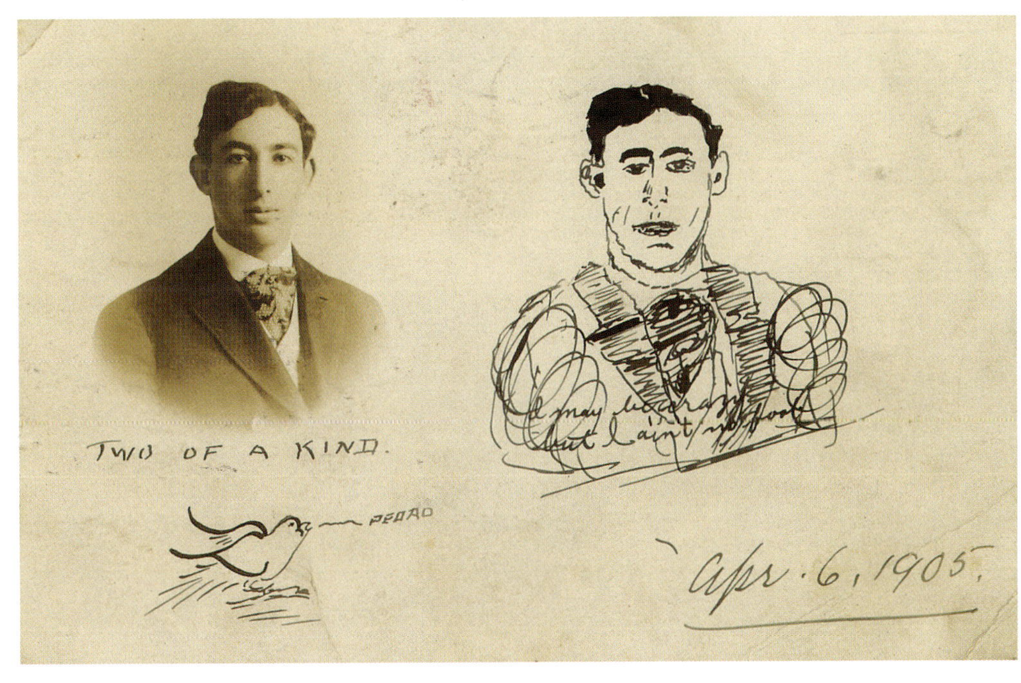

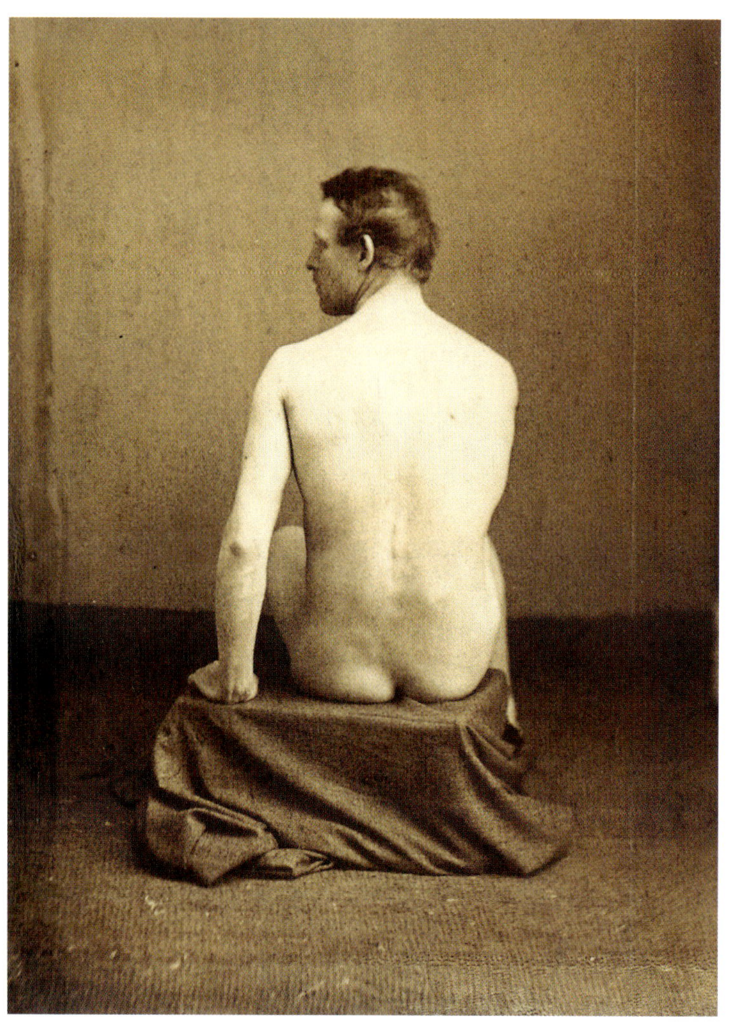

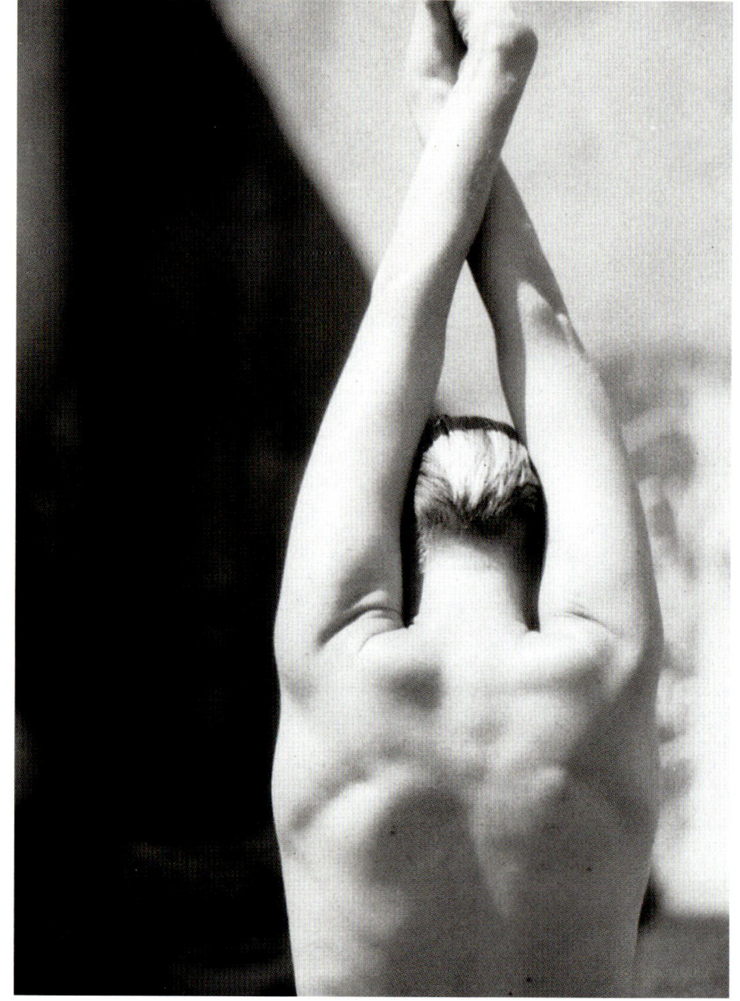

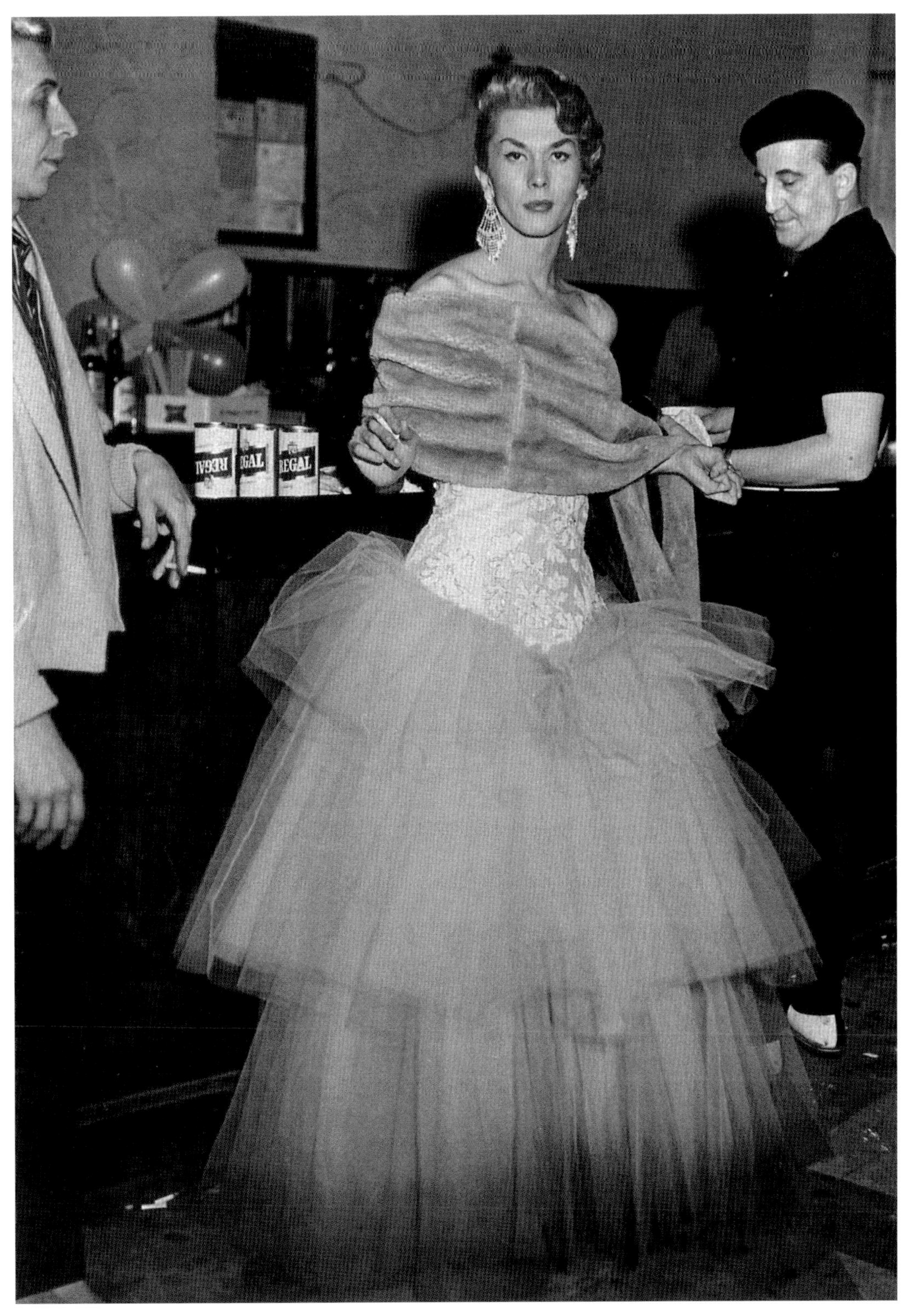
REGAL

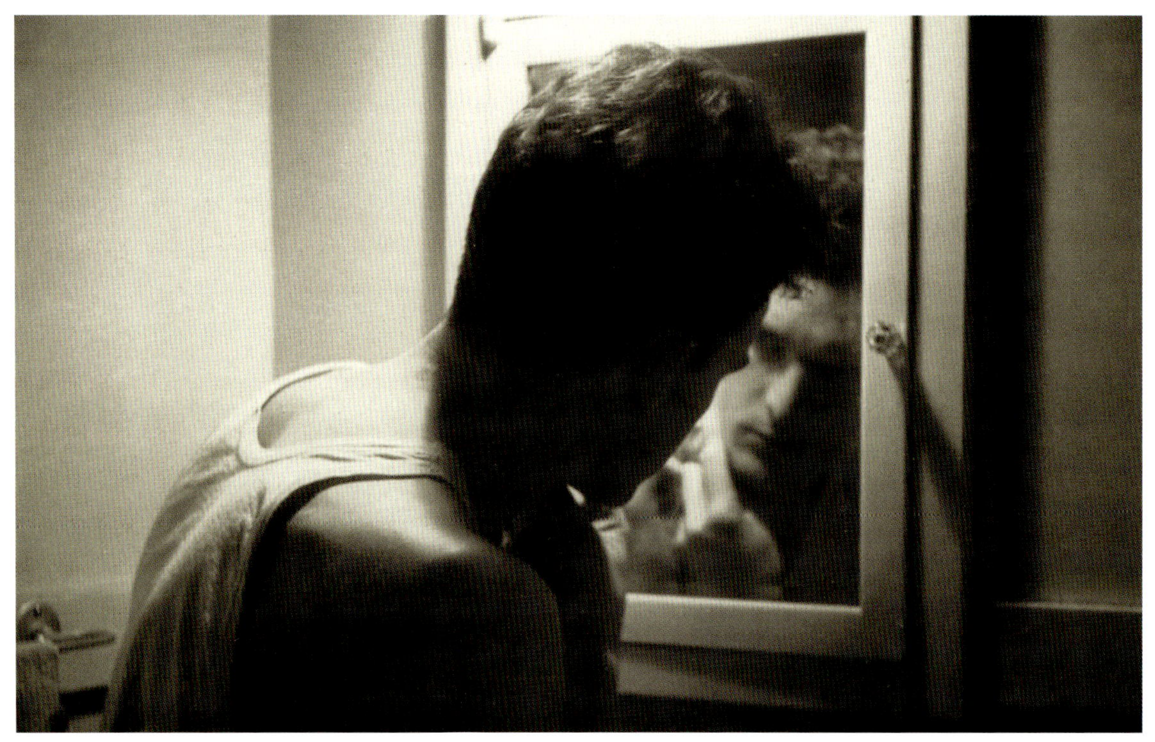

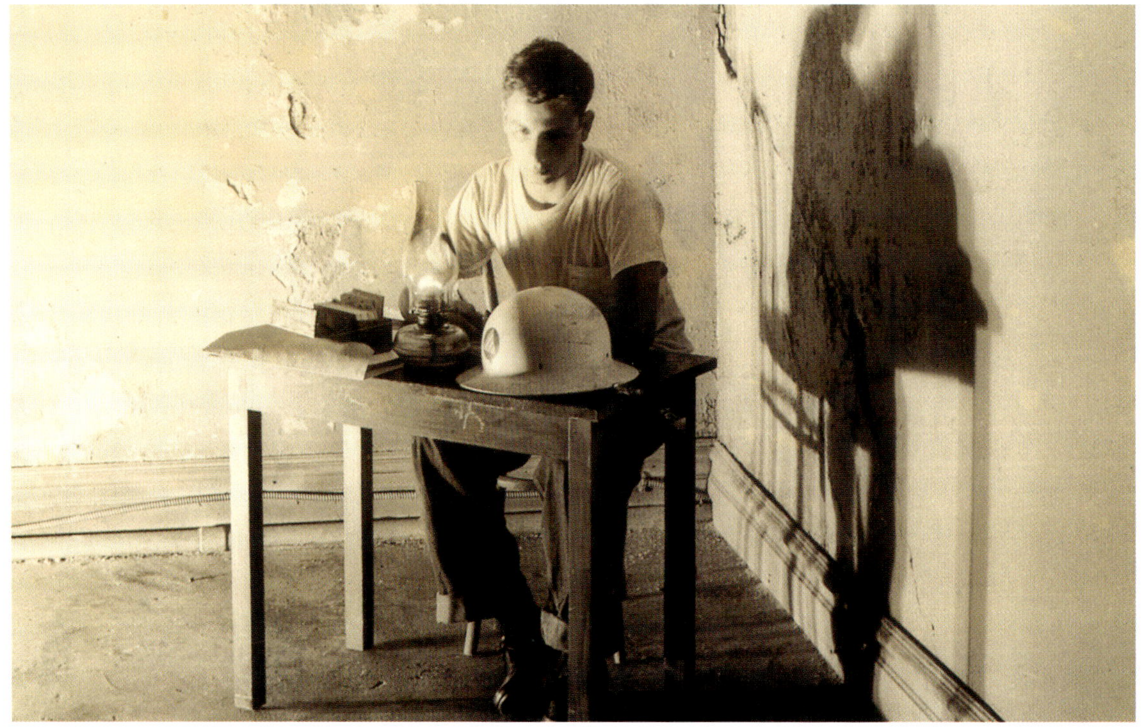

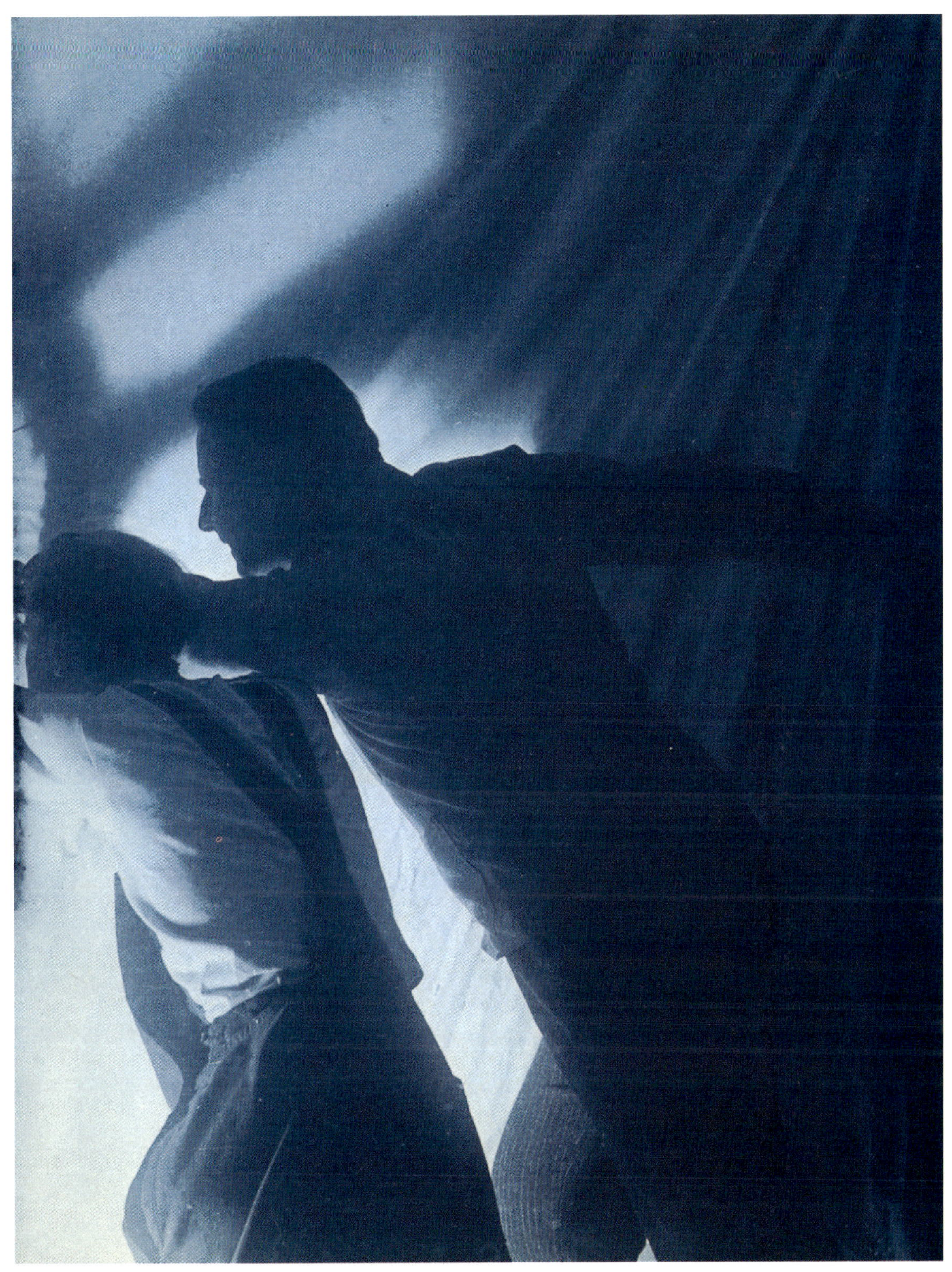

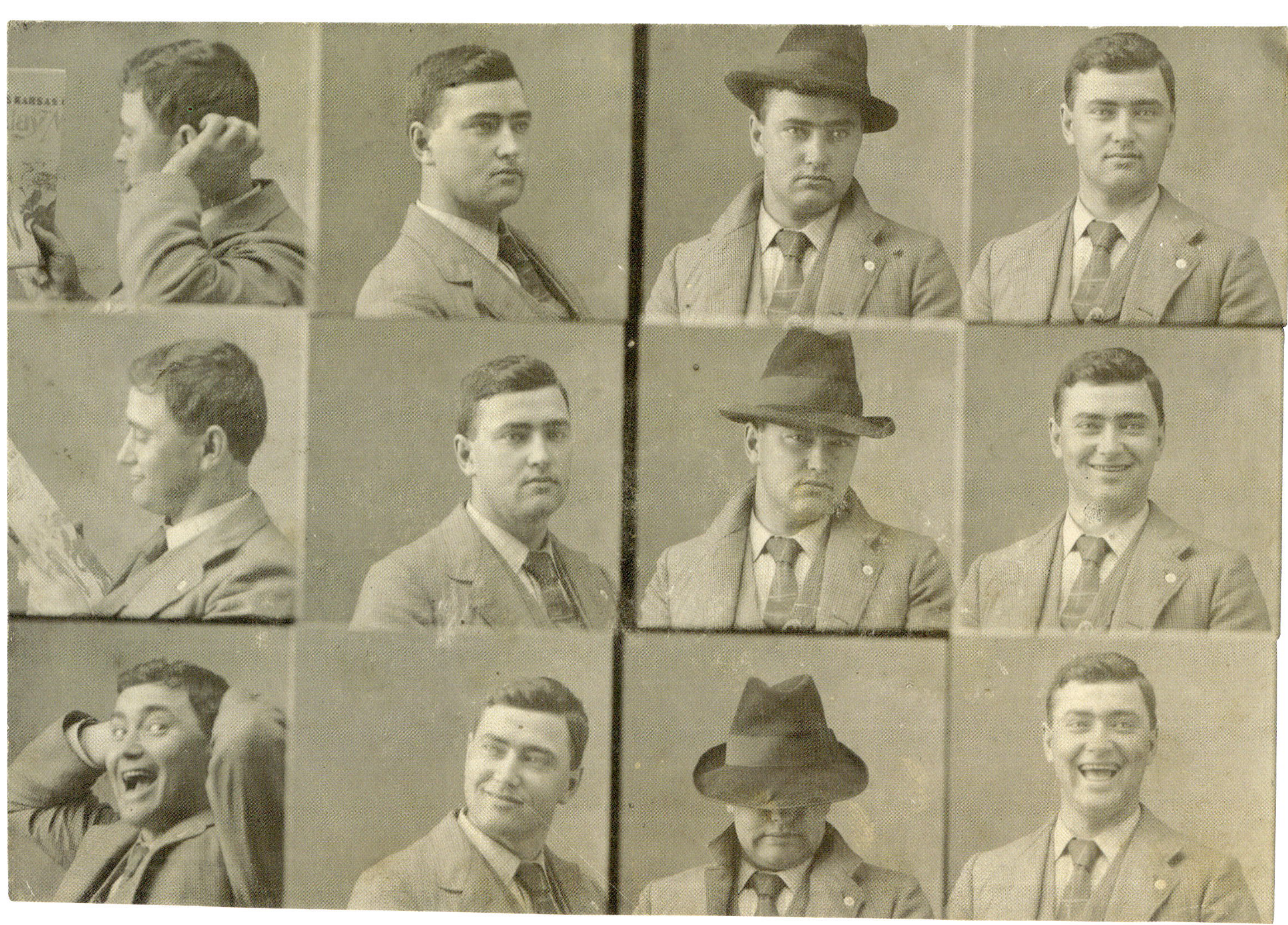

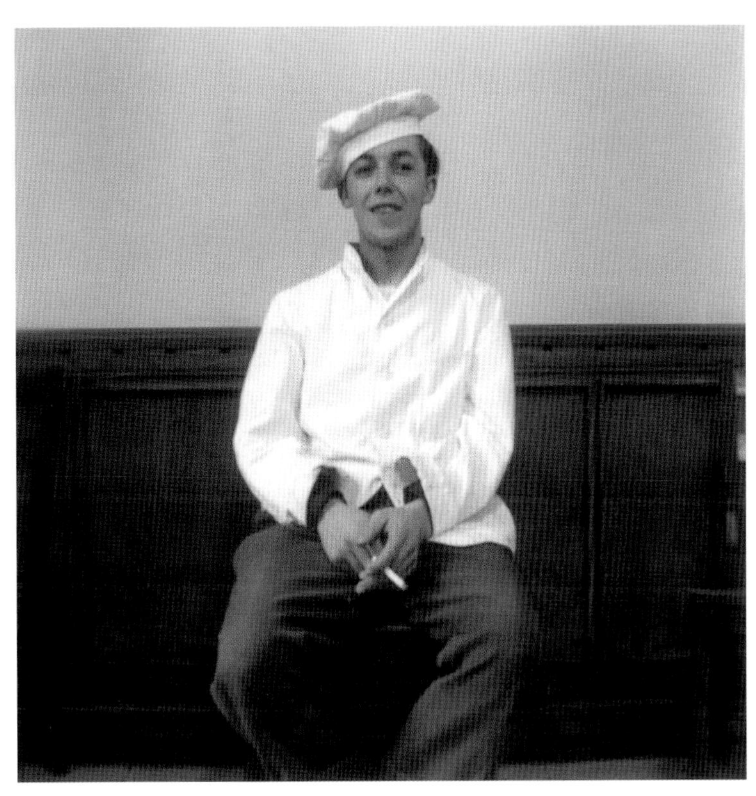

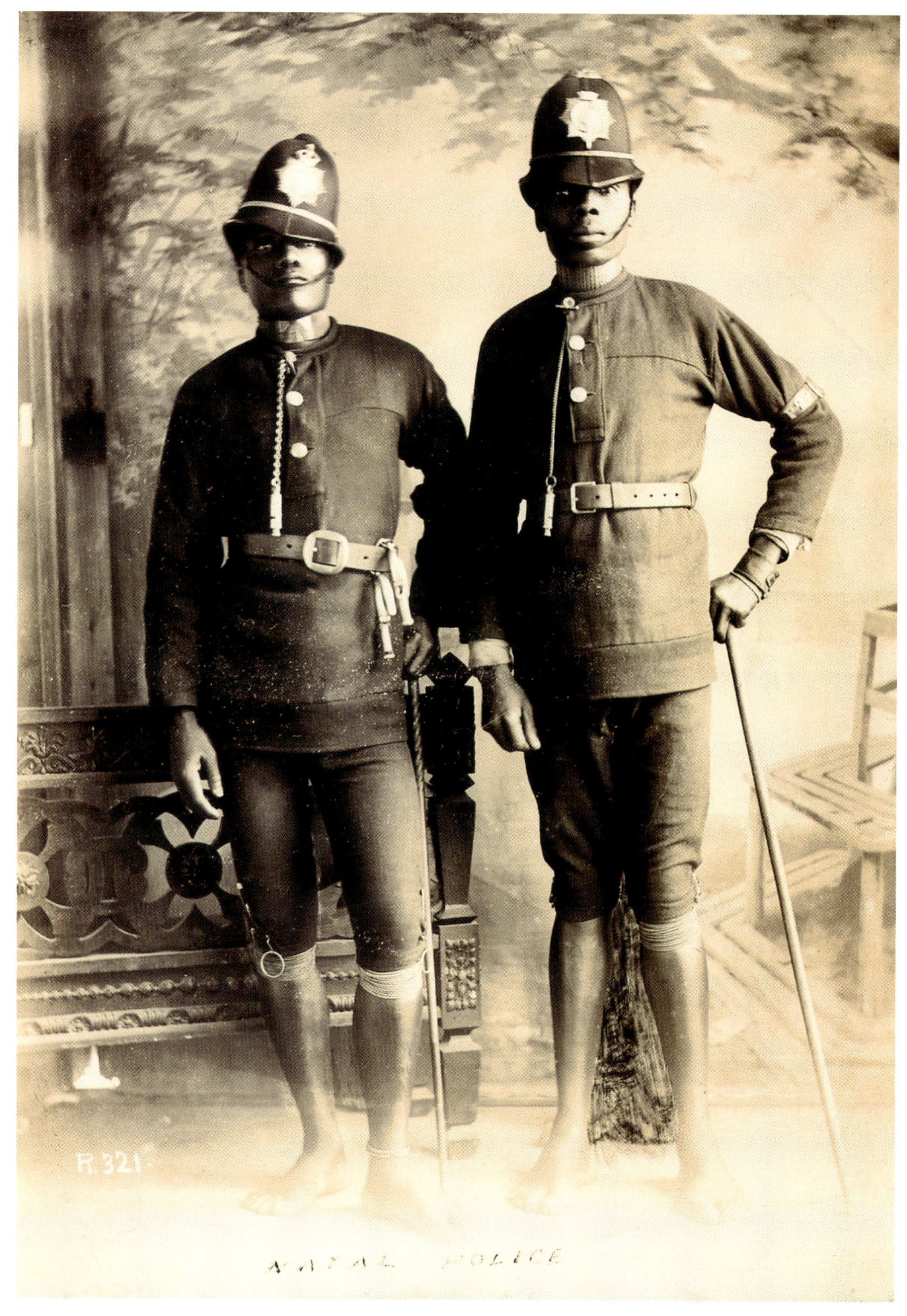
R.321.
NATAL POLICE

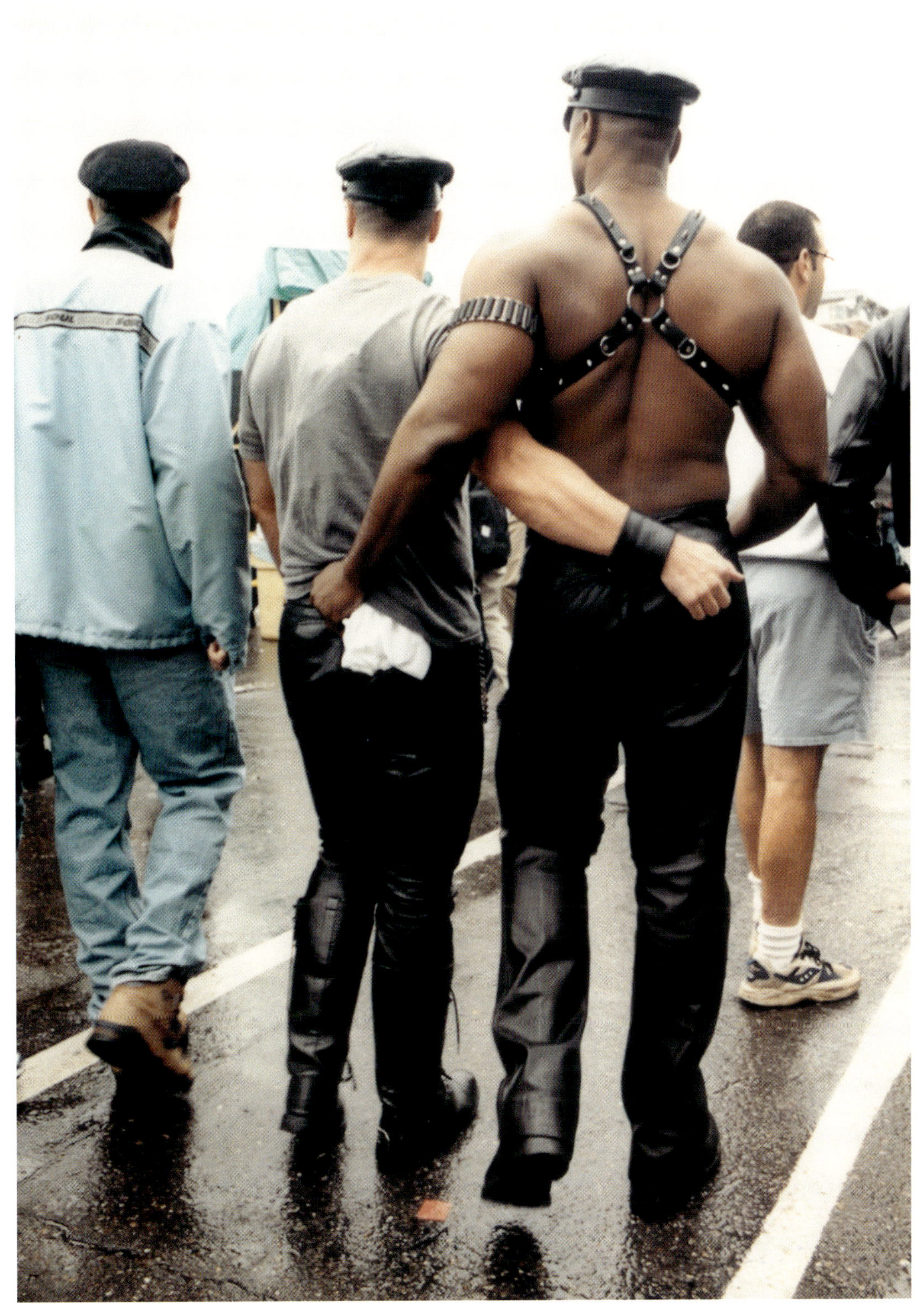

# Femininity

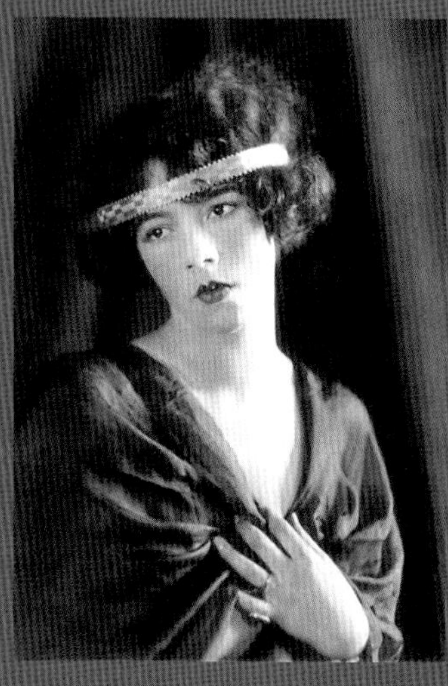

*'Women can change better'n a man. Man lives – well, in jerks. Baby born or somebody dies, that's a jerk. Gets a farm or loses one, an' that's a jerk. With a woman, it's all one flow, like a stream – little eddies, little waterfalls – but the river, it goes right on. Woman looks at it that way.'* Screenplay of *The Grapes of Wrath* by Nunnally Johnson, 1940, based on the novel by John Steinbeck

Women, in general, tend to look more relaxed, even self-assured, in photographs than men. Could it be that they are better prepared for the fickle judgment of the camera lens? Society has always placed a higher standard on the physical appearance of women than men. Consequently, whether they like it or not, women are conditioned to experience the frequent ritual of physical self-examination every time they view themselves in a mirror.

The variety of emotions and attitudes present in photographs of women is endless. They range from the reverential, reminiscent of saints, martyrs and stoics, to the lowdown, recalling temptresses, wenches and libertines. Costume, or the lack thereof, is often an obvious signal as to the character of the woman in a photograph. This implied moral judgment is rarely experienced in photographs of men.

The naked female form has been a constant staple of photography since the earliest daguerreotypes were made. Thoughtful aesthetic contemplation was usually the announced rationale for the creation of such images, while titillation and arousal were often closer to the truth. There is clearly a male objectification of women through the photography of their bodies. This is less a situation to be condemned than a visible recognition of the sensual female aura that women already know they possess but cannot always control. In photography there is often a fine line between a woman being placed on a pedestal and a woman being put on display.

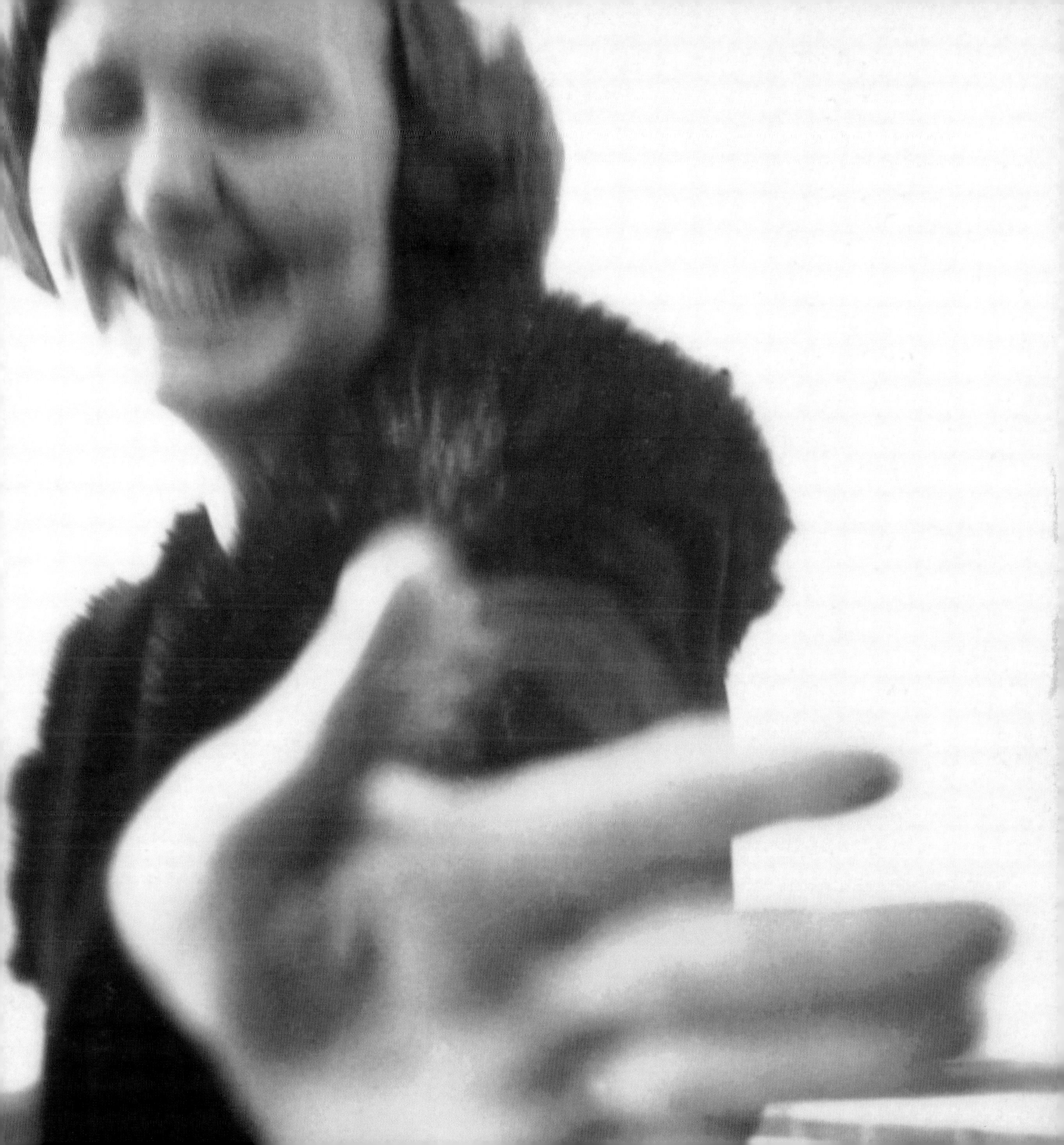

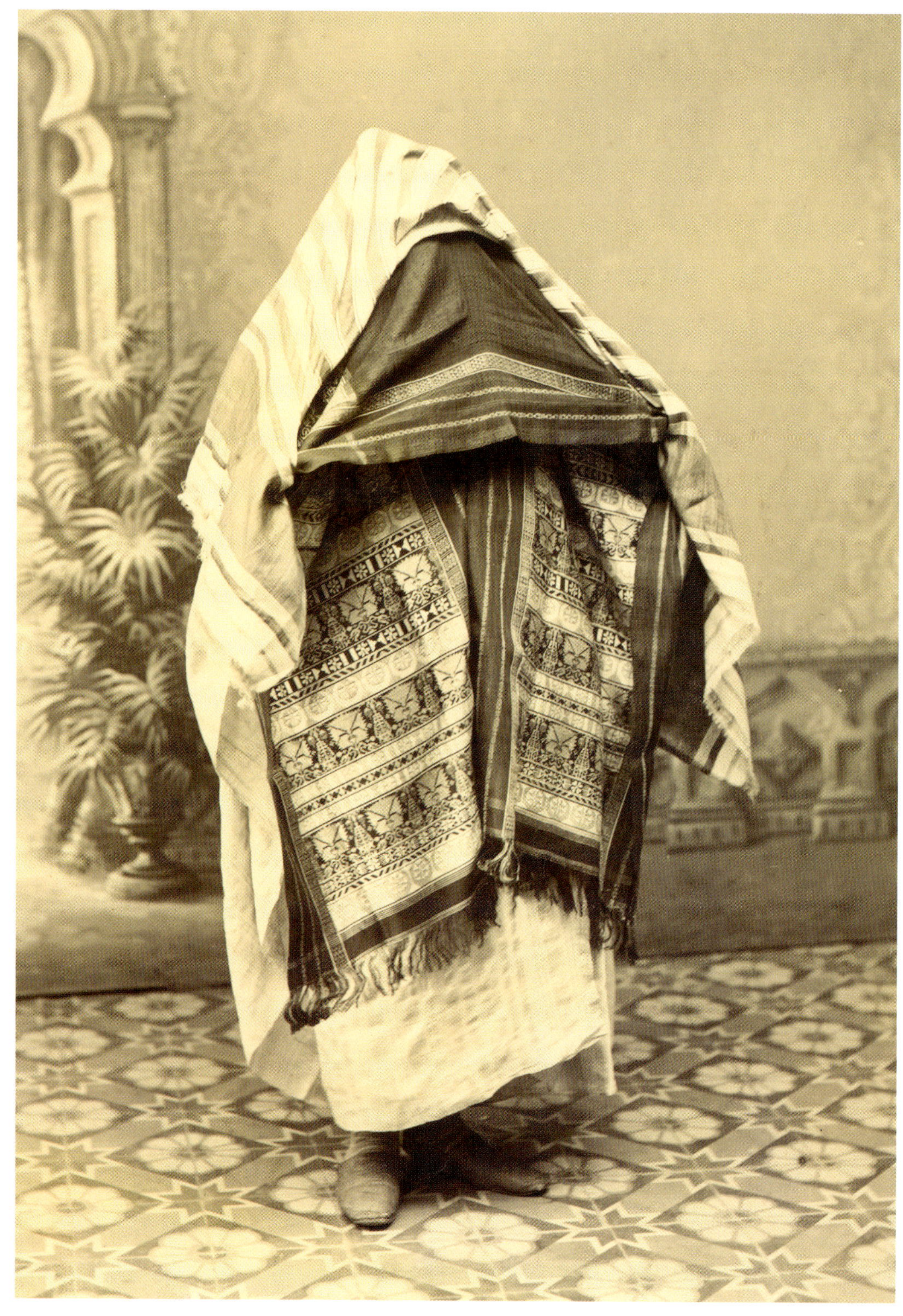

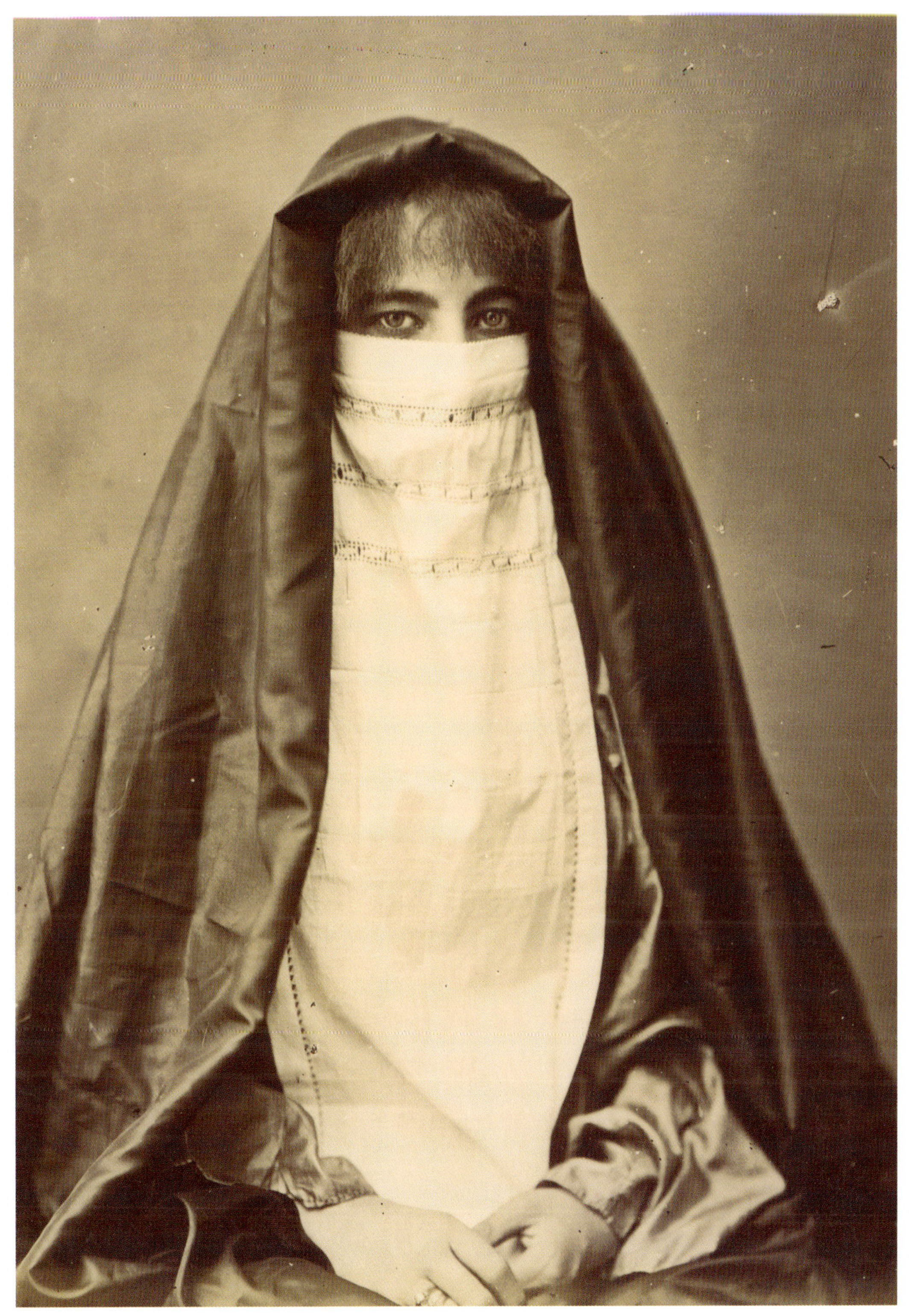

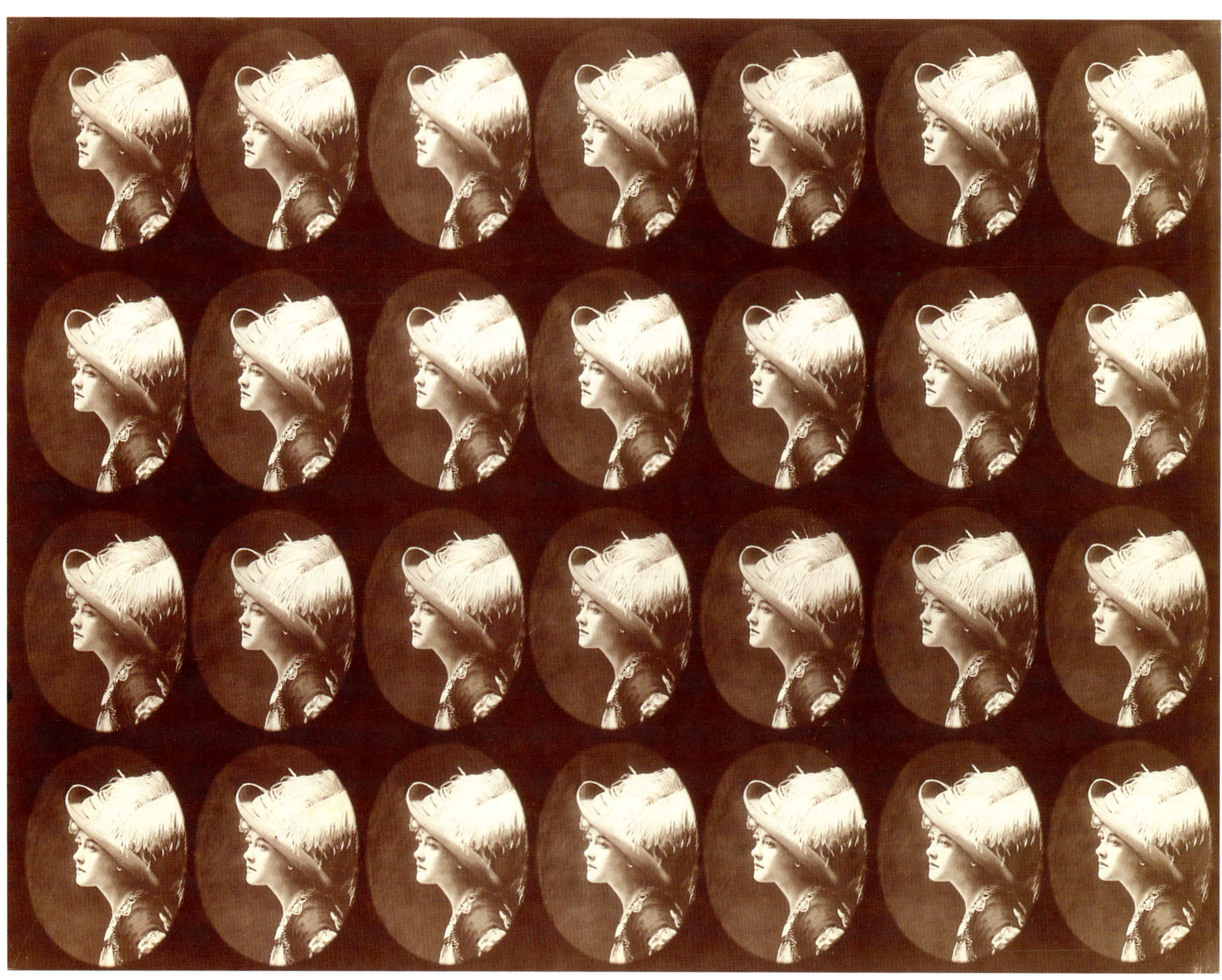

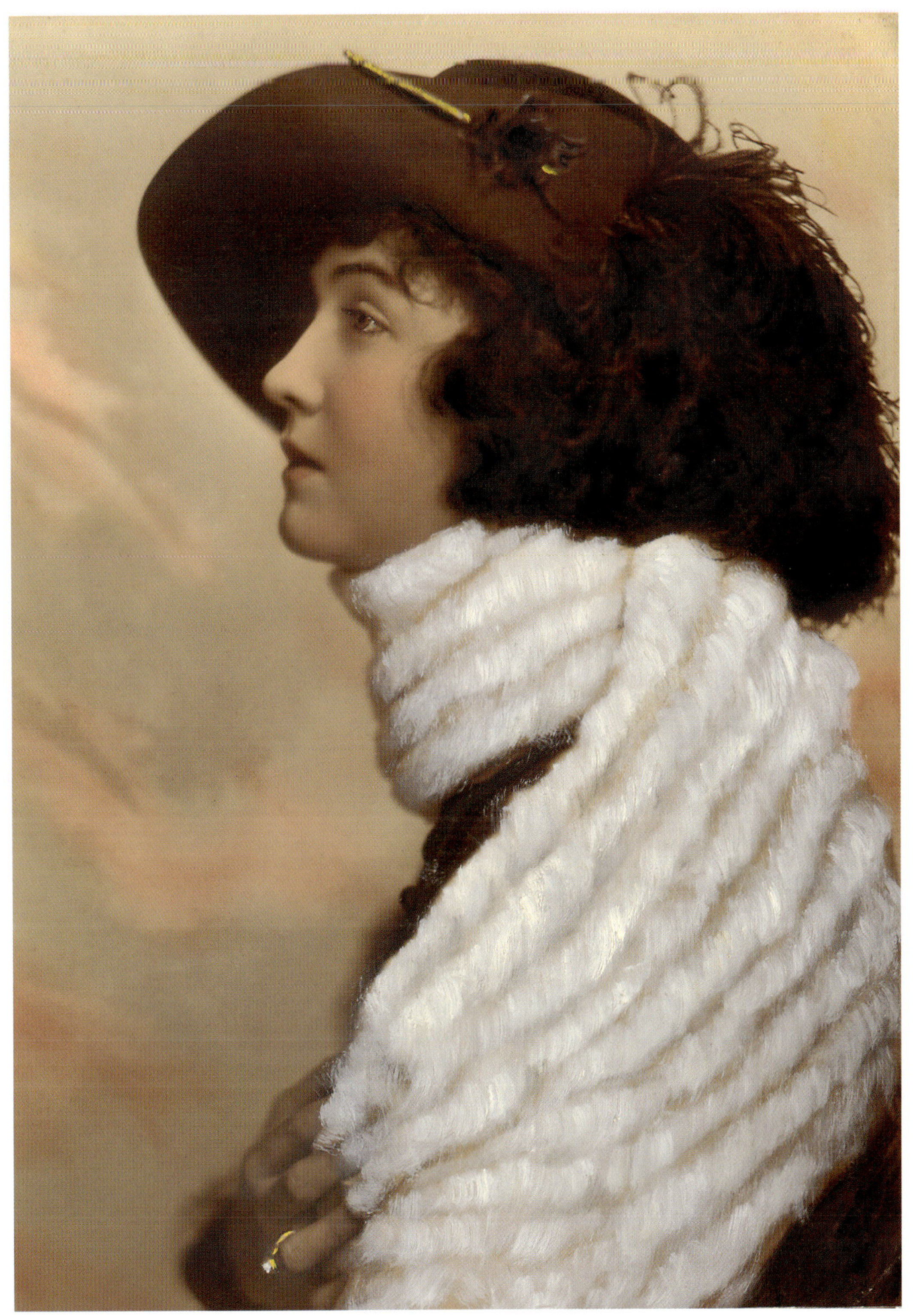

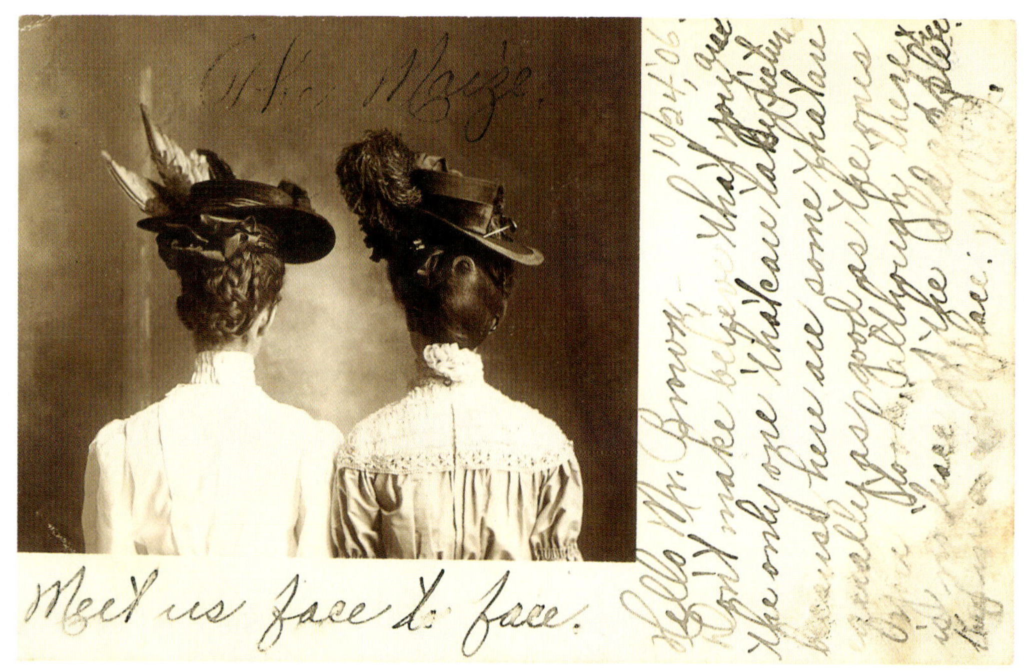
Meet us face to face.

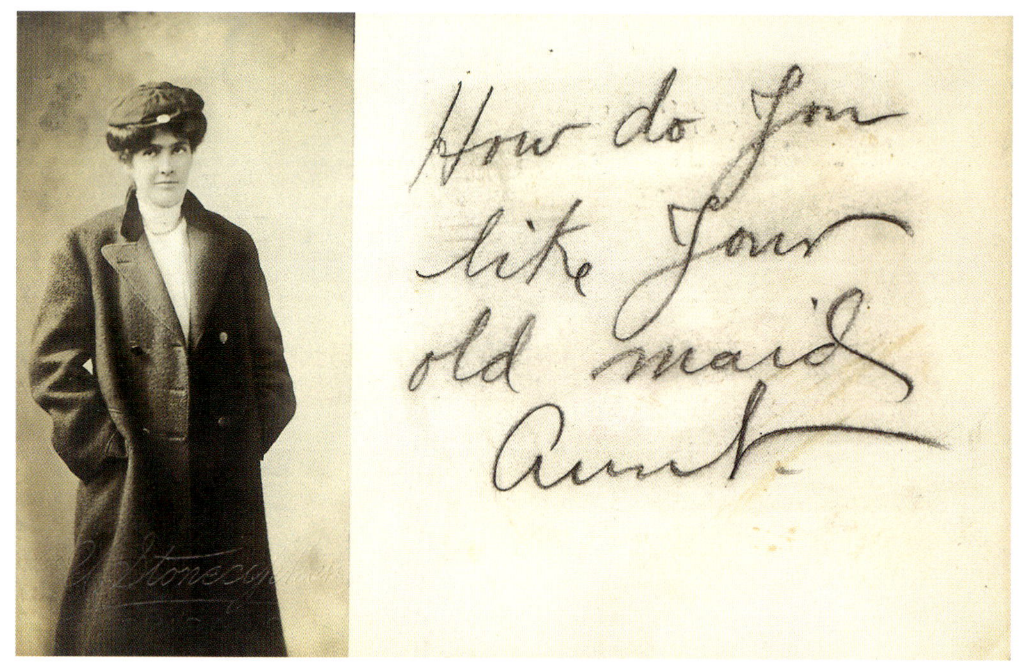
How do you
like your
old maid
Aunt

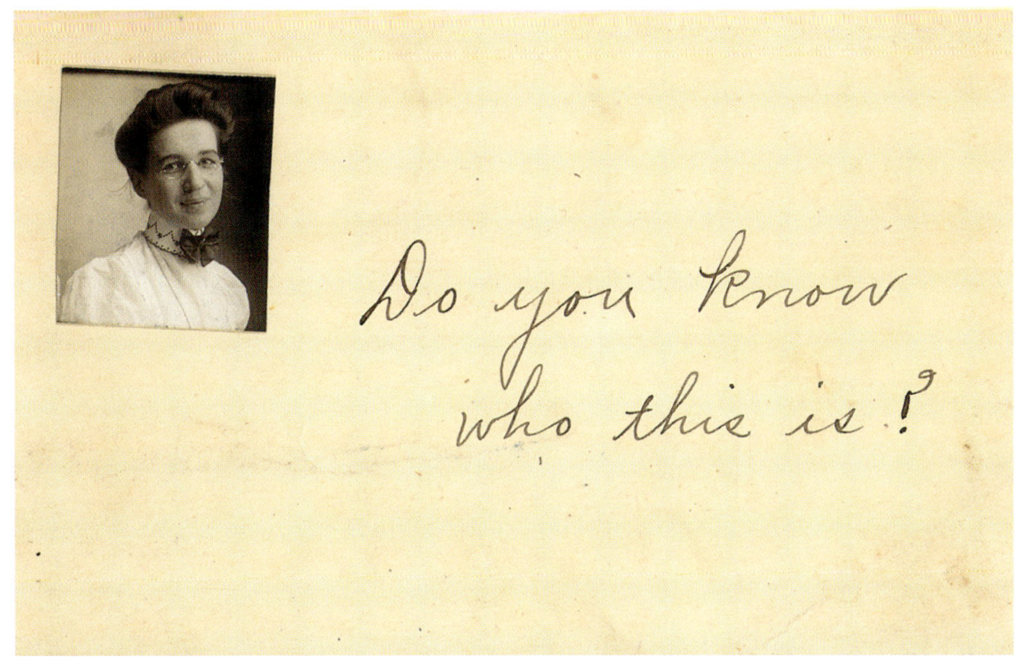
Do you know
who this is?

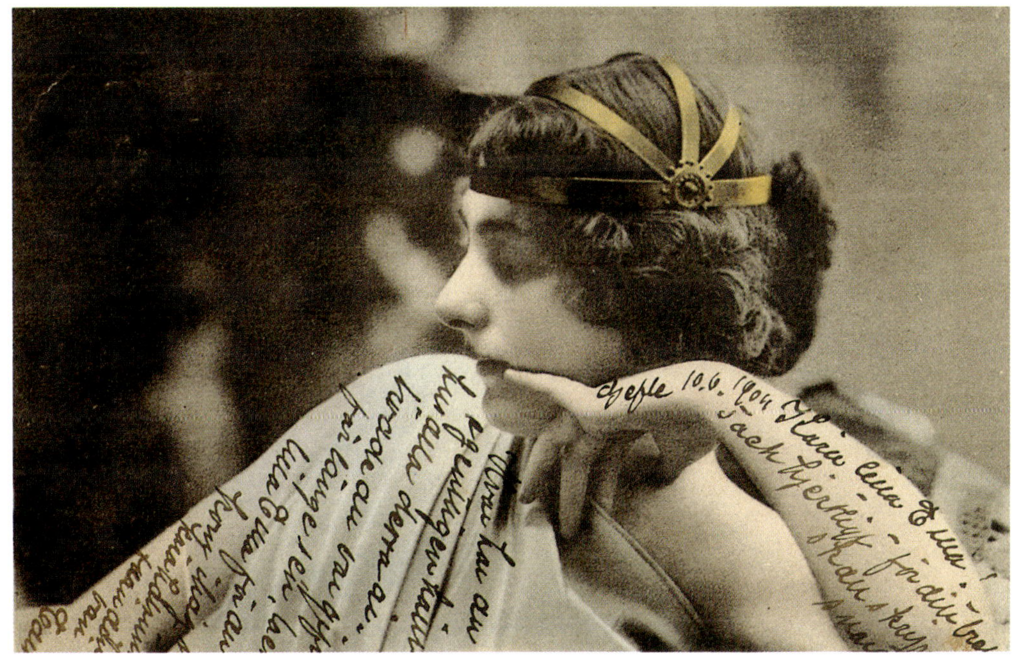

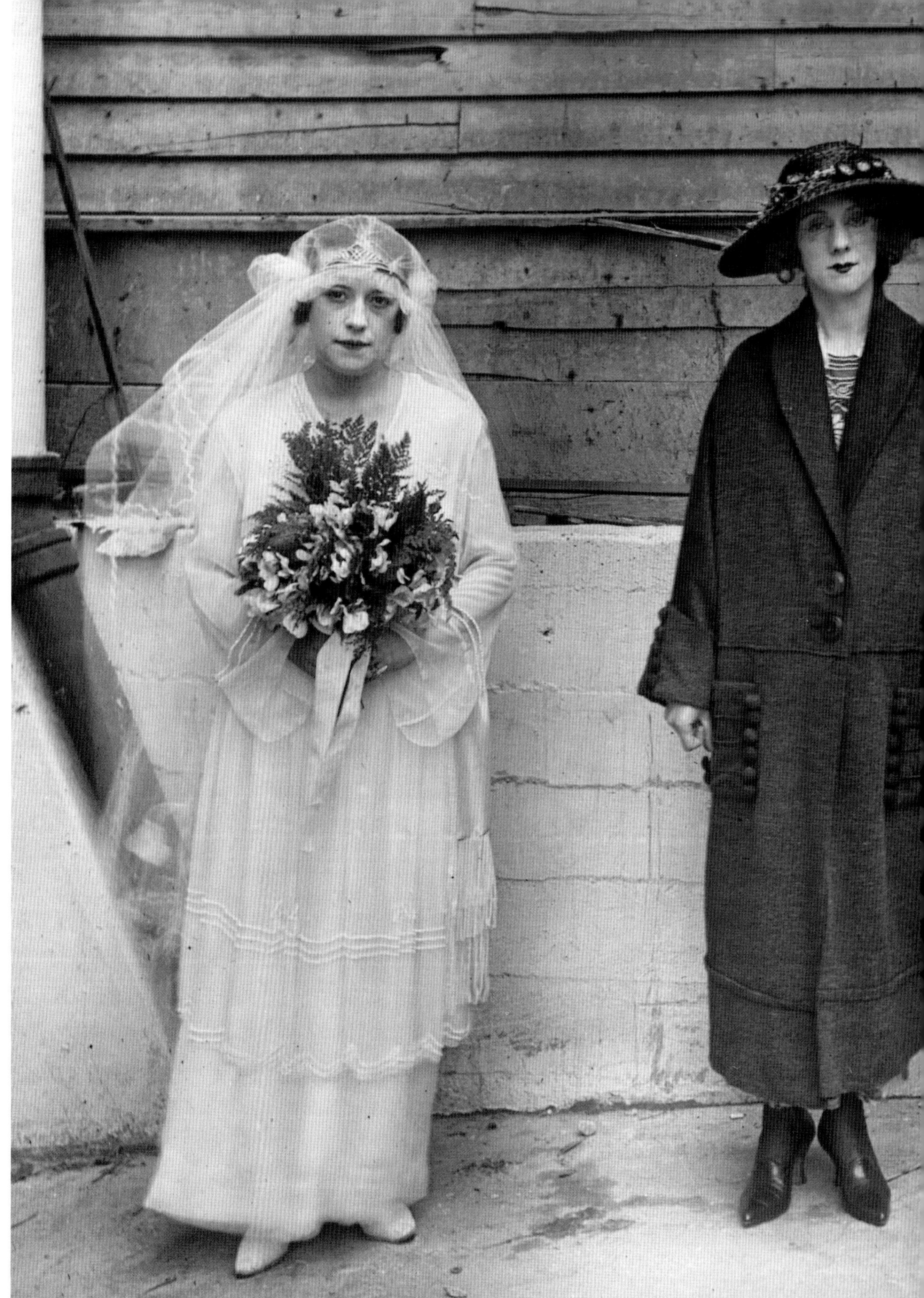

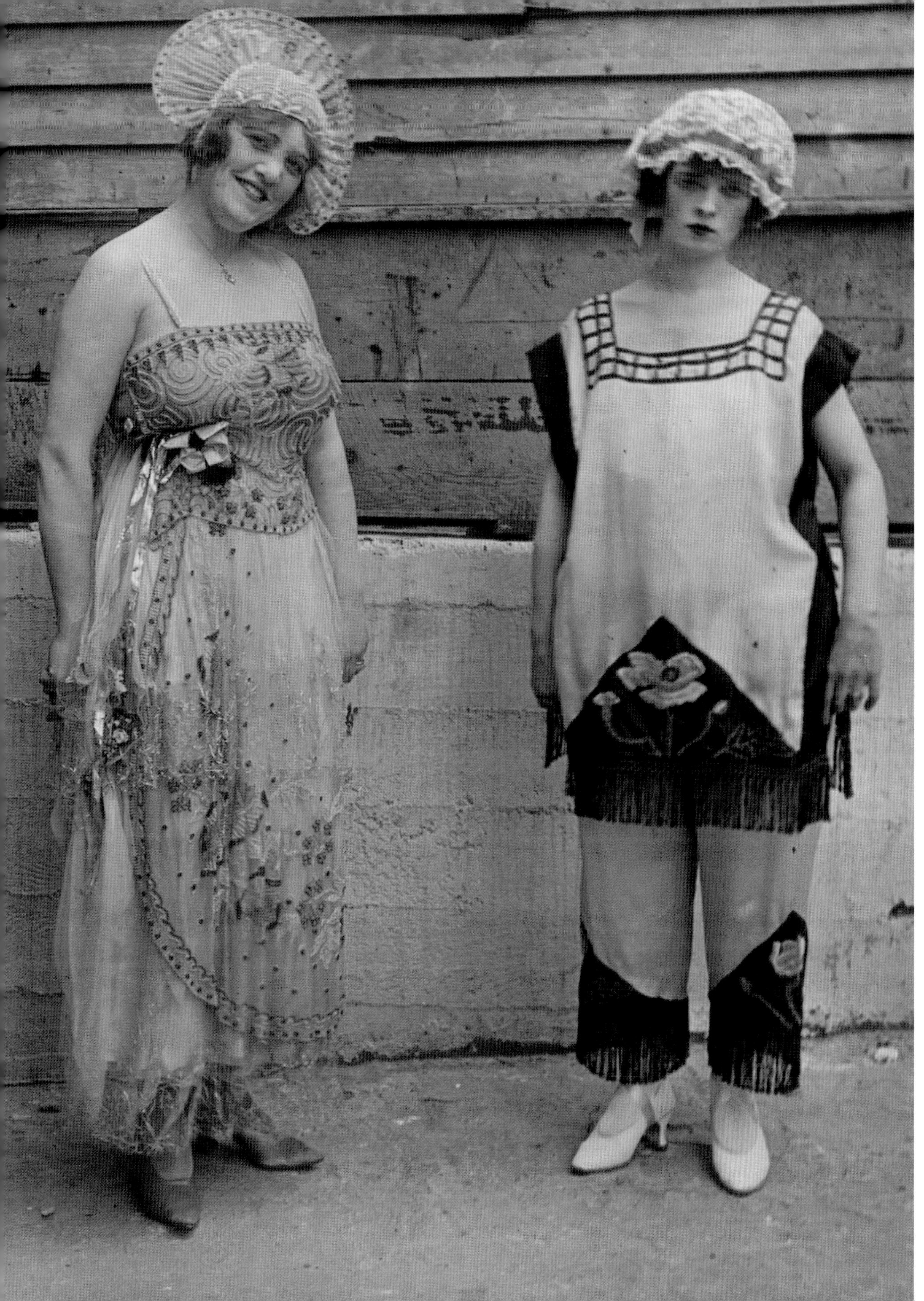

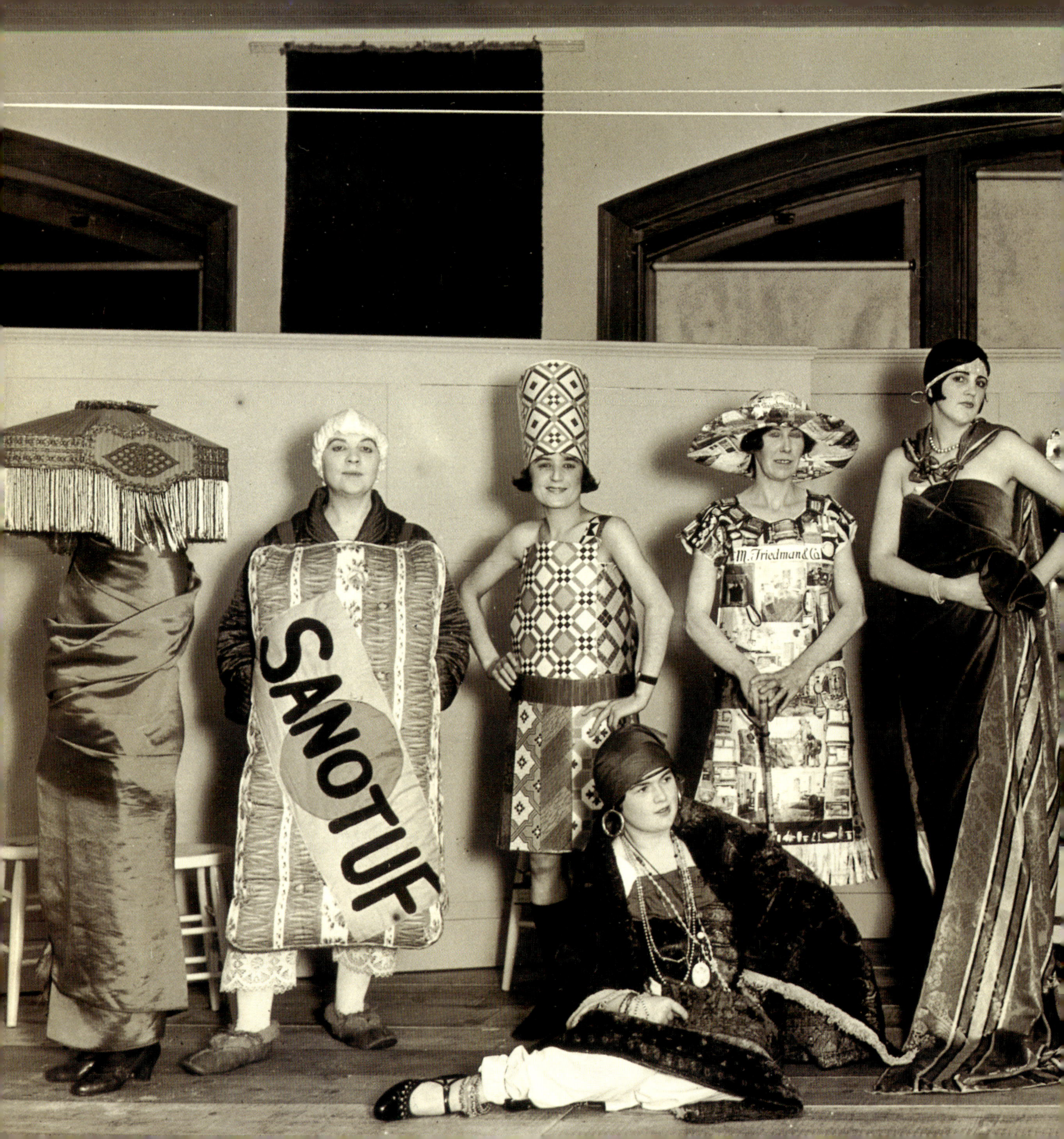
SANOTUF
M. Friedman & Co.

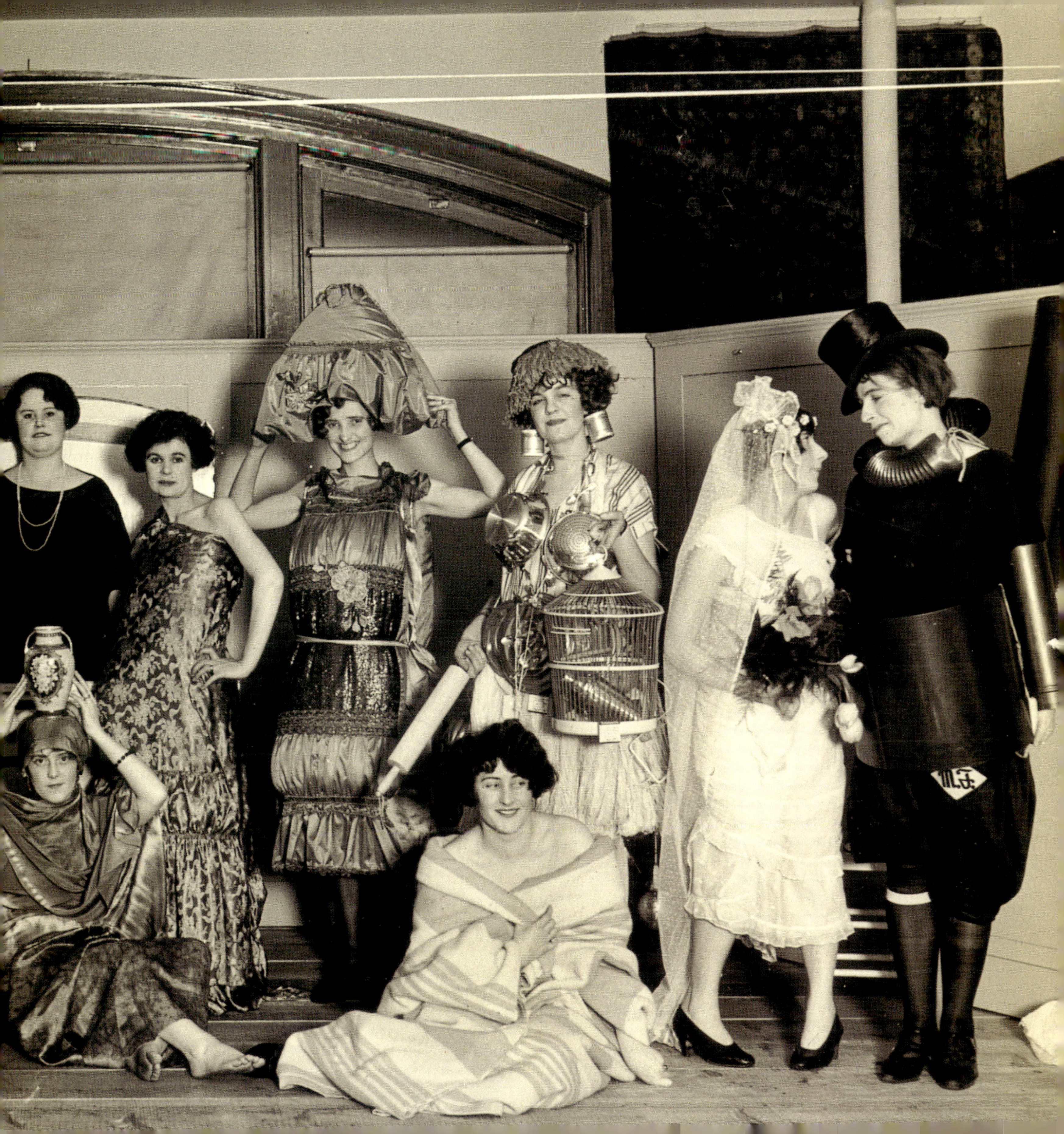

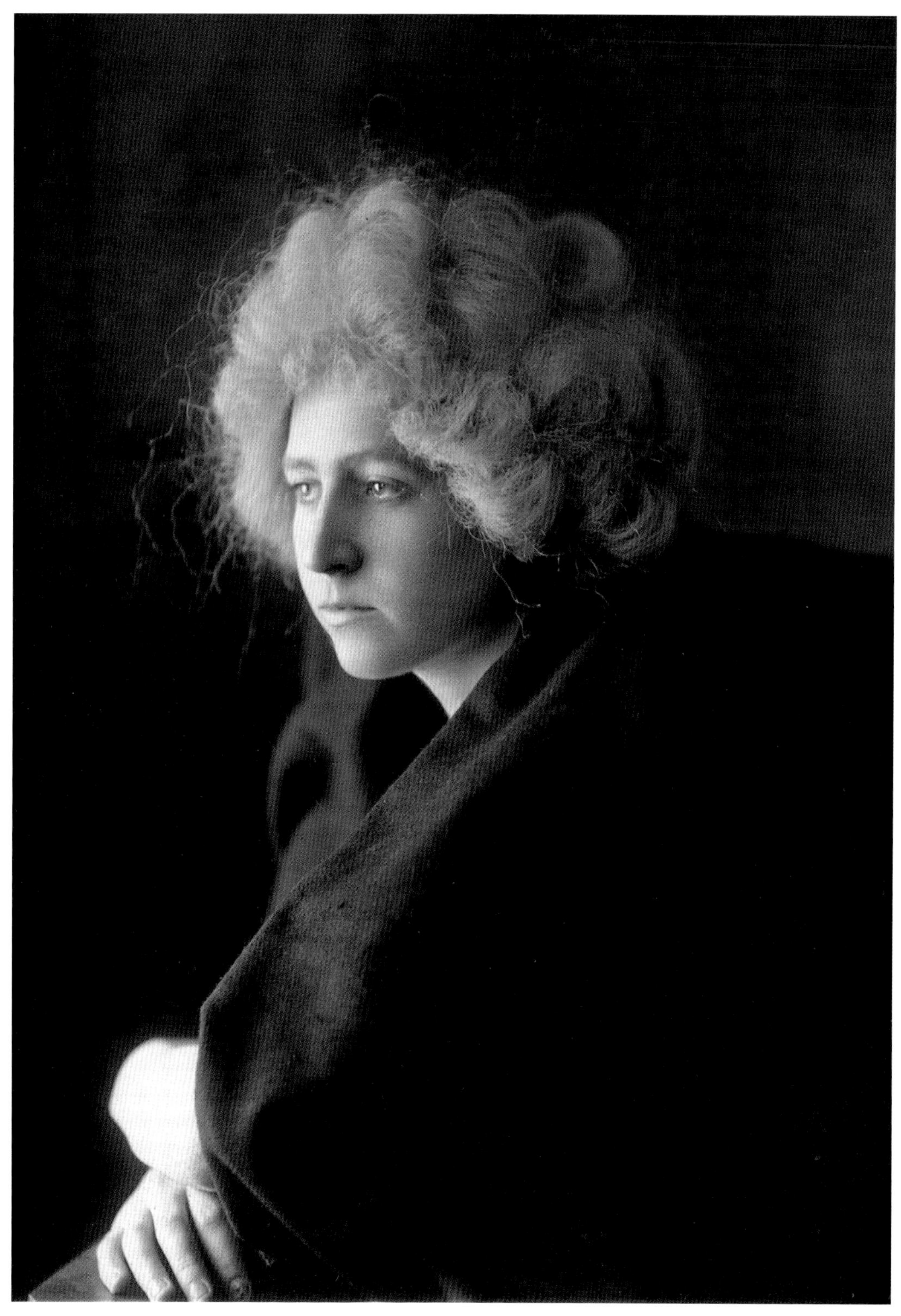

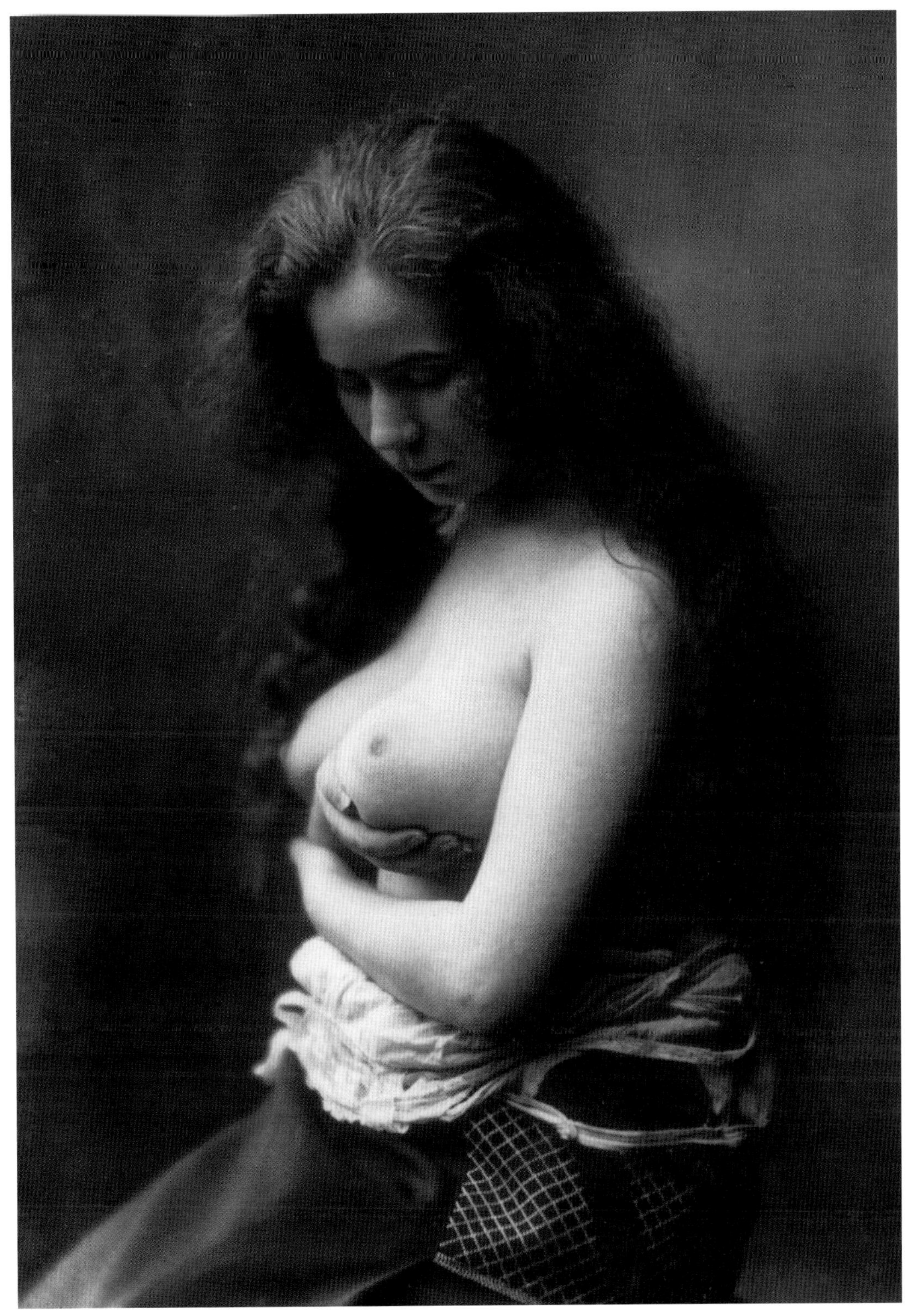

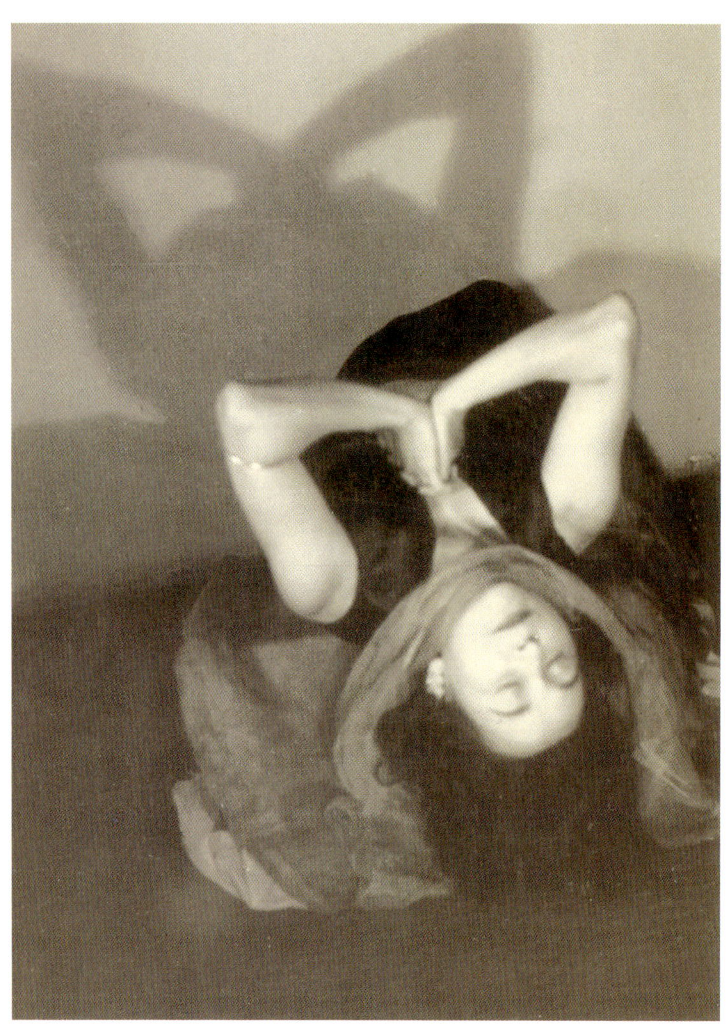

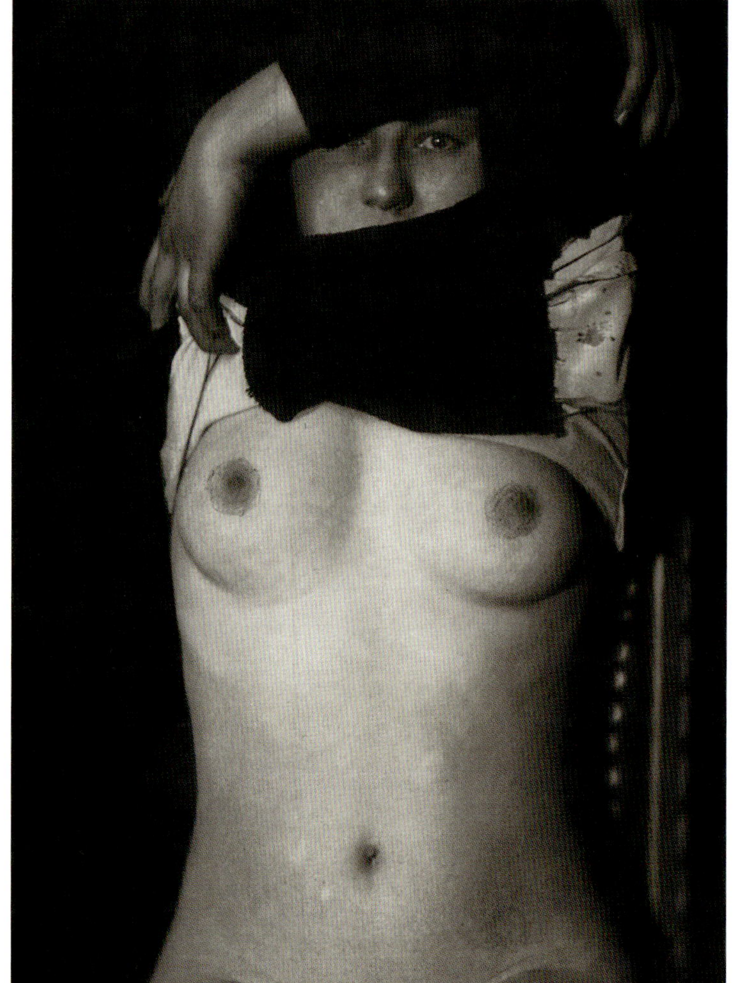

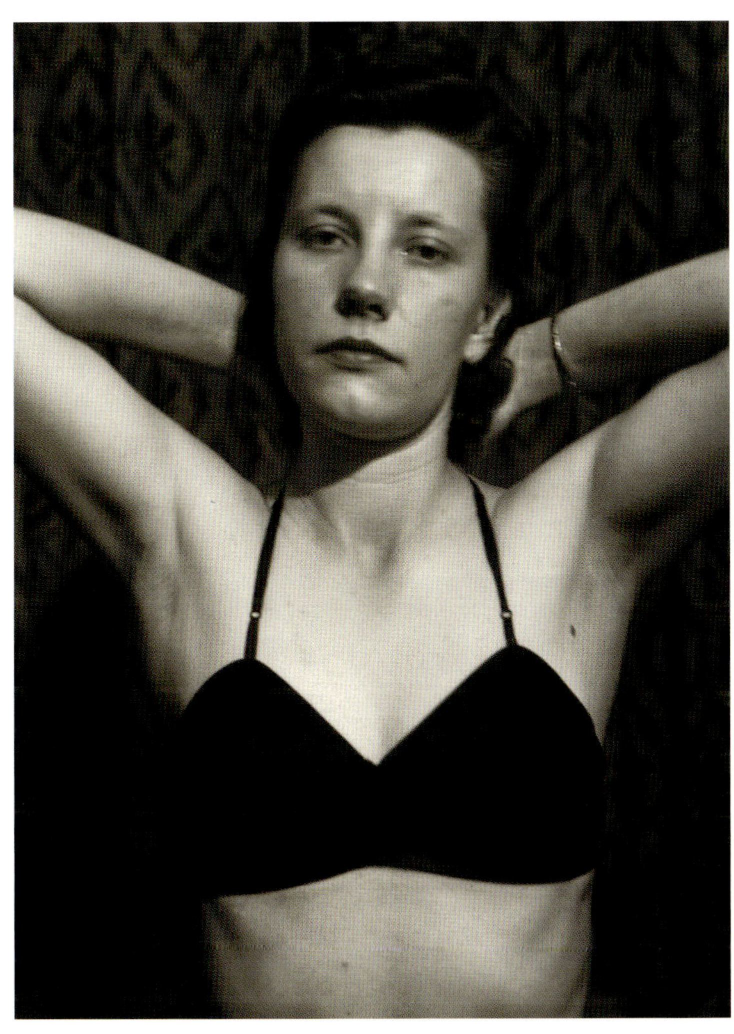

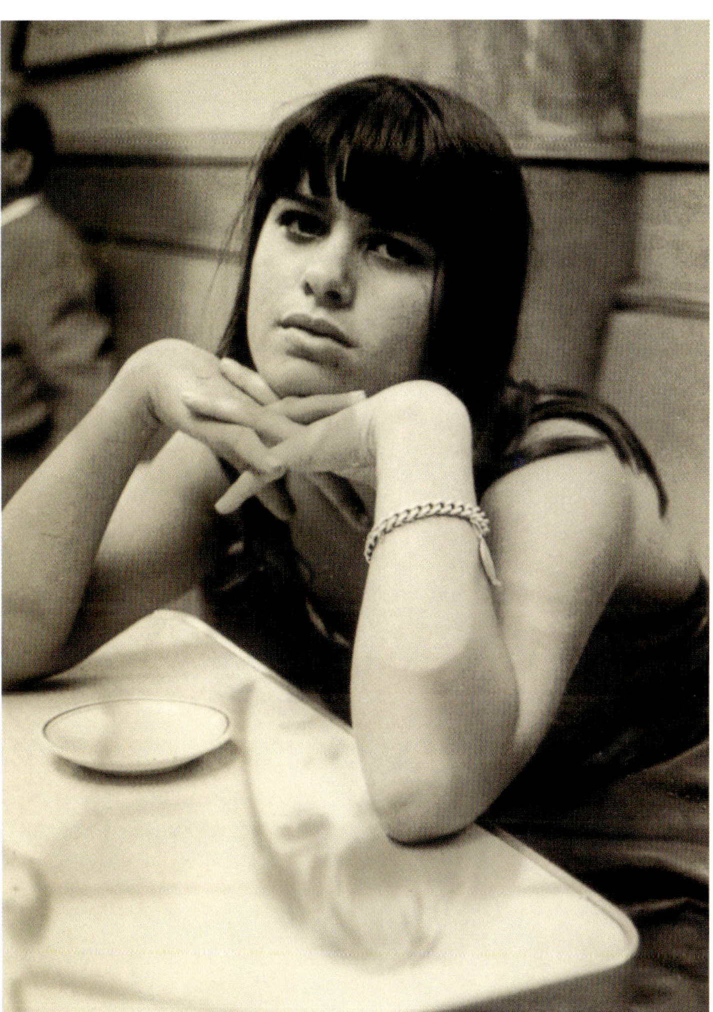

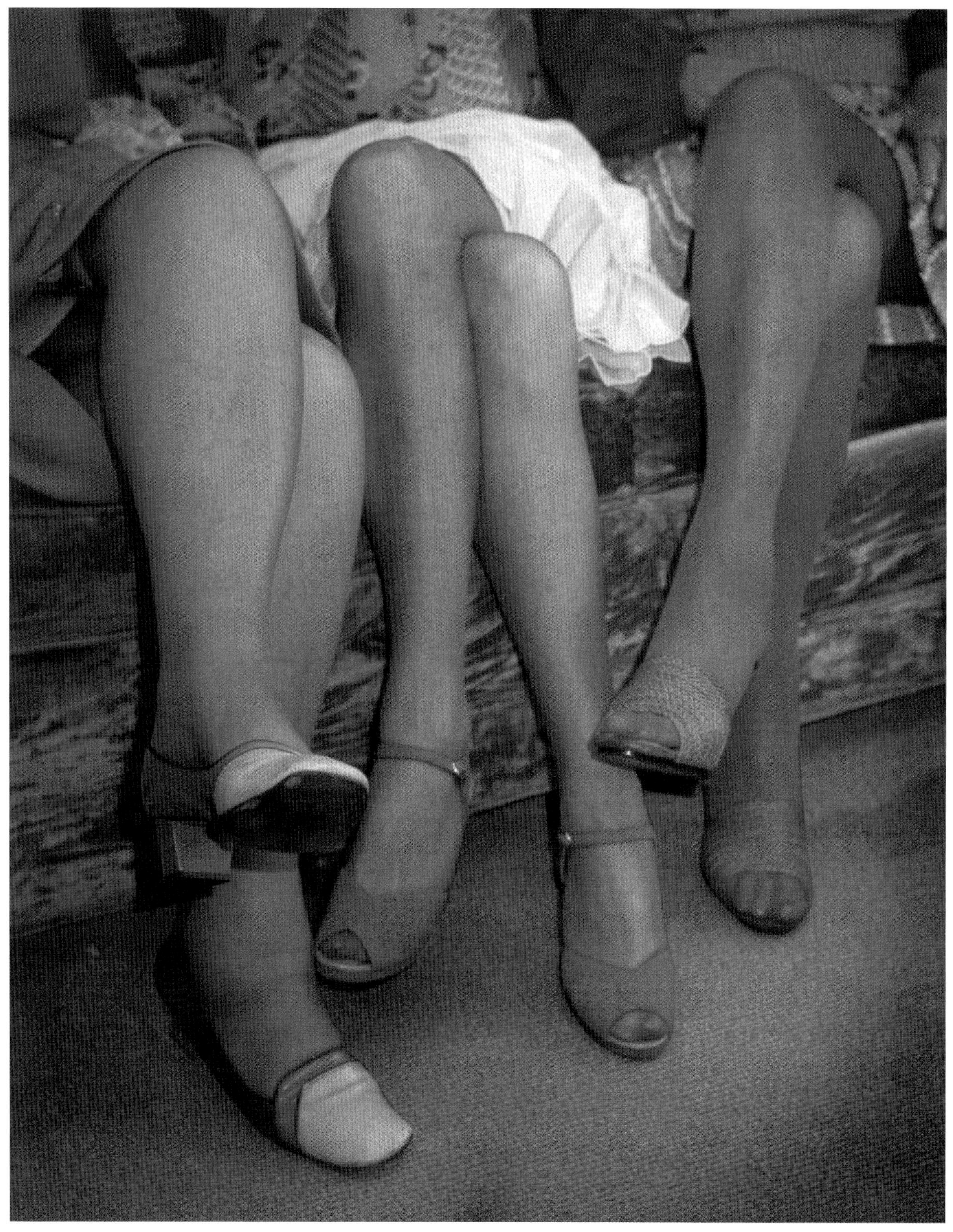

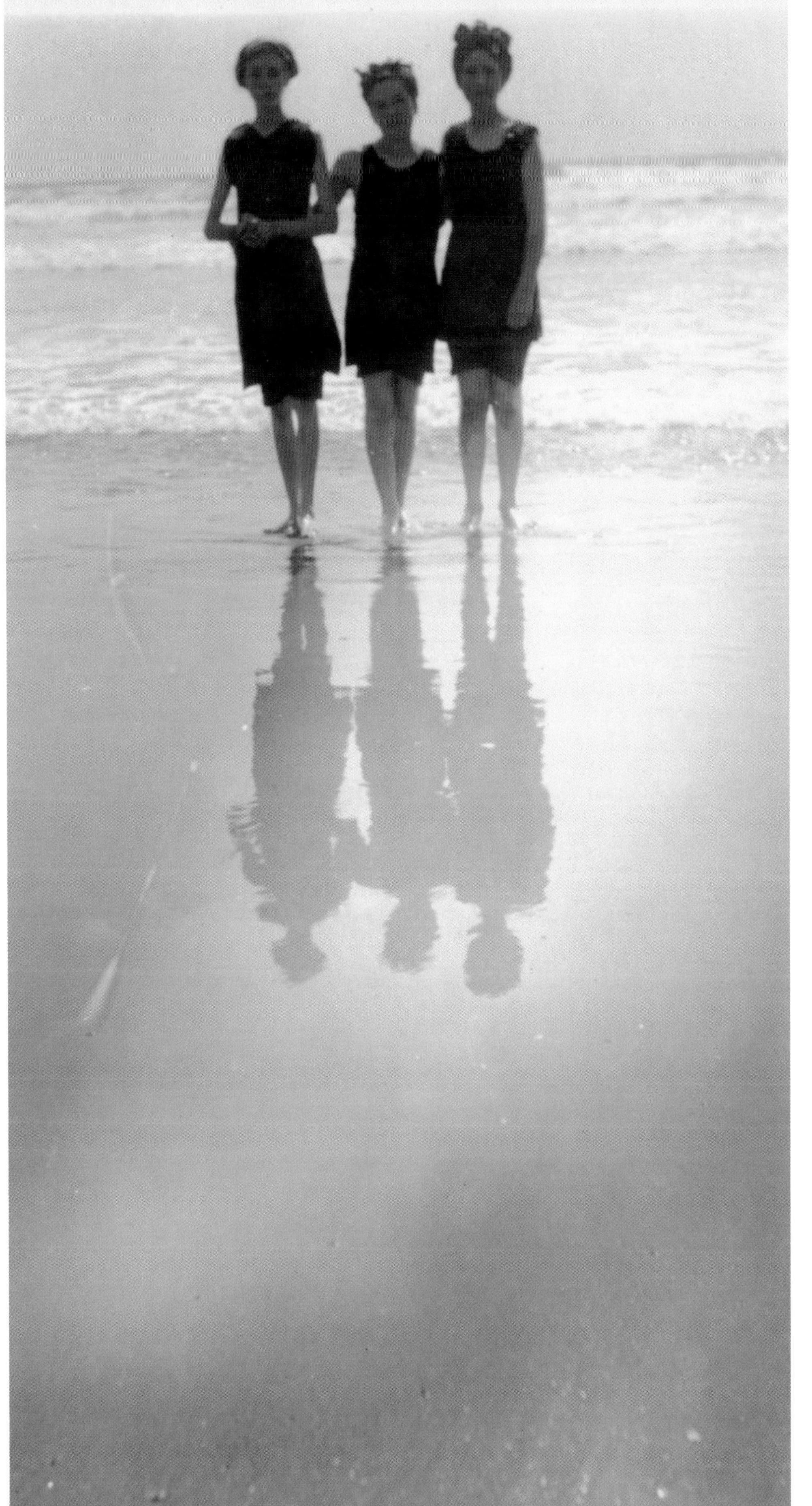

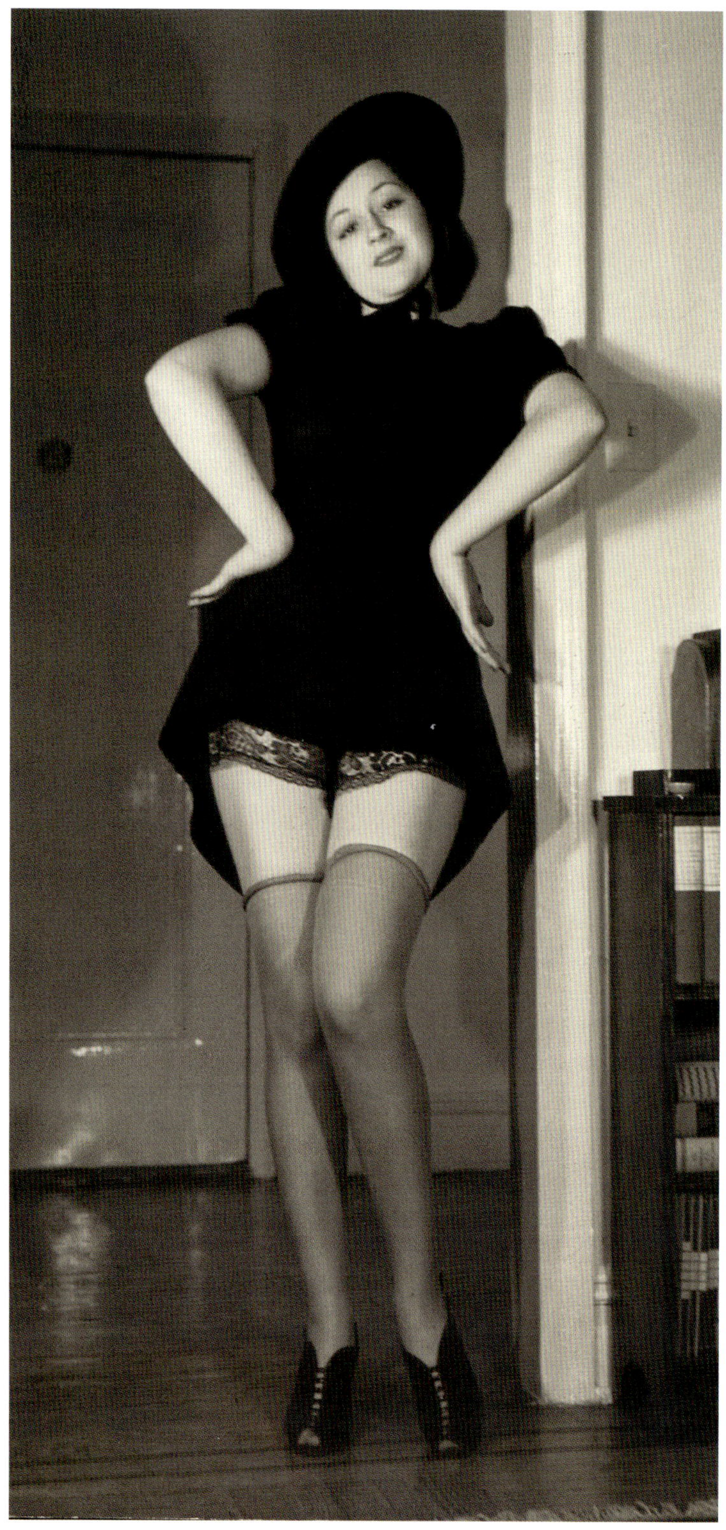

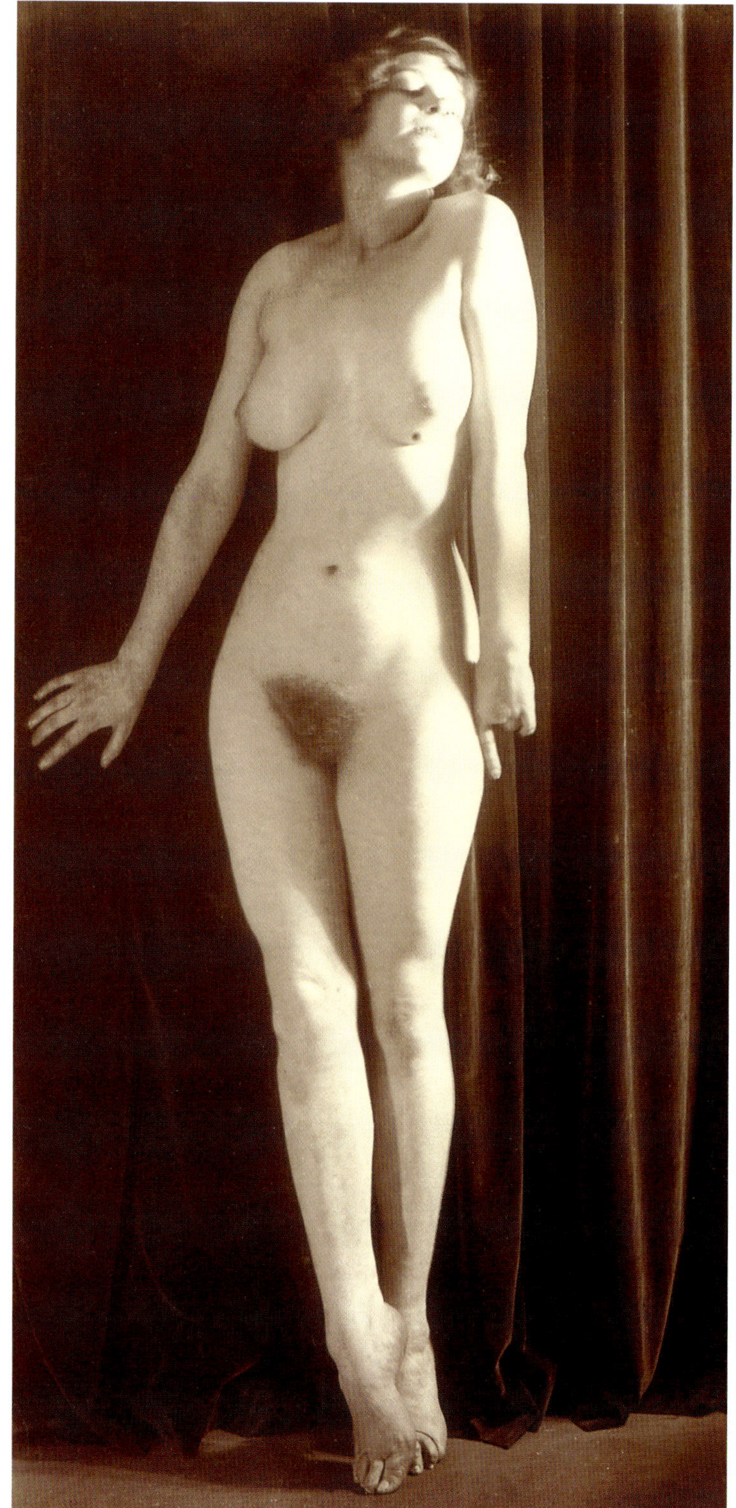

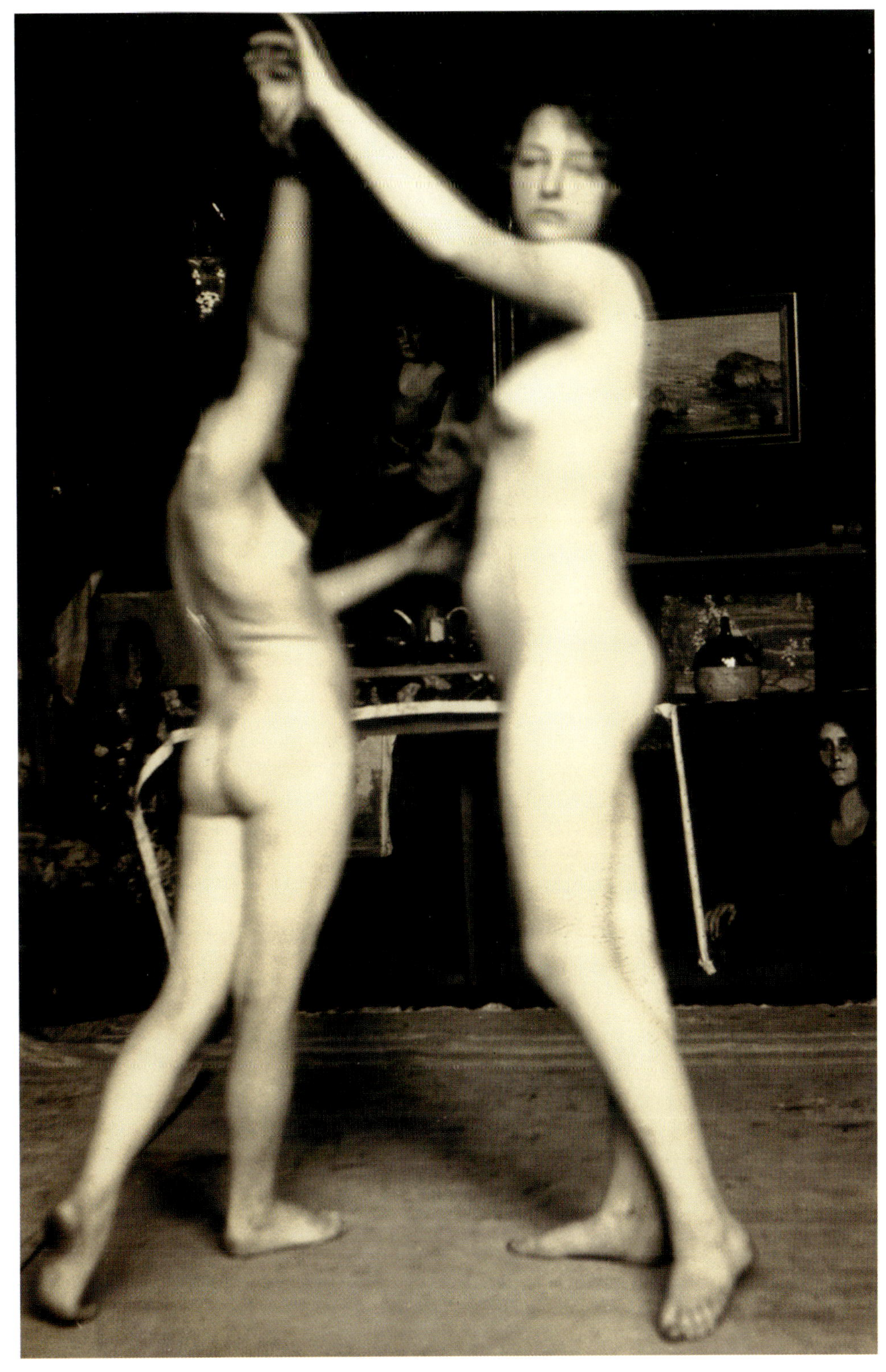

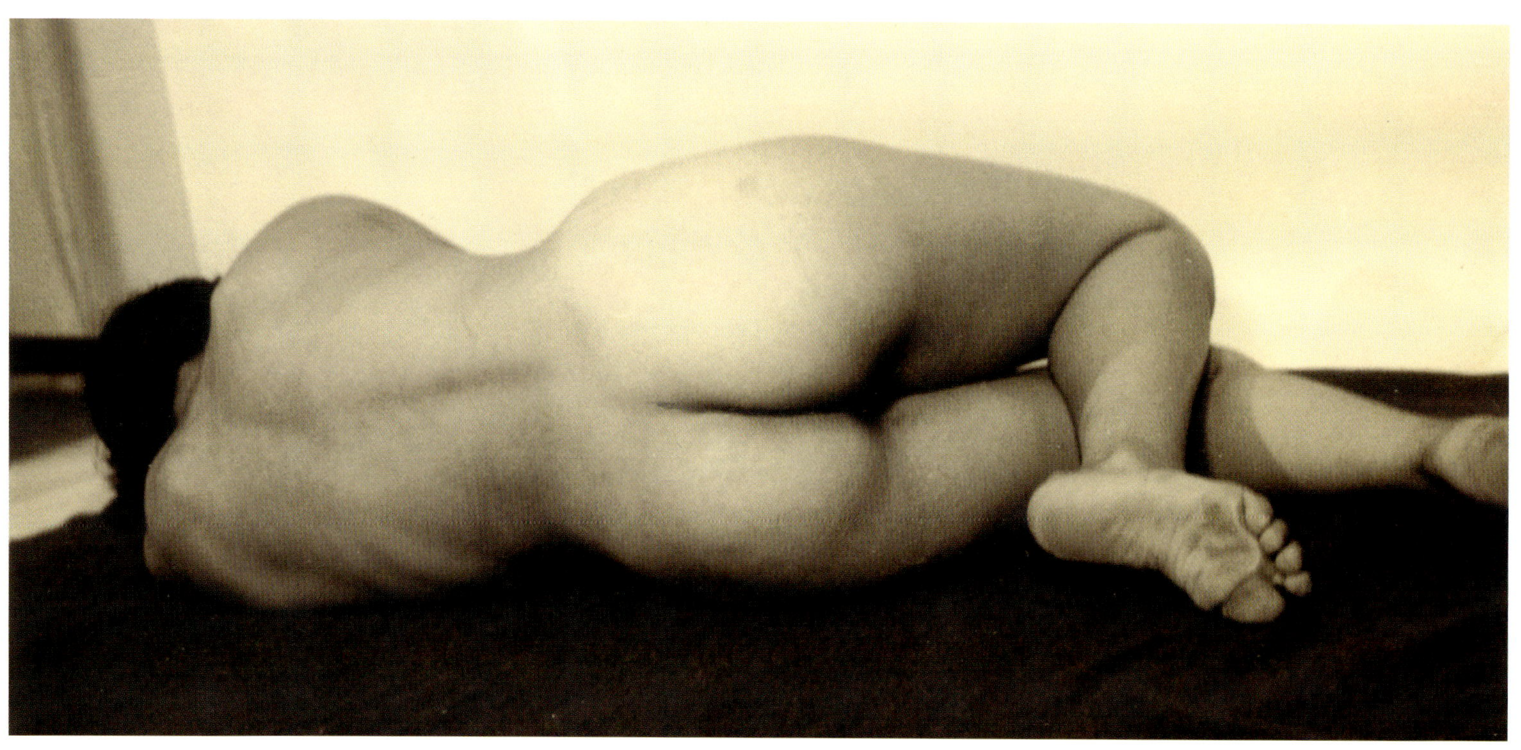

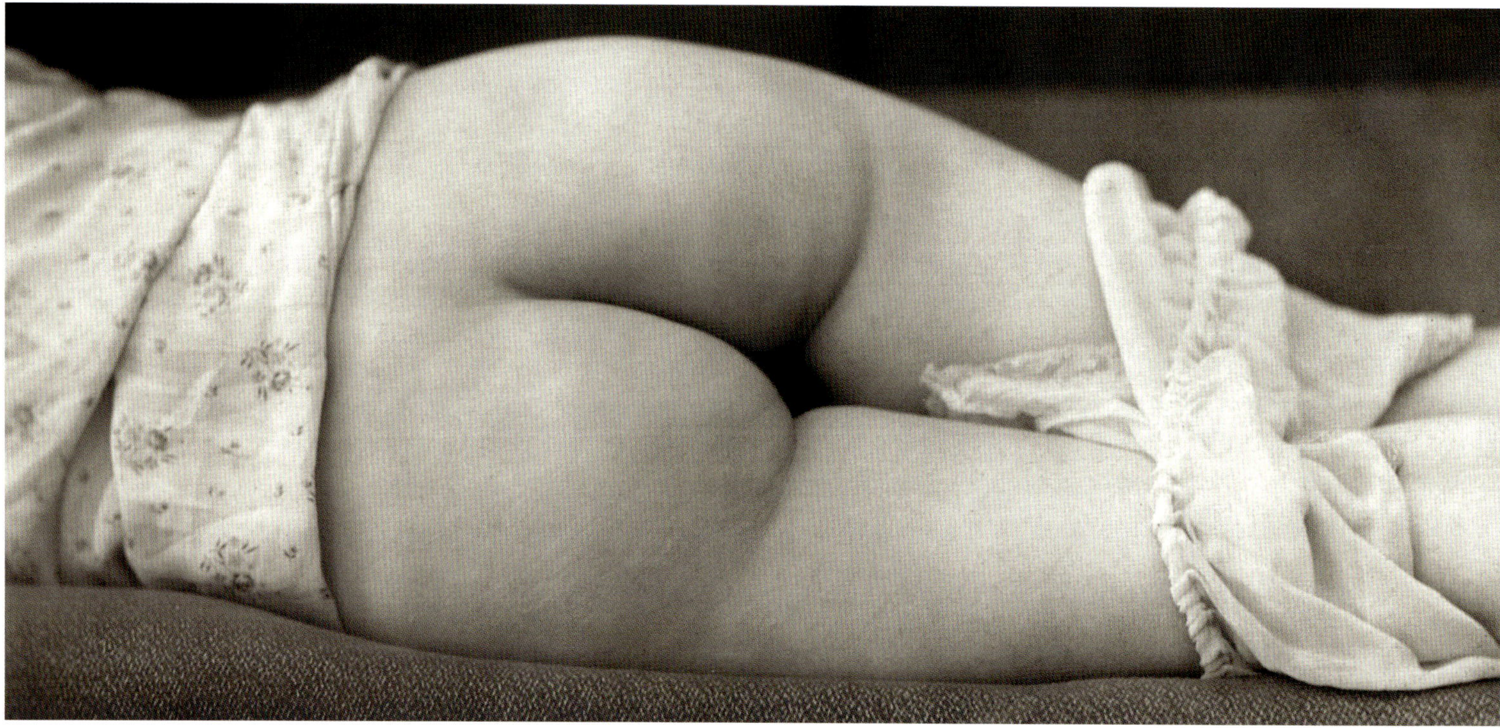

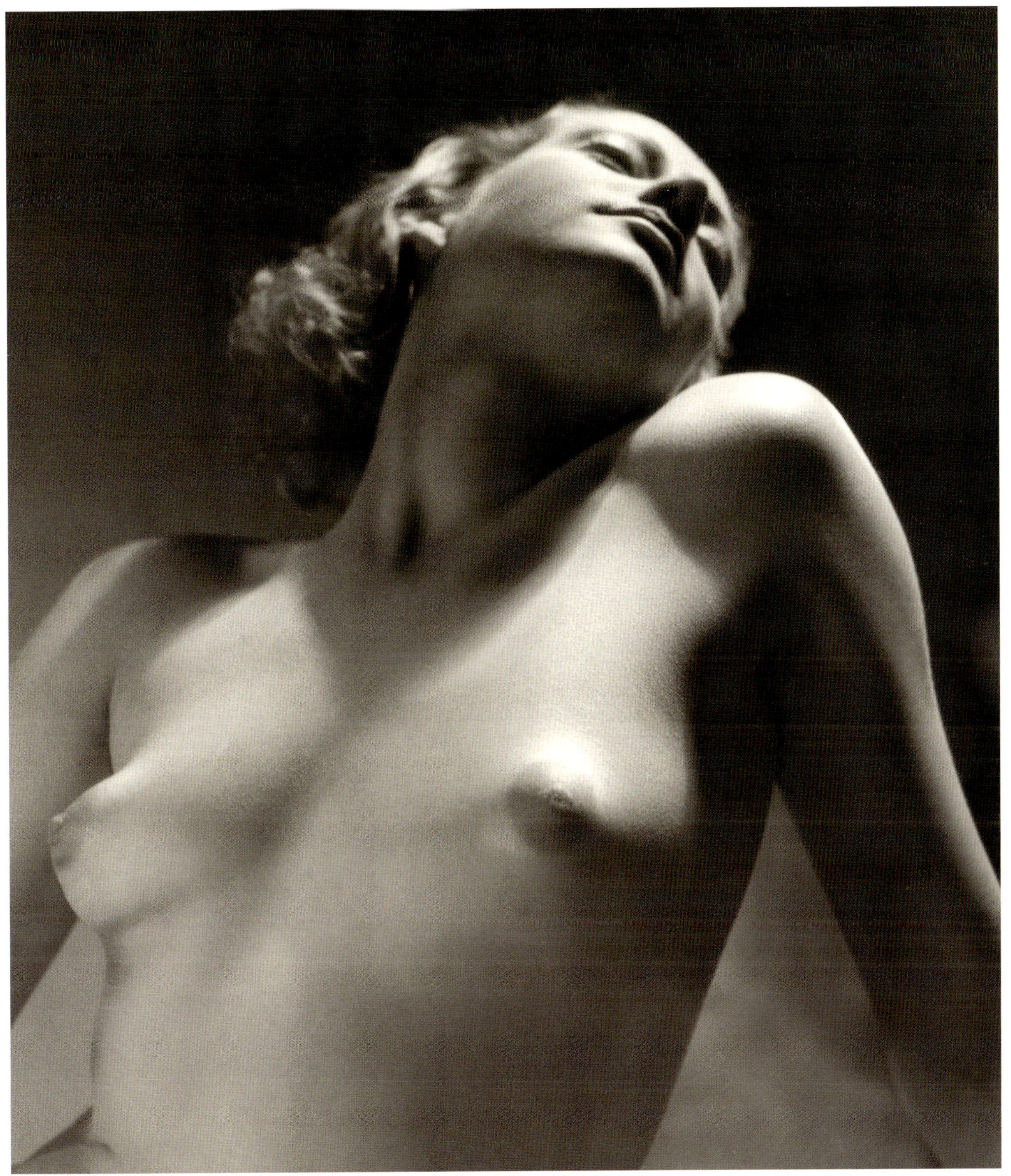

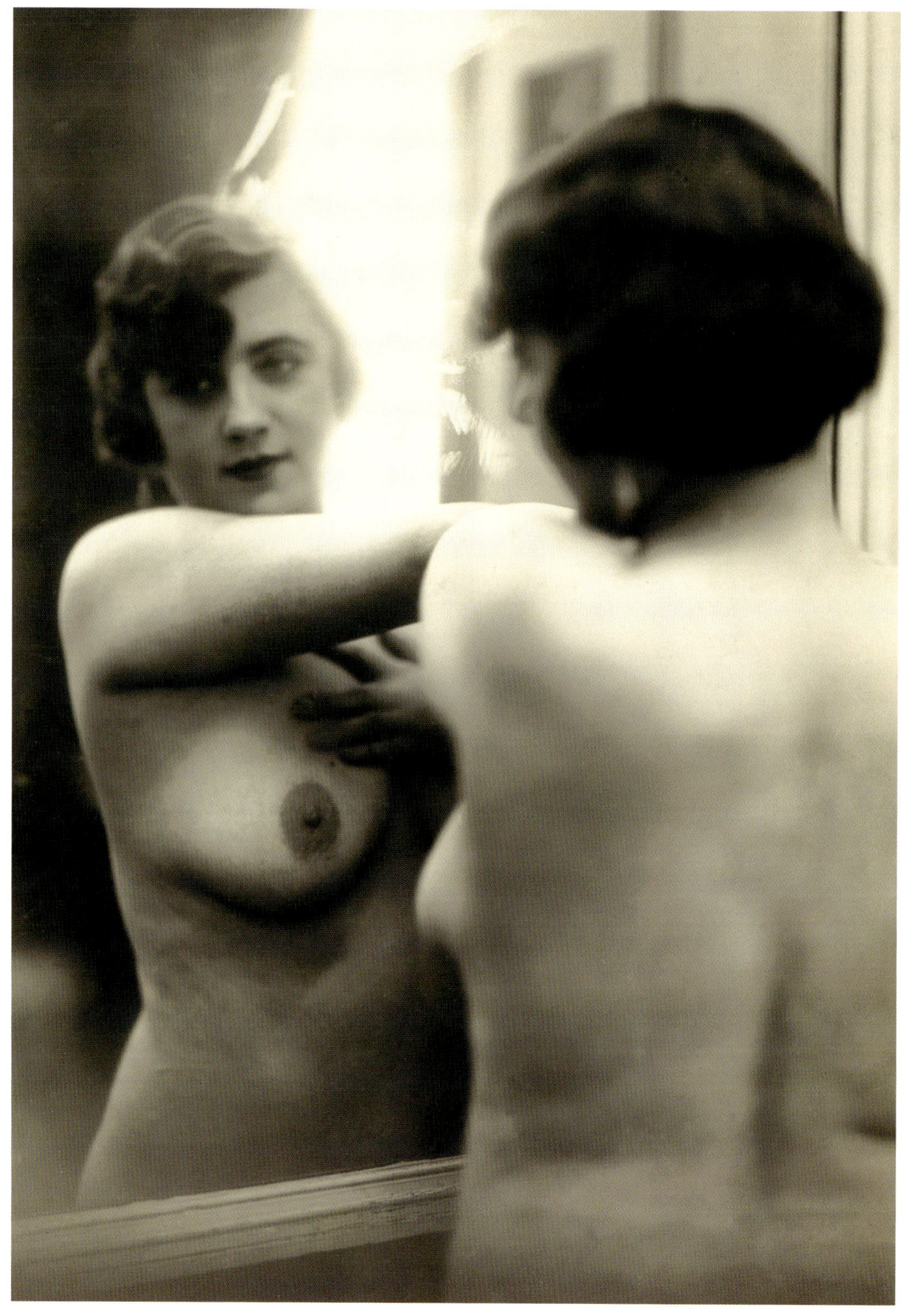

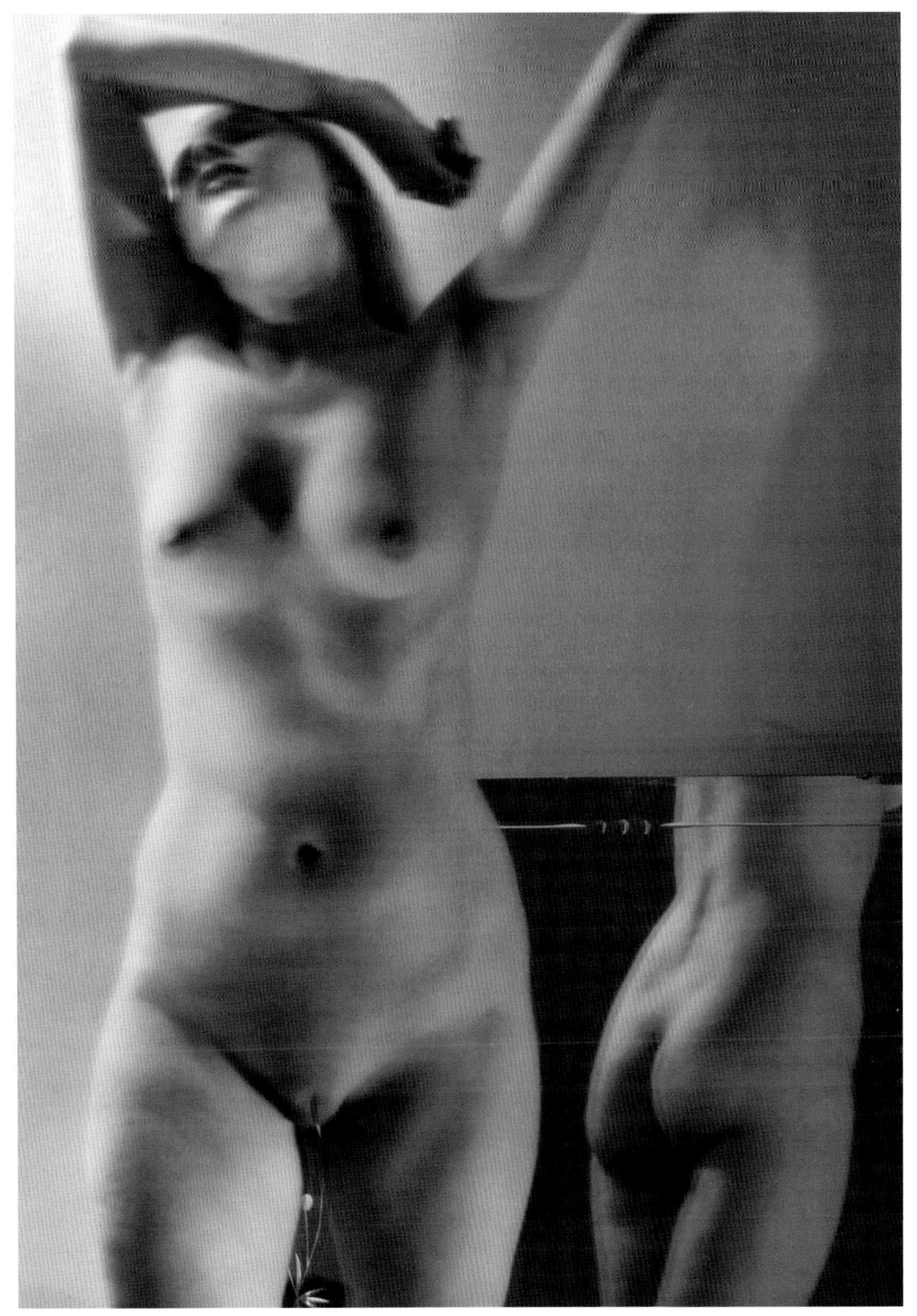

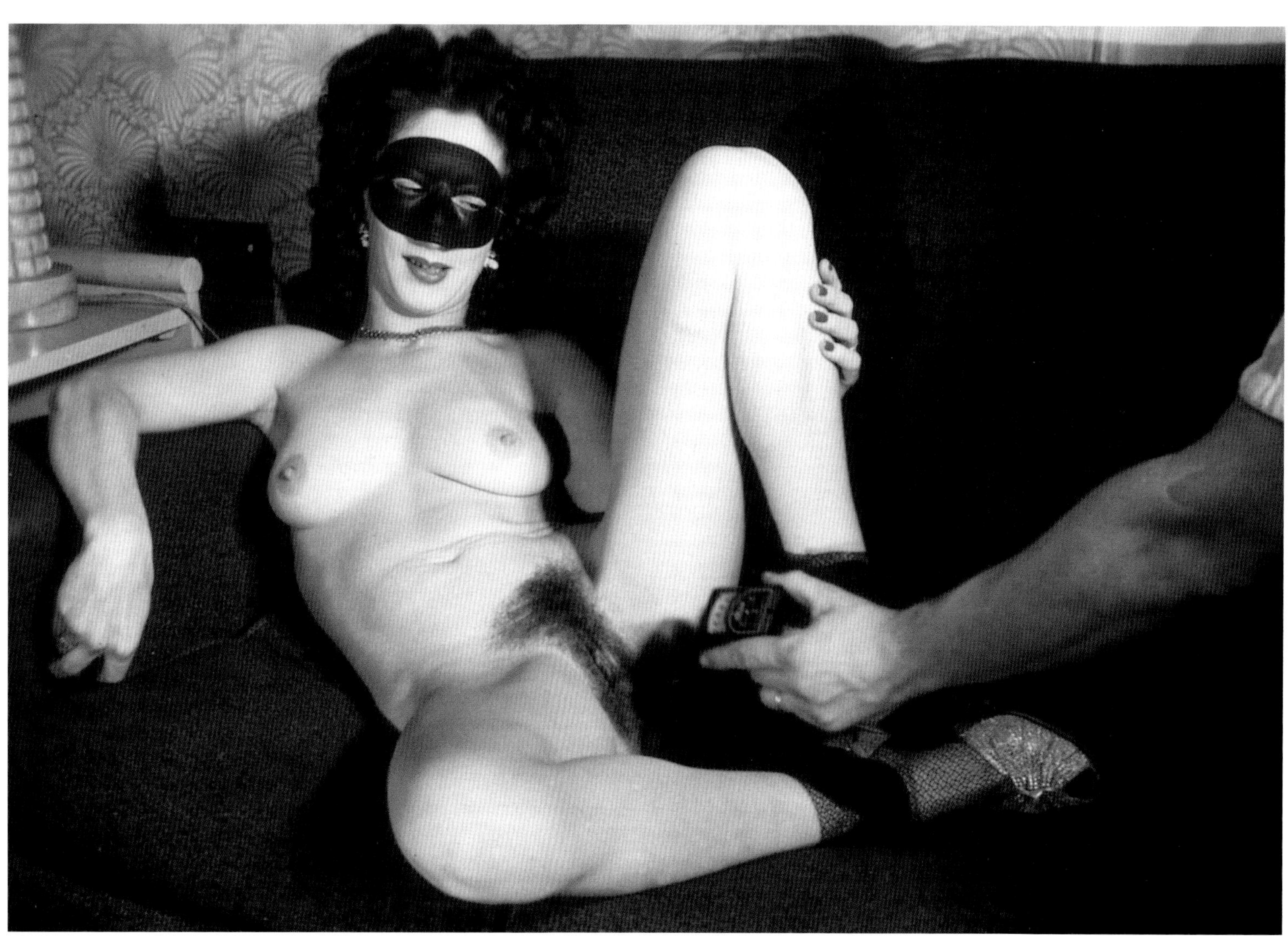

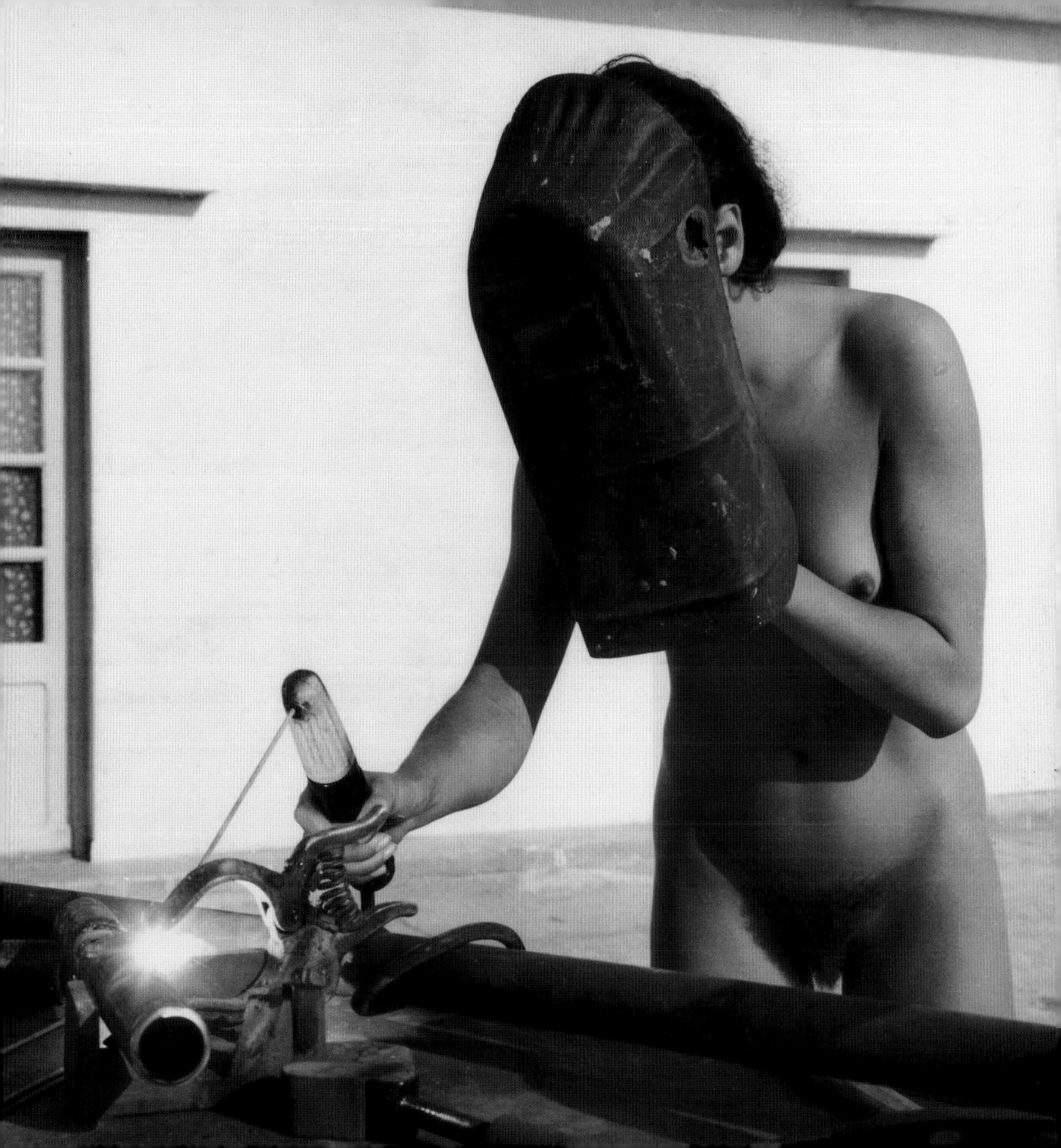

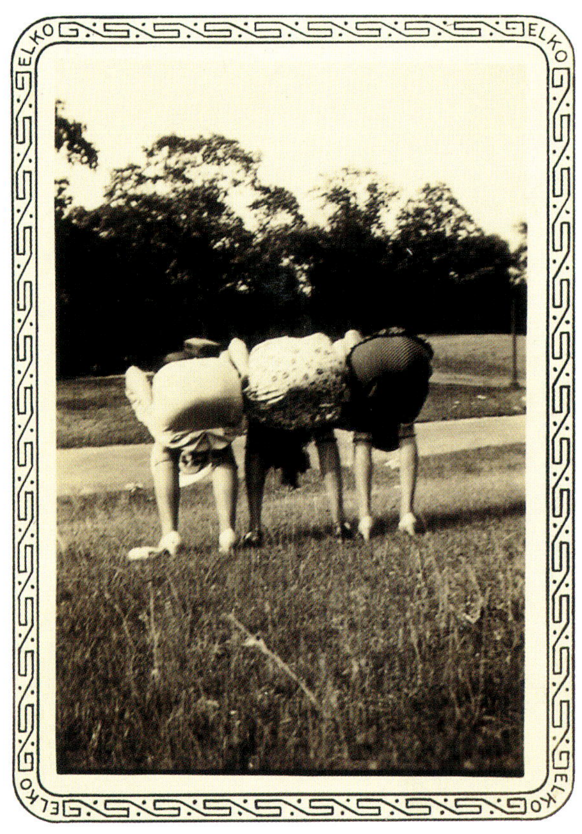
ELKO
ELKO
ELKO
ELKO

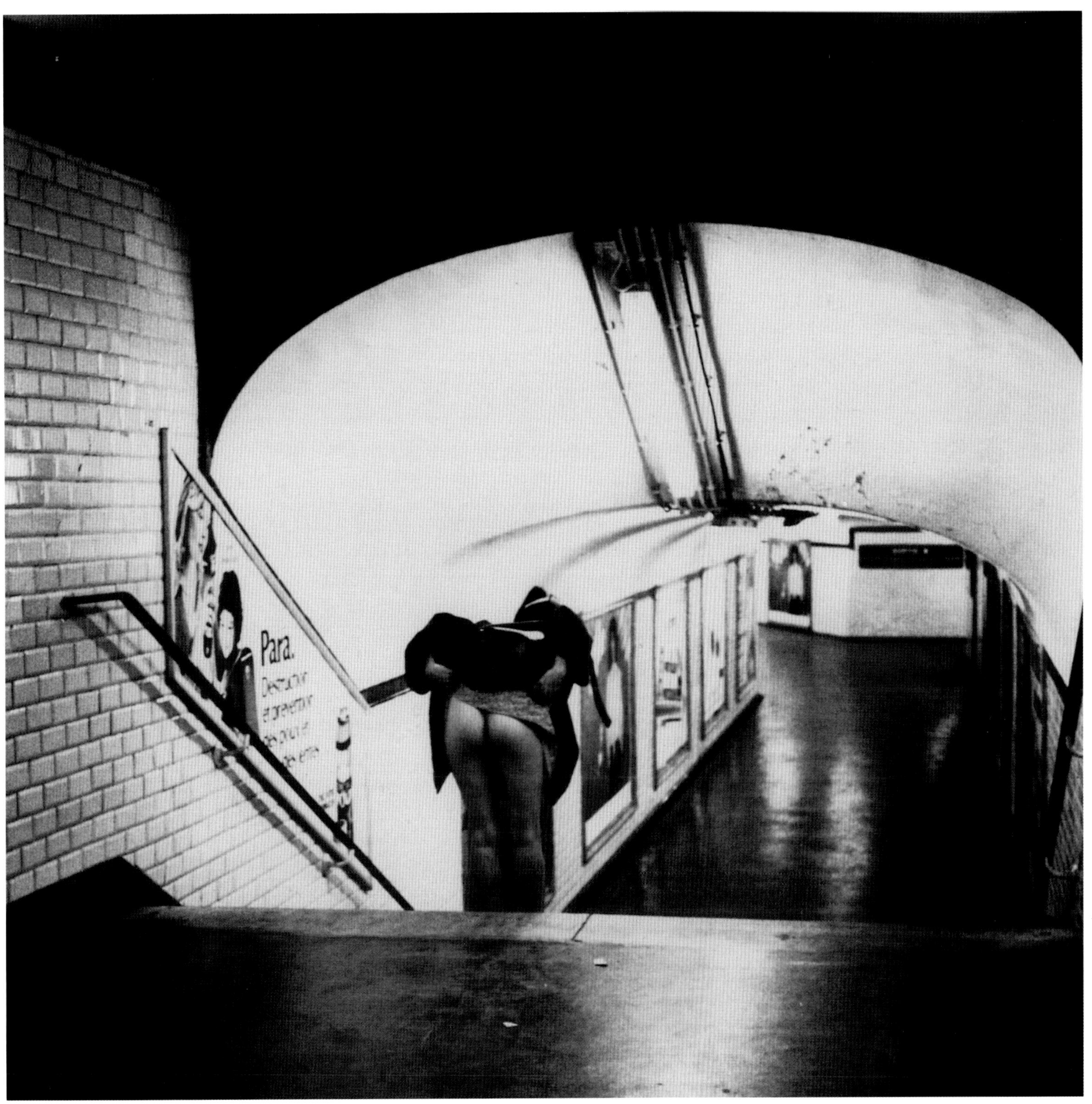
Para.

# Compatibility

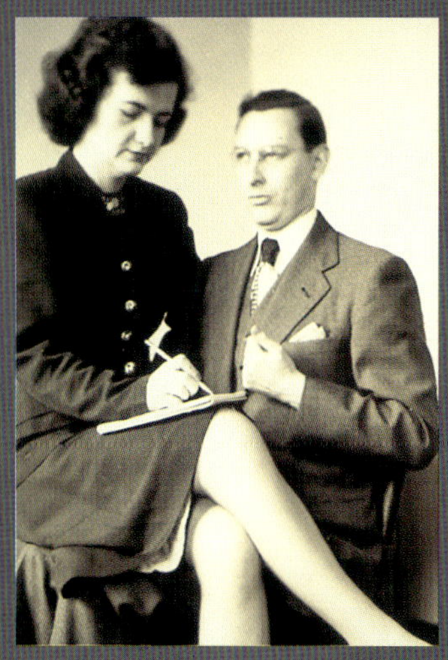

*'Love does not consist in gazing at each other but in looking outward together in the same direction.'*
Antoine de Saint-Exupéry

Photography has always been used to commemorate and attest to human emotional commitment through the reality of images preserved. Mortality, or the fleeting nature of the human heart, cannot erase the evidence of what – in the photograph – appeared to be true to one another, and to the world at large, at that specific moment in time.

It is an unstated truth that, whatever scene of intimacy takes place, it is done in the presence of at least one other witness, the photographer. In fact, there is a suspicion that occasions for picture-taking have been cause for a certain stage-managed creation of forced affection, instigated by the person with the camera. Wedding photographers are especially prolific in their frantic, all-encompassing documentation of formalized happiness.

Early photographs of couples exhibit the grim-faced charm of people being led before a firing squad, as the exposure time permitted no relaxed smile or gesture. Later technology allowed for a greater level of relaxation and shedding of inhibitions.

Ultimately, many of these photographs hover between public declarations of fidelity and private gestures of feeling. John Updike wrote, 'Like novels and scandal sheets, snapshots are windows, however smeary, into other lives.' It is a sad fact that, although fragile, photographs often outlive the attraction, passion, love and commitment they were once thought to immortalize.

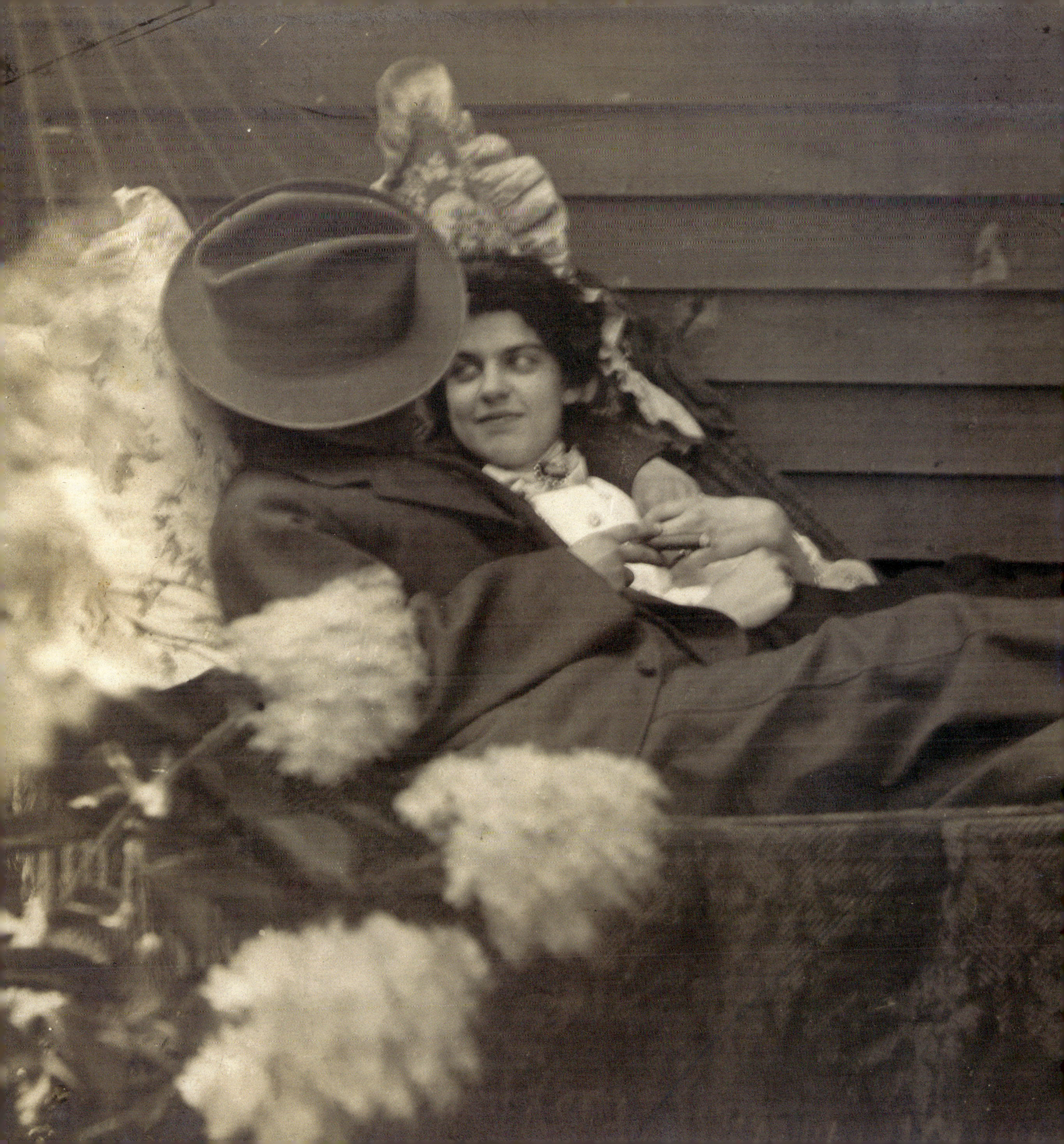

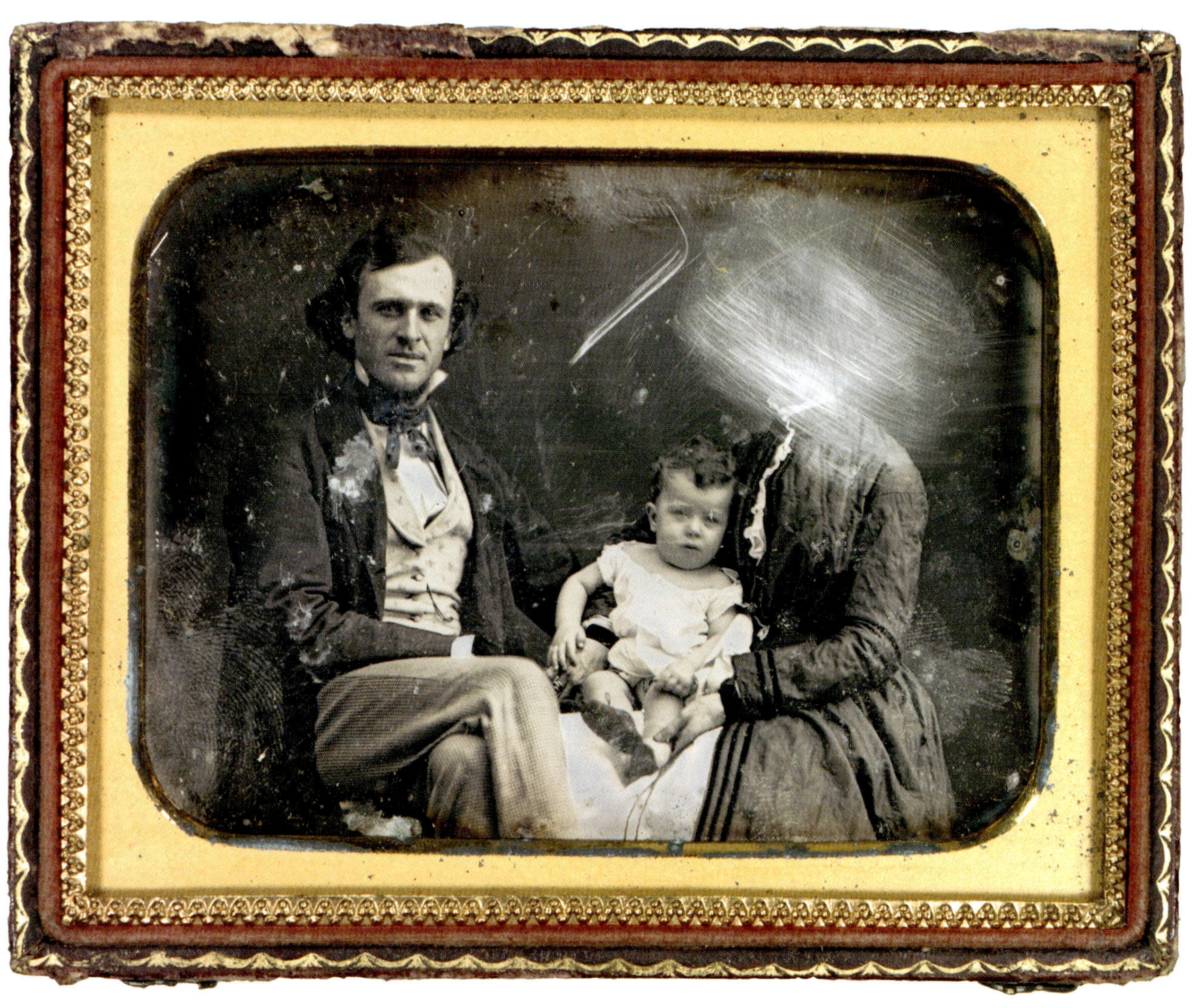

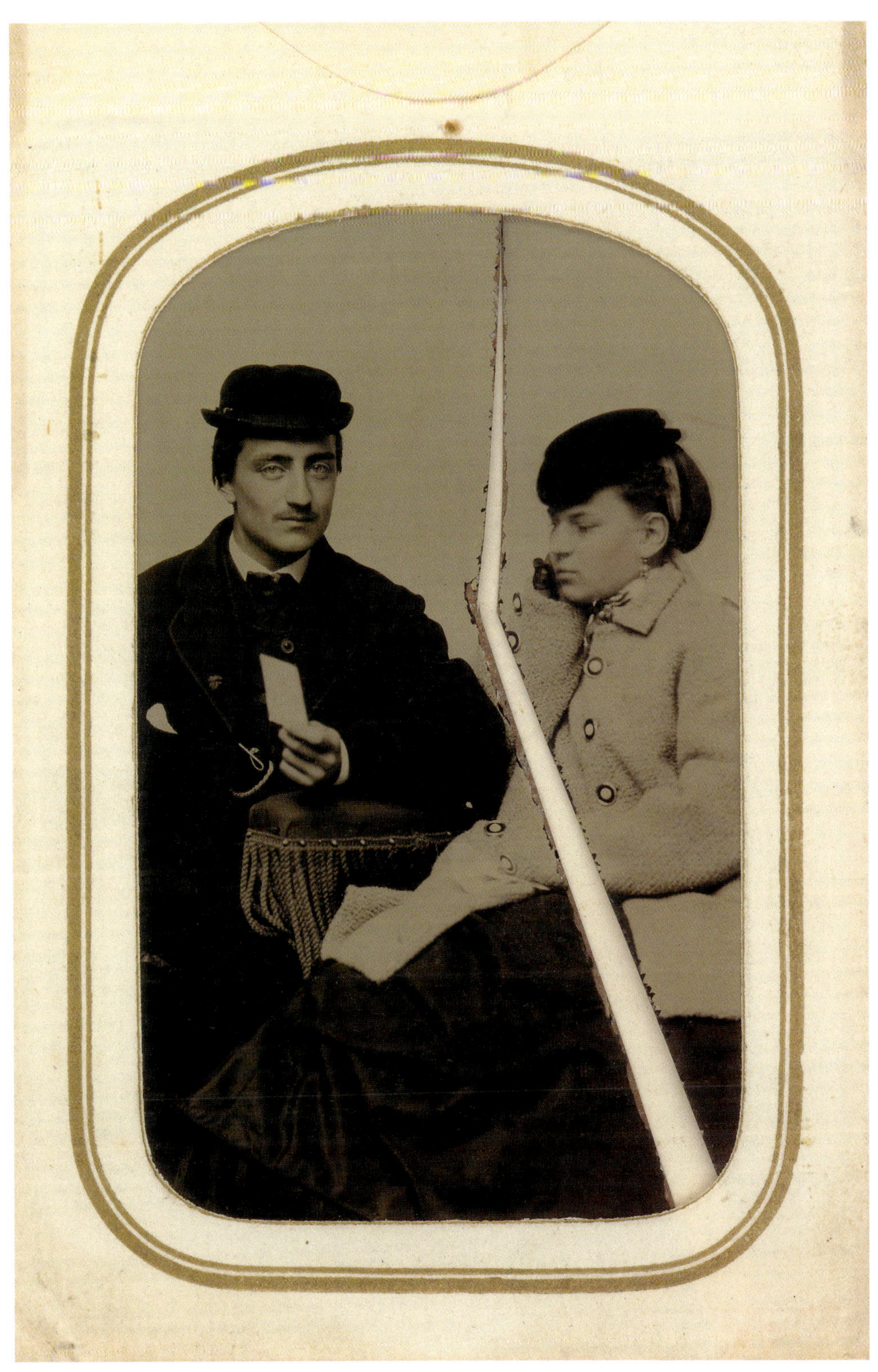

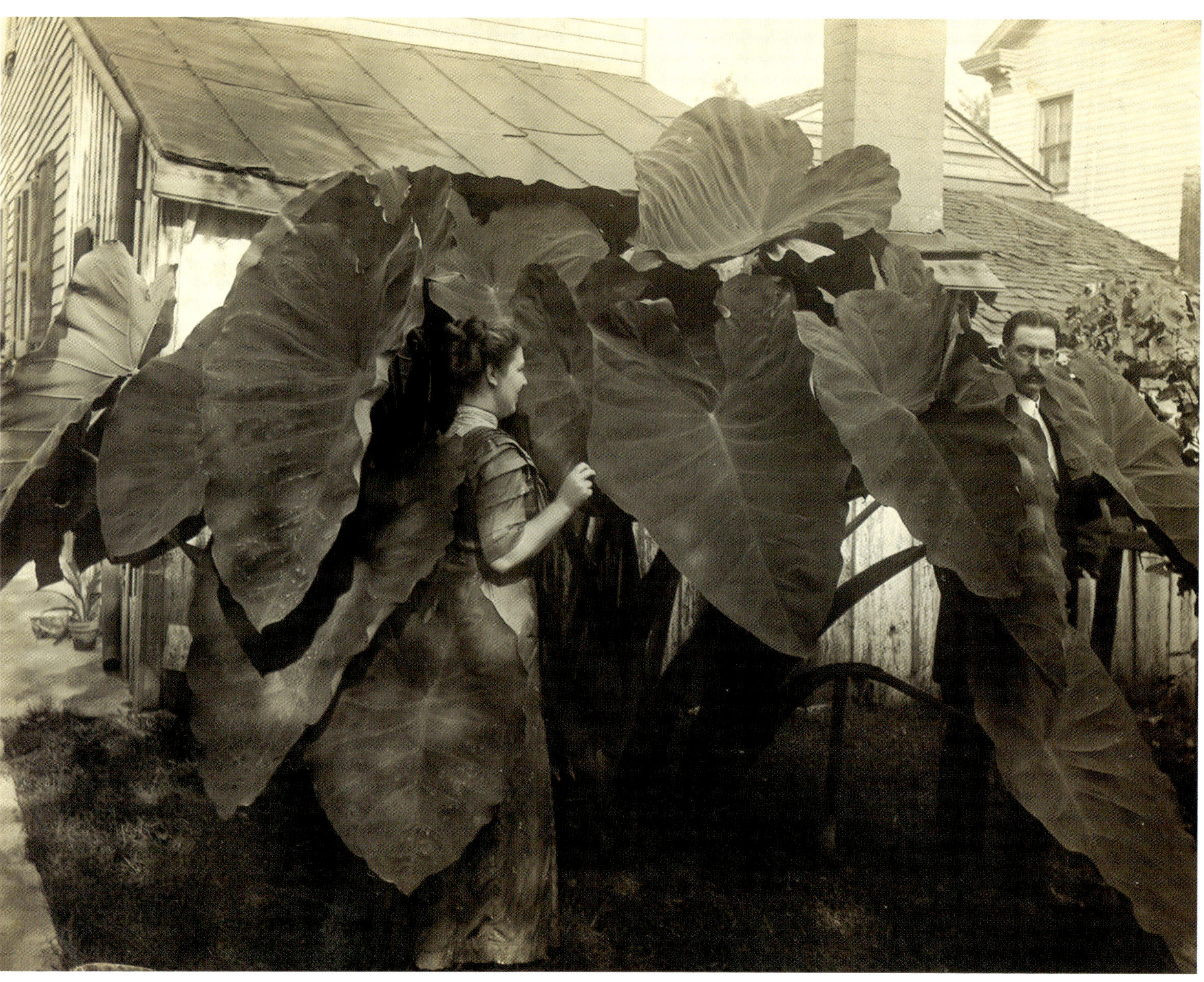

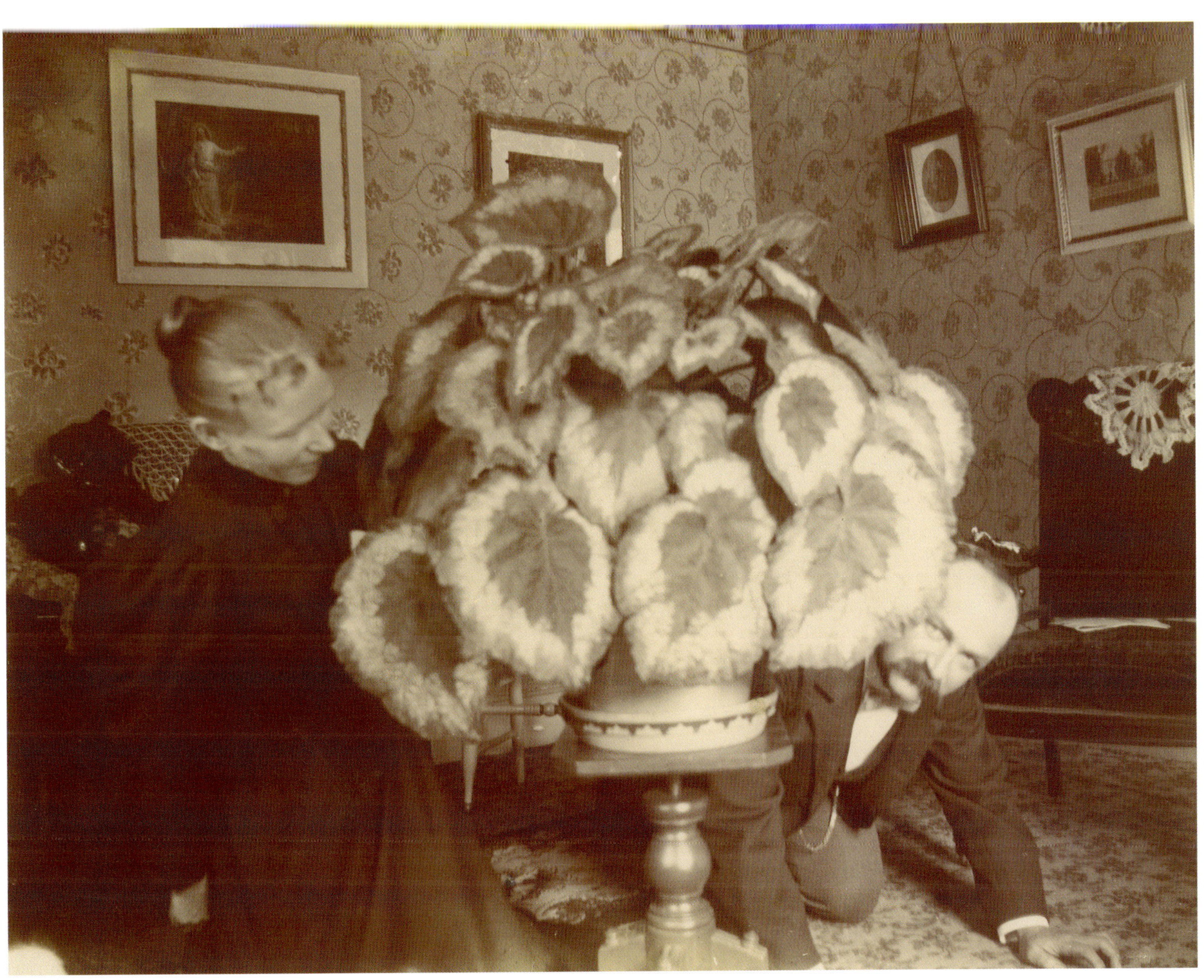

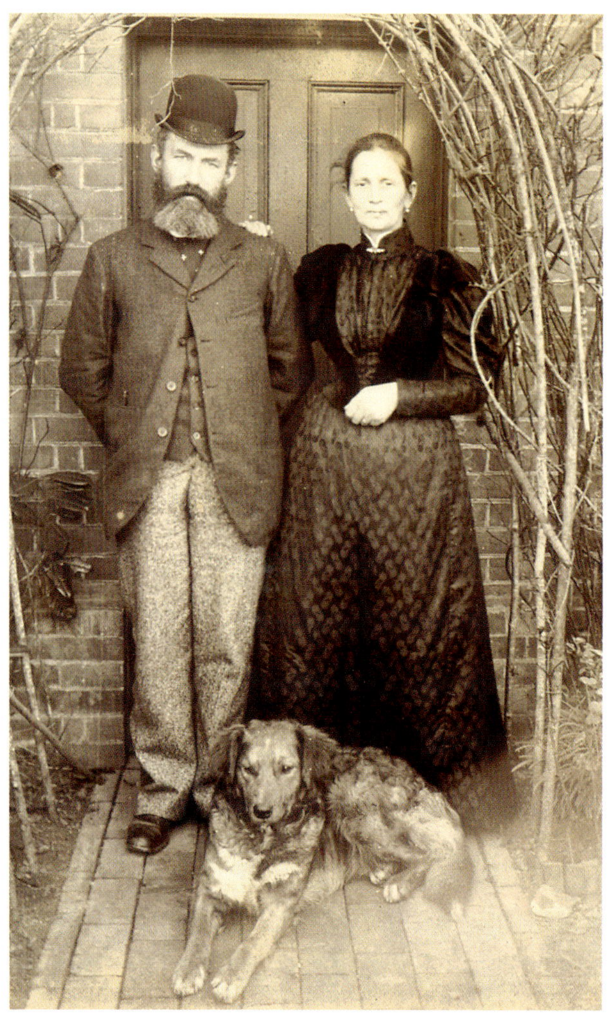

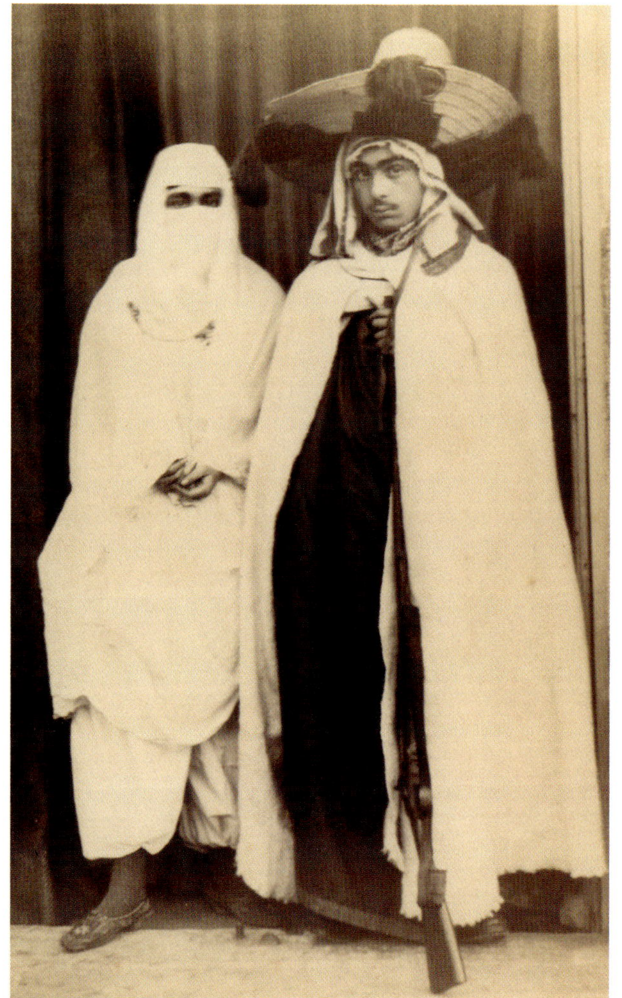

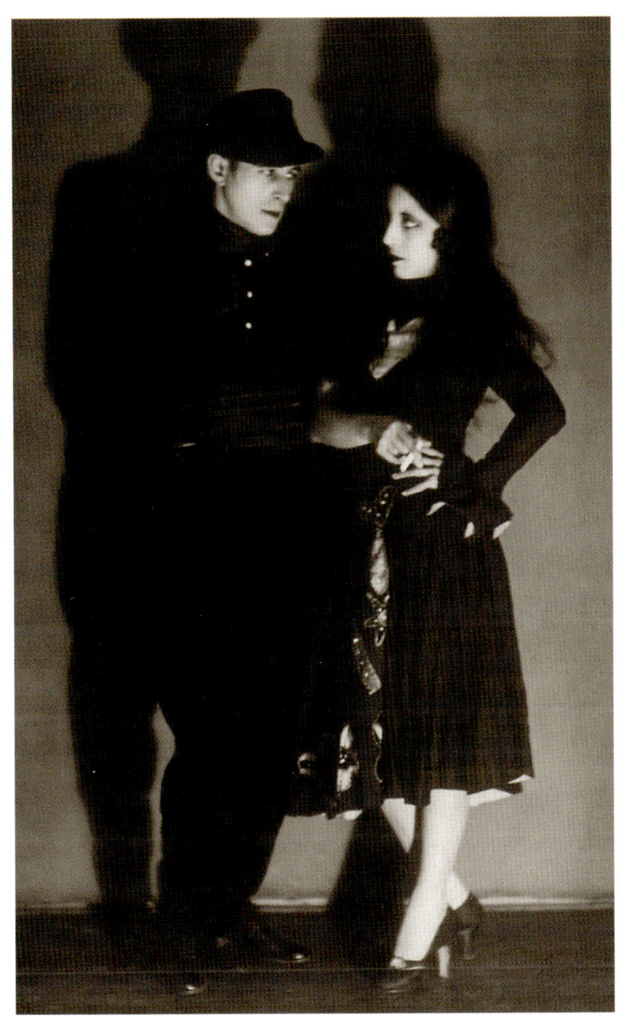

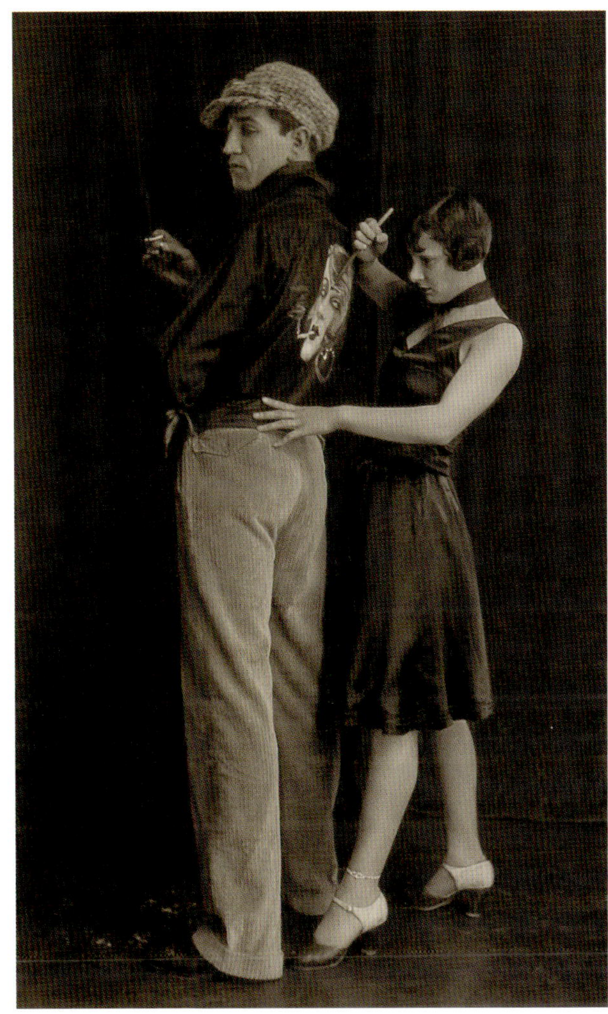

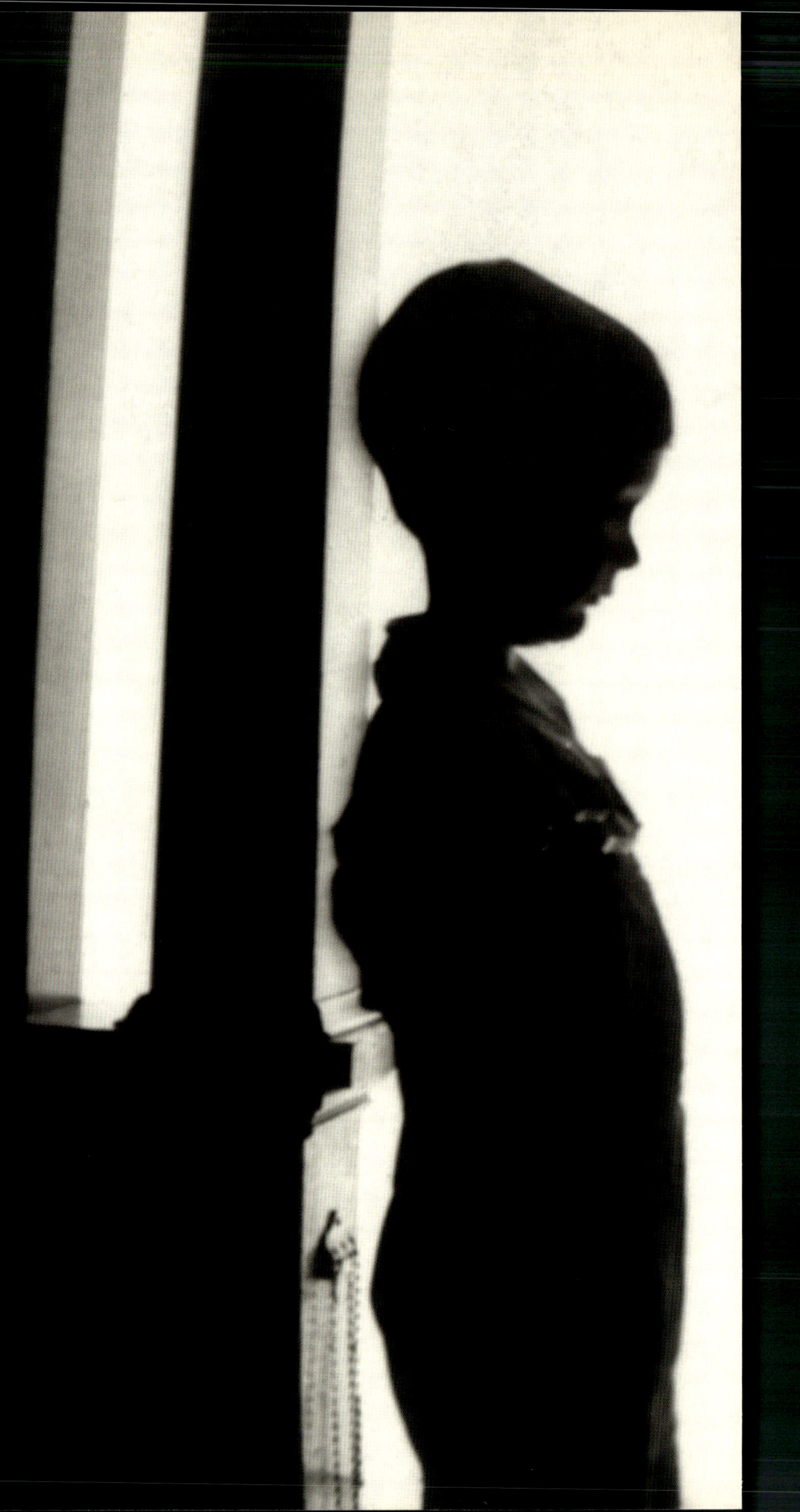

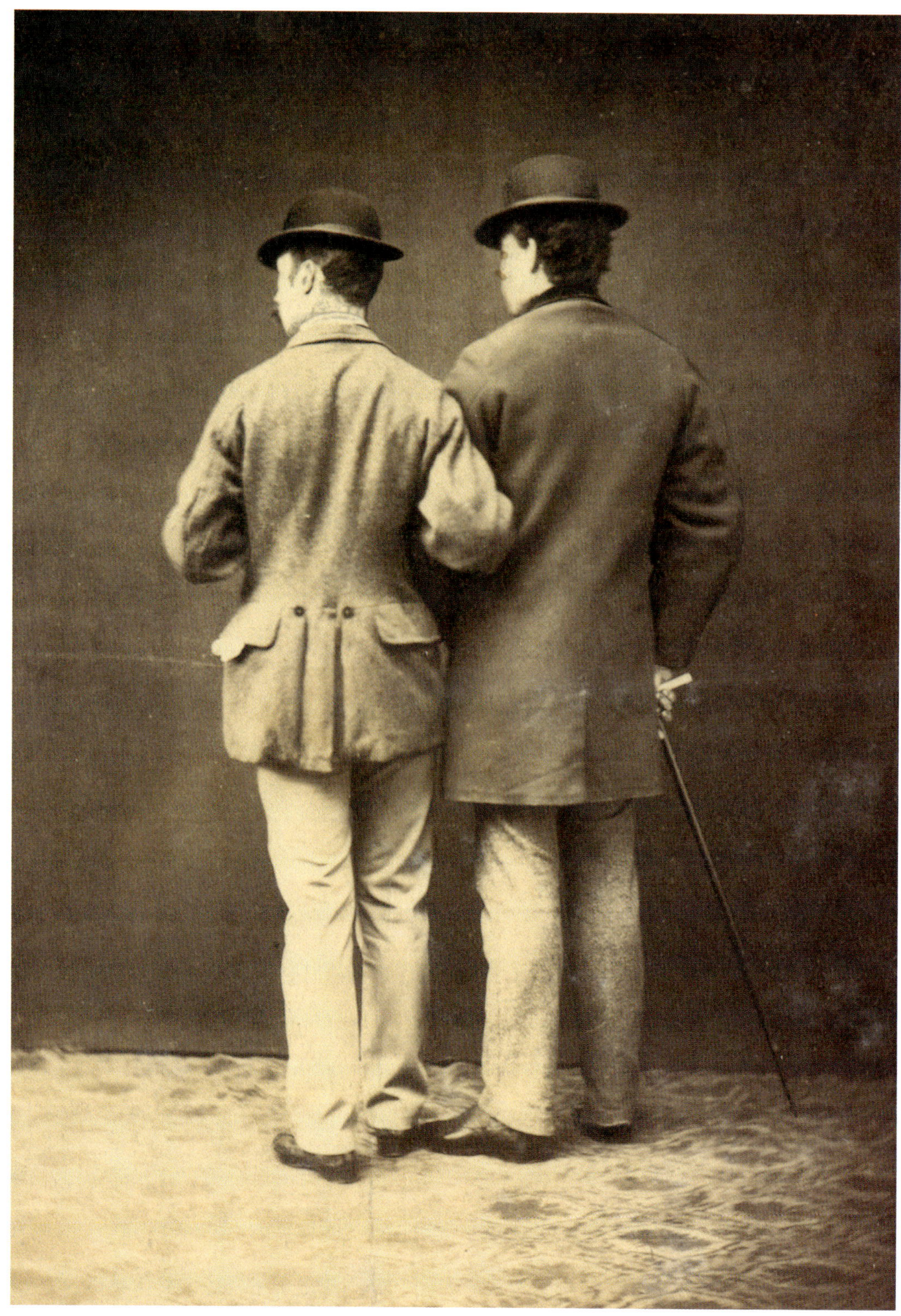

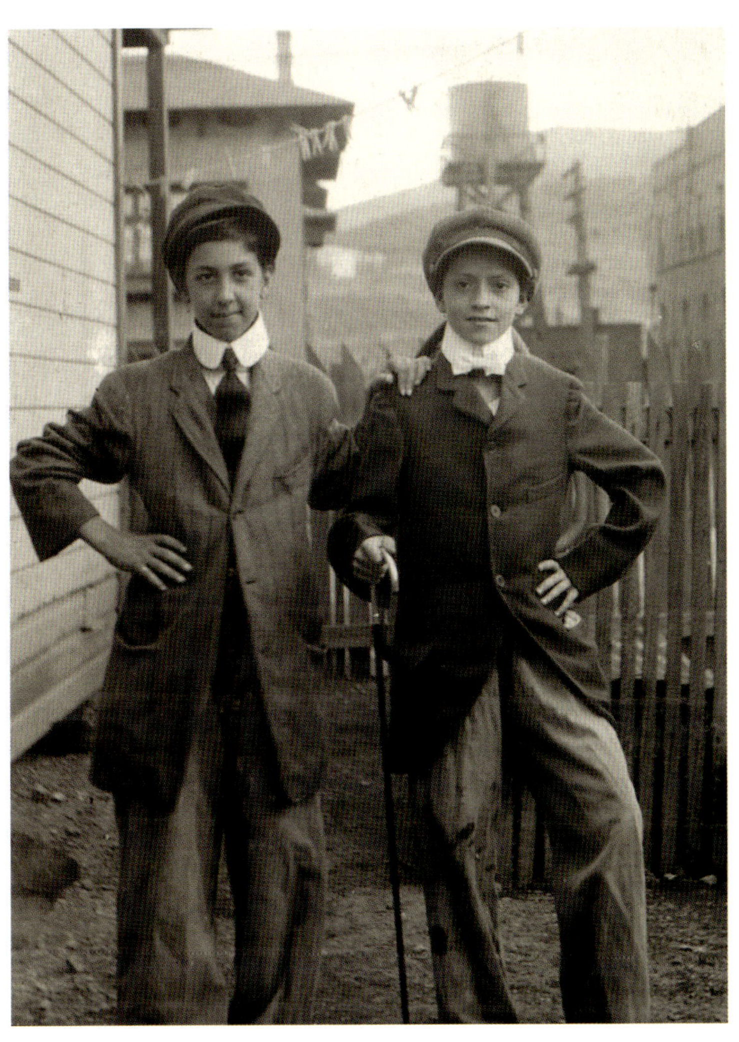

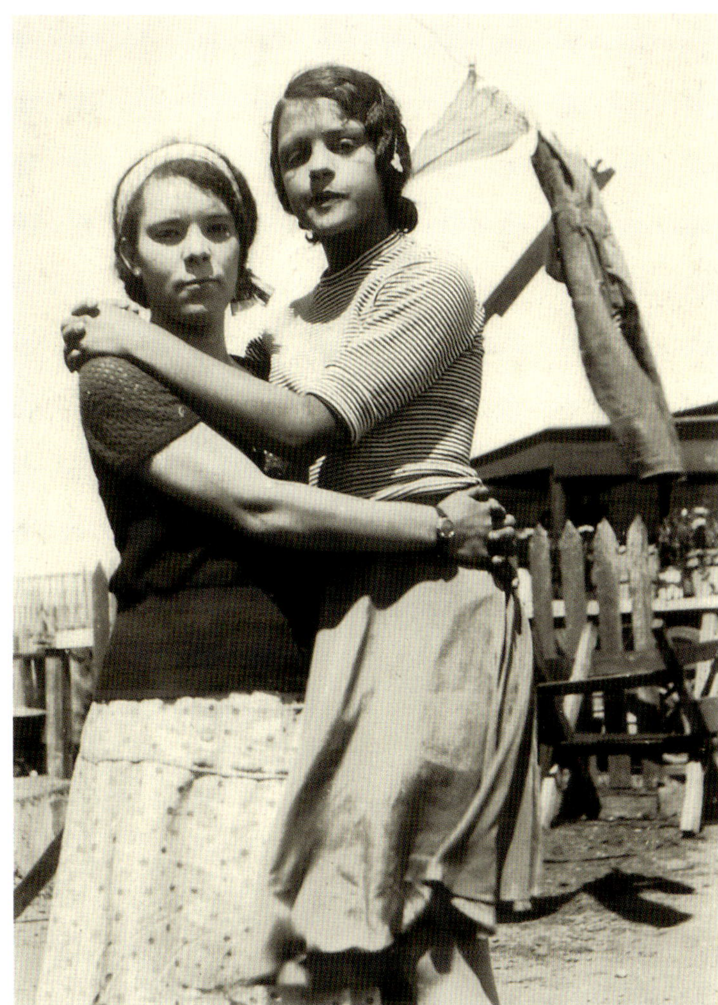

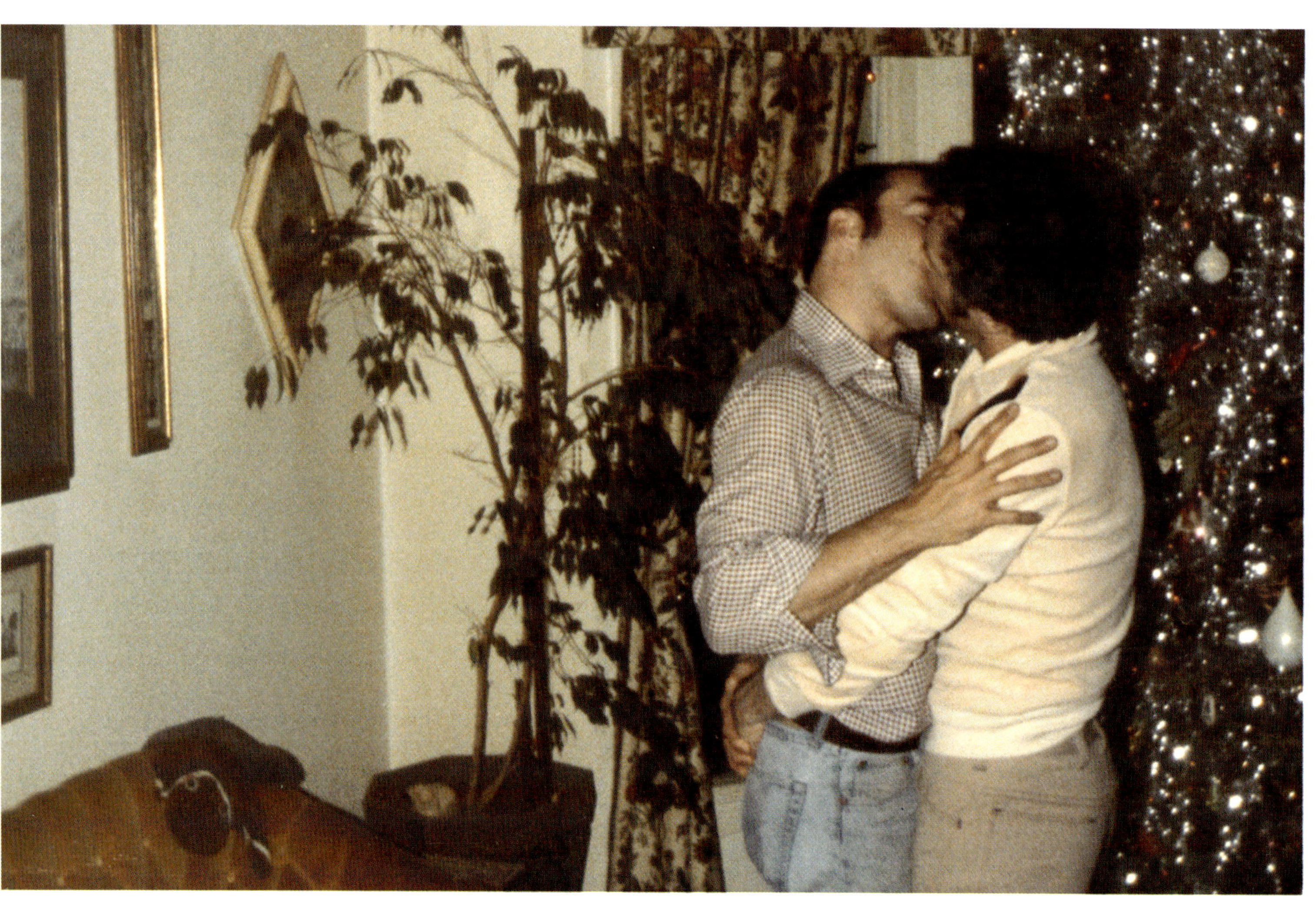

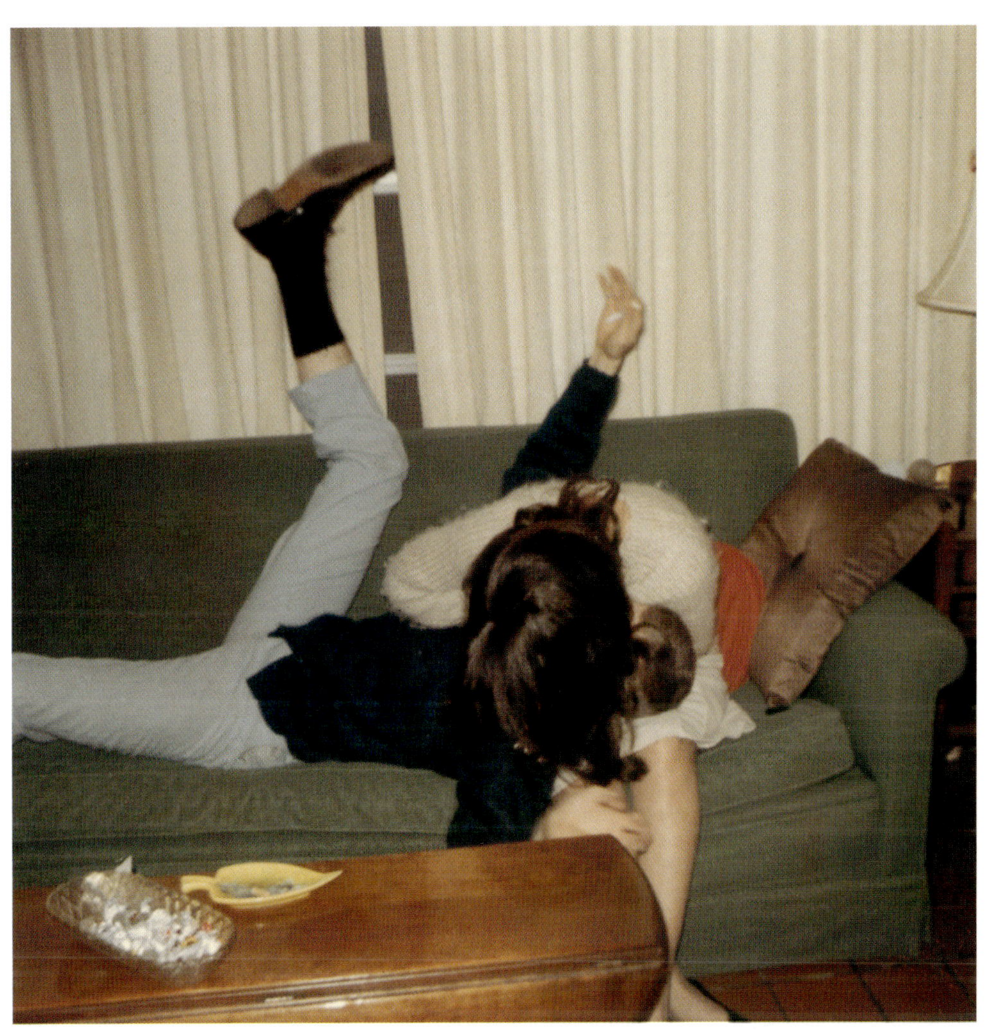

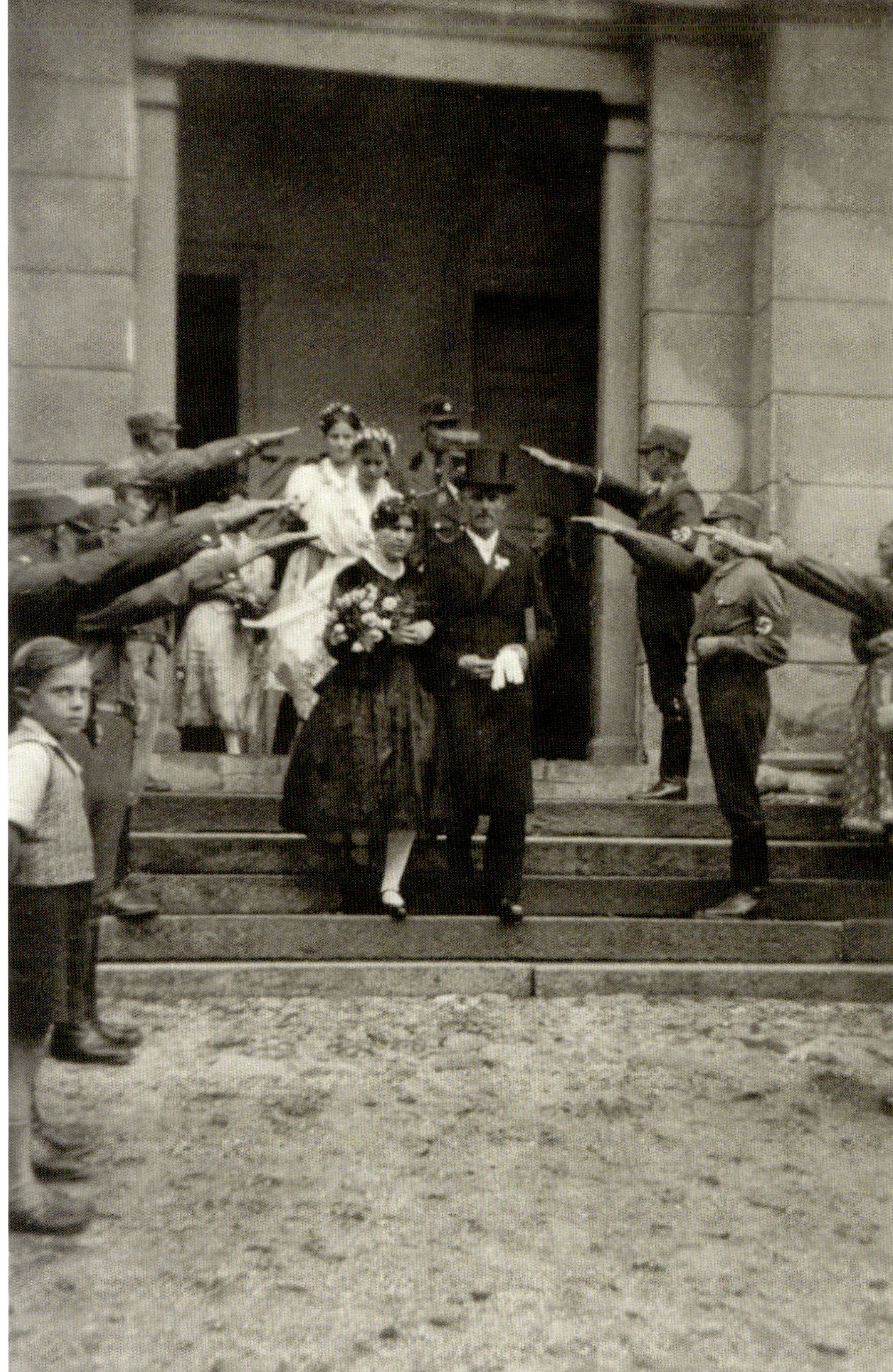

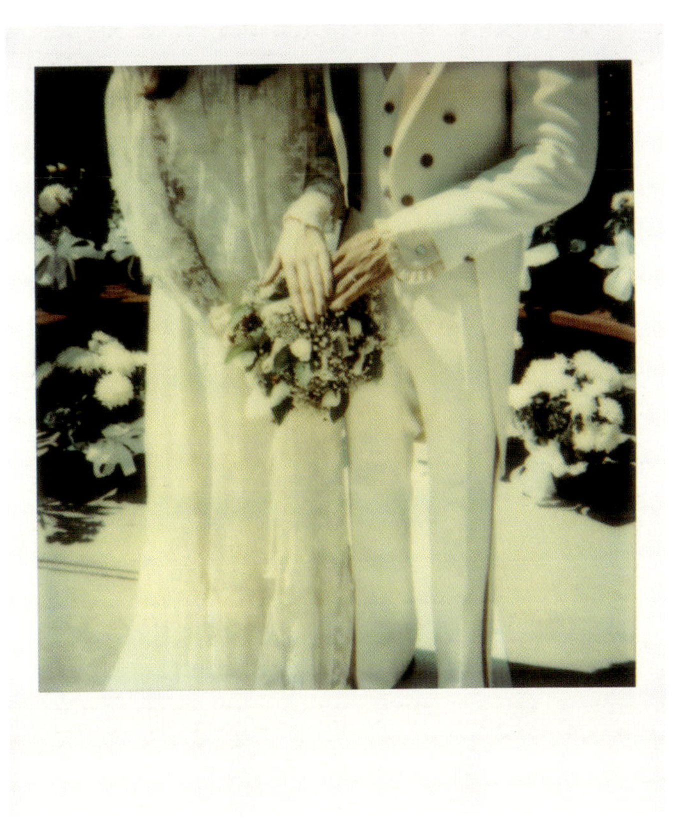

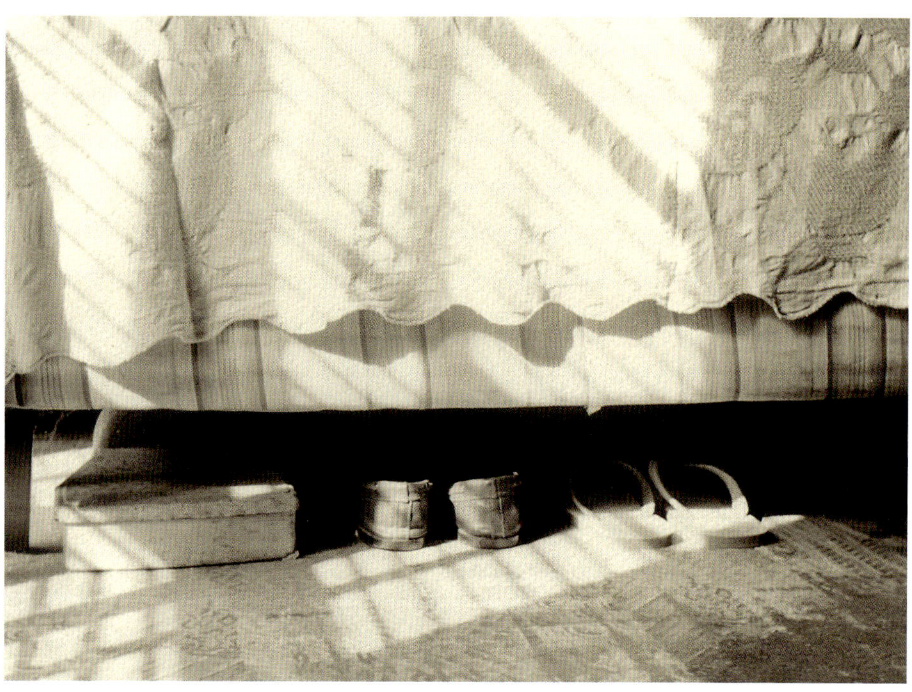

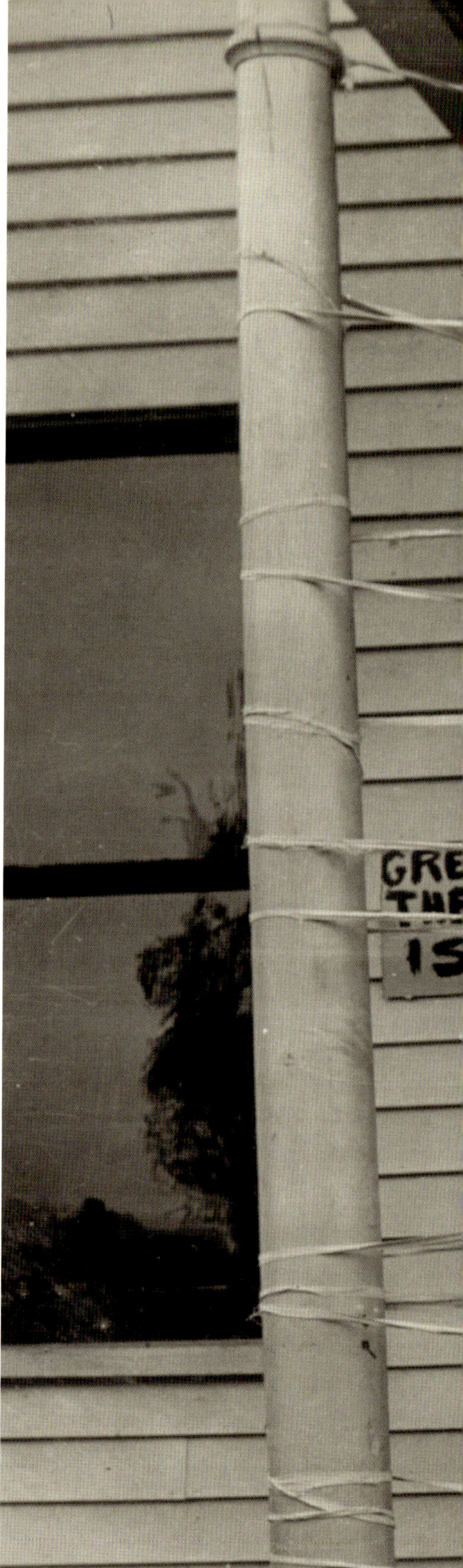

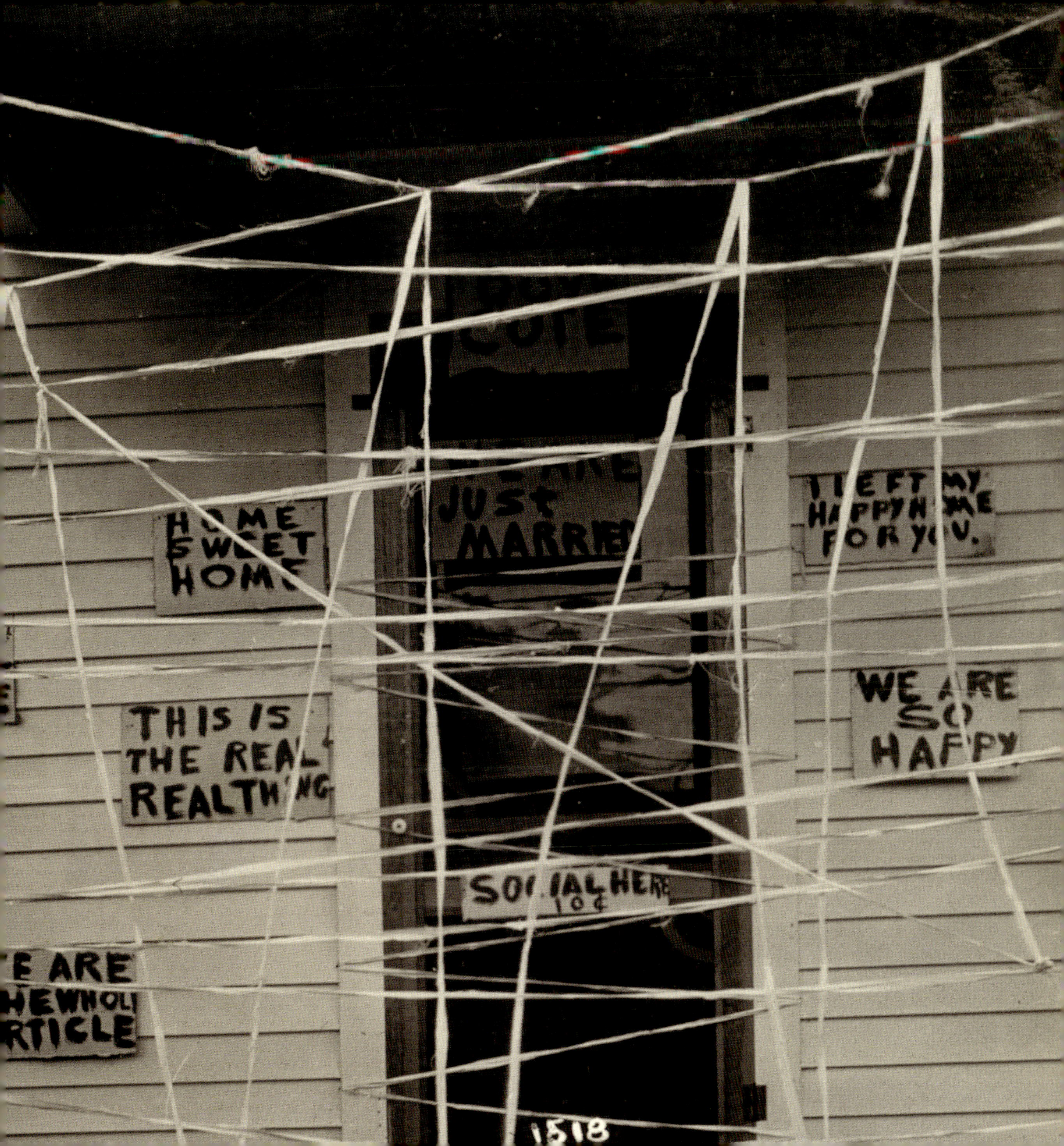

HOME
SWEET
HOME
JUST
MARRIED
I LEFT MY
HAPPY HOME
FOR YOU.
THIS IS
THE REAL
REALTHING
WE ARE
SO
HAPPY
SOCIAL HERE
10¢
E ARE
HEWHOL
RTICLE
1518

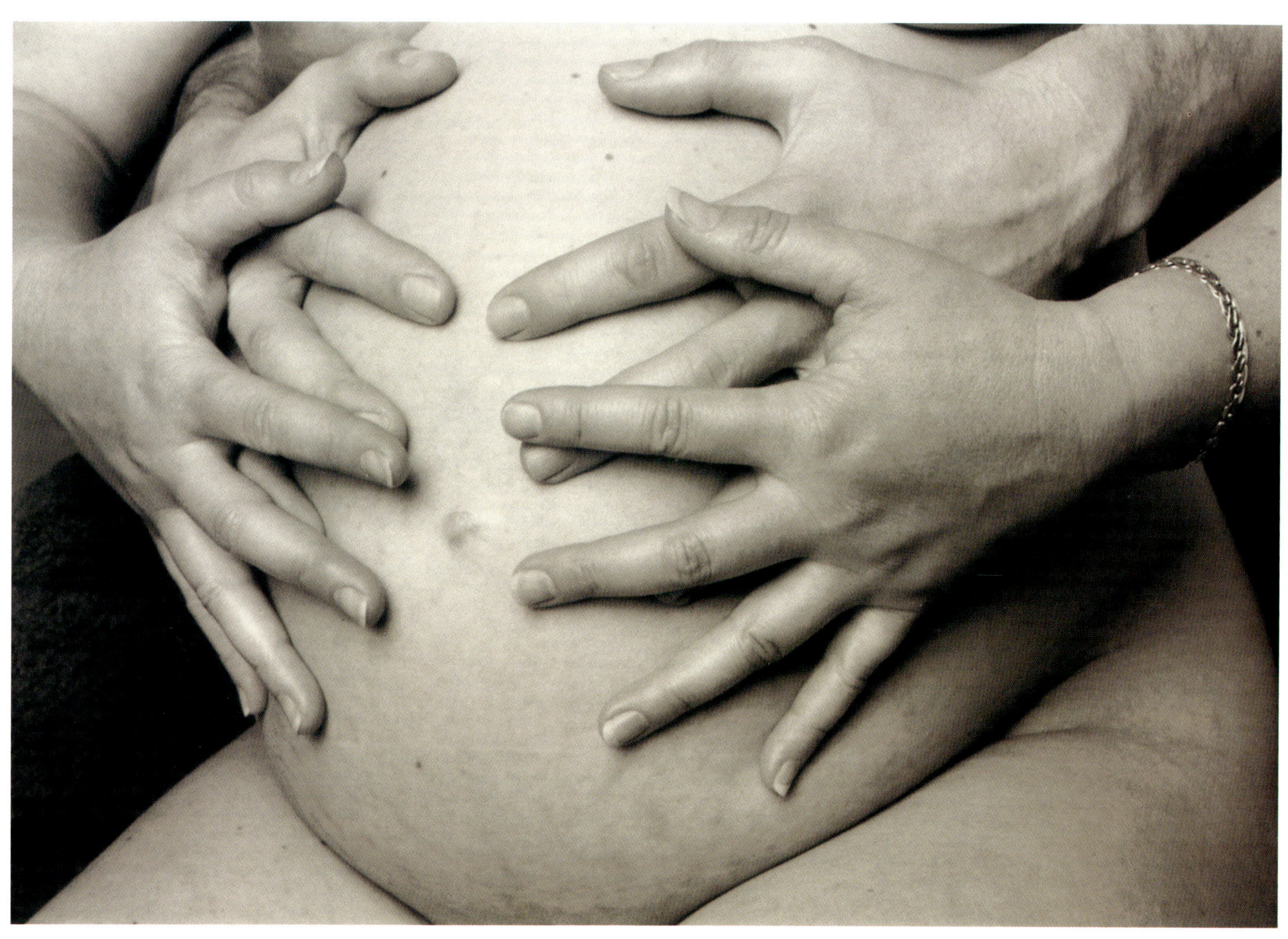

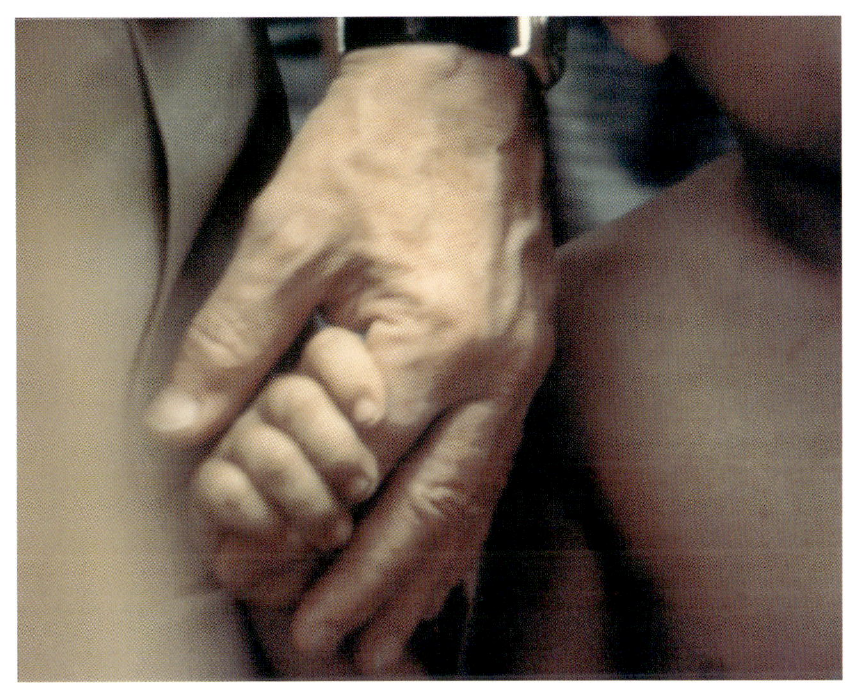

# Celebrity

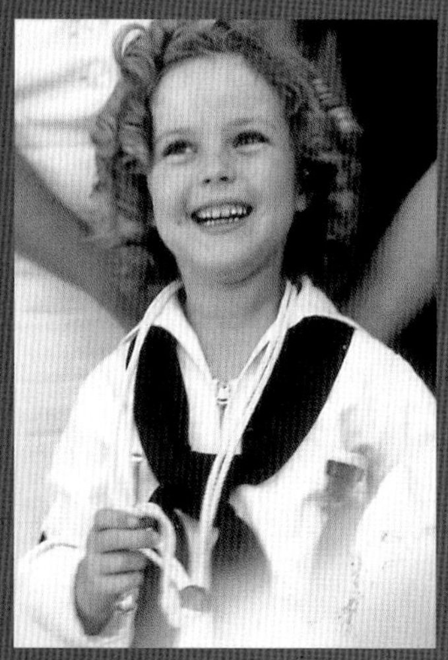

*'A celebrity is a person who works hard all his life to become well known, and then wears dark glasses to avoid being recognized.'*
Fred Allen

The patenting in 1854 by André-Adolphe-Eugène Disdéri of the carte-de-visite – an inexpensive, mass-produced photographic format – marked the point at which photography began to serve as a vehicle to advance fame and celebrity. In earlier times, such individuals as Queen Victoria and Napoleon III had actually been seen by very few of their countrymen. The advent of the carte-de-visite acted as a propagandist and unifying tool, binding subjects to their rulers.

For those in the spotlight, the world's flirtation with celebrity is a two-edged sword. Unwelcome intrusion into one's privacy is usually more than compensated by the opportunity to enhance one's political or economic power, cultural fame or social standing. Photography has played a pivotal role in the promotion (and sometimes demise) of reputations. Luminaries are hardened veterans of exposure to the camera. They are accustomed to providing a predictable pose during dutiful photo opportunities.

Under such conditions insightful images can generally be made only through chance, luck or stealth. Knowing their love of animals, Richard Avedon once lied to the Duke and Duchess of Windsor at a photo session, saying that he was late because his taxi had run over a dog. Avedon's classic recording of their stricken expressions momentarily removed the masks that they, like most famous people, keep firmly in place. It is only in snapshots or candid unposed photographs that reputation gives way to revelation with regard to the recording of the basic human qualities that even the most famous among us possess.

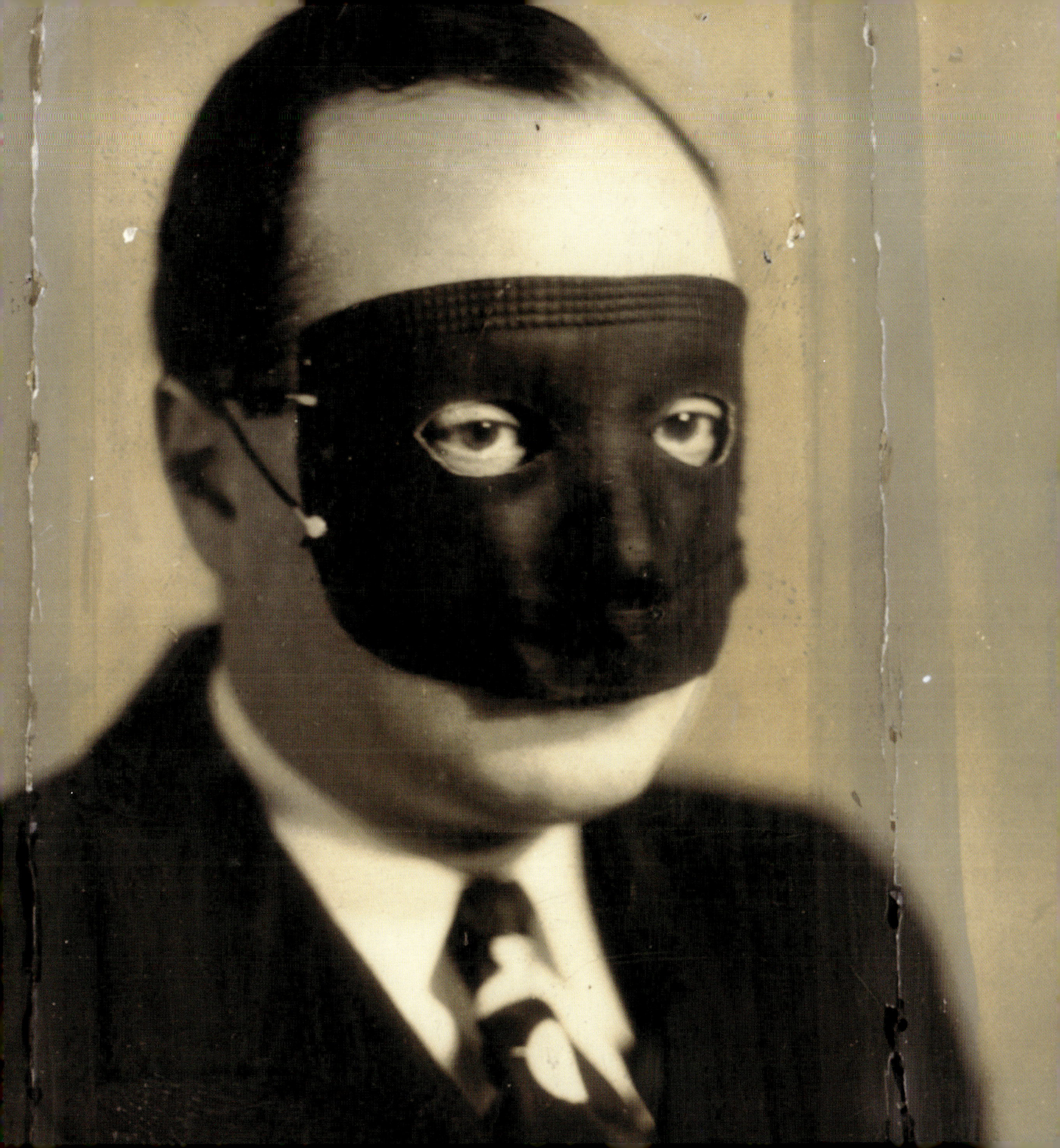

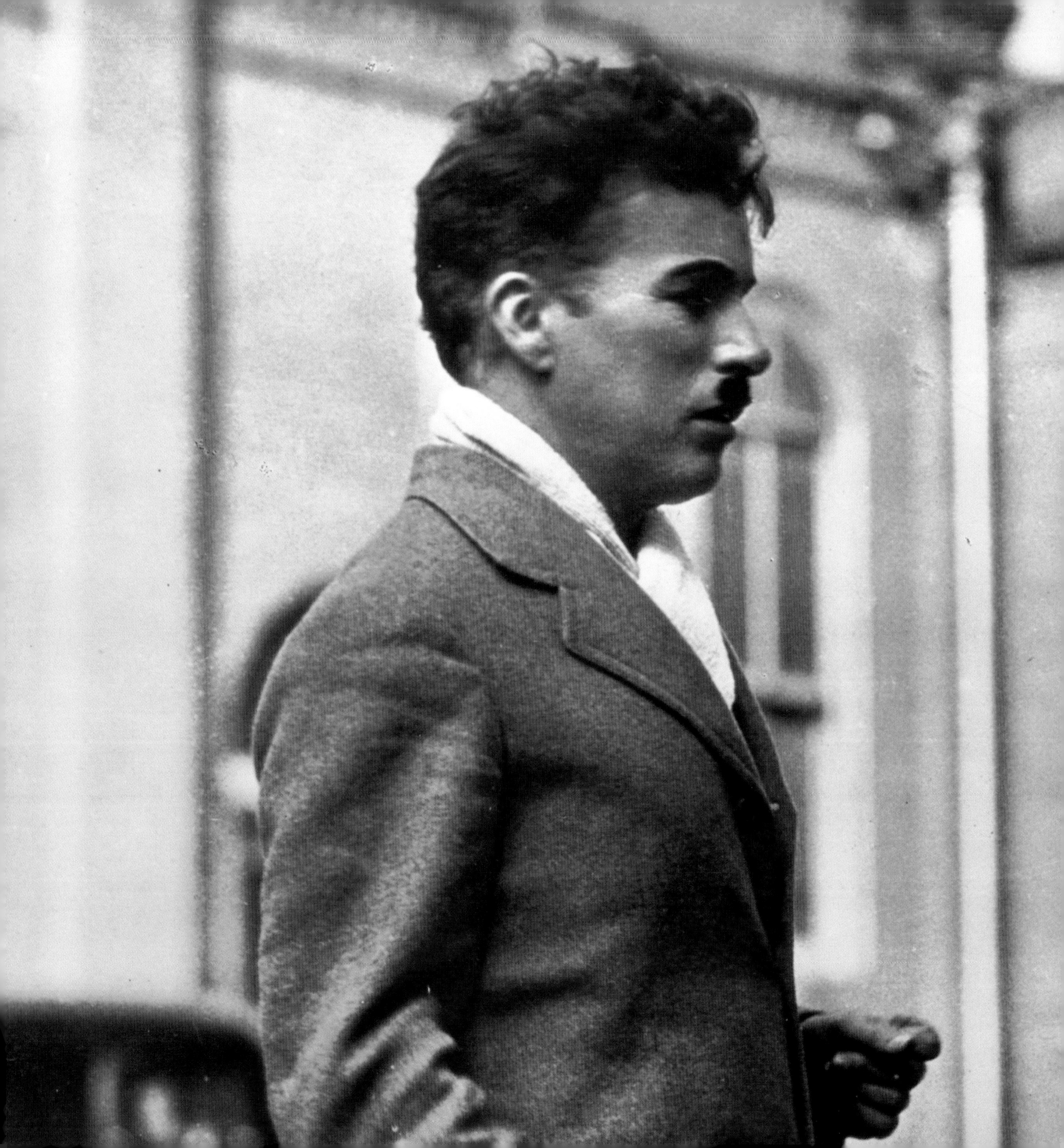

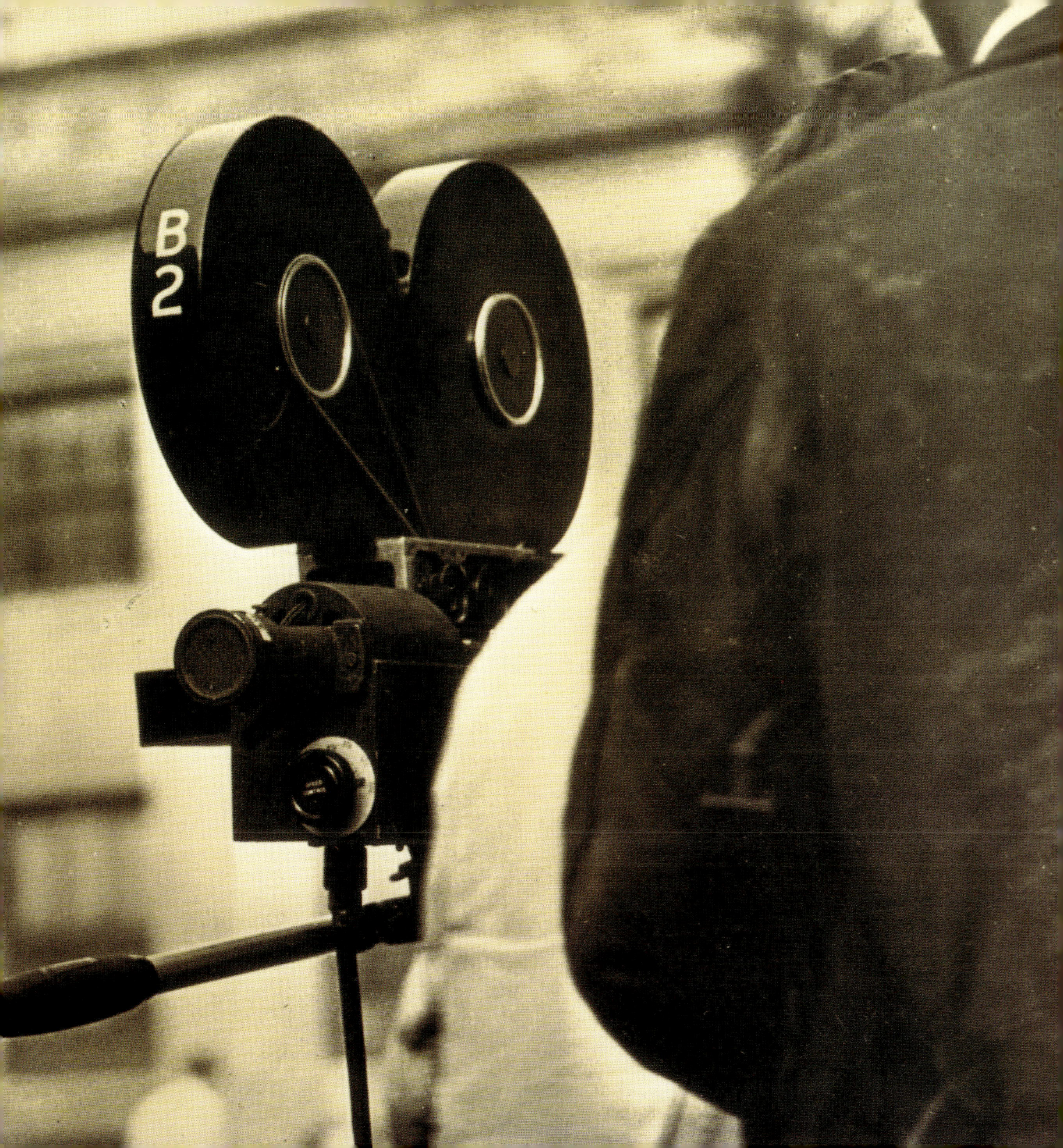
B2

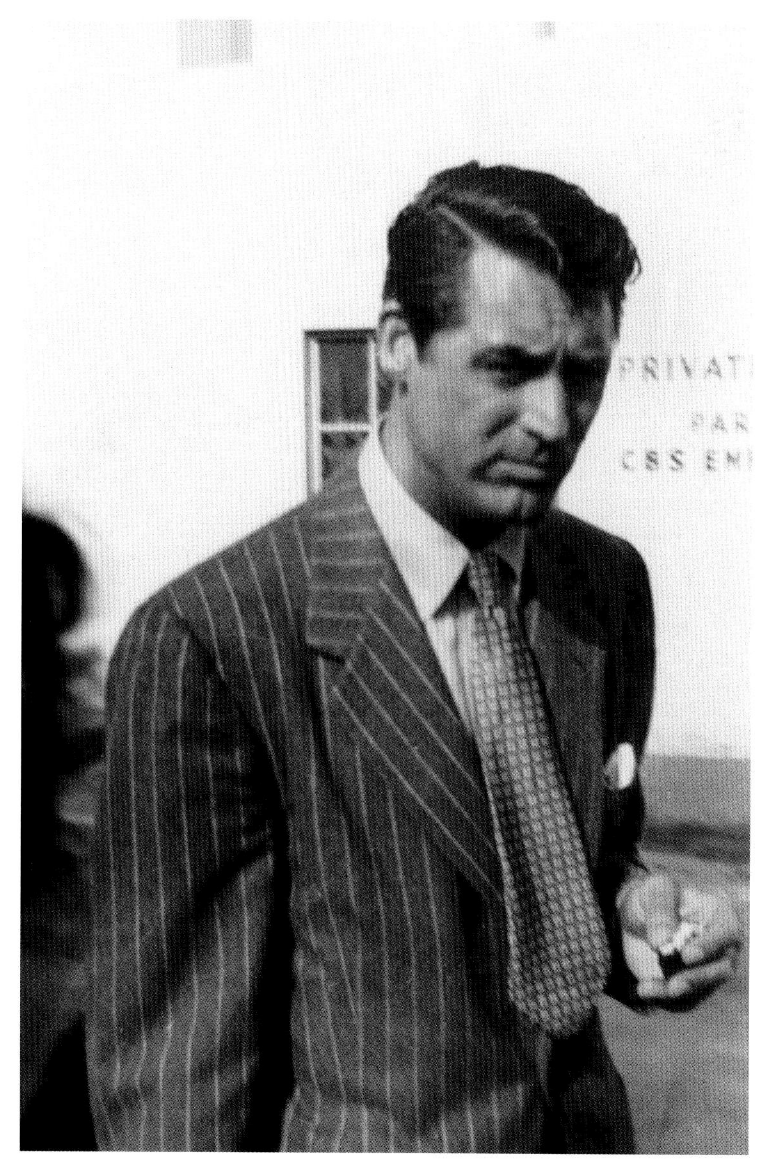
PRIVAT
PAR
CBS EM

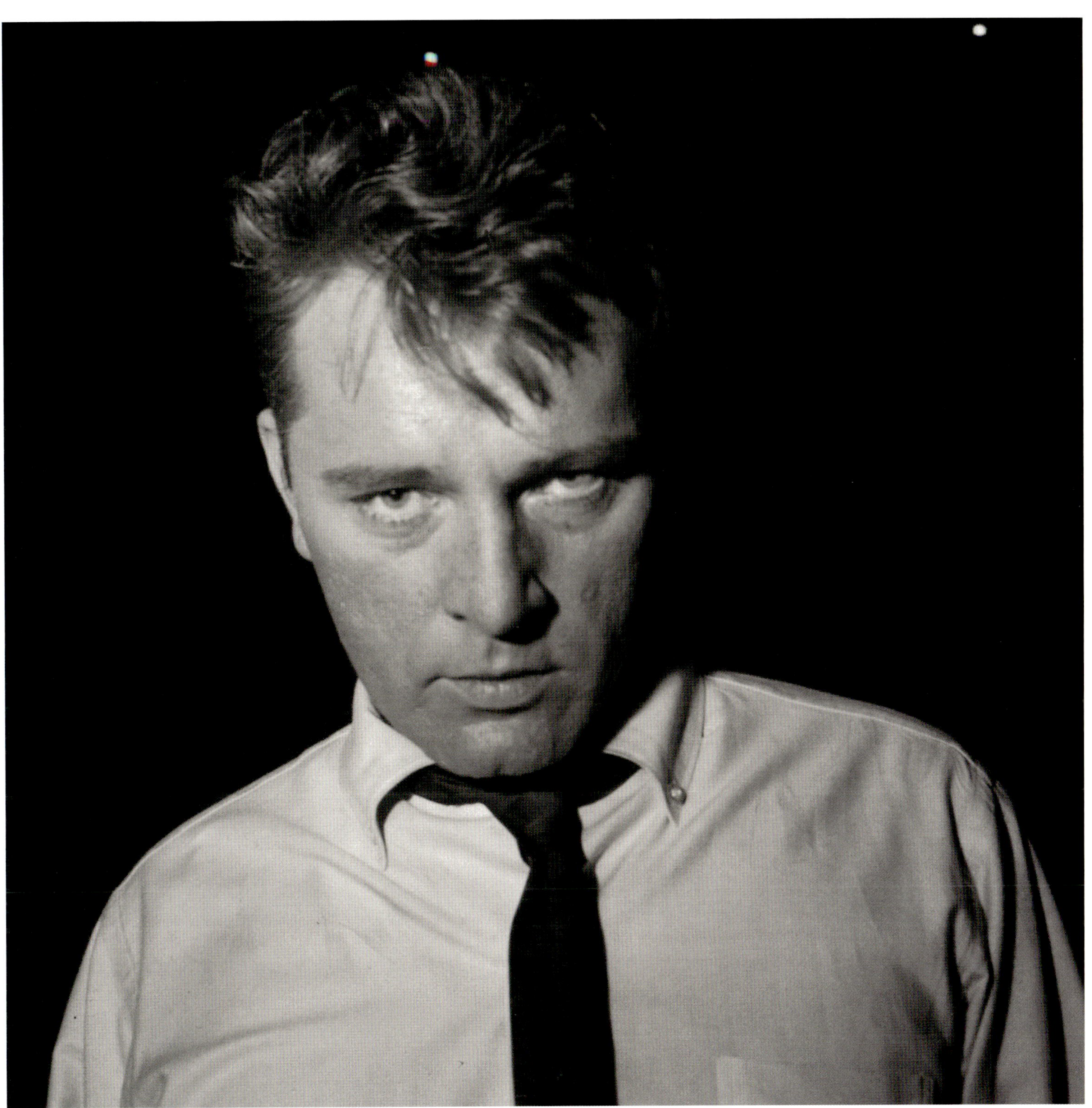

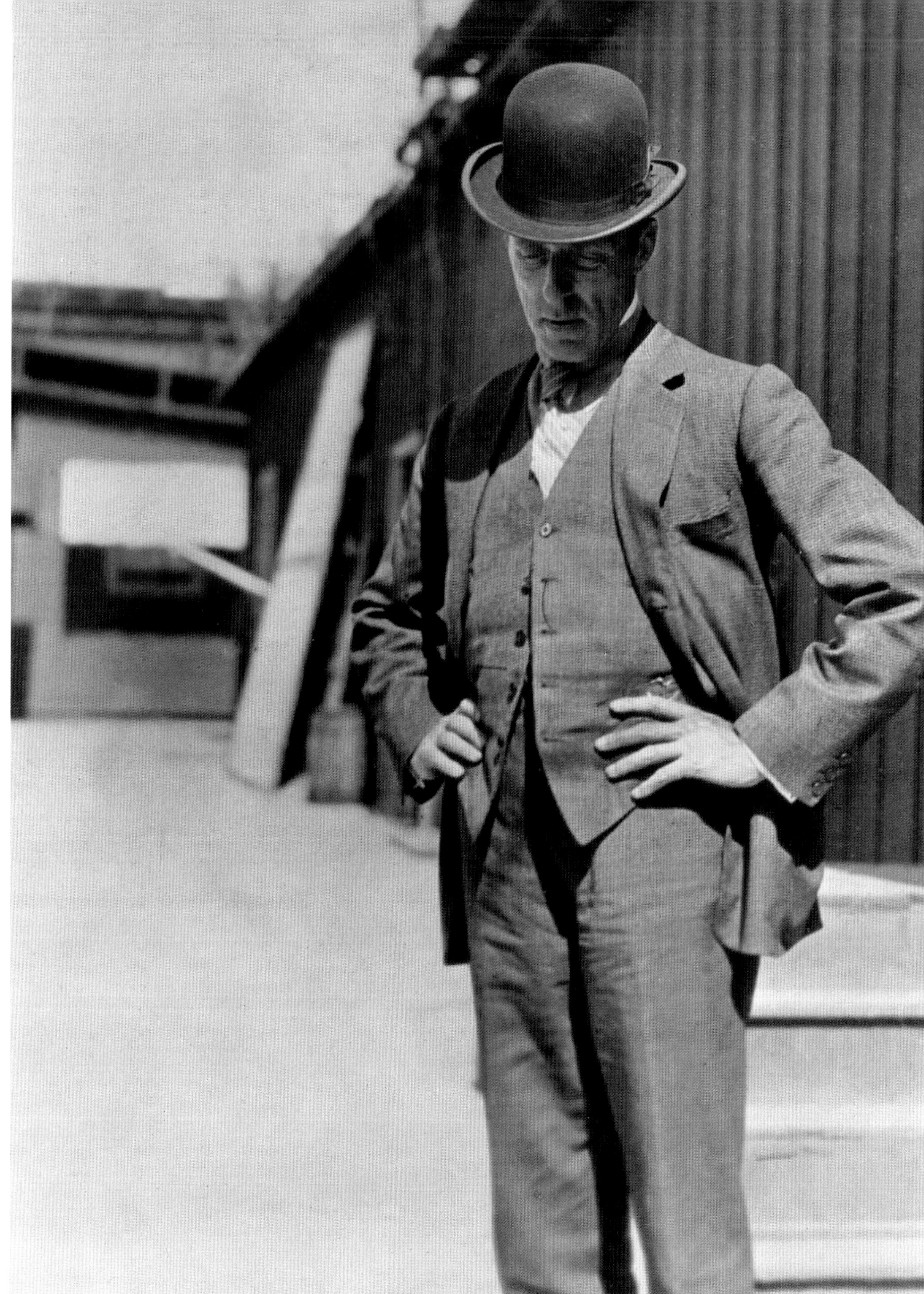

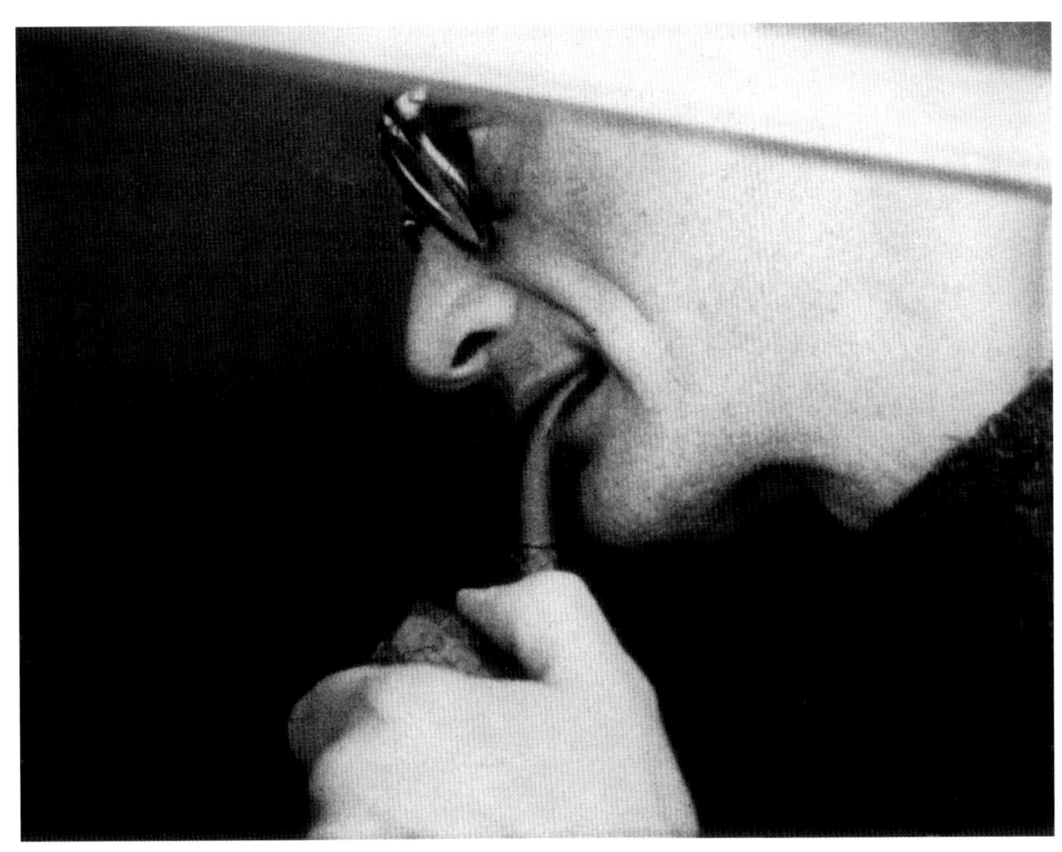

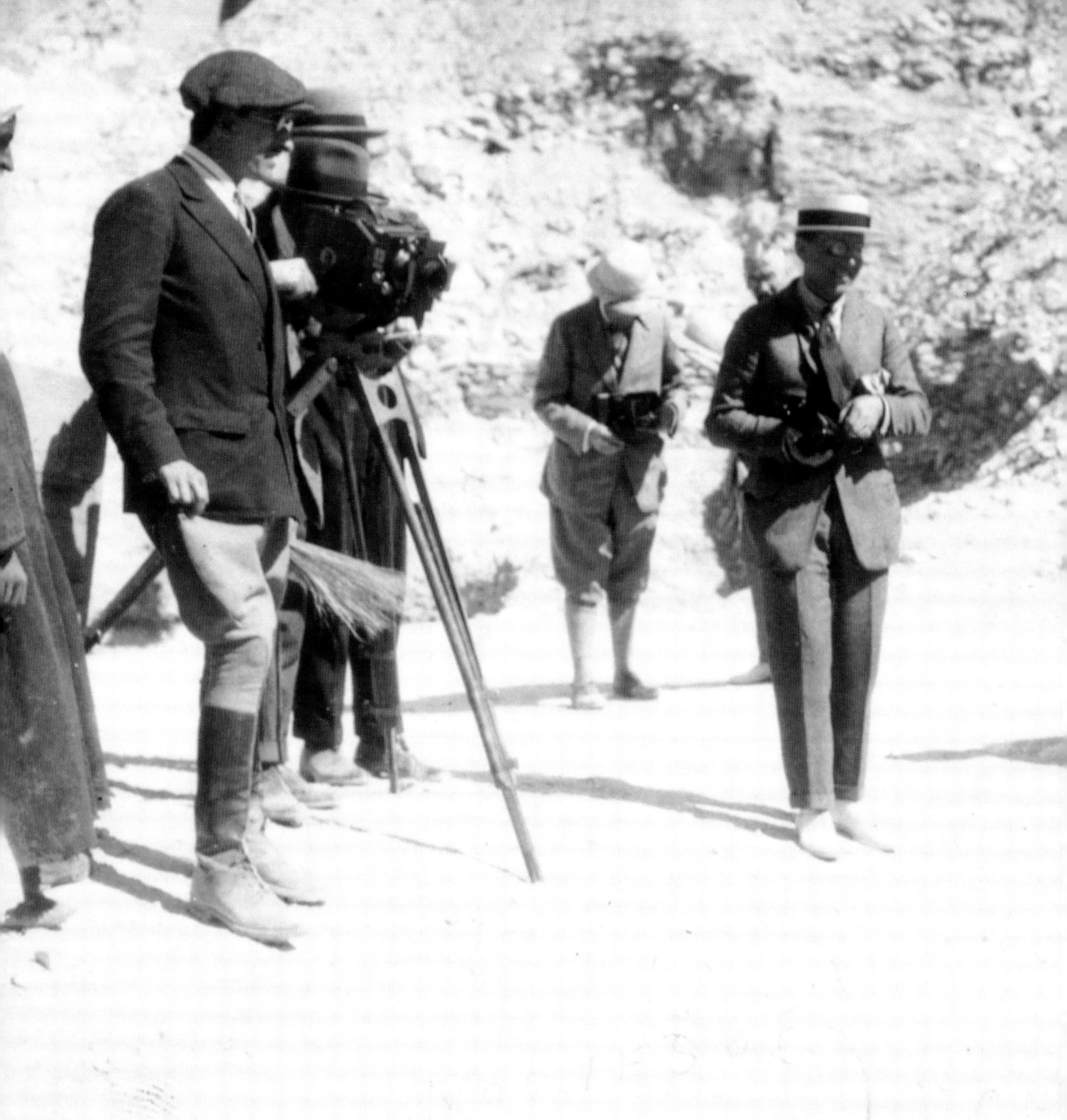

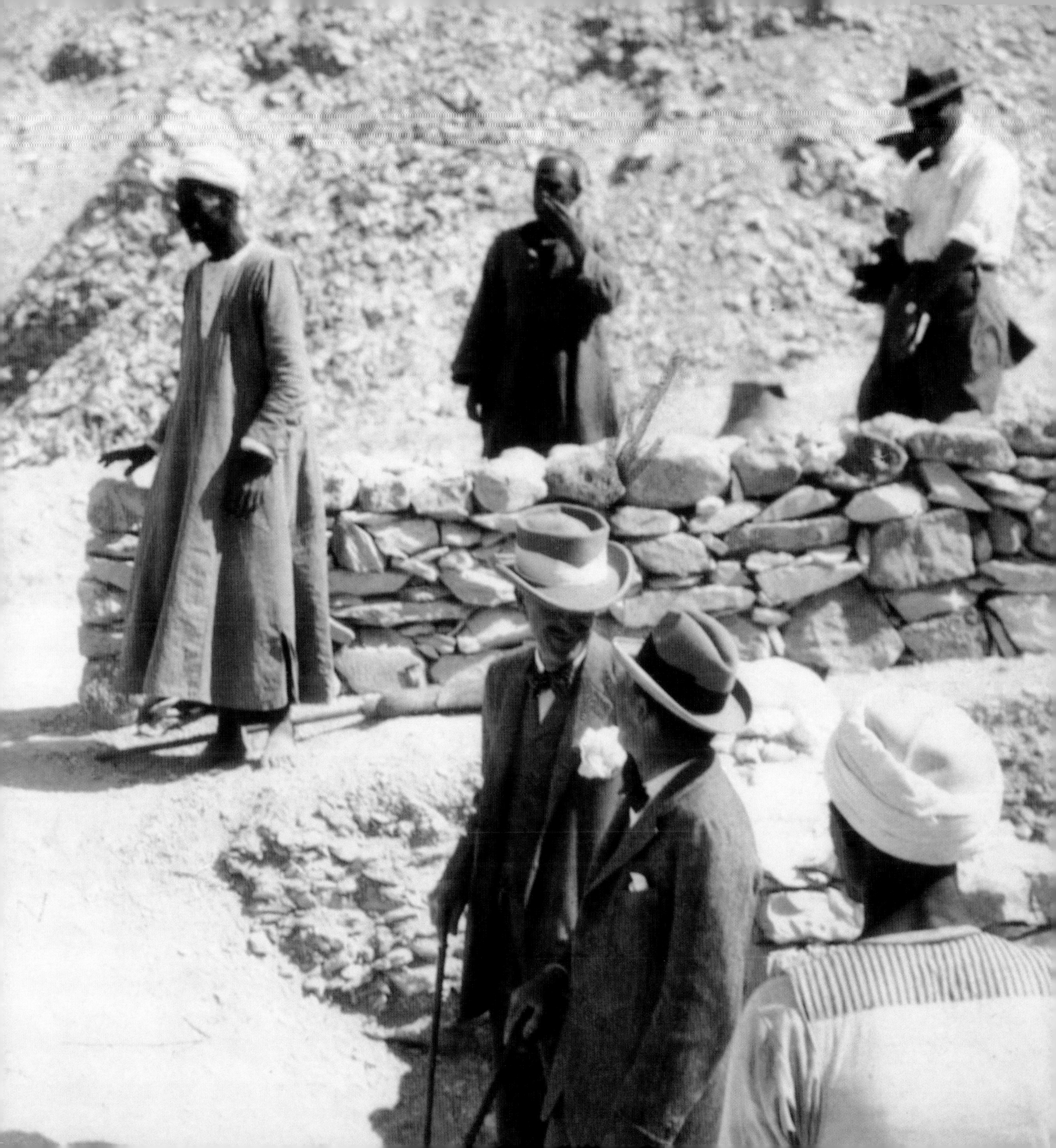

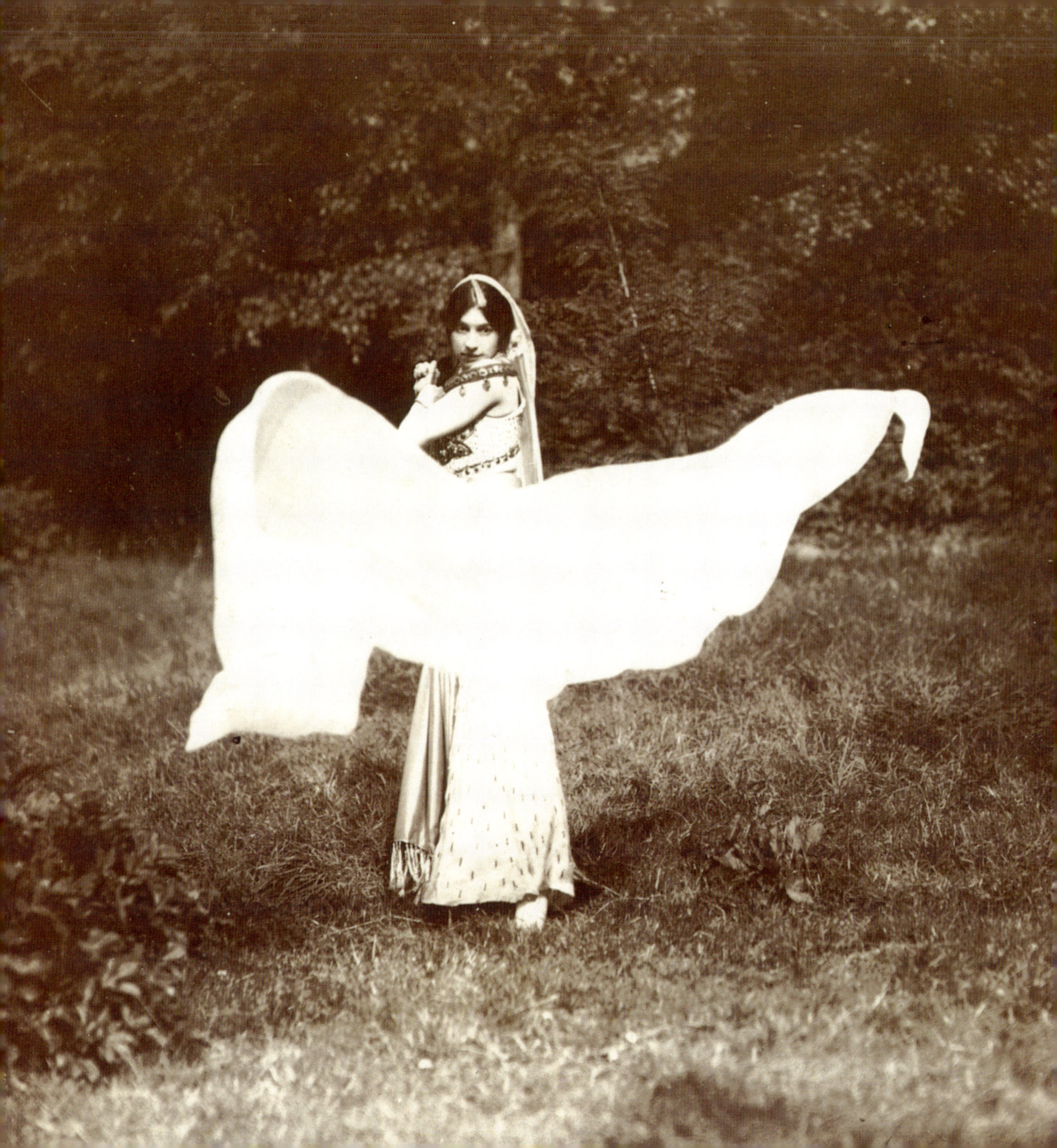

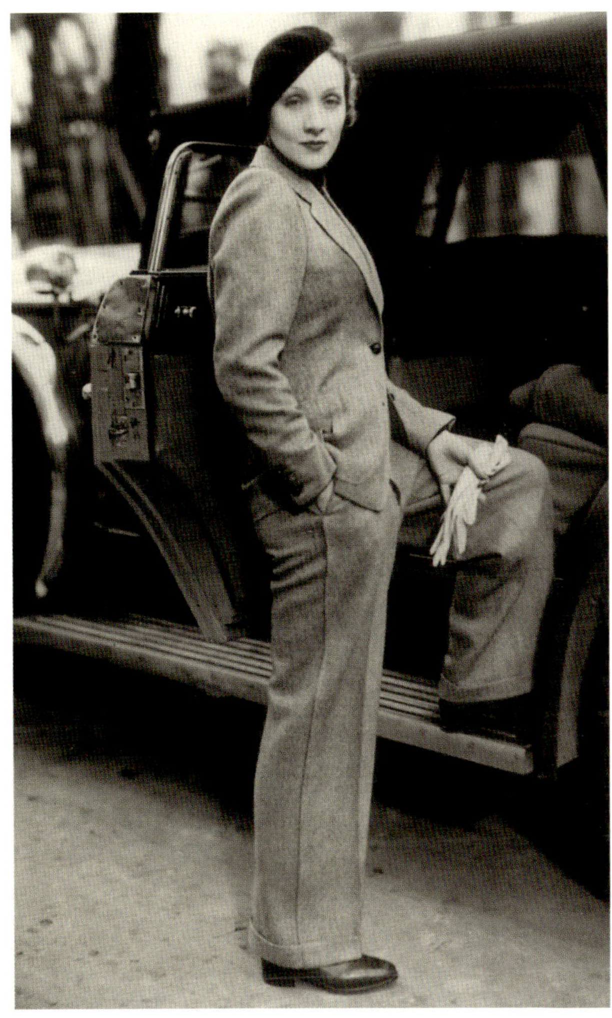

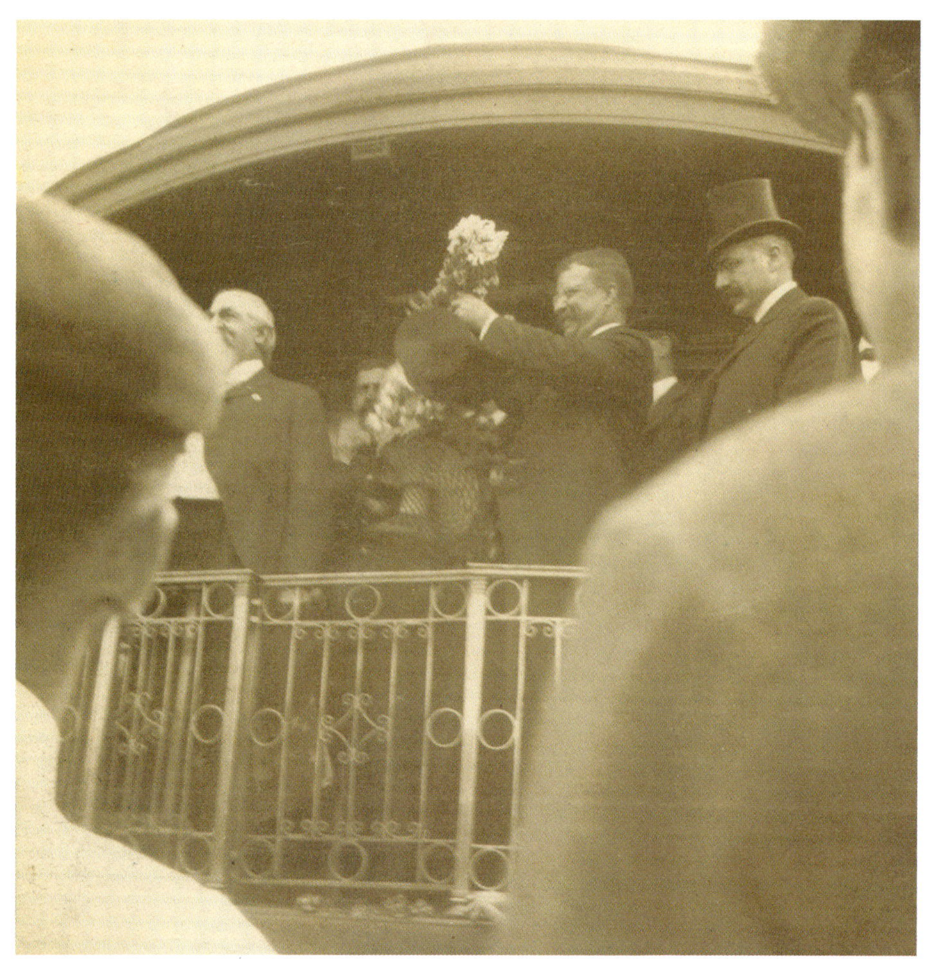

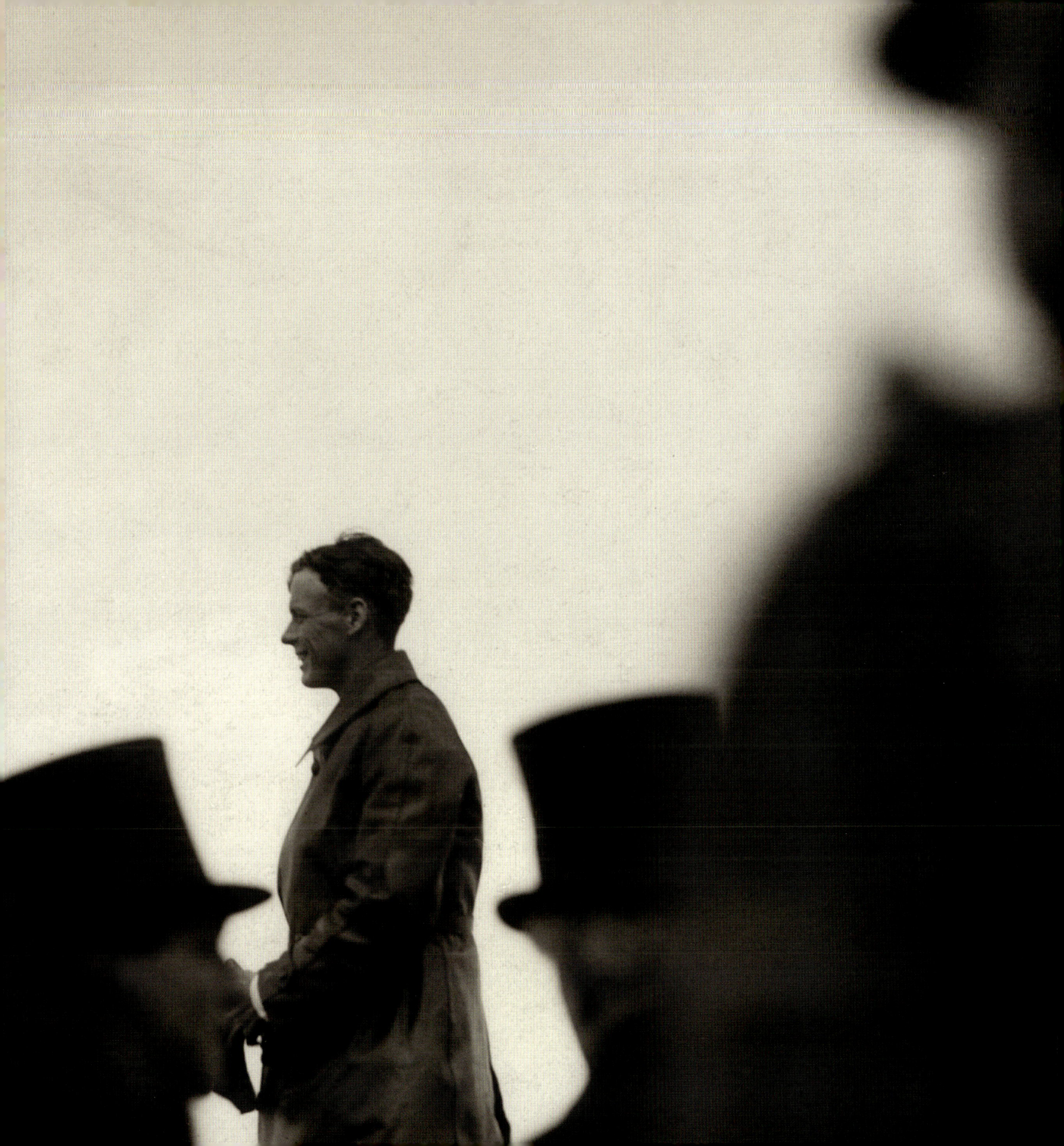

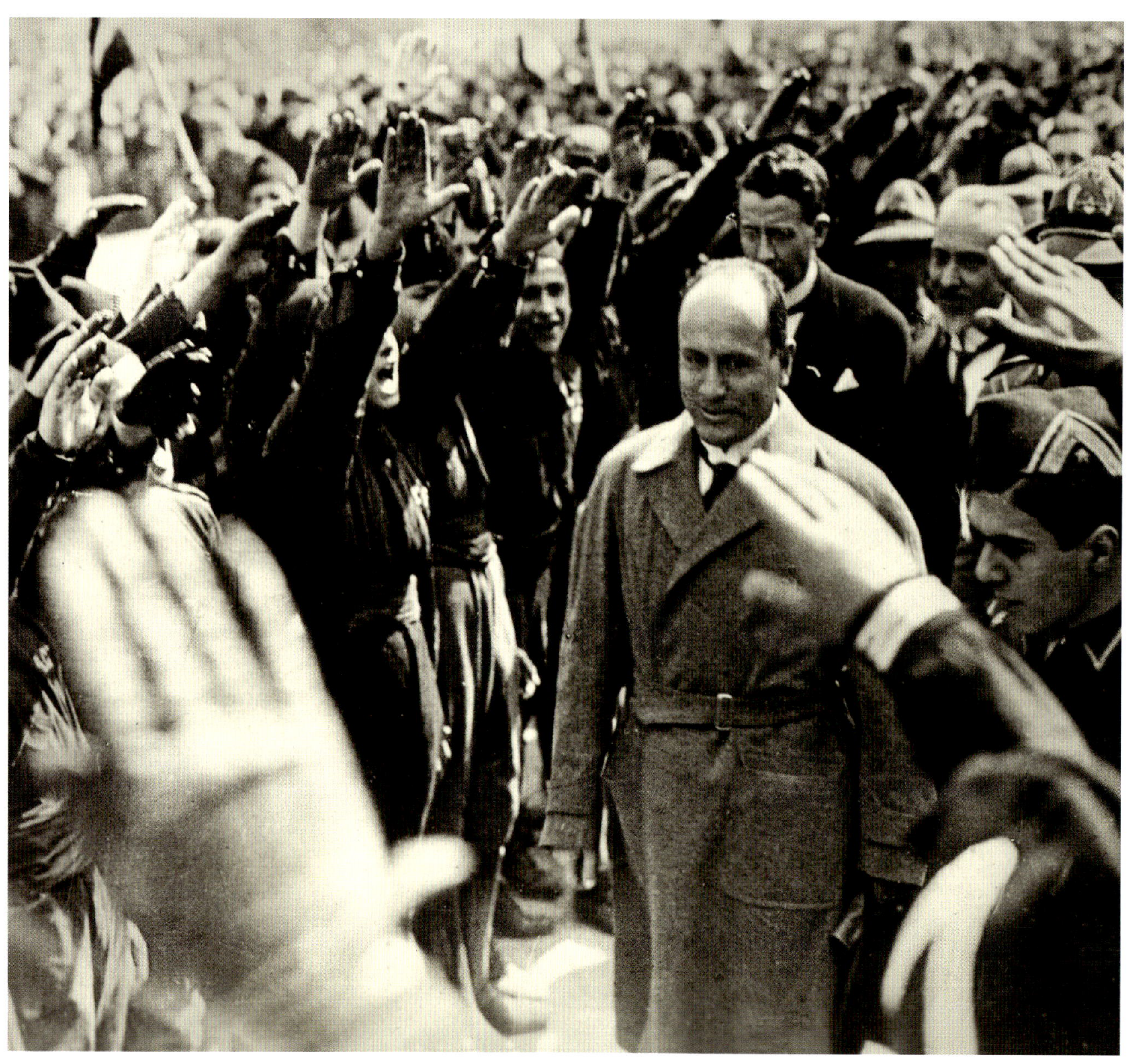

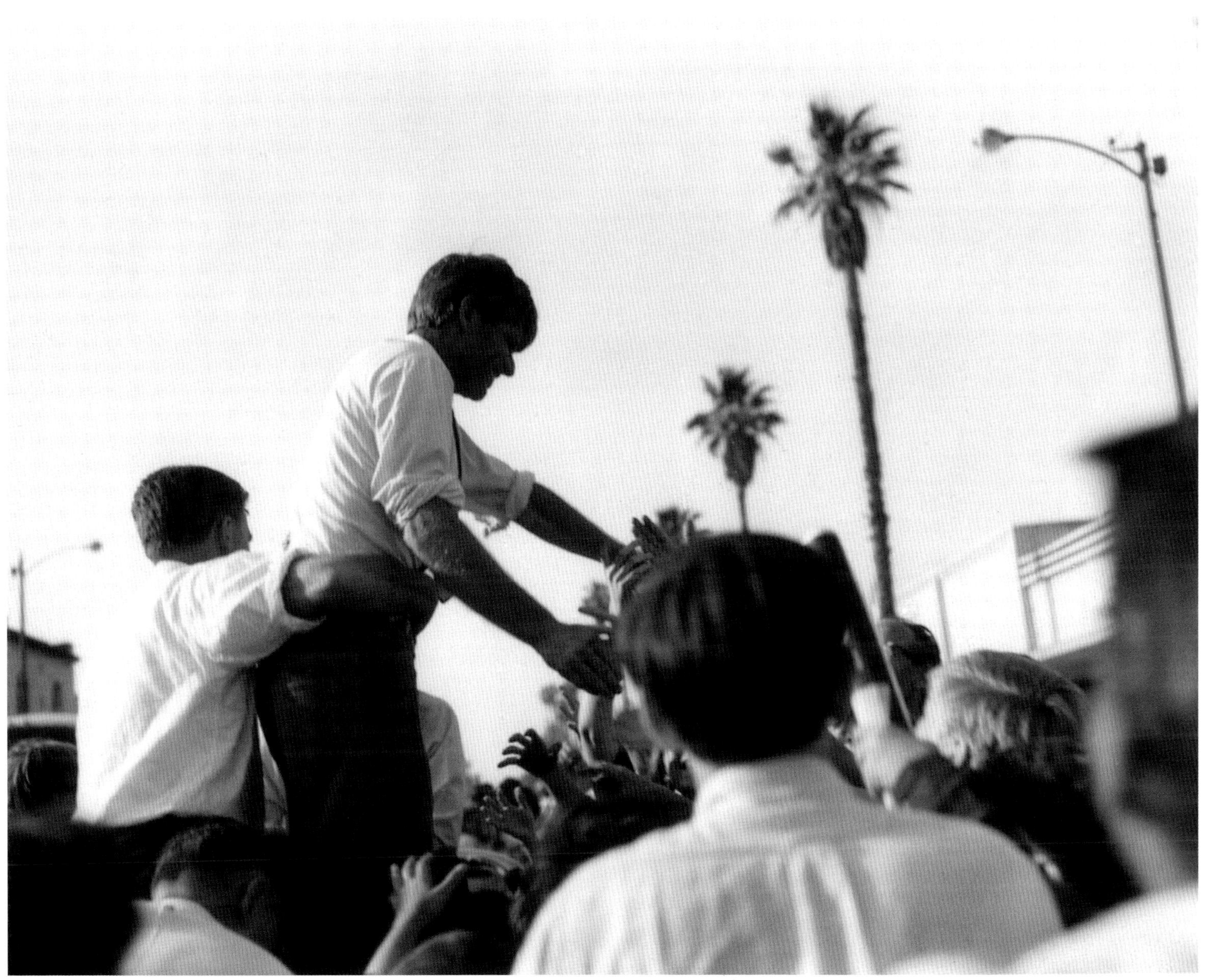

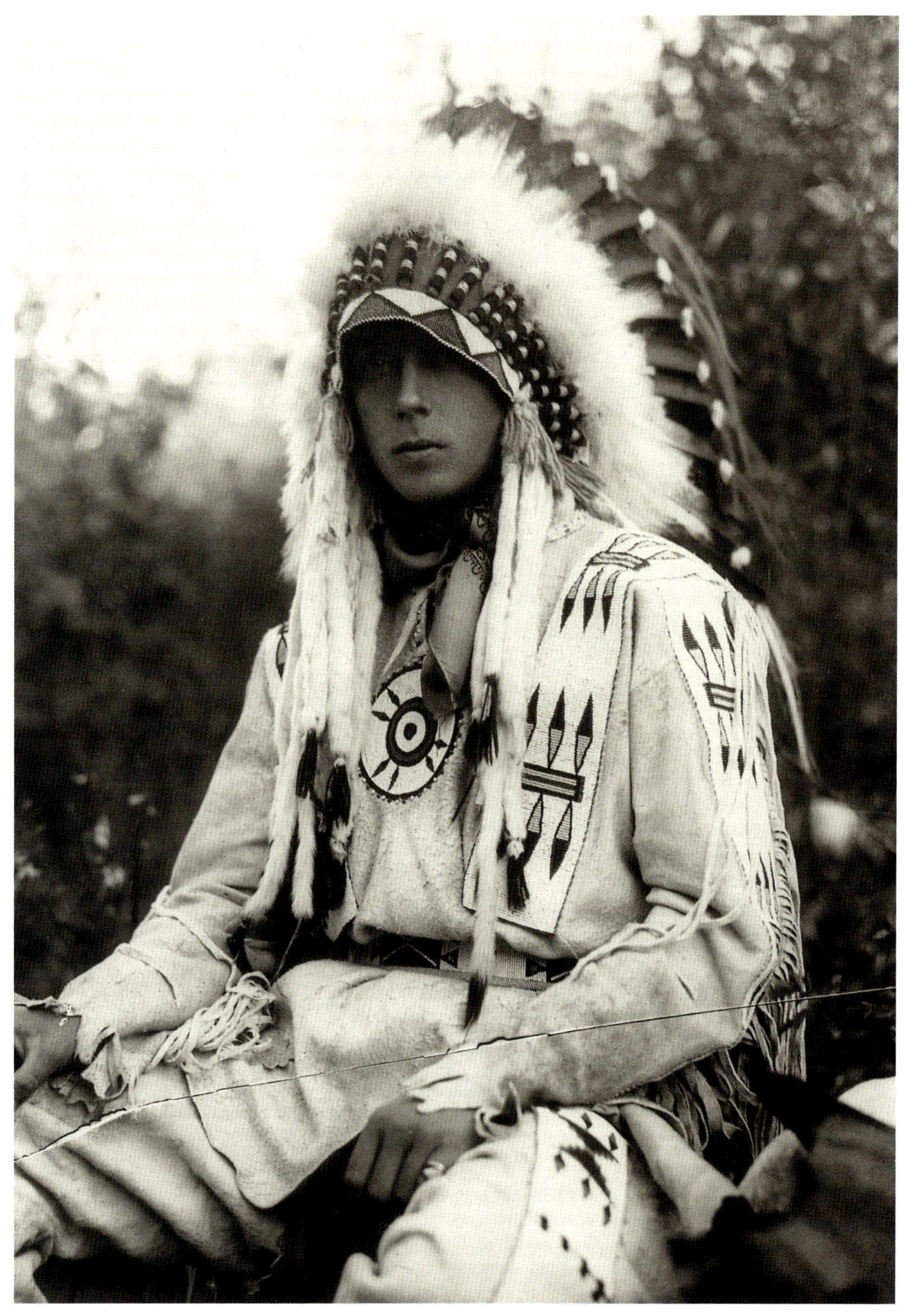

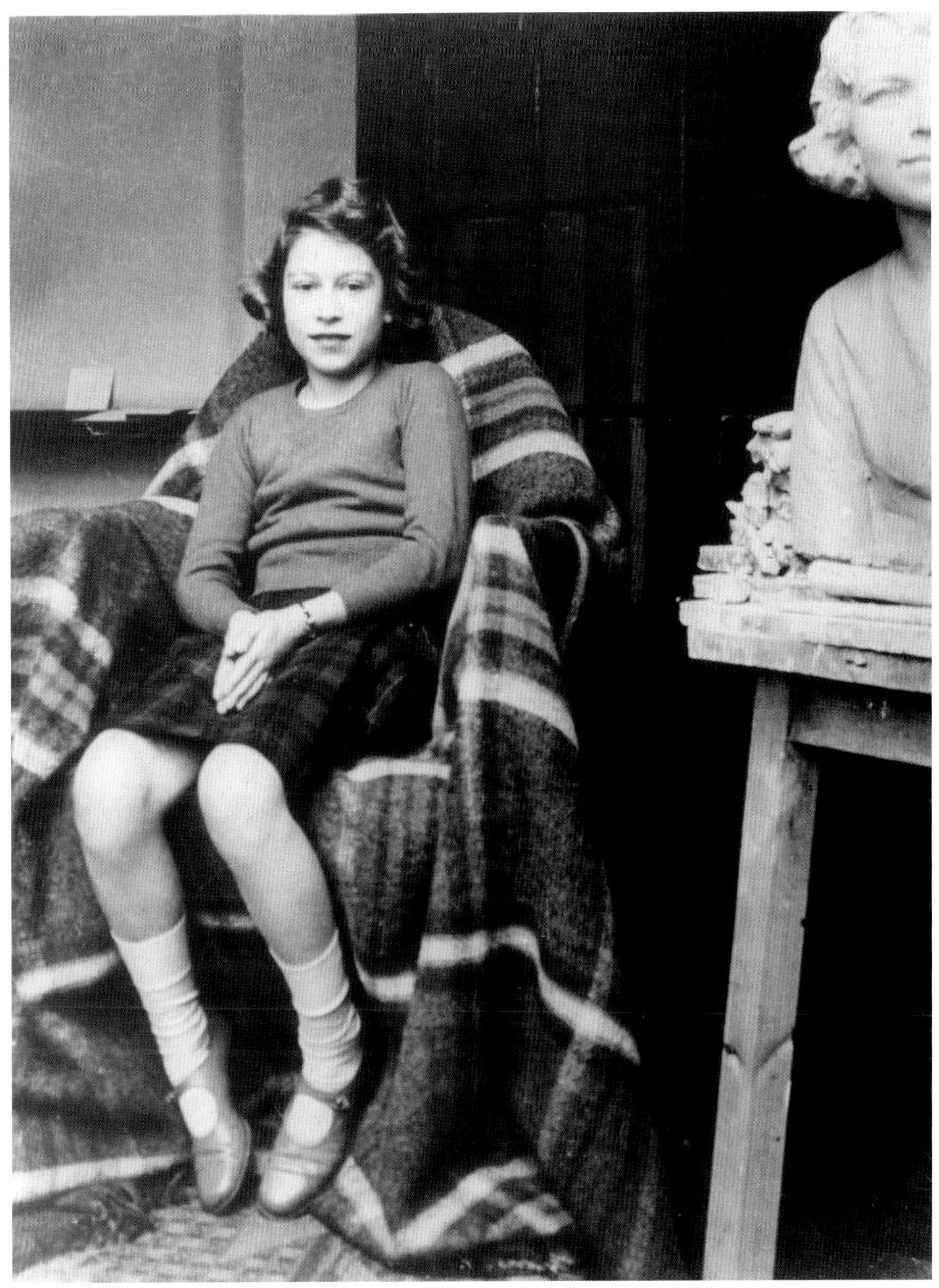

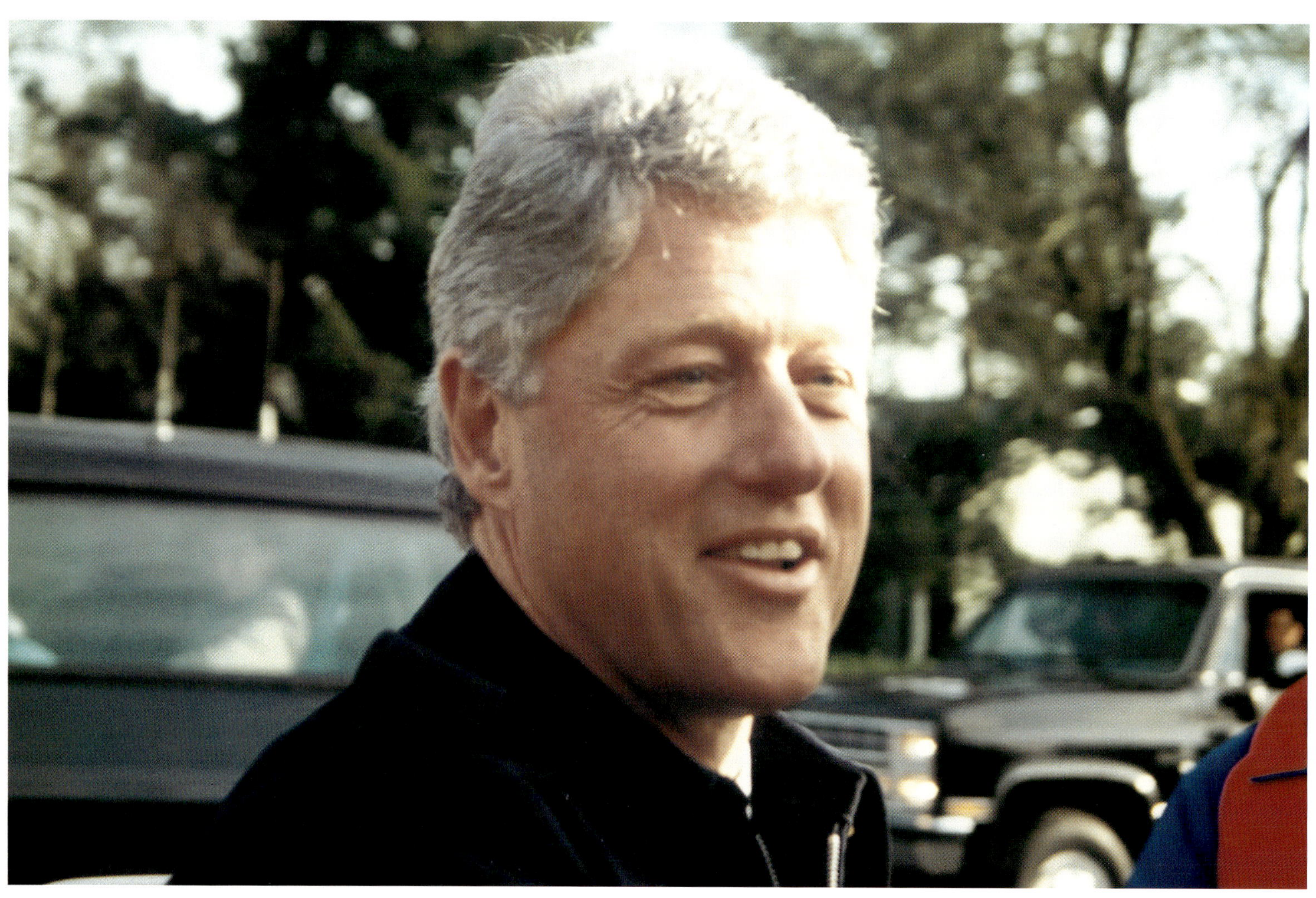

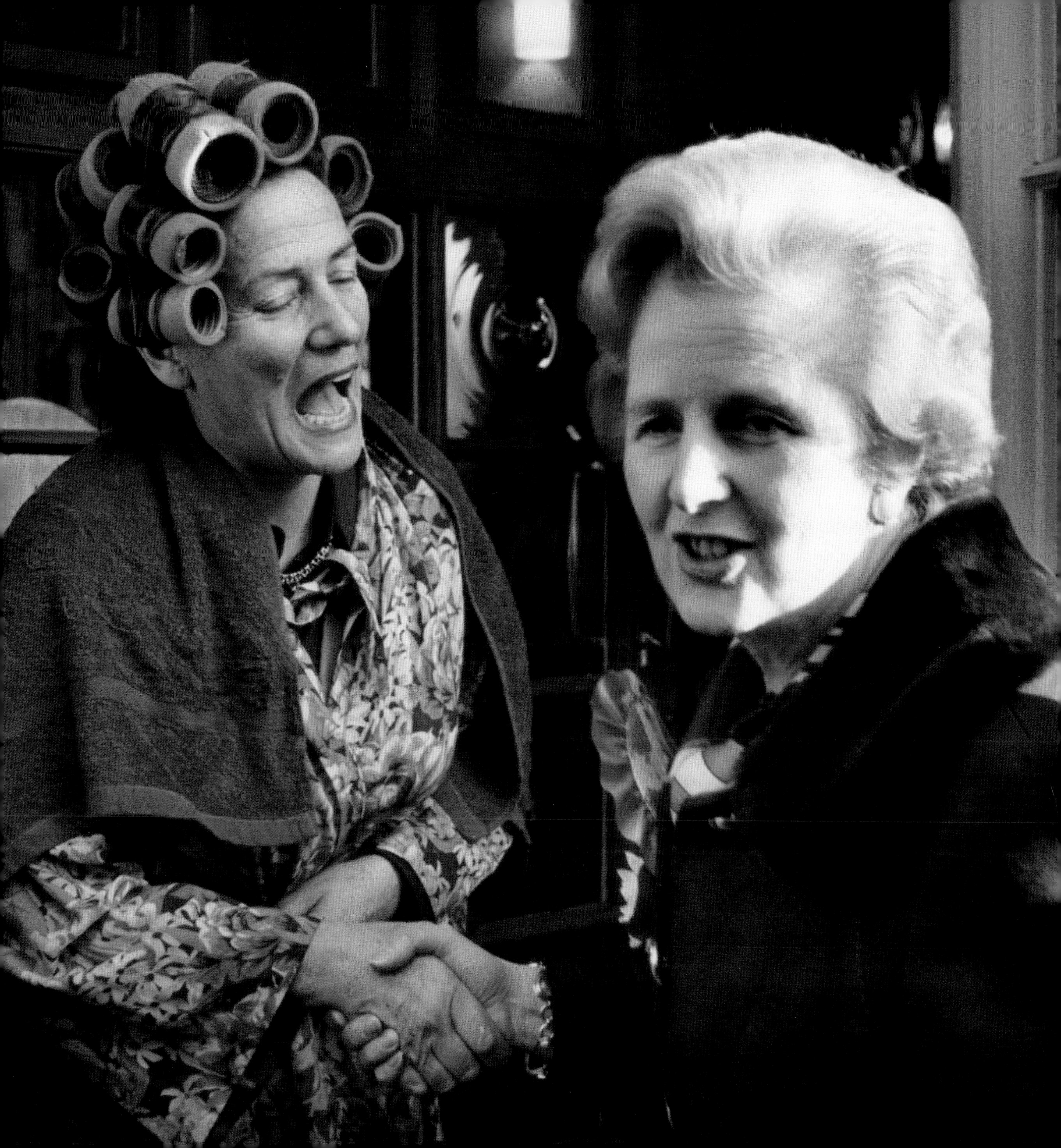

# Singularity

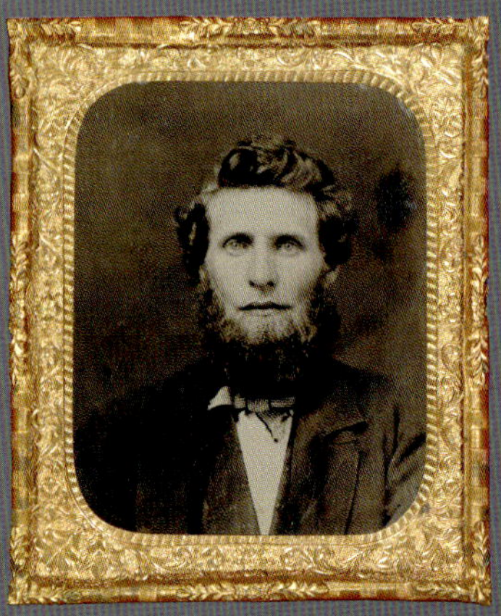

*'It is hard to laugh at the need for beauty and romance, no matter how tasteless, even horrible, the results of that need are. But it is easy to sigh. Few things are sadder than the truly monstrous.'*
Nathanael West
*The Day of the Locust*, 1939

In earlier times, if fate had decreed a person to be born extraordinarily tall, short, fat, thin, or with some outstanding physical deformity, a career in a circus or sideshow was encouraged as an acceptable occupation. In the past century, however, society has turned on this subculture with disgust. Susan Sontag commented, 'As the inhabitants of deviant underworlds are evicted from their restricted territories – banned as unseemly, a public nuisance, obscene, or just unprofitable – they increasingly come to infiltrate consciousness as the subject of art, acquiring a certain diffuse legitimacy and metaphoric proximity which creates all the more distance.'

Diane Arbus, more than any other photographer, conditioned and expanded our comprehension of subtle abnormality amongst those who had previously been perceived to be forgettably ordinary. What is remarkable about her body of work is not her disturbing portraits of freaks and outsiders but her uncanny ability to have sought out and photographed seemingly normal people who, through her lens, appear to our eyes as dangerous, deranged or merely desperate human beings.

Through the sensational or dispassionate recording of unfortunate truths, photography has always been a vehicle for satisfying puerile visual curiosity, albeit at a safe distance. Whether via technical tricks, props or juxtapositions, clever practitioners have, since the invention of the camera, taken advantage of the public's neverending appetite for photographs displaying the strange or the absurd. Lowbrows might consider such images a novelty, while highbrows would solemnly regard them as Surreal.

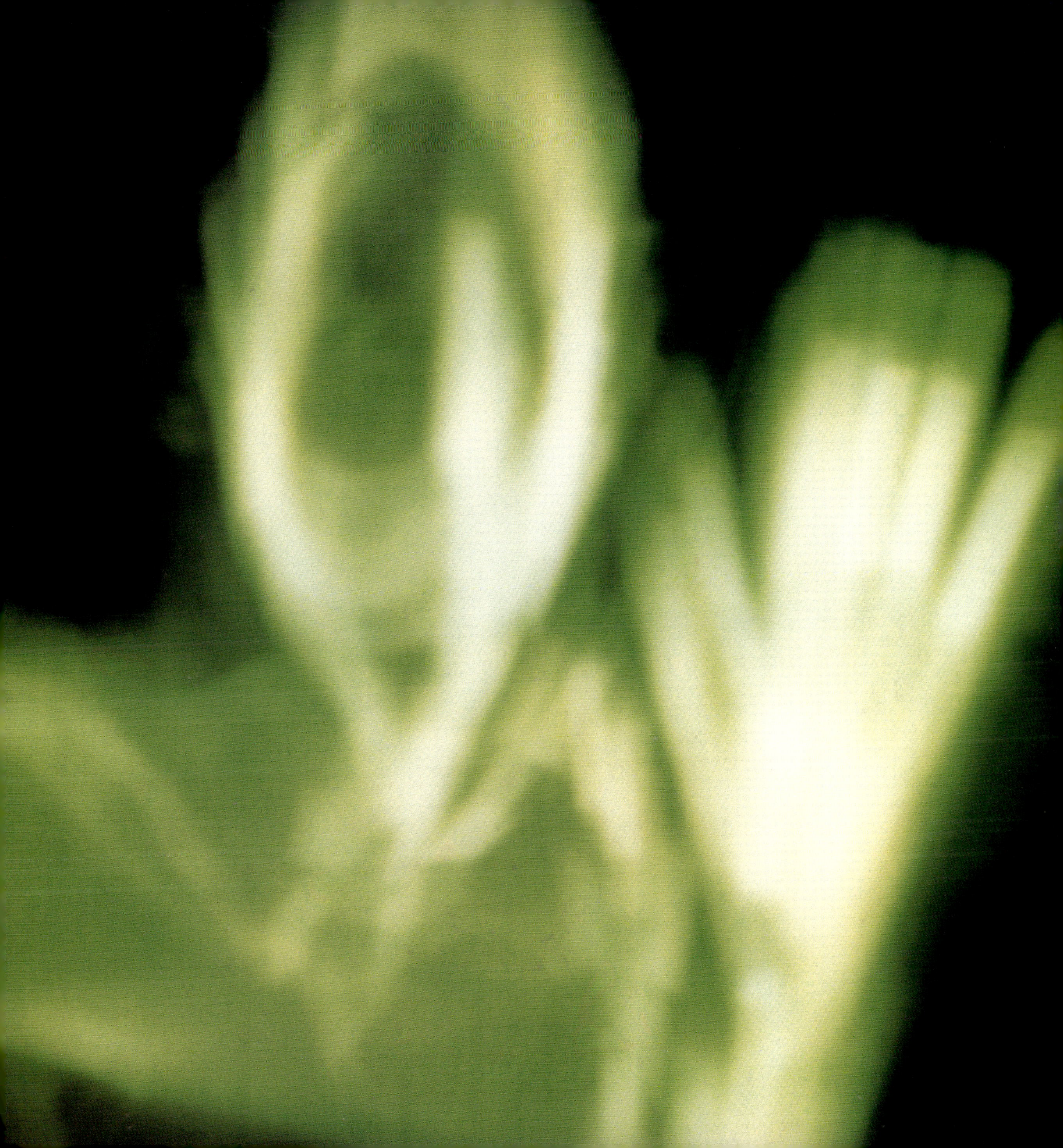

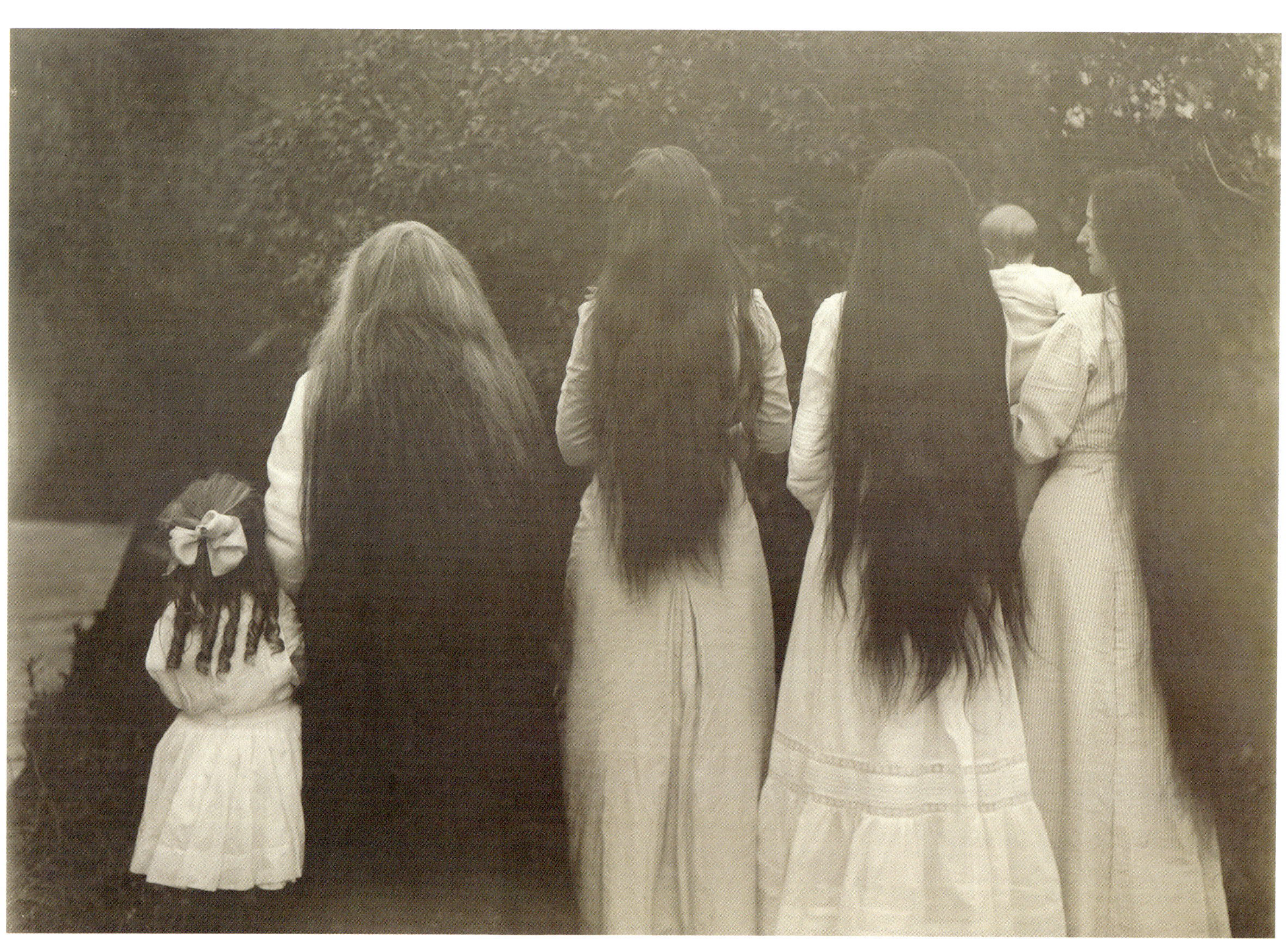

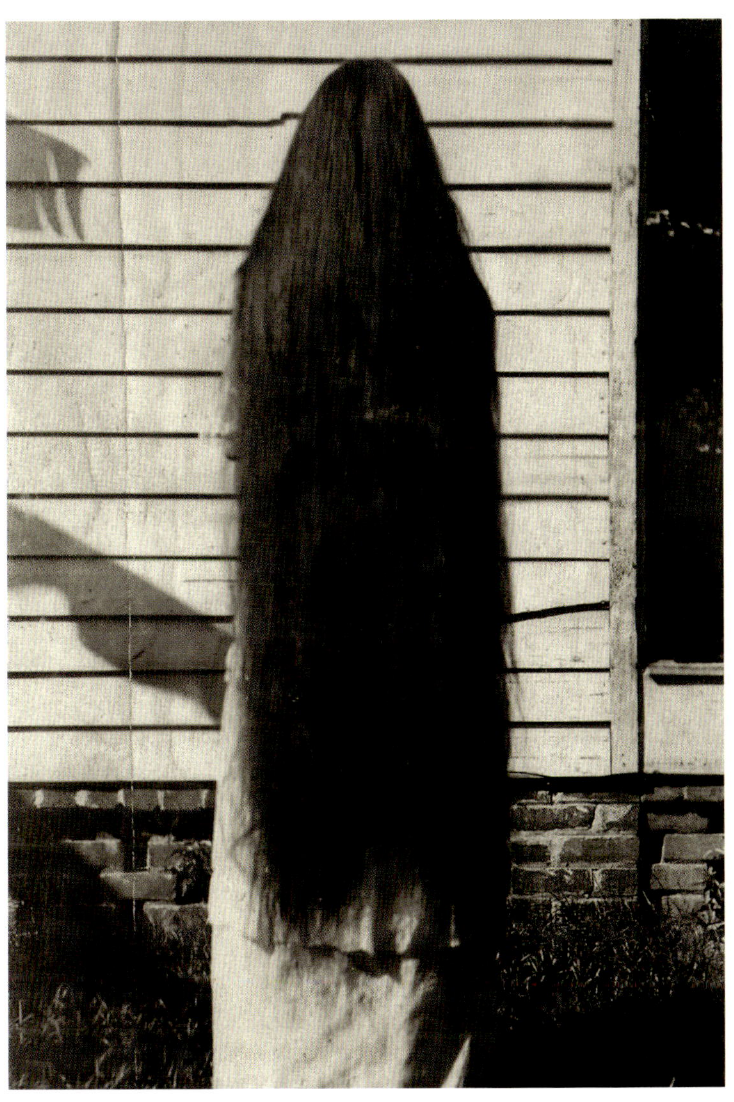

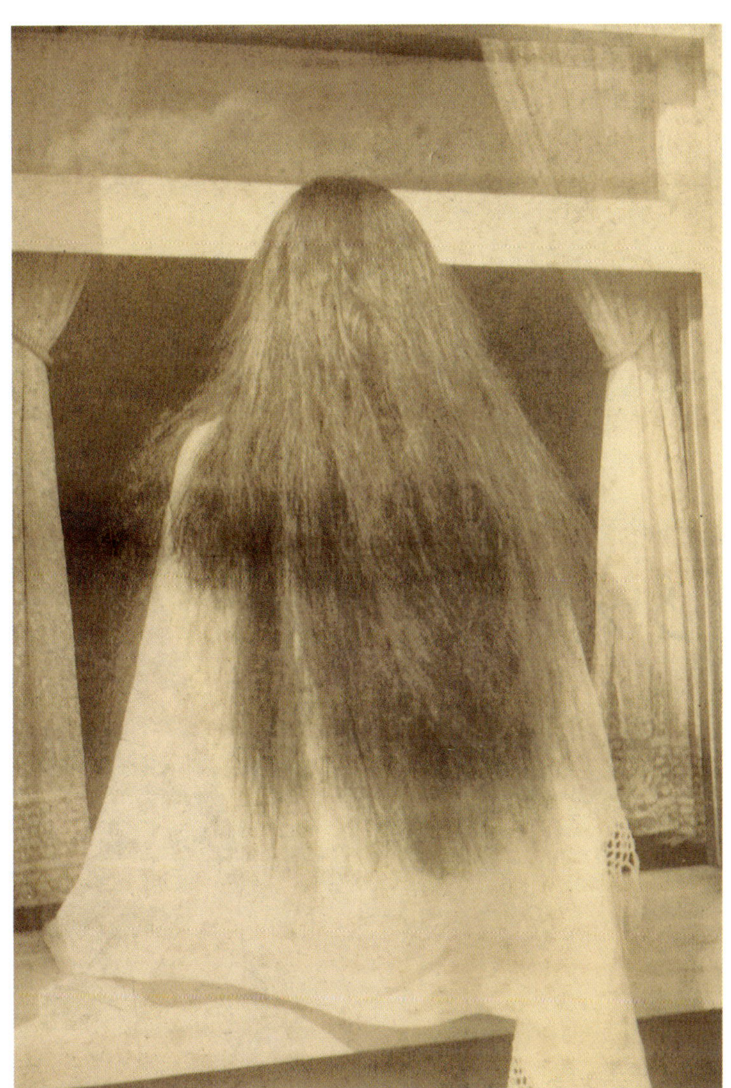

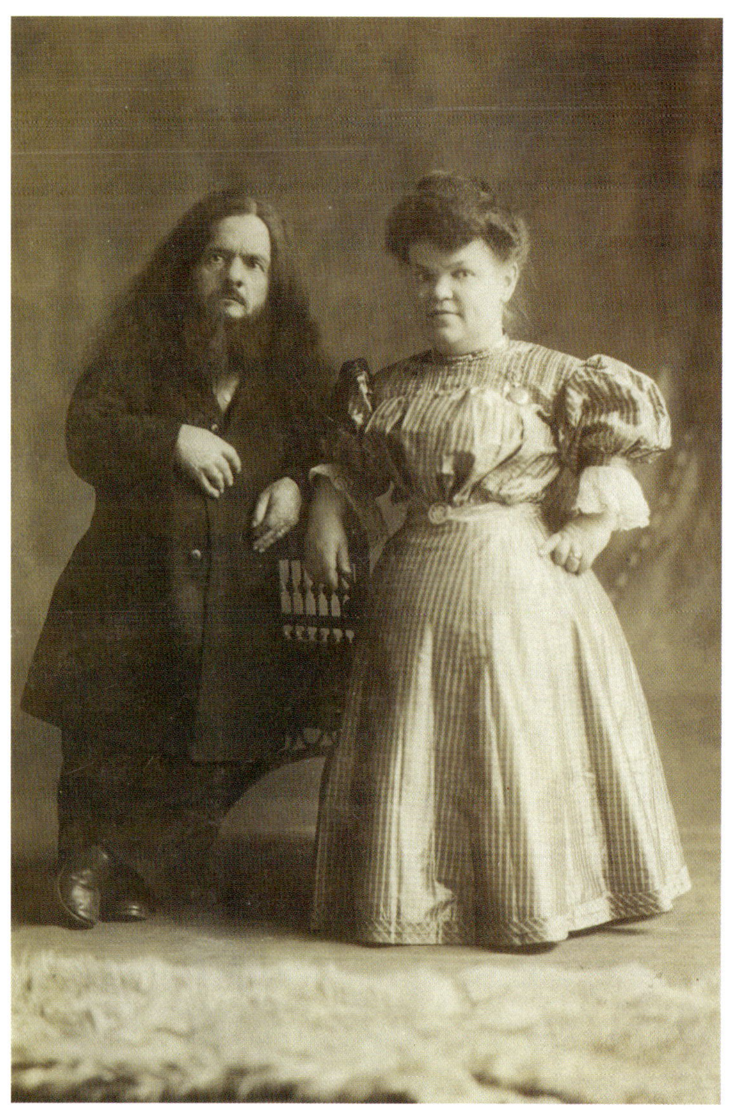

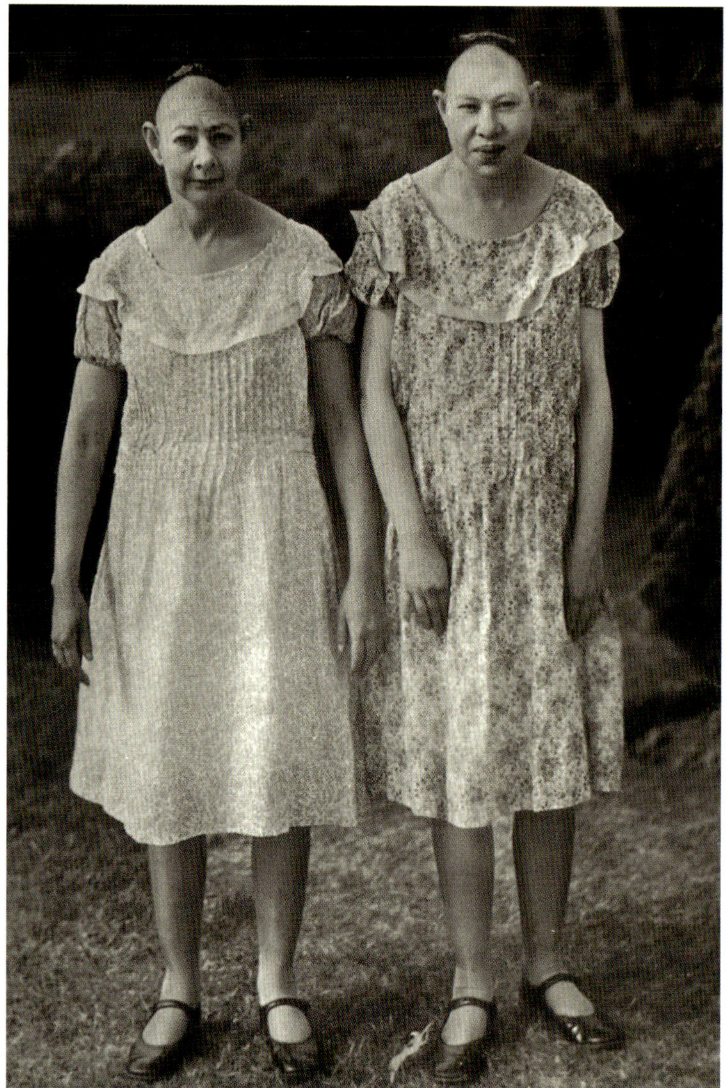

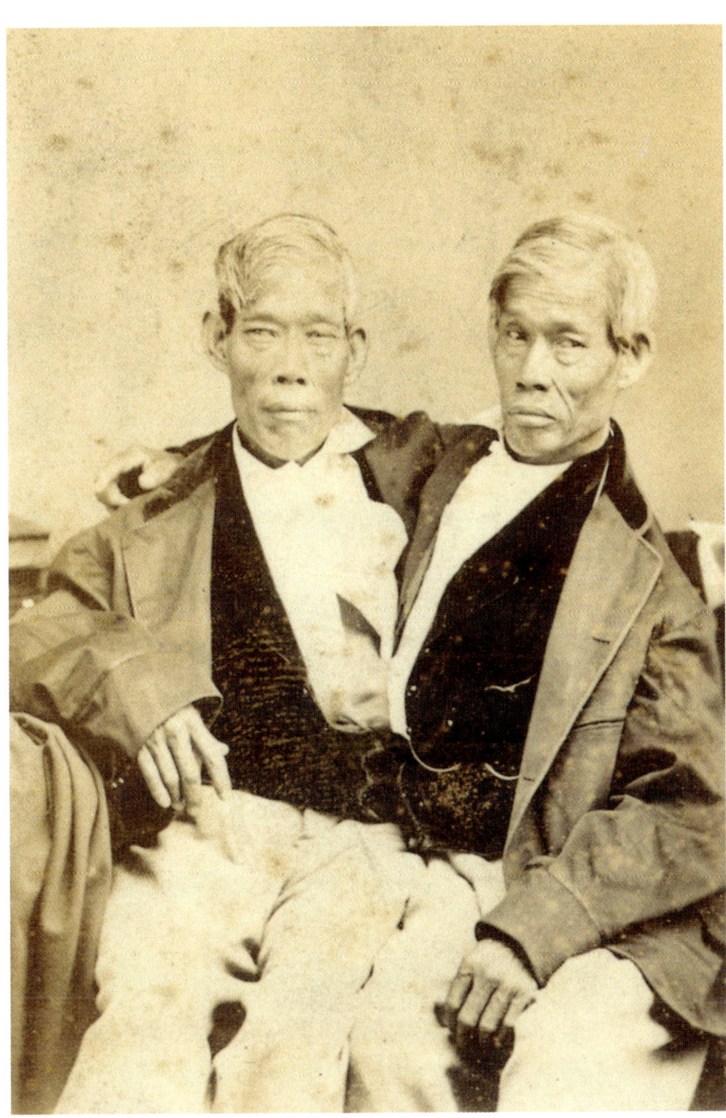

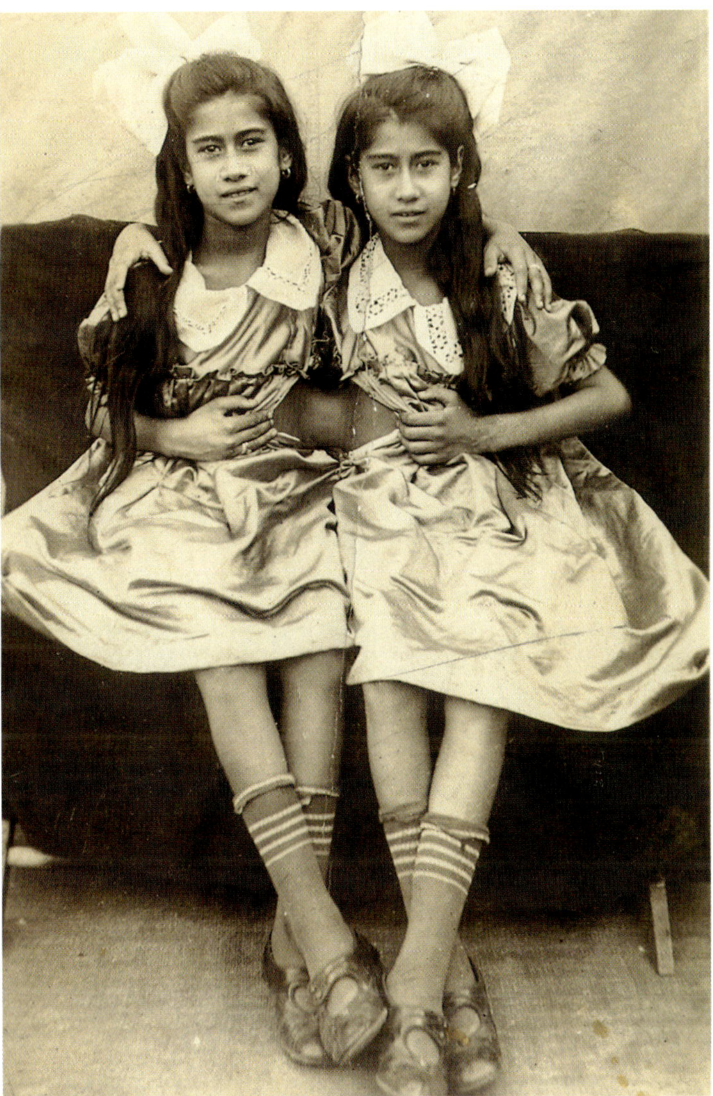

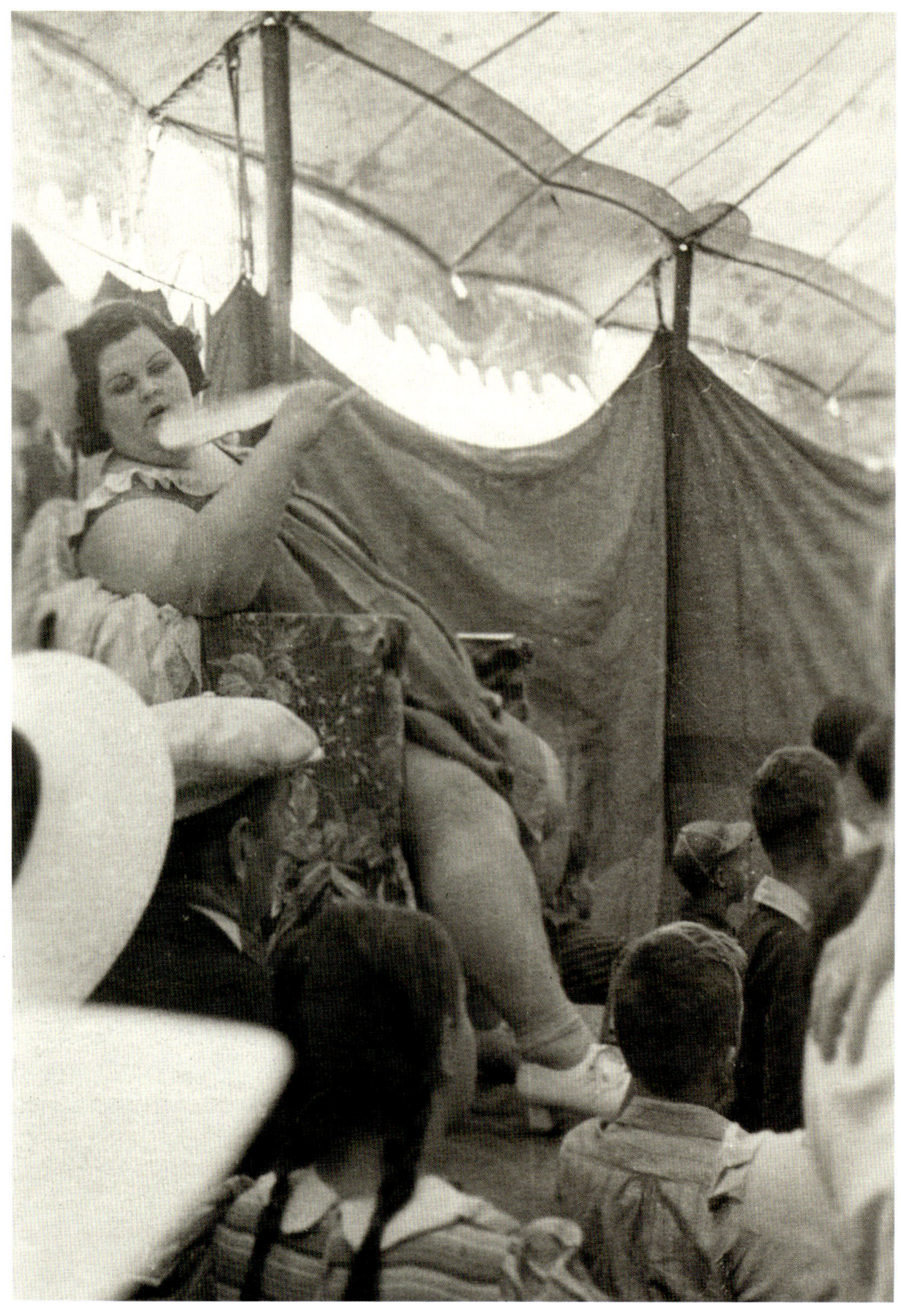

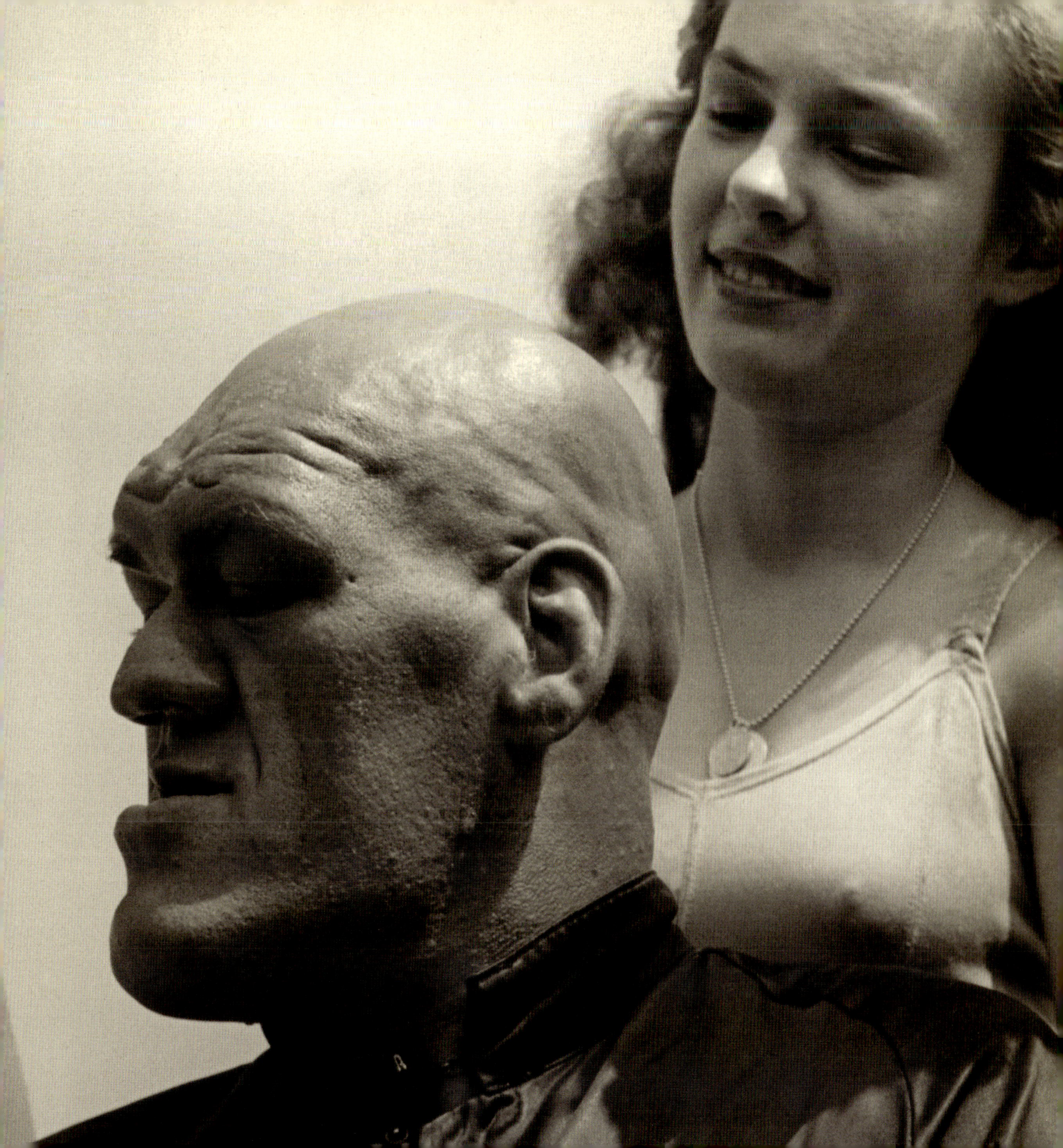

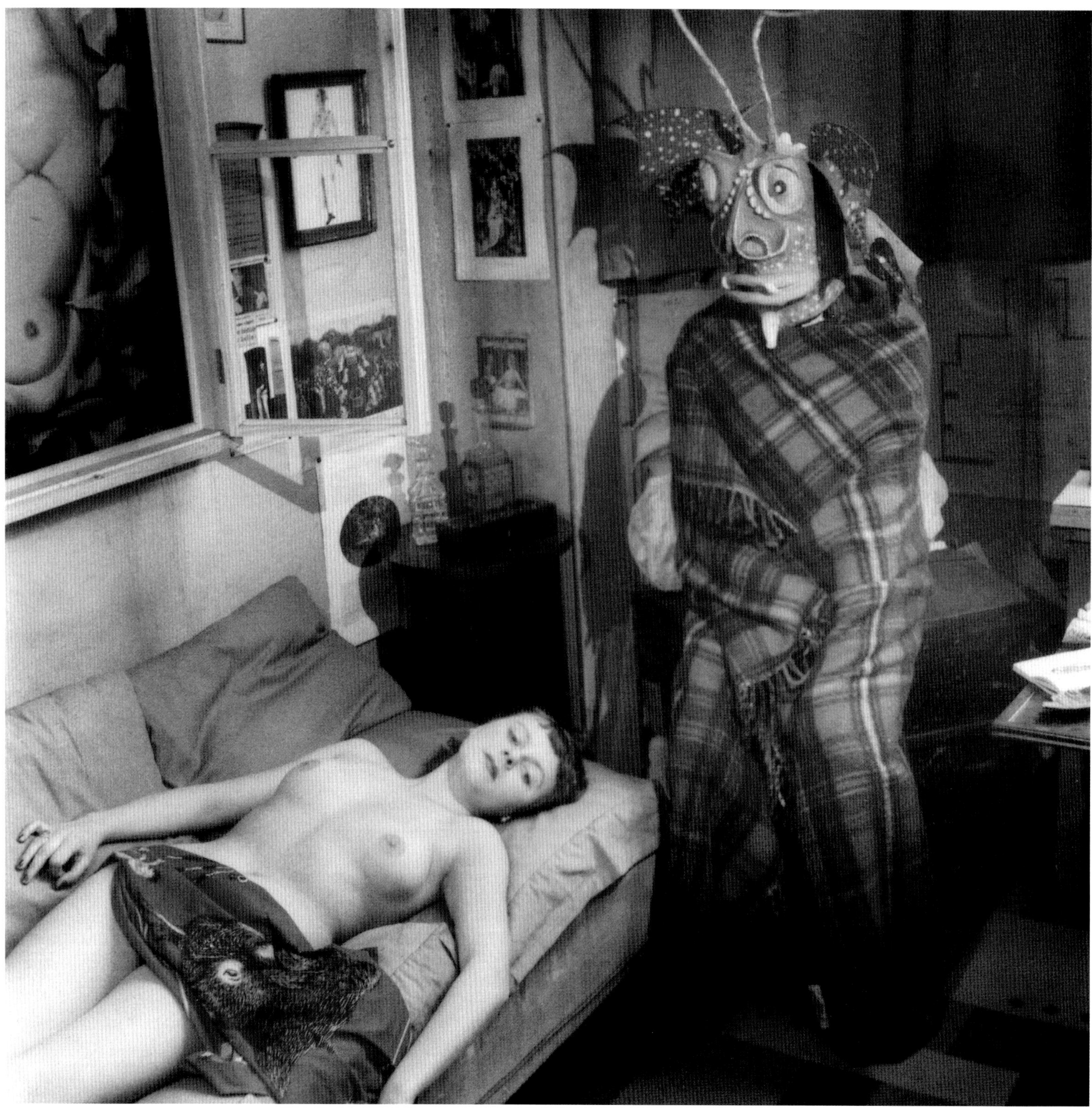

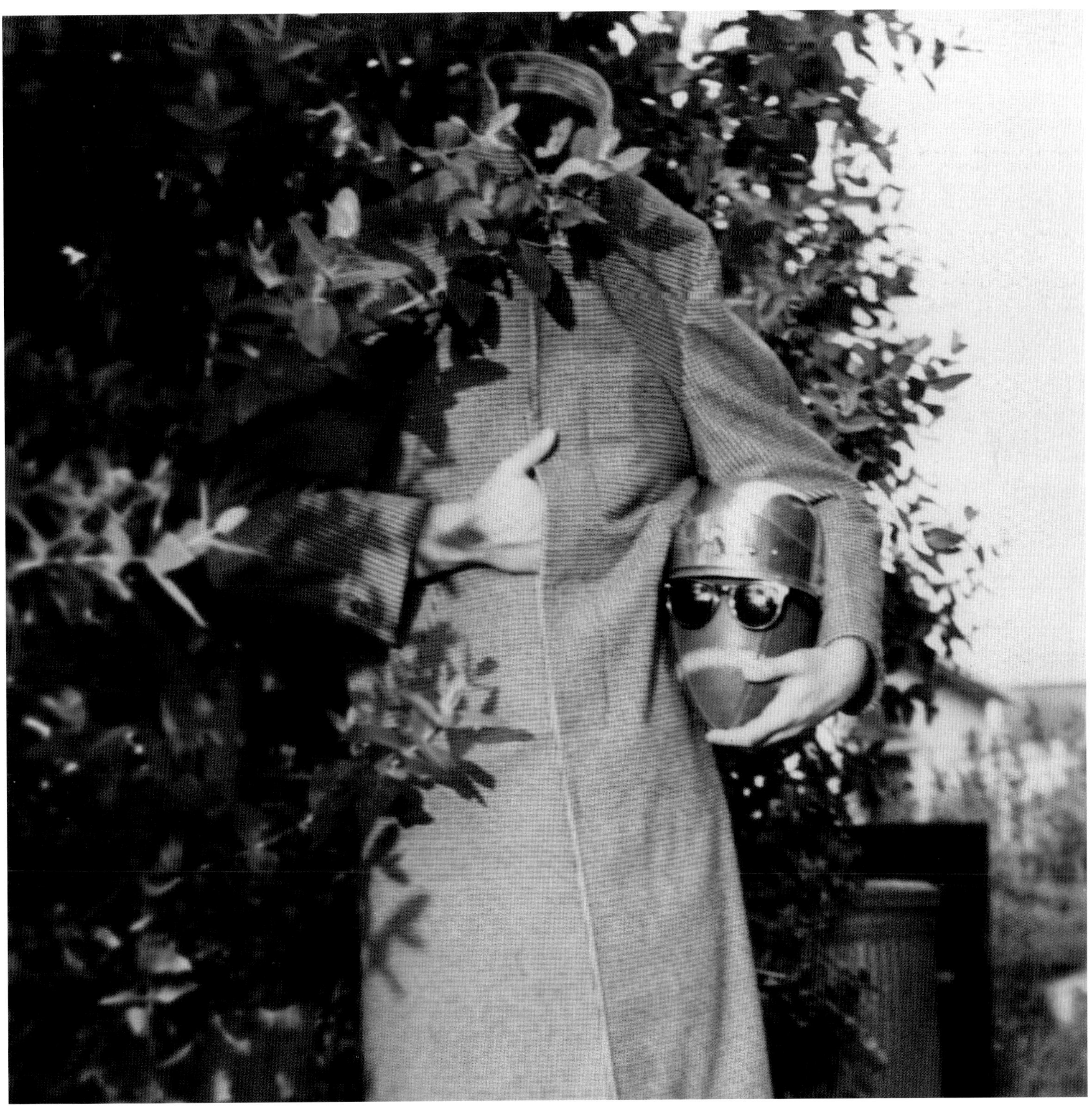

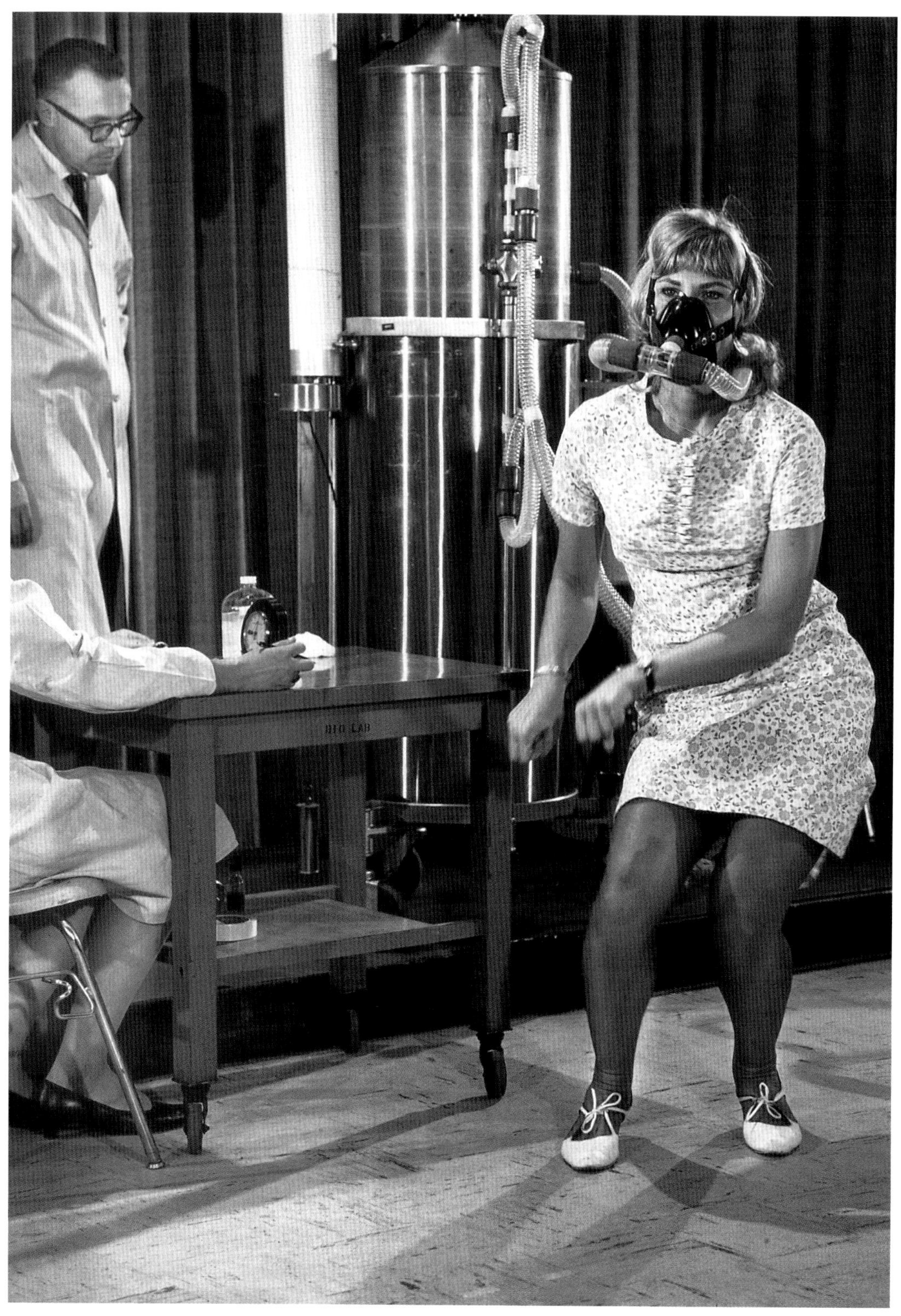

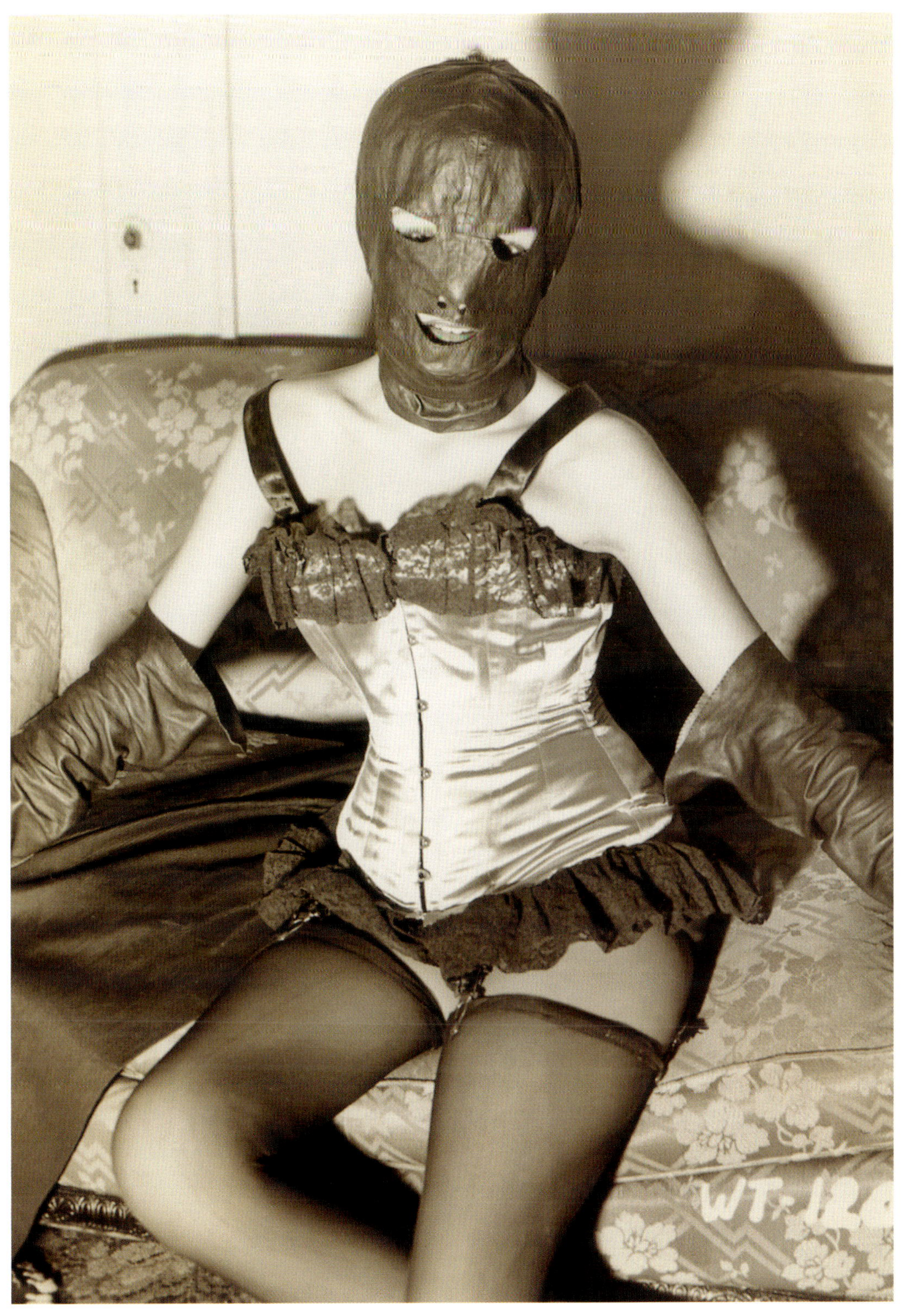
WT-12

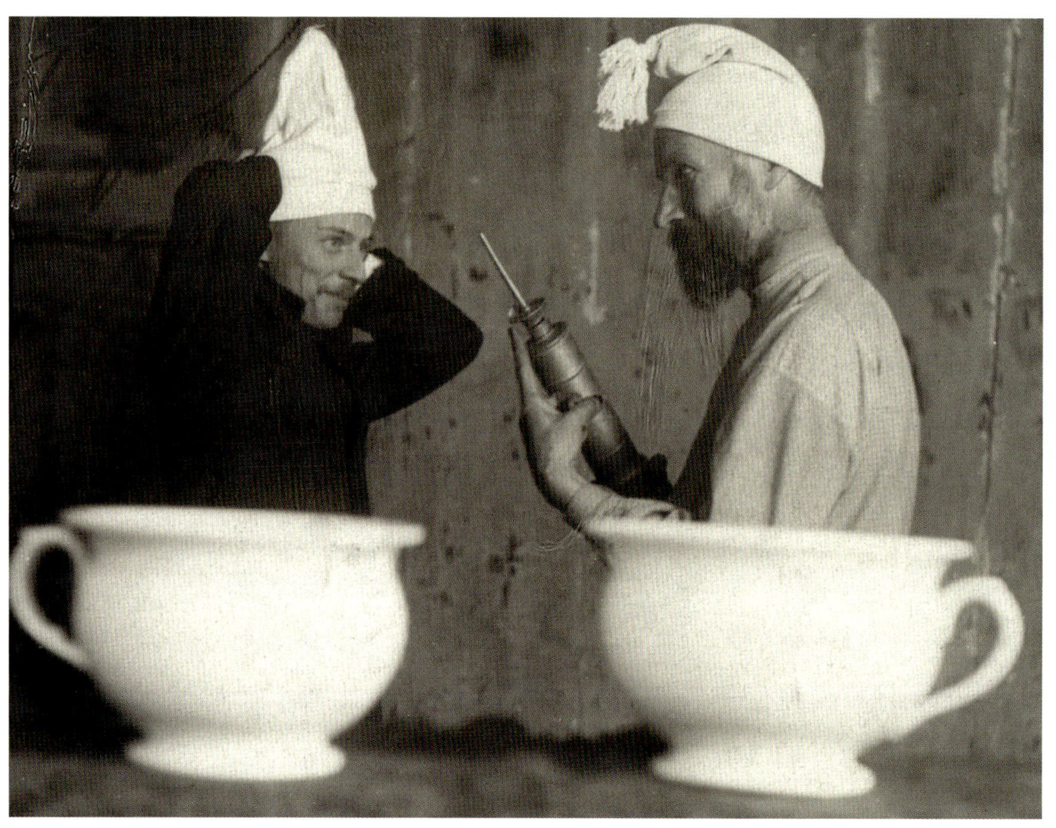

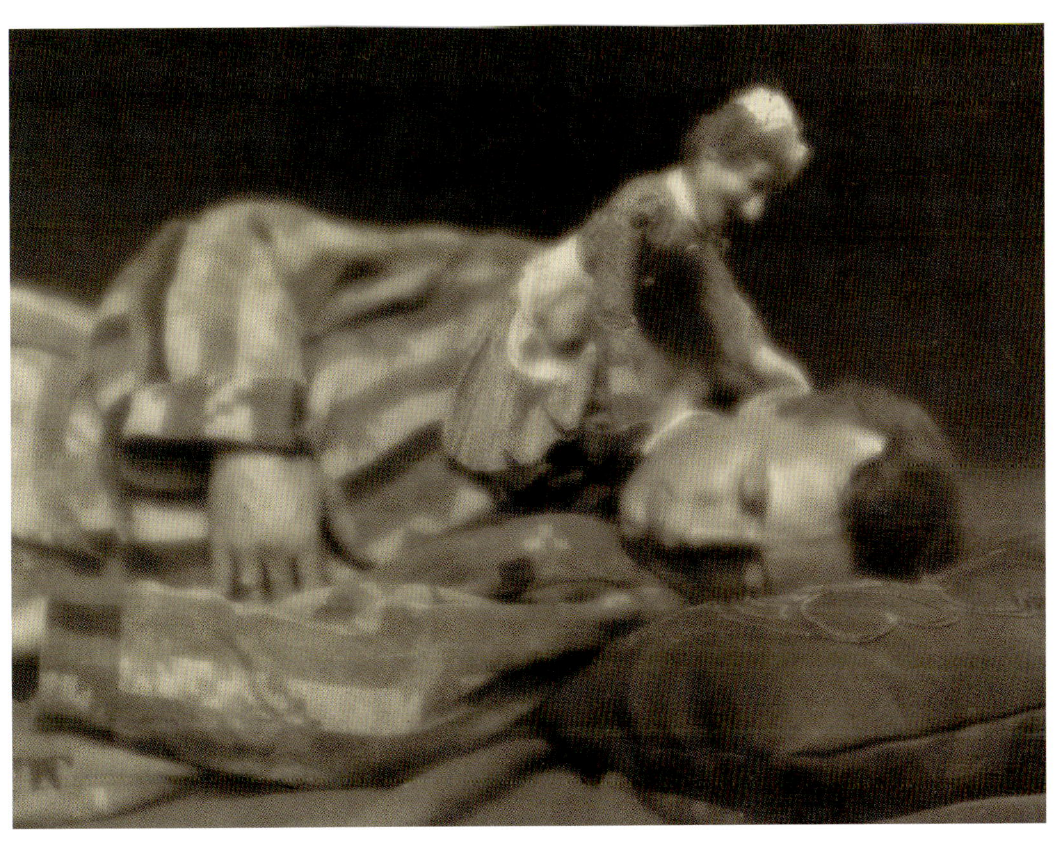

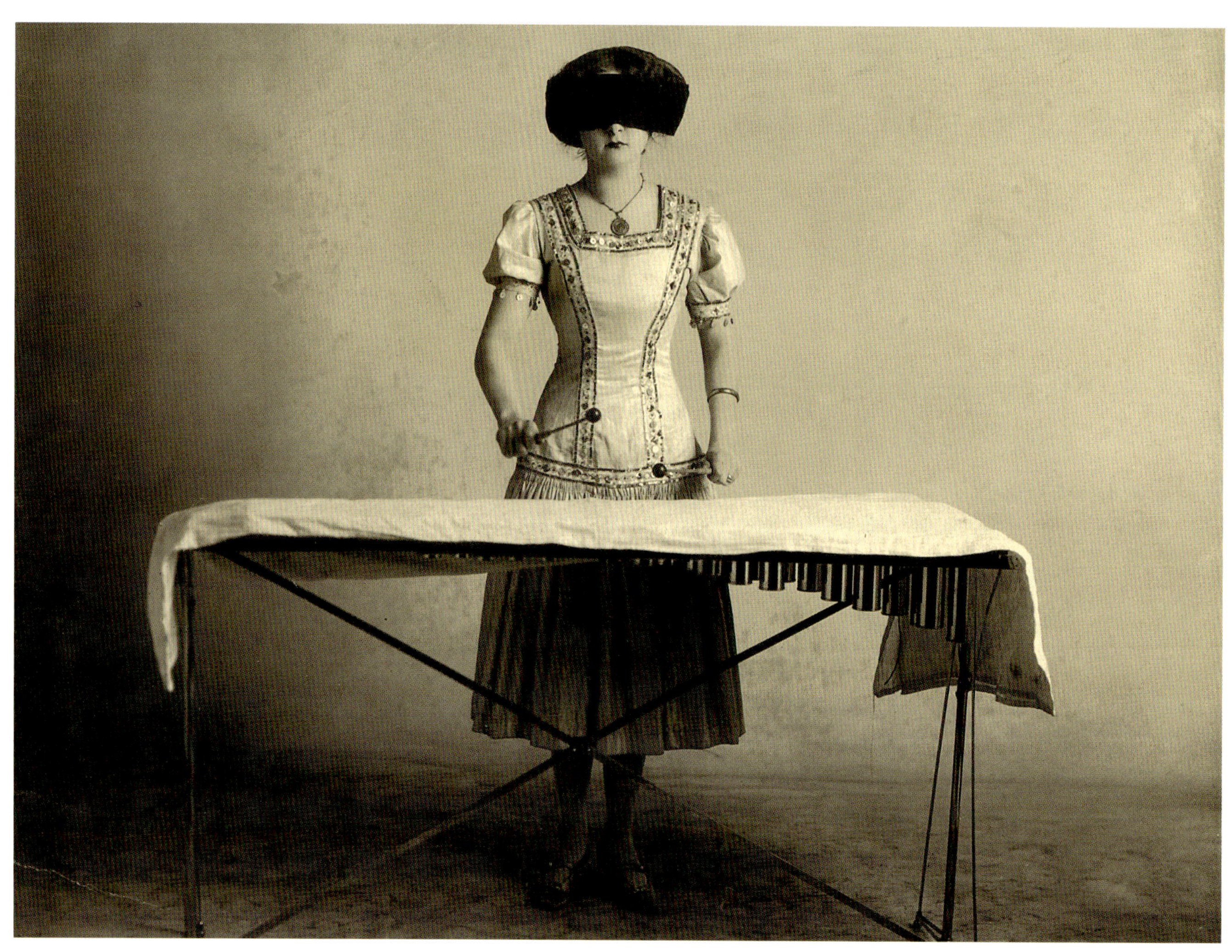

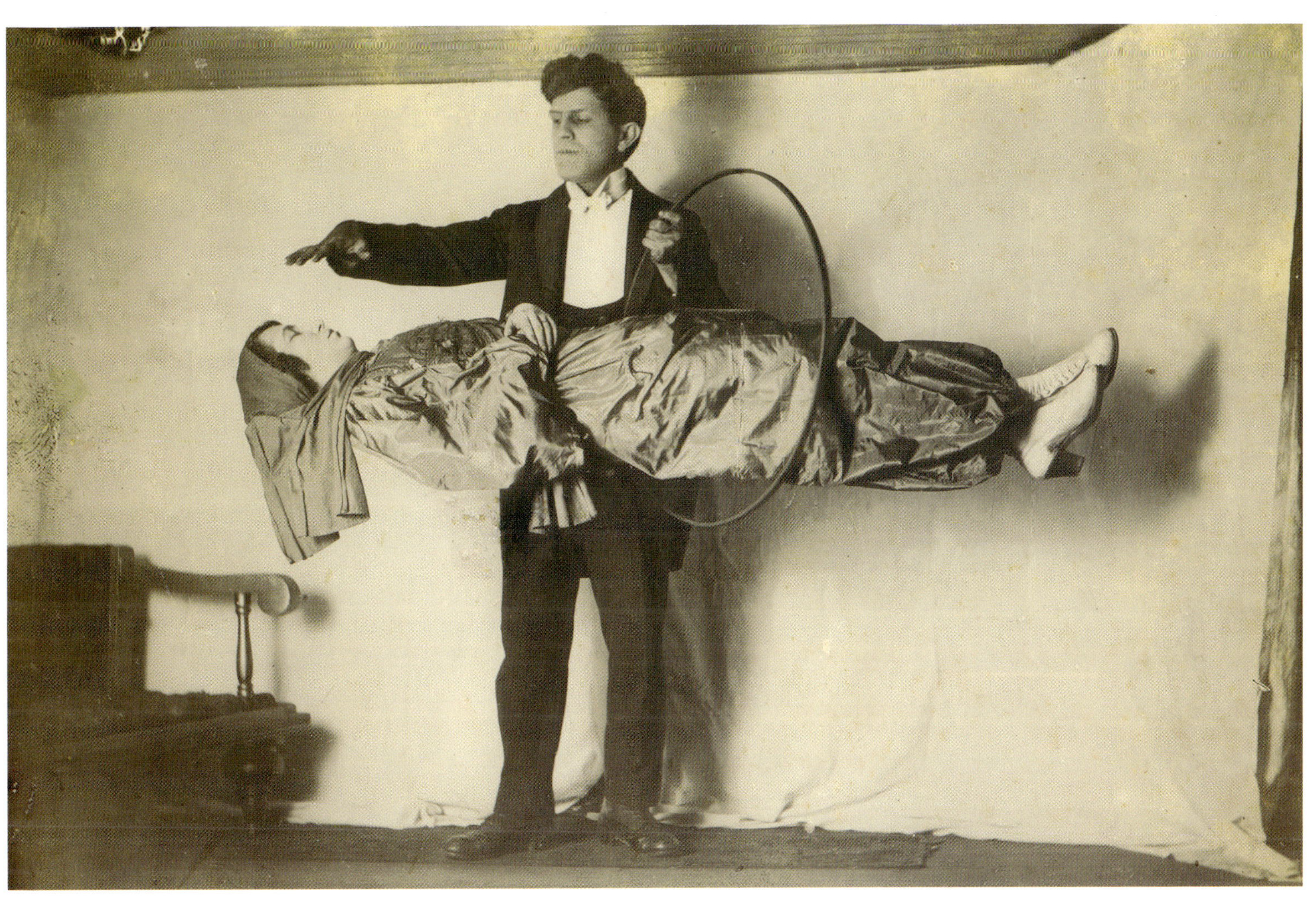

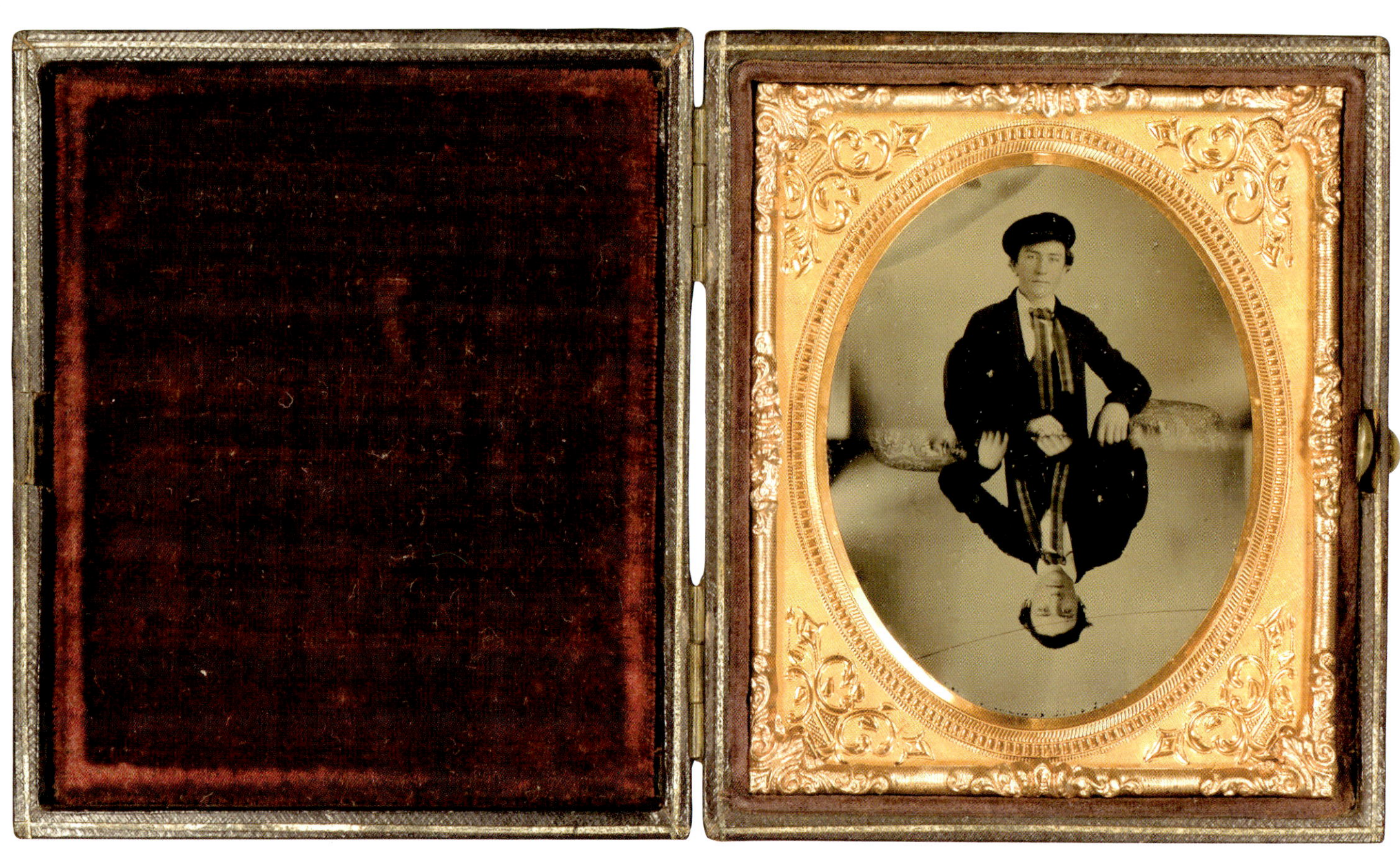

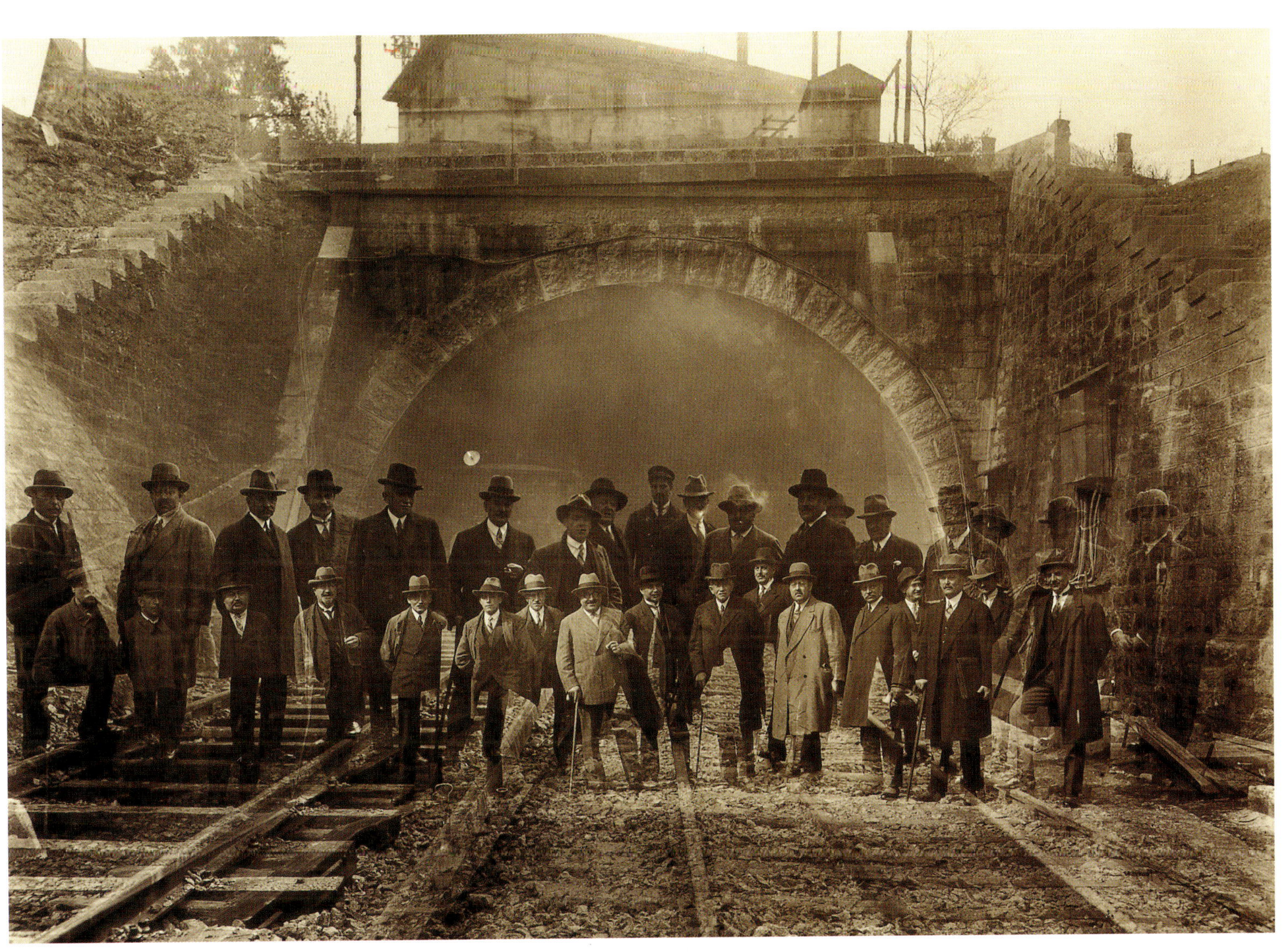

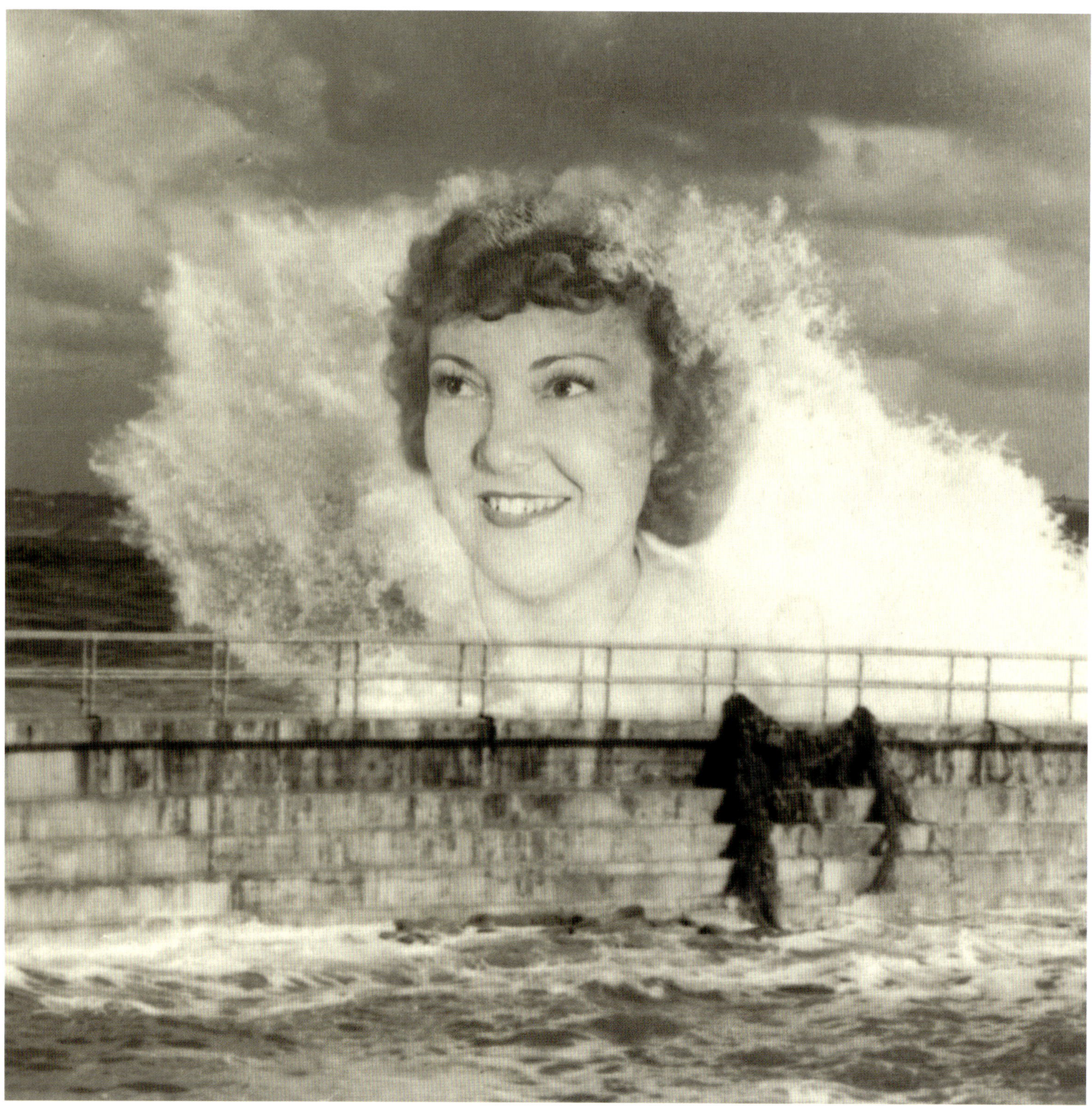

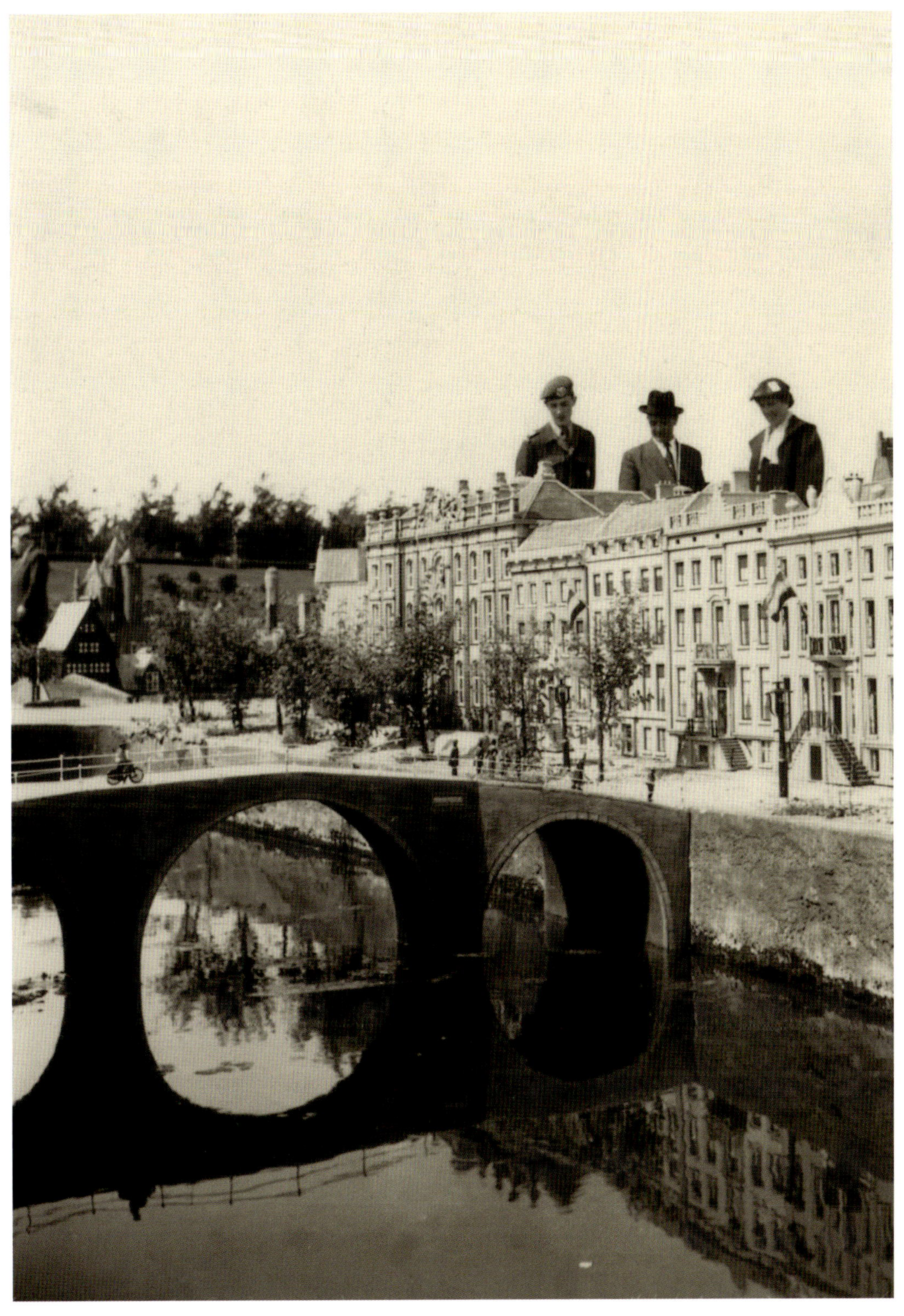

# Activity

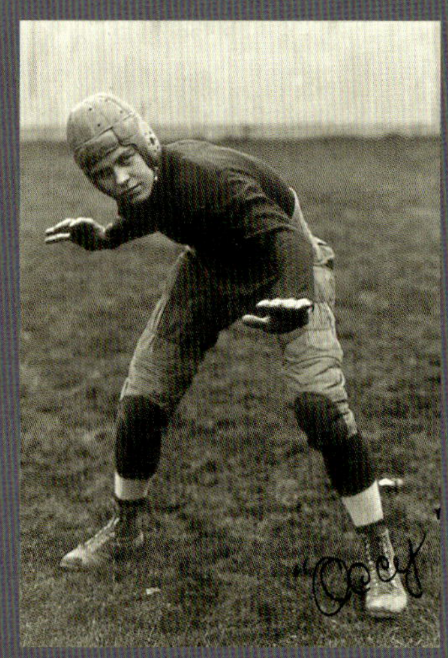


*'... like watching people dancing through an open window. They seem a little mad at first, until you realize they hear the song that you are watching.'*
Sam Wagstaff
*A Book of Photographs*, 1978

It took technical innovations developed at the end of the nineteenth century to allow instantaneous motion to be routinely captured on film. Although most photographs of people continued to be stiffly static, the idea that the activity of a person could serve as an important aspect of a picture began to take hold. Long before the term 'body language' was in common parlance, photographs of people in the act of daily activities revealed different facets of their personality.

What appears to the casual observer to be a pastime can, in fact, to the person in the photograph be hard and serious labour. Images of professional athletes, performers, sailors, fishermen and farmers come to mind in this category. 'Occupationals' is the photographic term for pictures that have long been taken of people posing in front of, or within, their place of employment. One can often notice on their faces a sense of pride of profession. These images serve as a visible affirmation that their vocations were an important component of society through the necessary services they provided.

By contrast, it is fascinating to see how individuals diminish and dissolve into mere parts of a whole in photographs of crowds. This brings to mind the cynical comment of Harry Lime (Orson Welles) to Holly Martins (Joseph Cotten) in the 1949 movie *The Third Man*, when, at the top of a ferris wheel in post-war Vienna, Lime looks at the distant pedestrians below and says, 'Look down there. Would you really feel any pity if one of those dots stopped moving forever? If I offered you £20,000 for each dot that stopped, would you really, old man, tell me to keep my money? Or would you calculate how many dots you could afford to spare?'

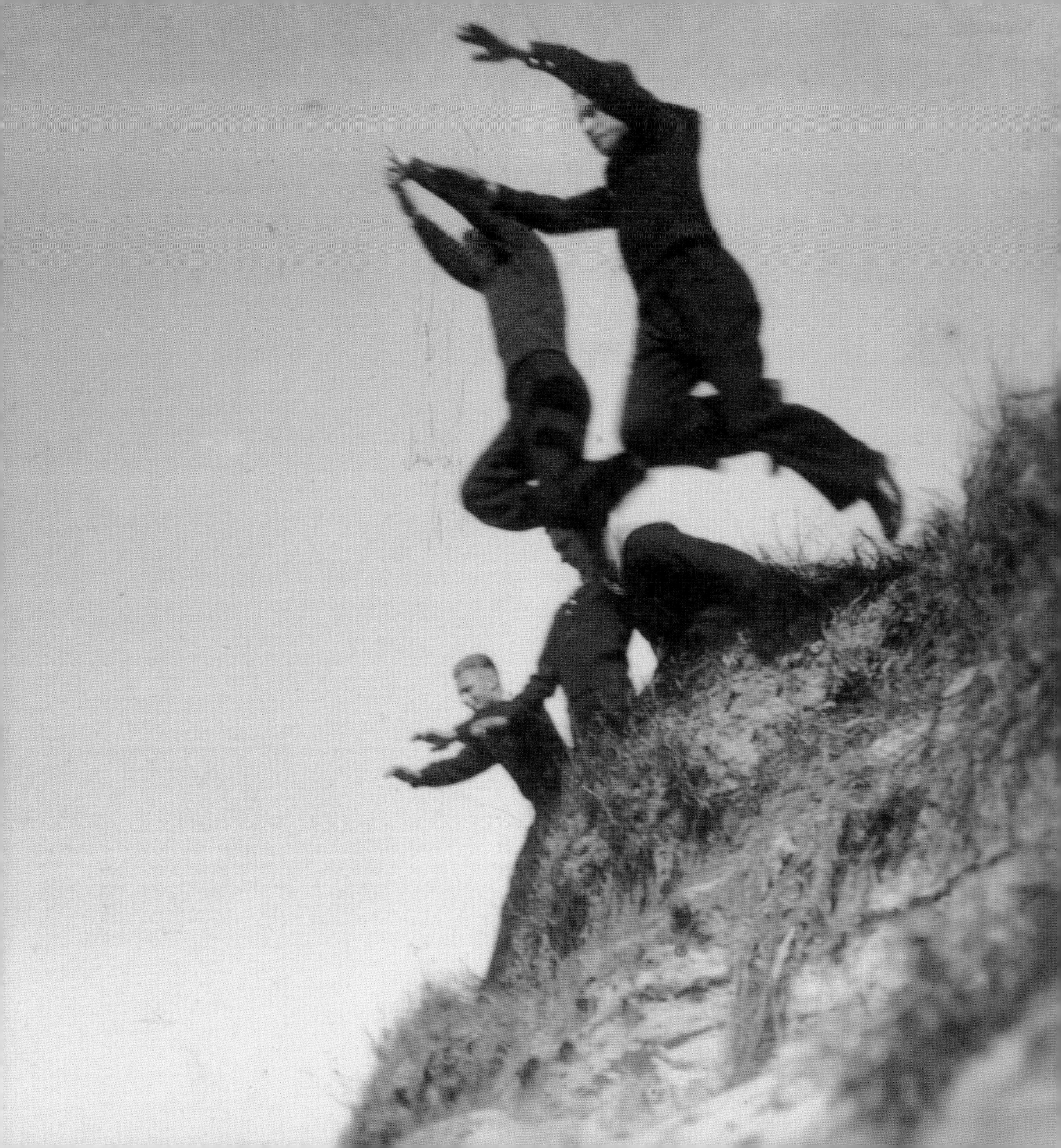

DES

# QUATRE DANSEURS EXCENTRIQUES

Qui ont paru **CENT FOIS** sur le théatre de la GAITÉ

DANS

# PARIS

## LA NUIT

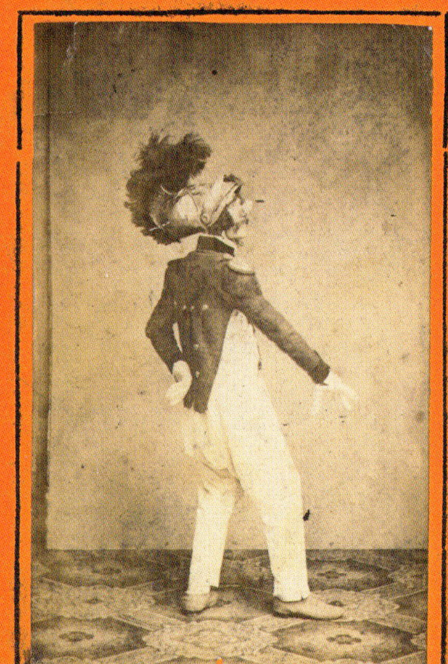

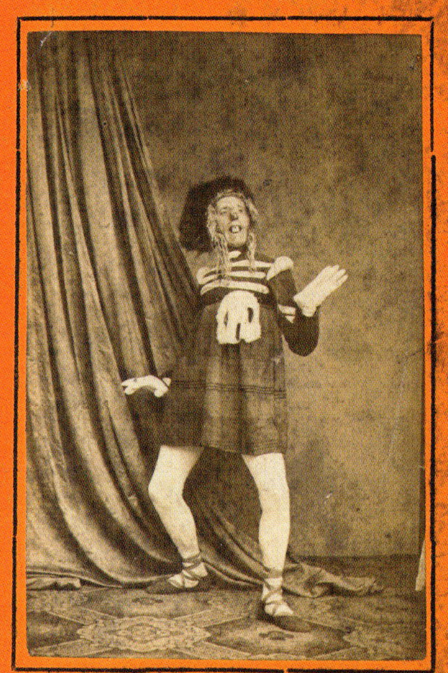

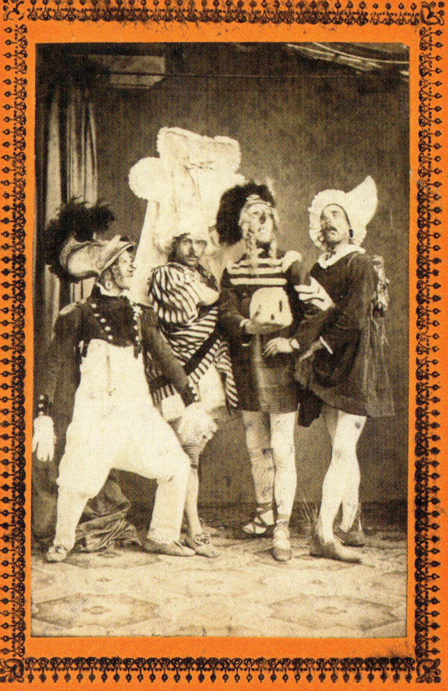

FLAGEOLET

CLODOCHE

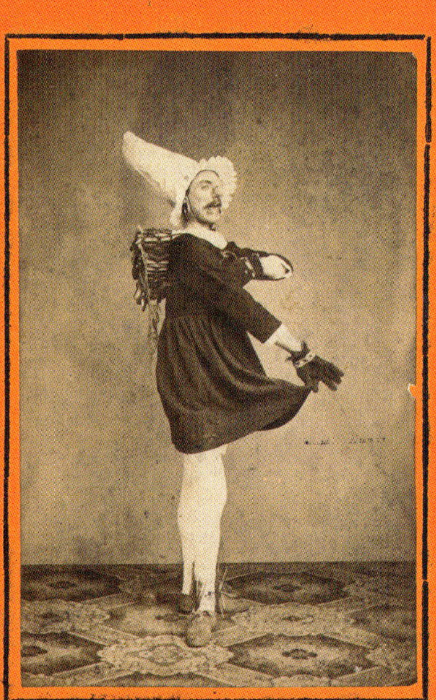

LA

## PASTOURELLE

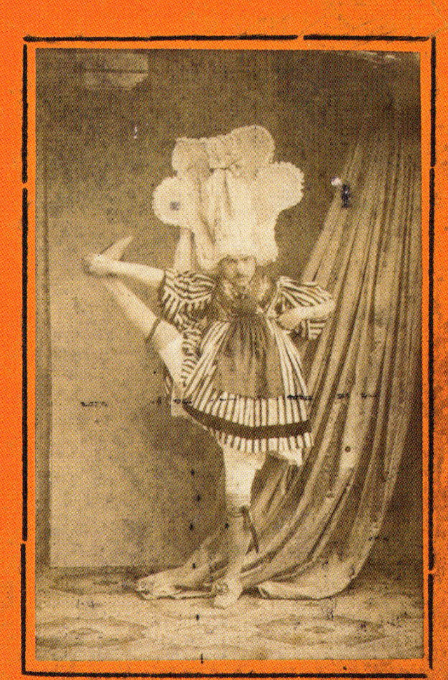

LACOMÈTE

NORMANDE

Lyon. — Typ. d'Aimé VINGTRINIER, rue de la Belle-Cordière, 14.

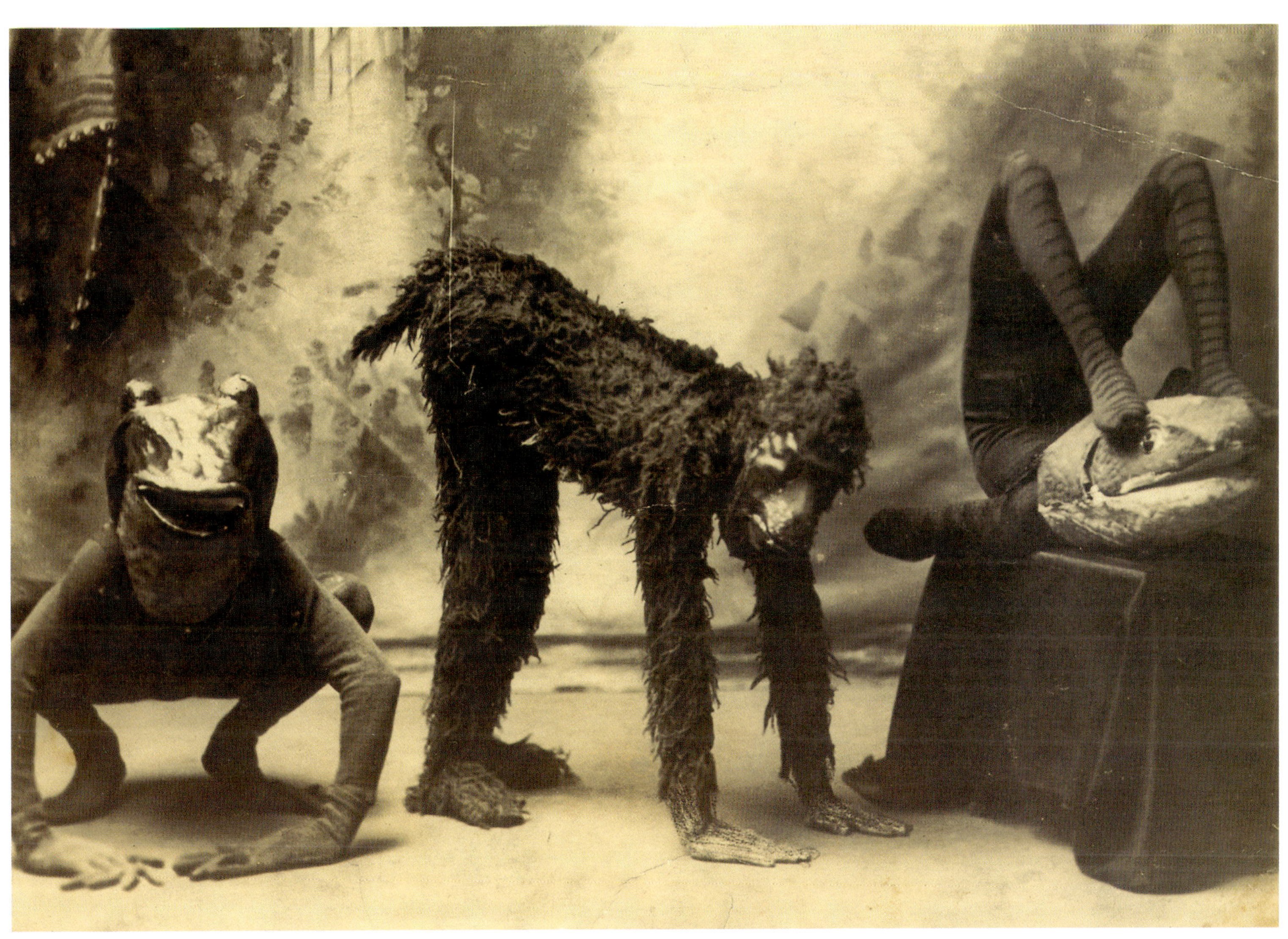

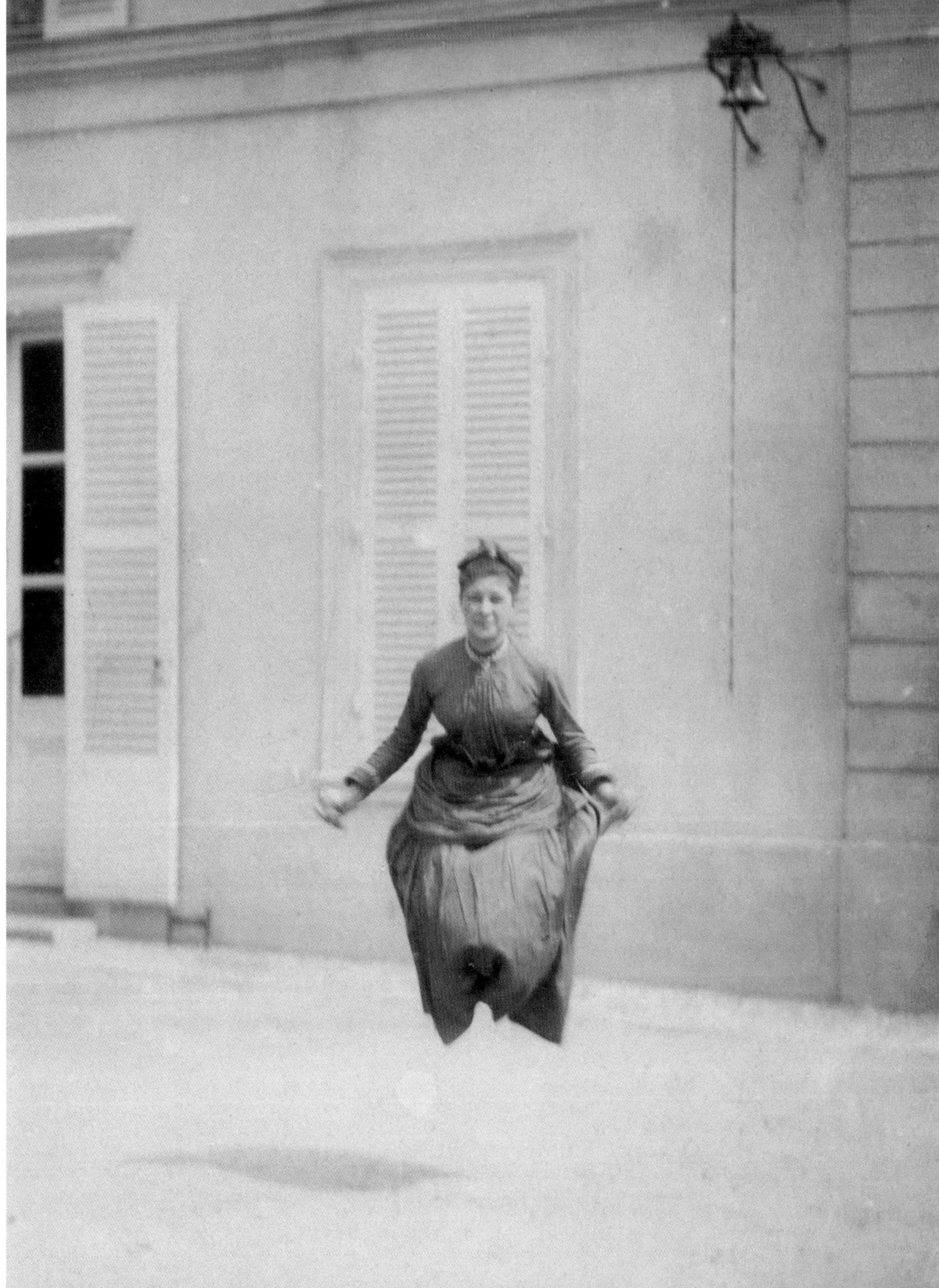

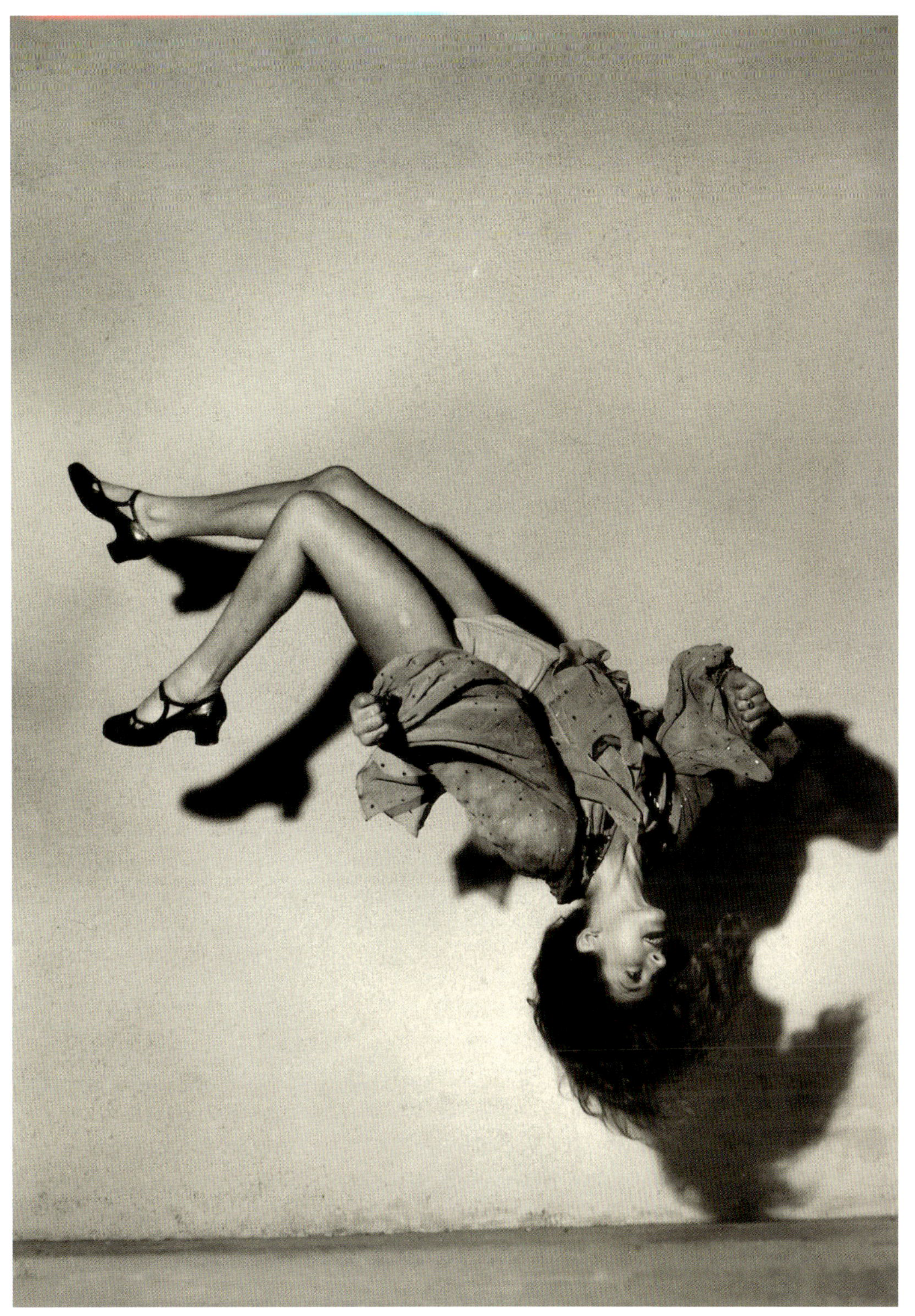

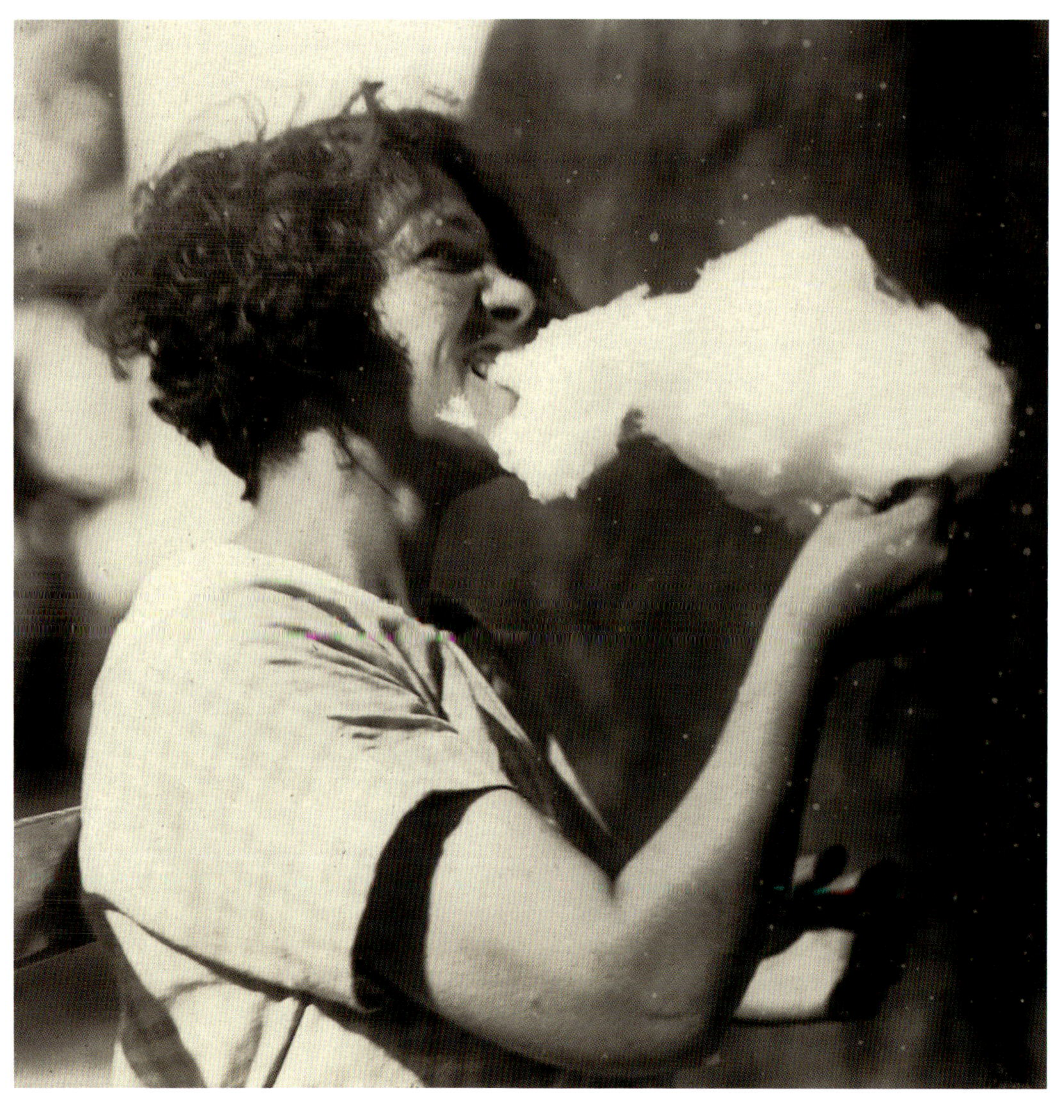

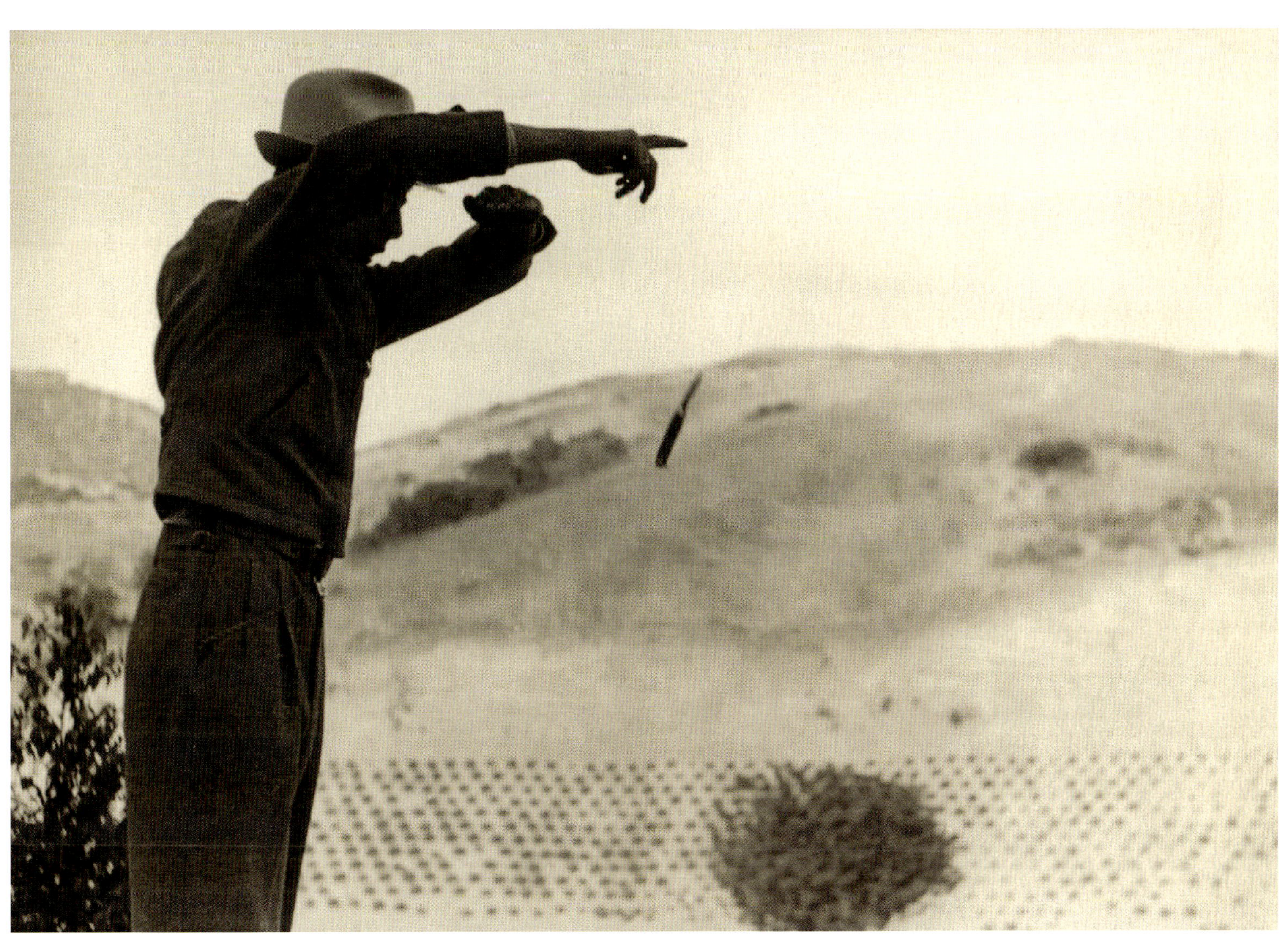

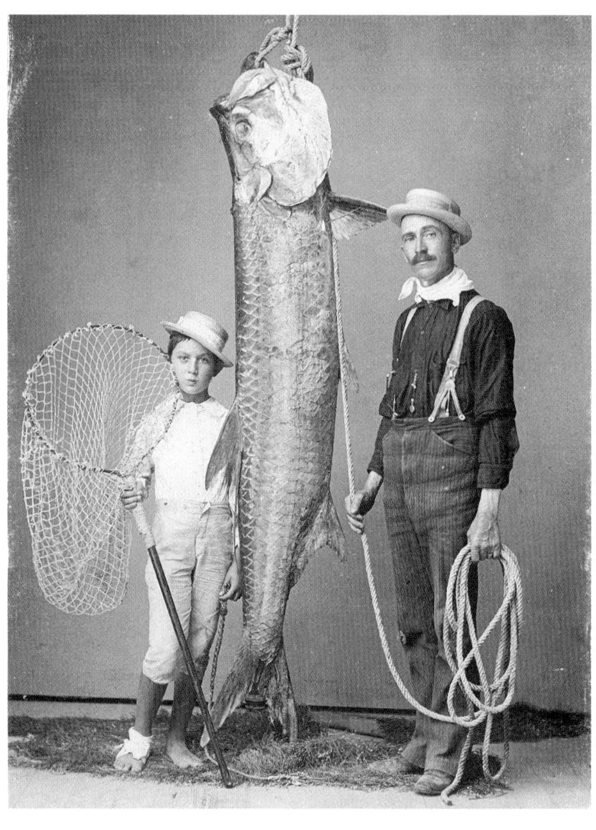

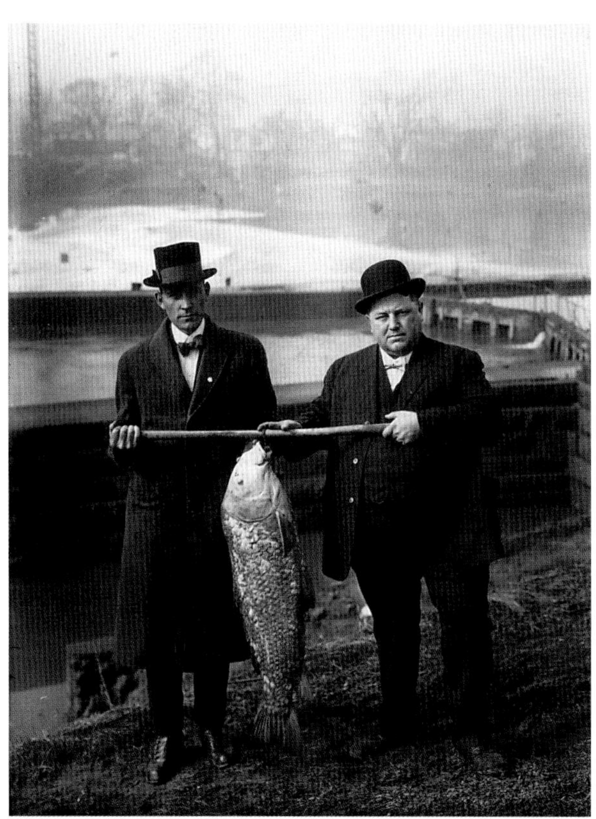

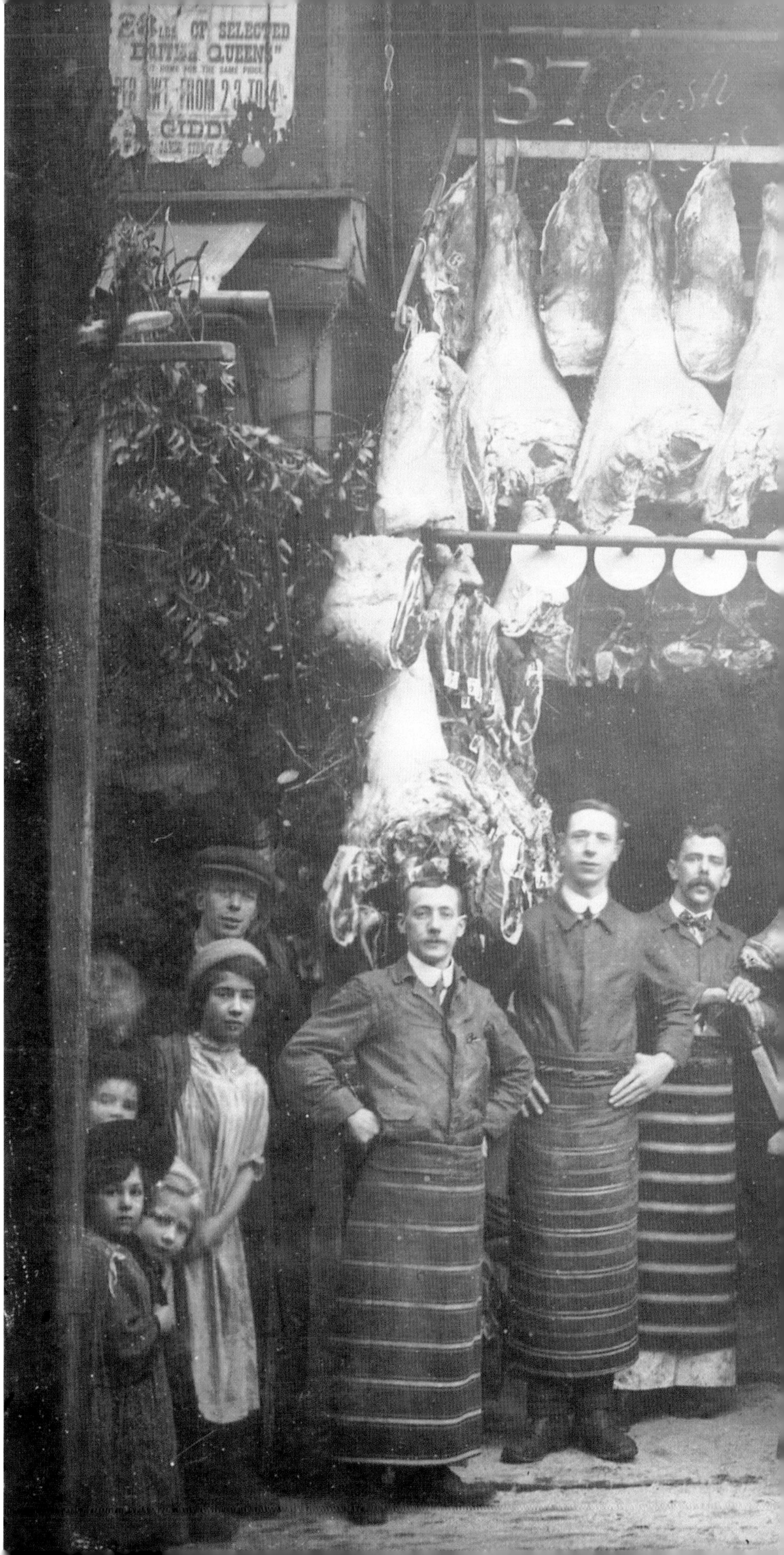

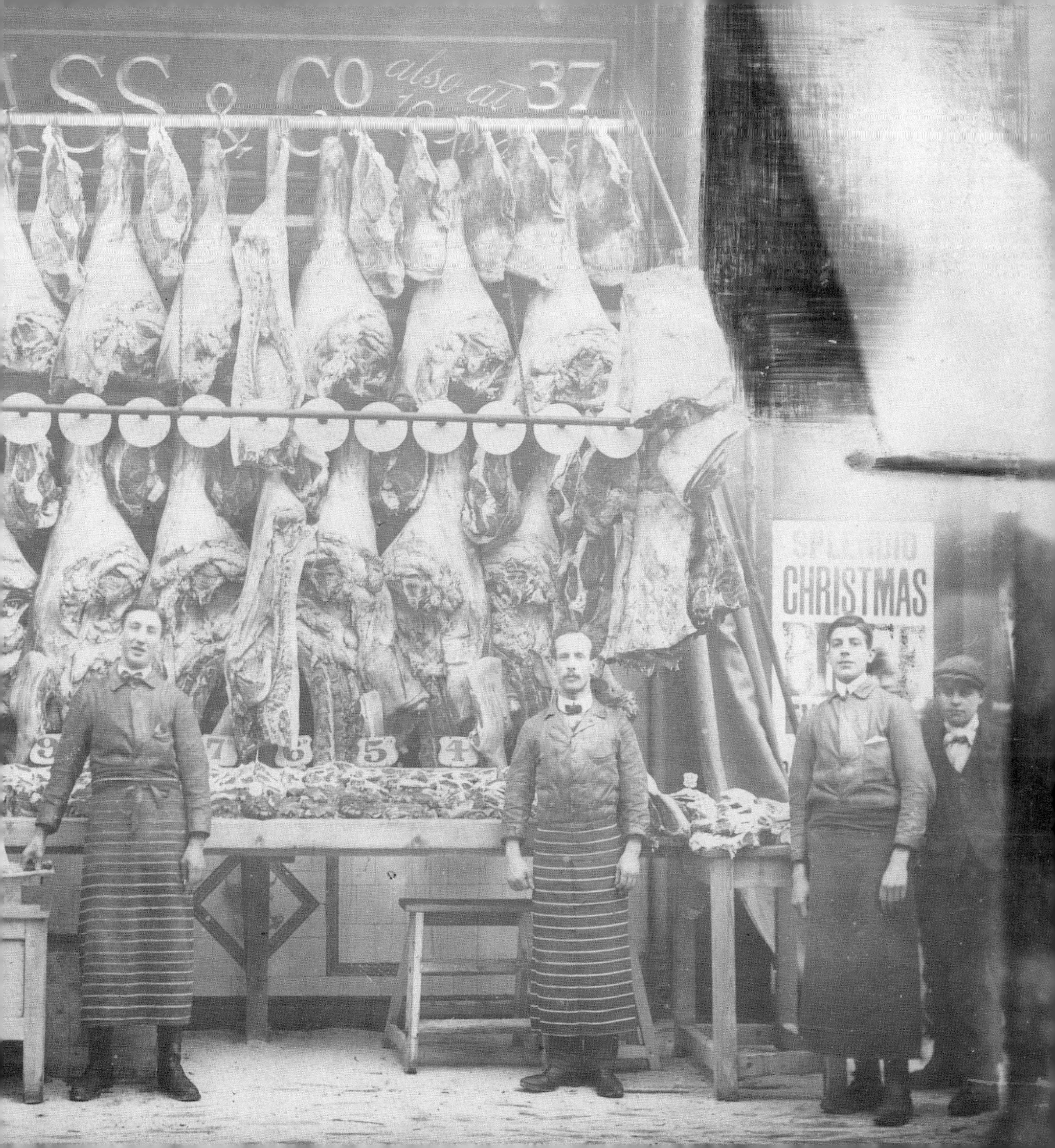

SS & Co also at 37
SPLENDID
CHRISTMAS

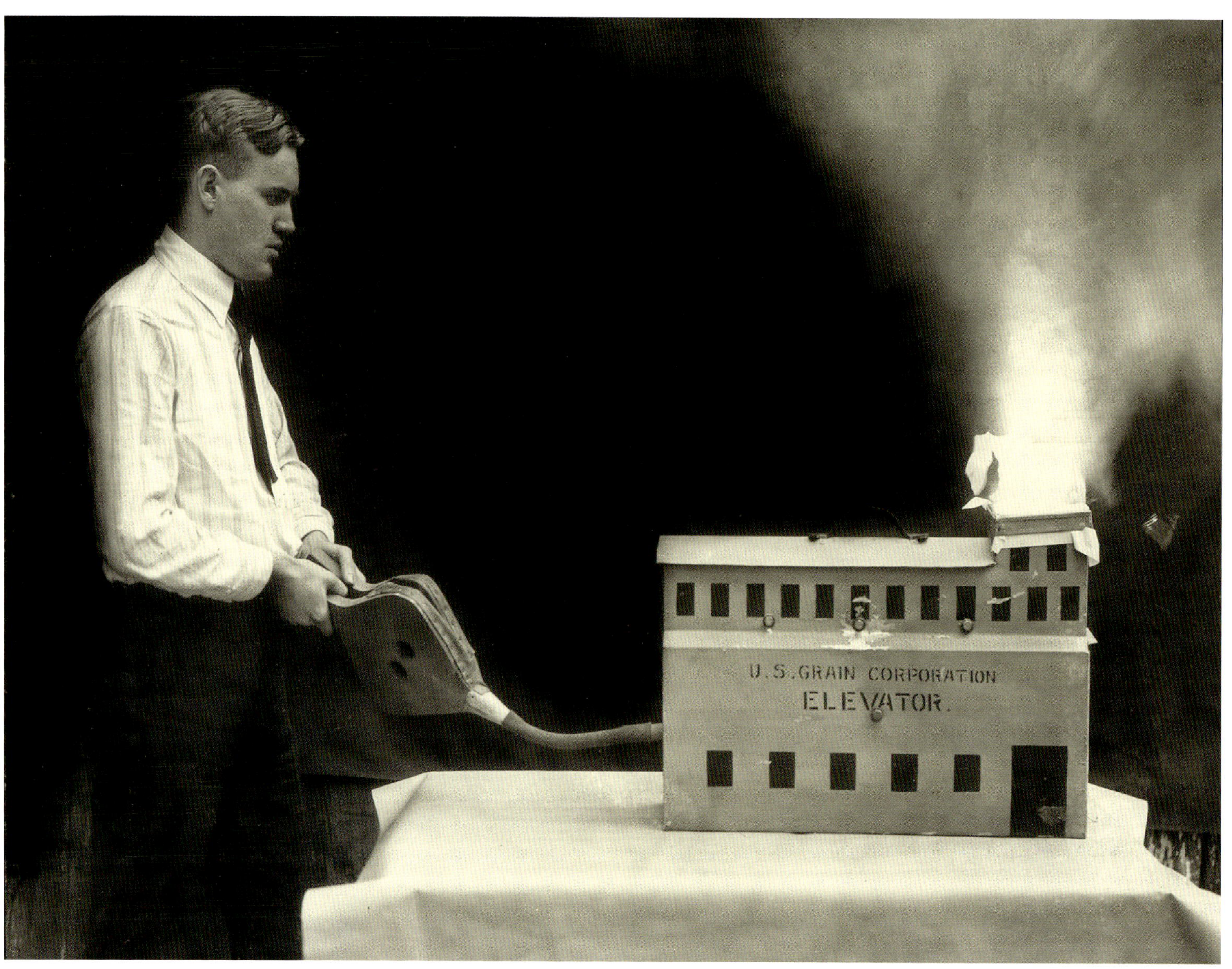
U.S.GRAIN CORPORATION
ELEVATOR.

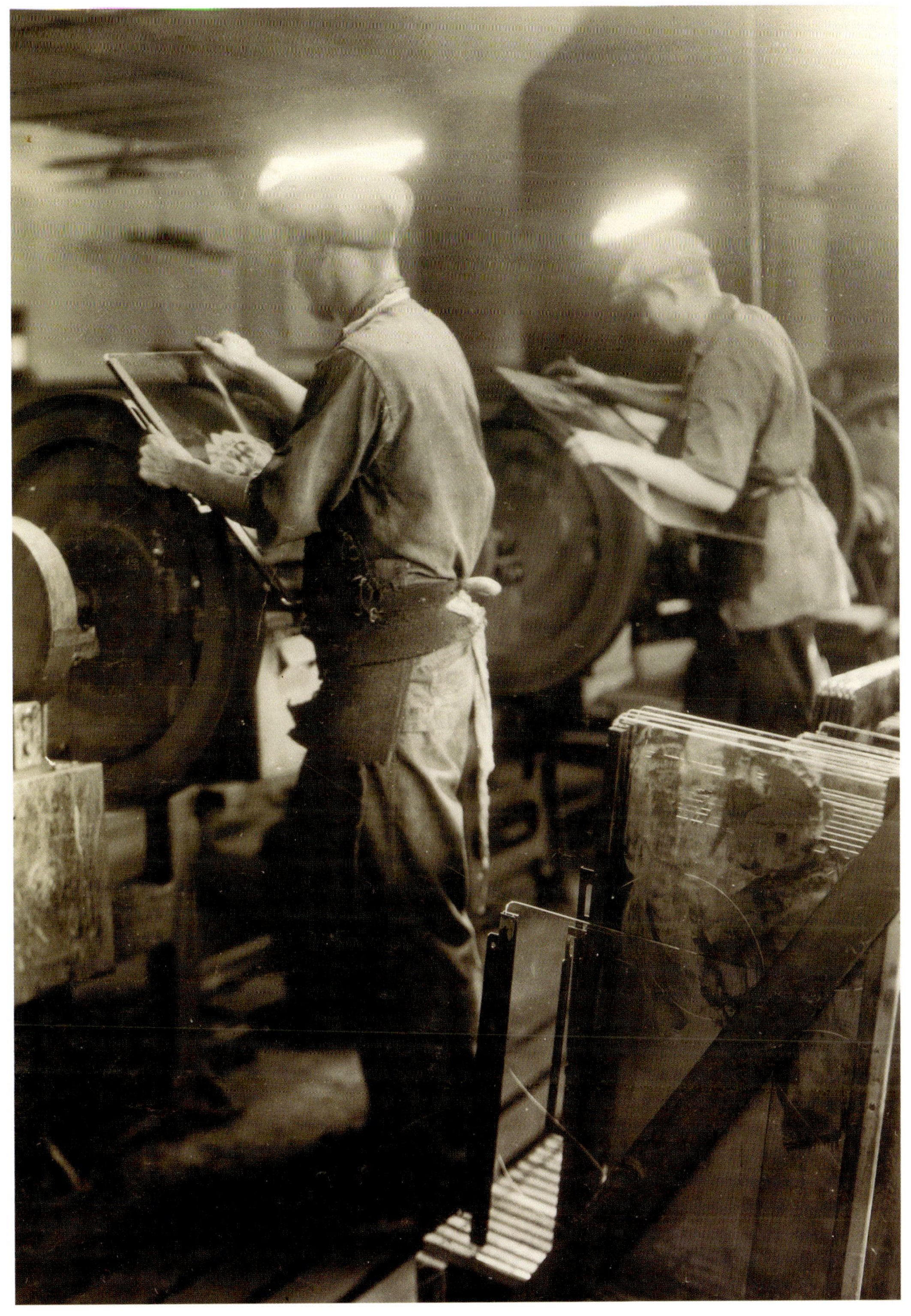

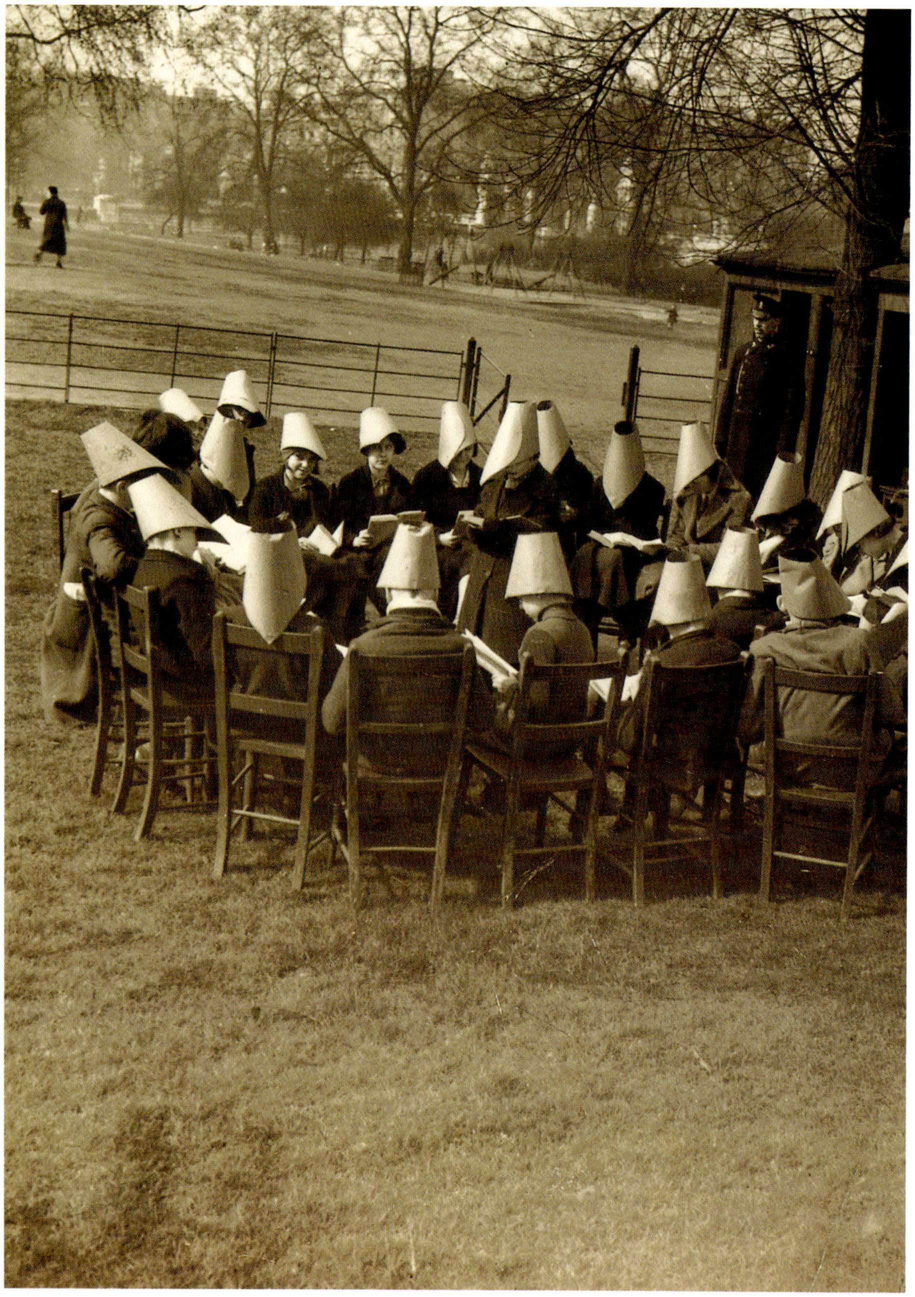

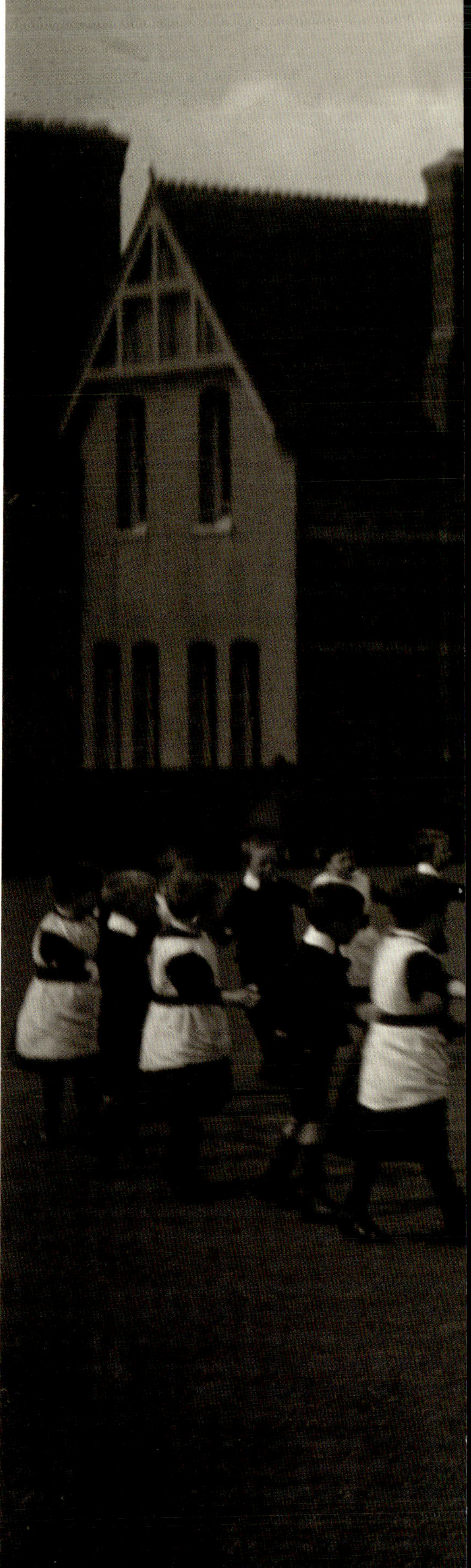

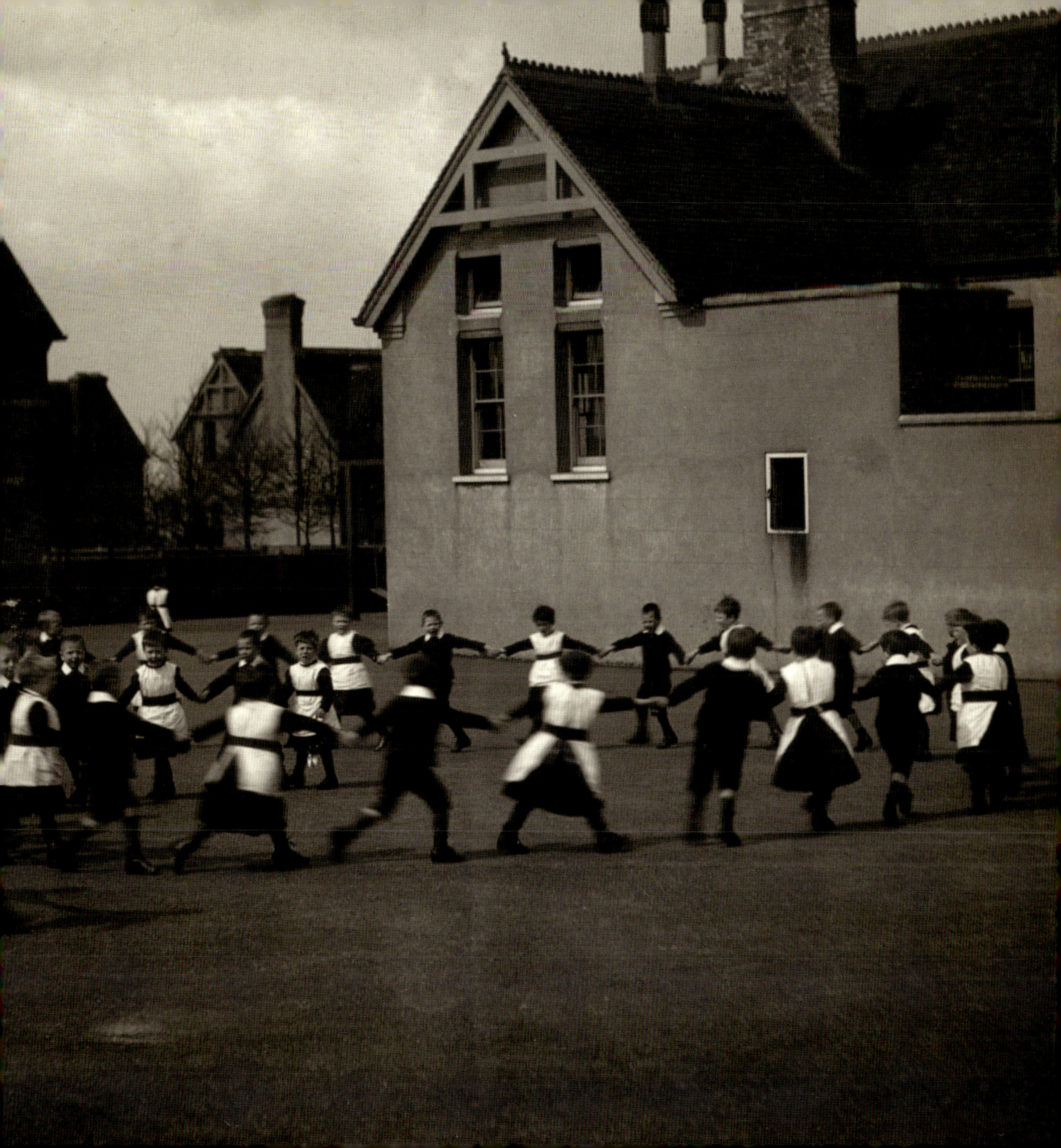

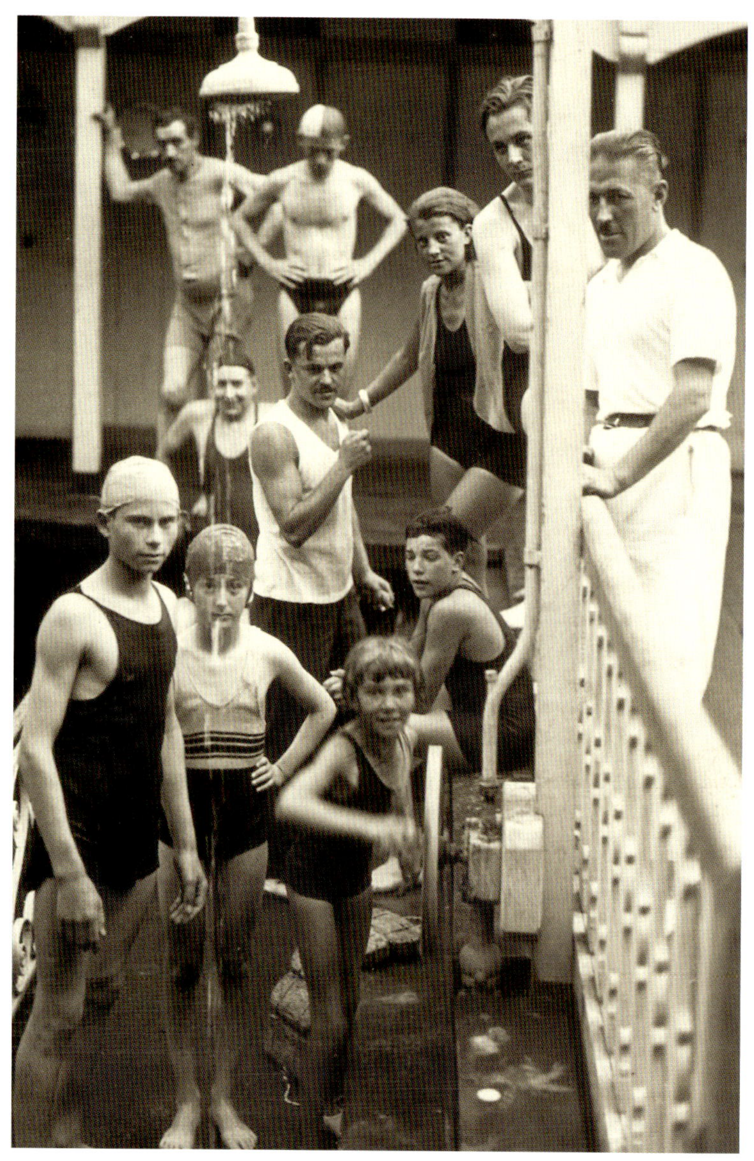

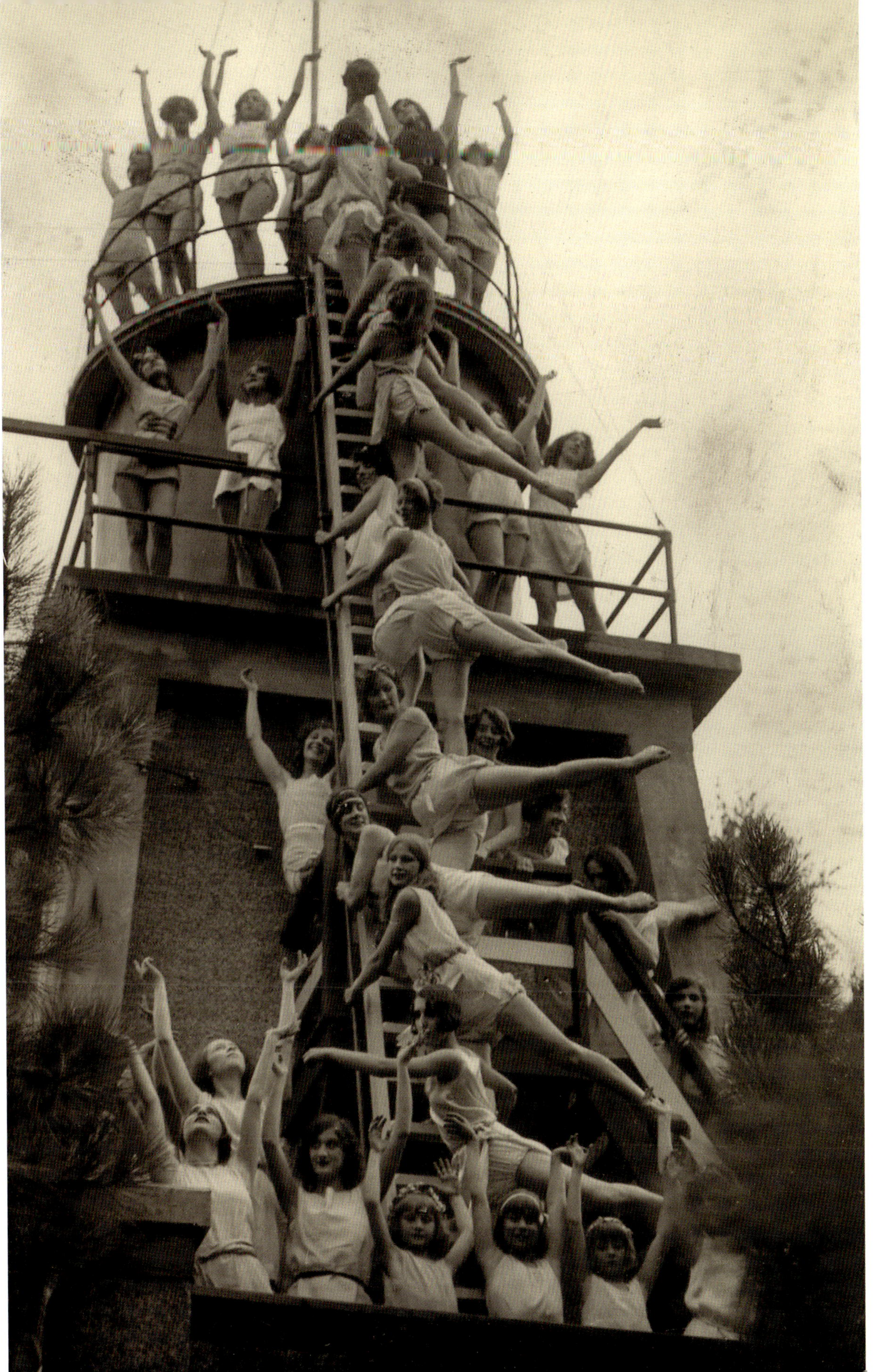

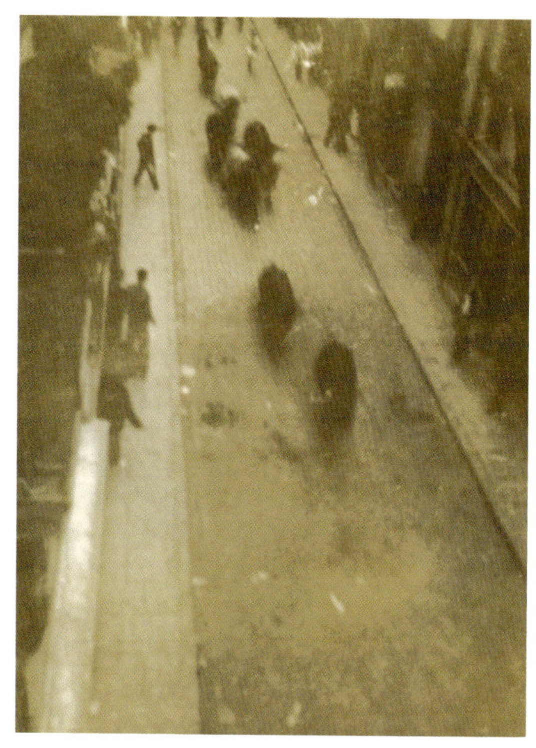

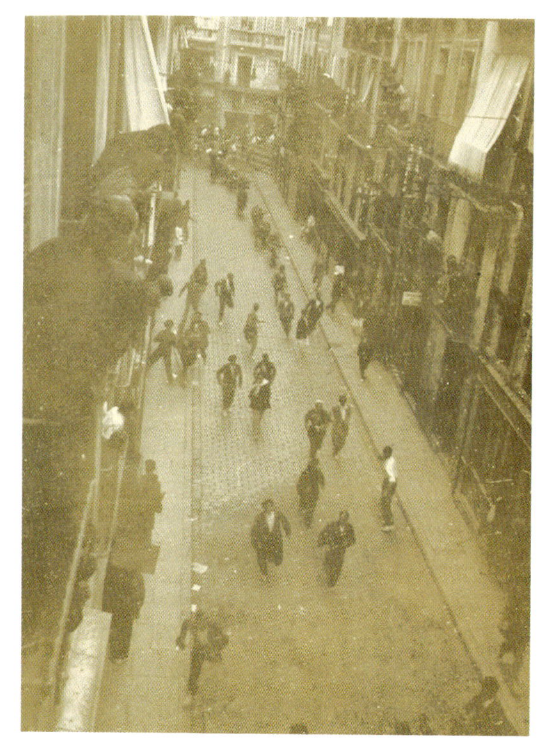

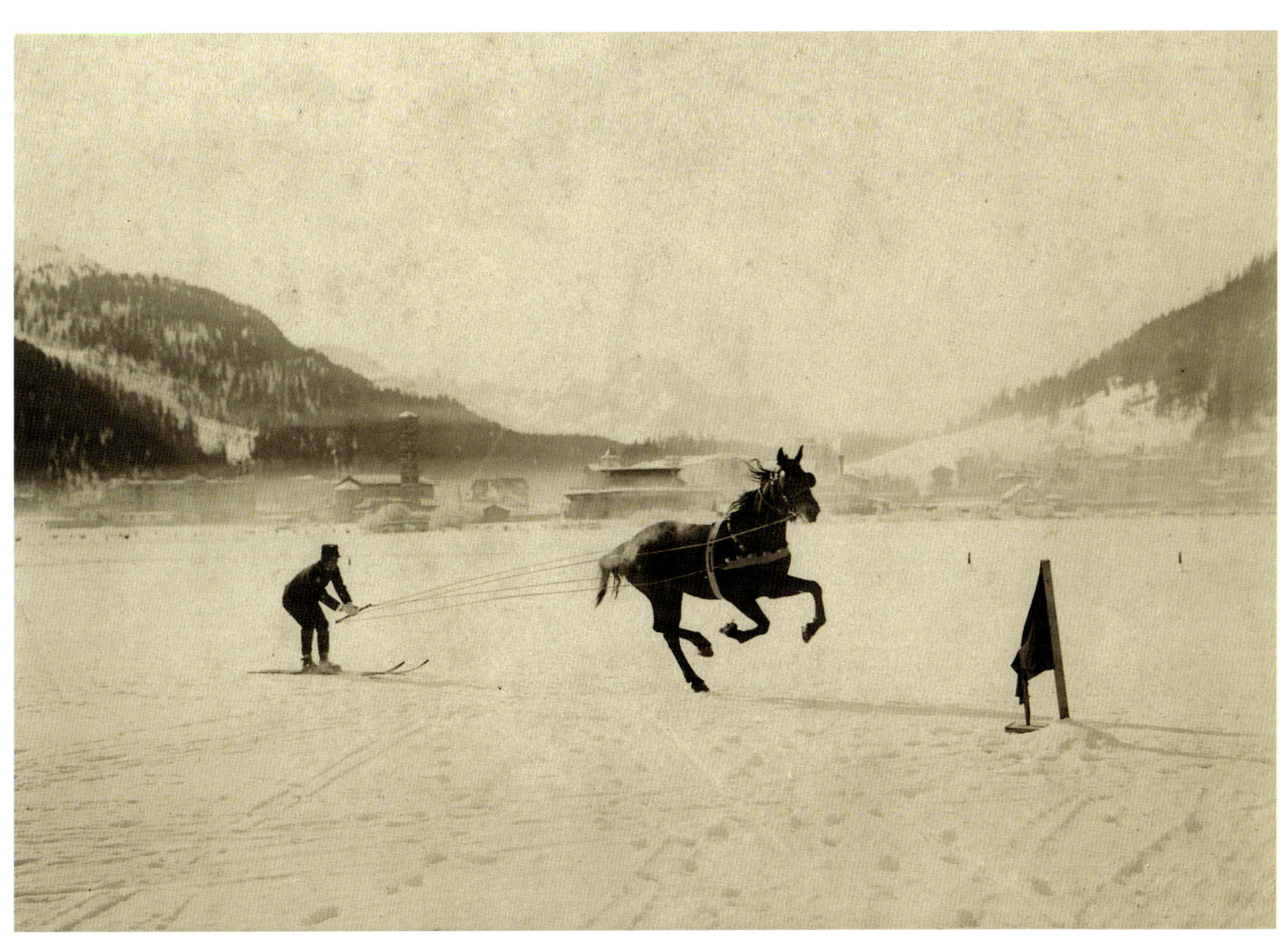

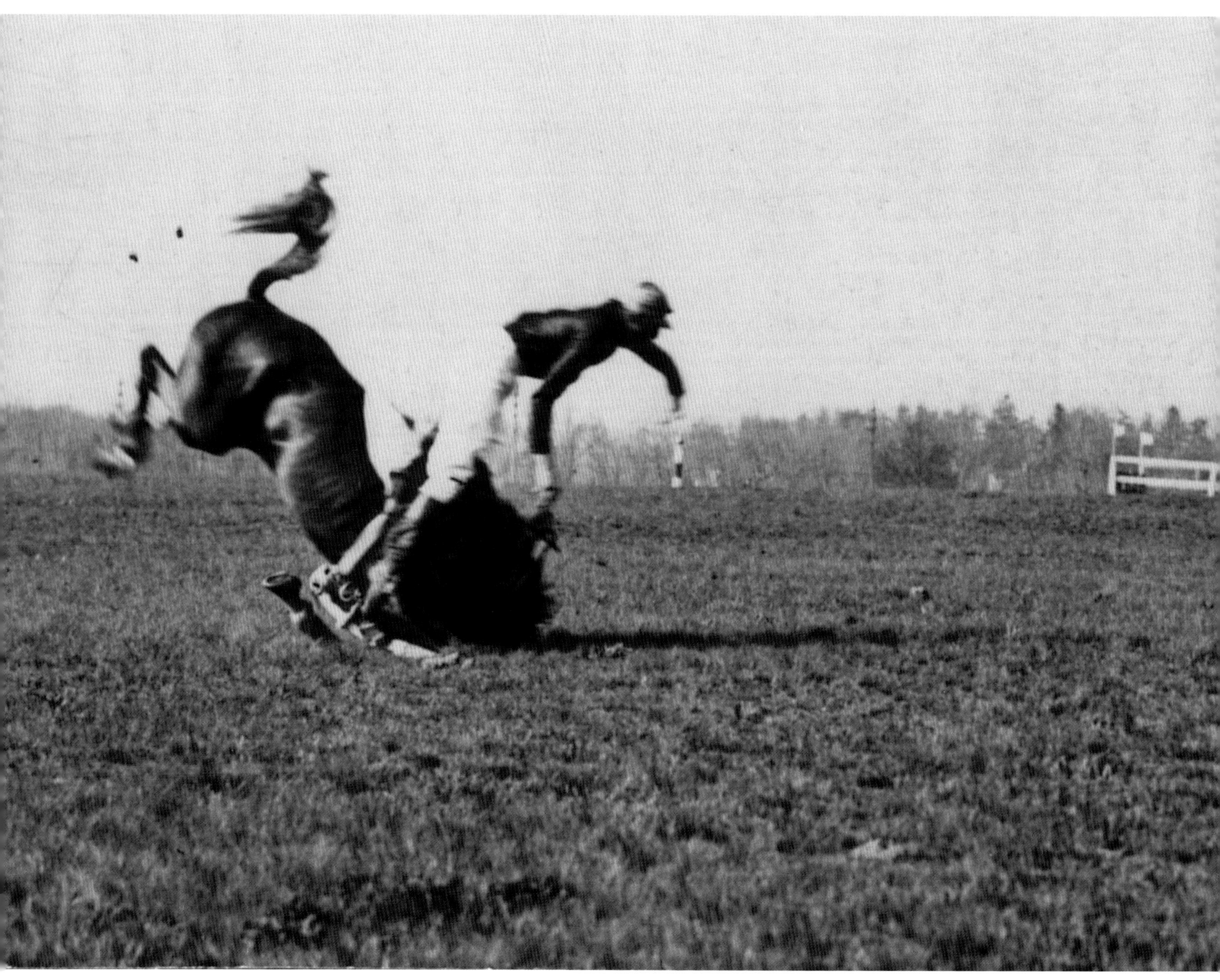

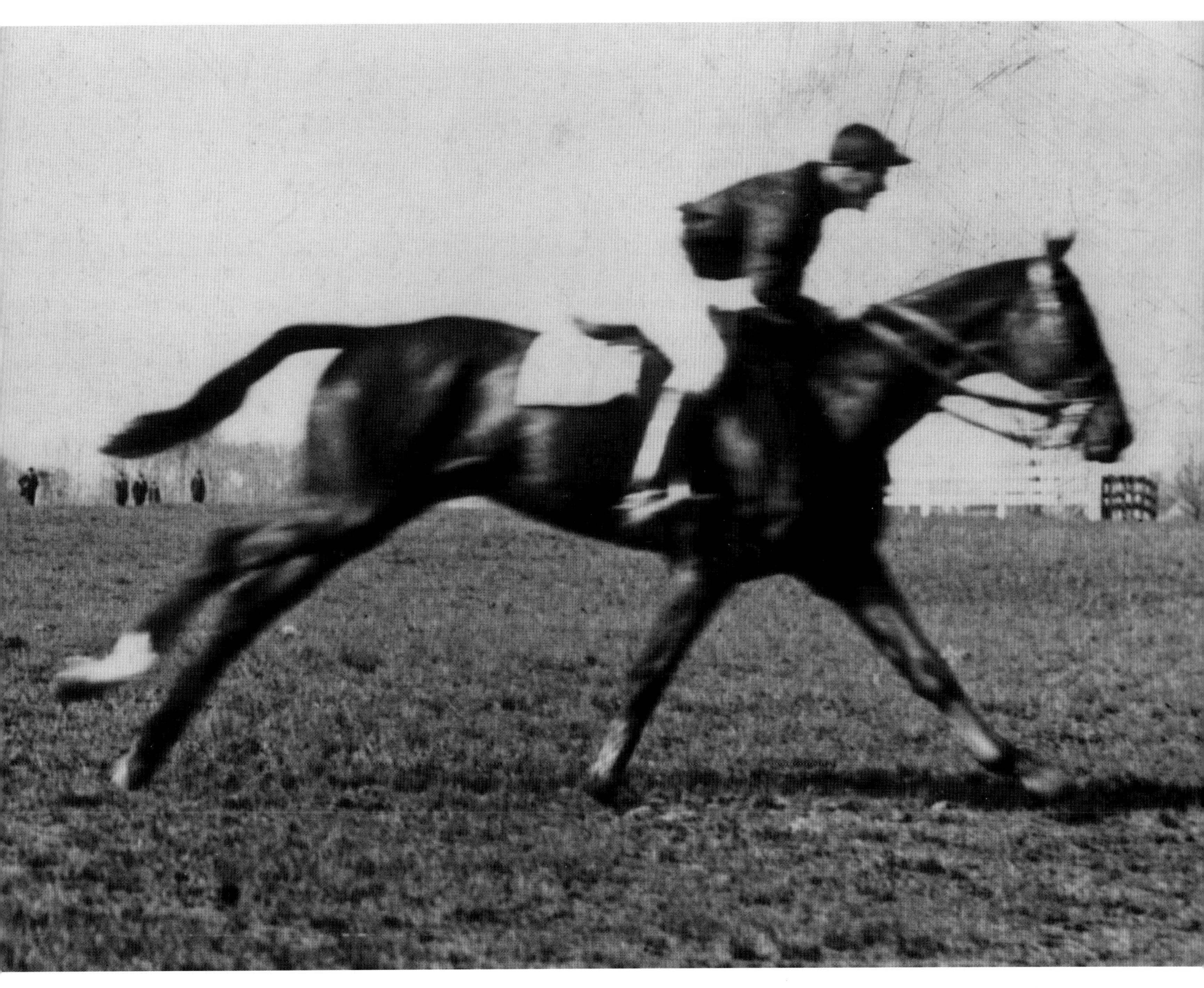

# Festivity

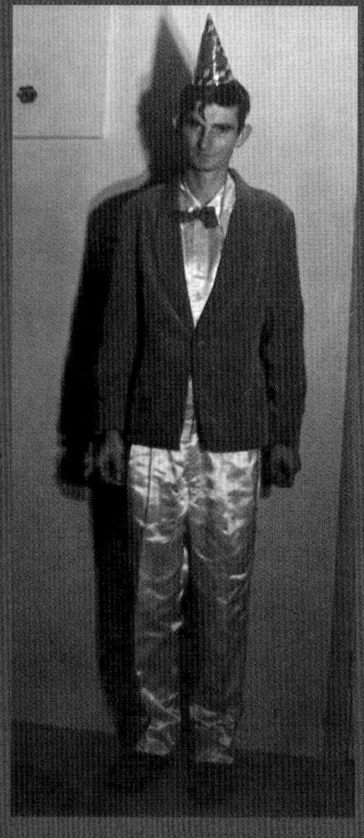

*'It seemed the world was divided into good and bad people. The good ones slept better … while the bad ones seemed to enjoy the waking hours more.'*
Woody Allen

Celebrations and special events have always given people a chance to dress up and get out. Through the anticipation of festivity, they are permitted to escape for a time what Henry David Thoreau memorably referred to as 'lives of quiet desperation'. The costumes of festivity range from the stiff uniforms of class structure, such as ball gowns and formal white tie and tails, to the colourful dress of ethnic minorities. The similar outfits that are worn by each group signal a special occasion in which all are linked in a communal ritual of mutual recognition and commemoration.

A transformative aspect of festivity is the wearing of masks. The hiding of one's true self, combined with the aggressive visual impact of an artificial visage, usually makes for powerful photographic imagery. Masks, when worn by children on Halloween, birthdays or other gatherings, create an aura of innocence and fantasy, while the similar wearing of masks by adults conveys decidedly more sinister connotations.

It is notable how in many photographs of festivities there is a sense of crowd control and manipulation – an attempt to get everyone into a designated area, keep their attention, and make them stand still until the picture has been taken. Also present in many images is a kind of forced levity, as if the photographer was egging on his or her subjects to register a good impression of the event for posterity.

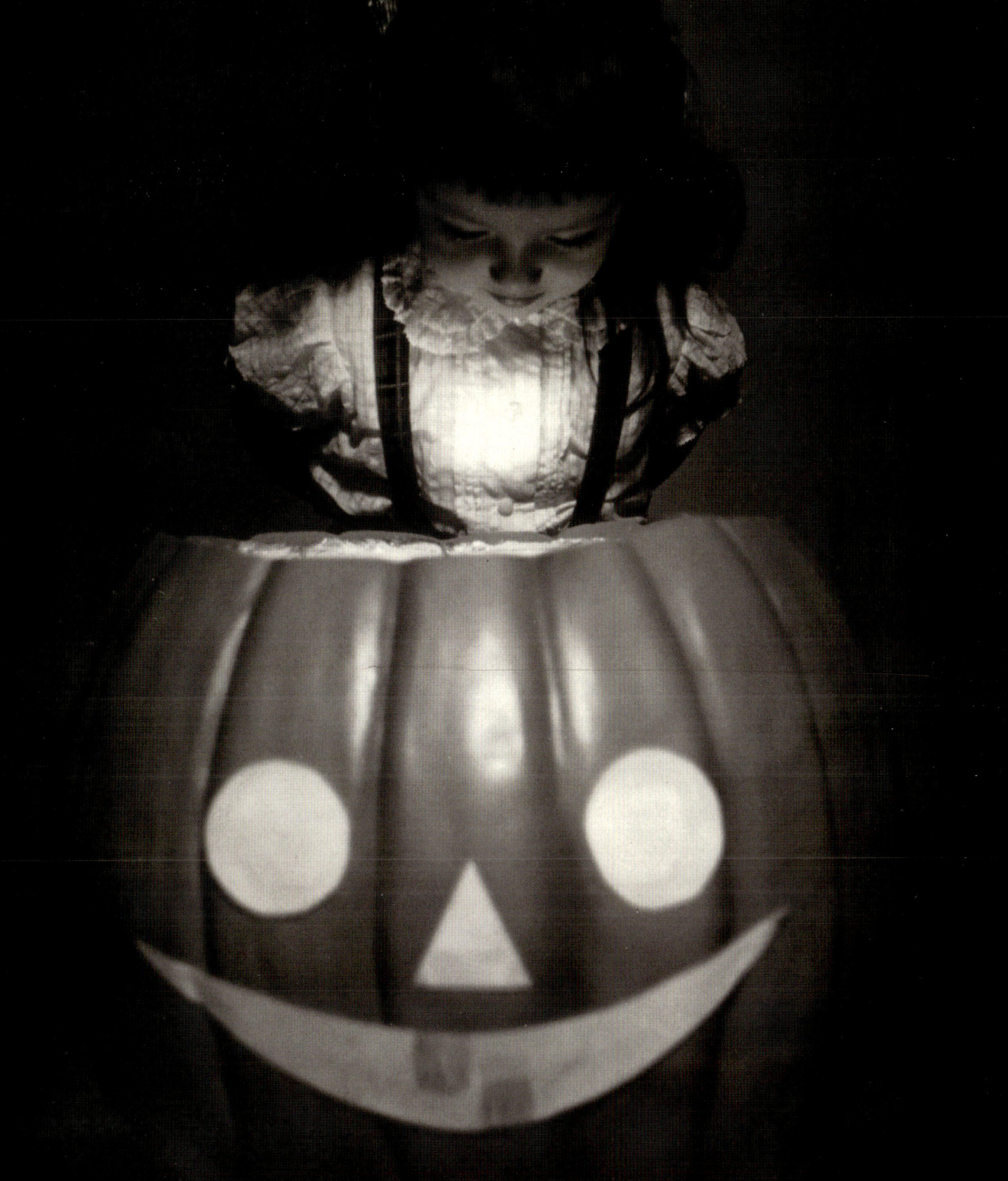

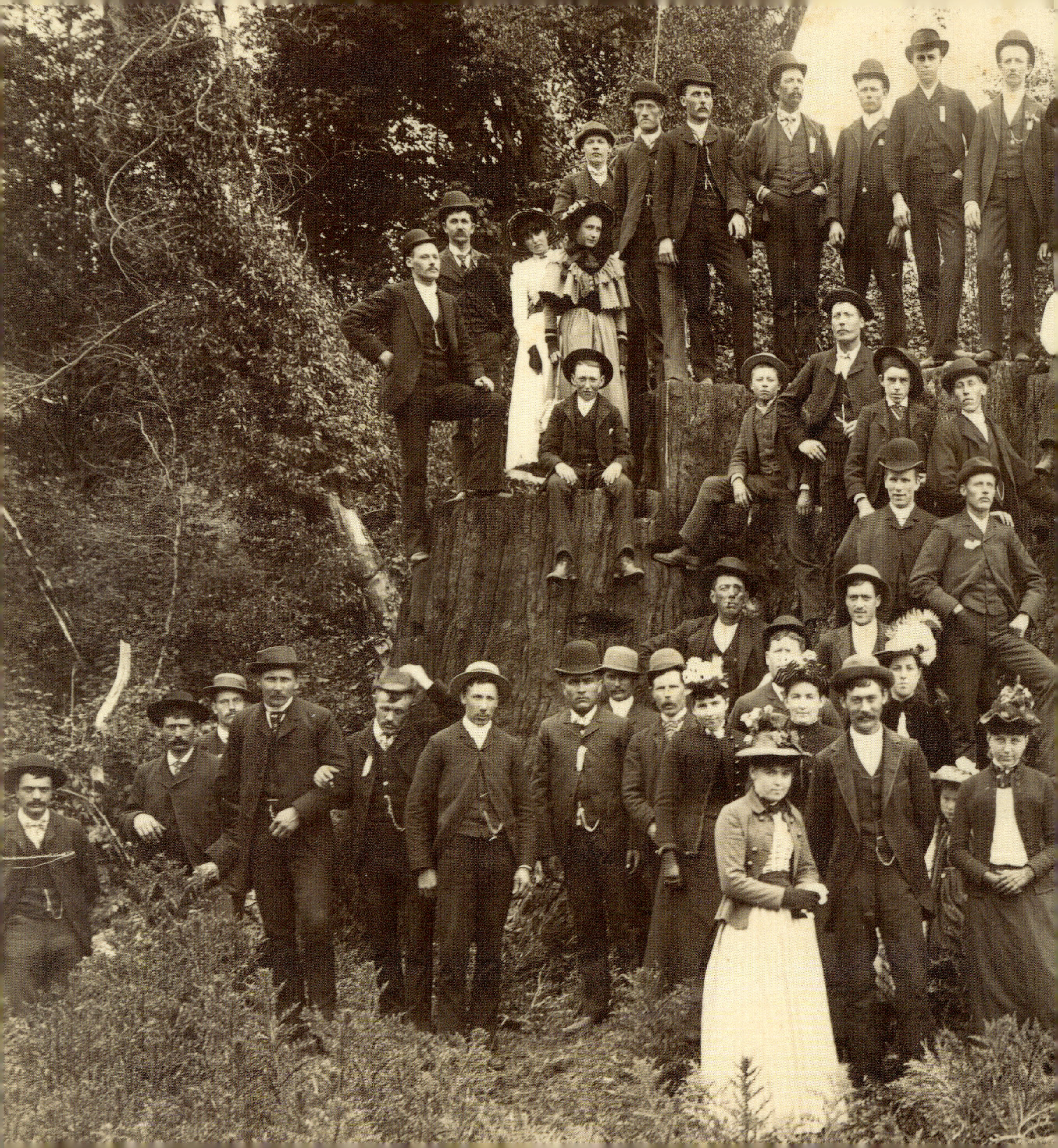

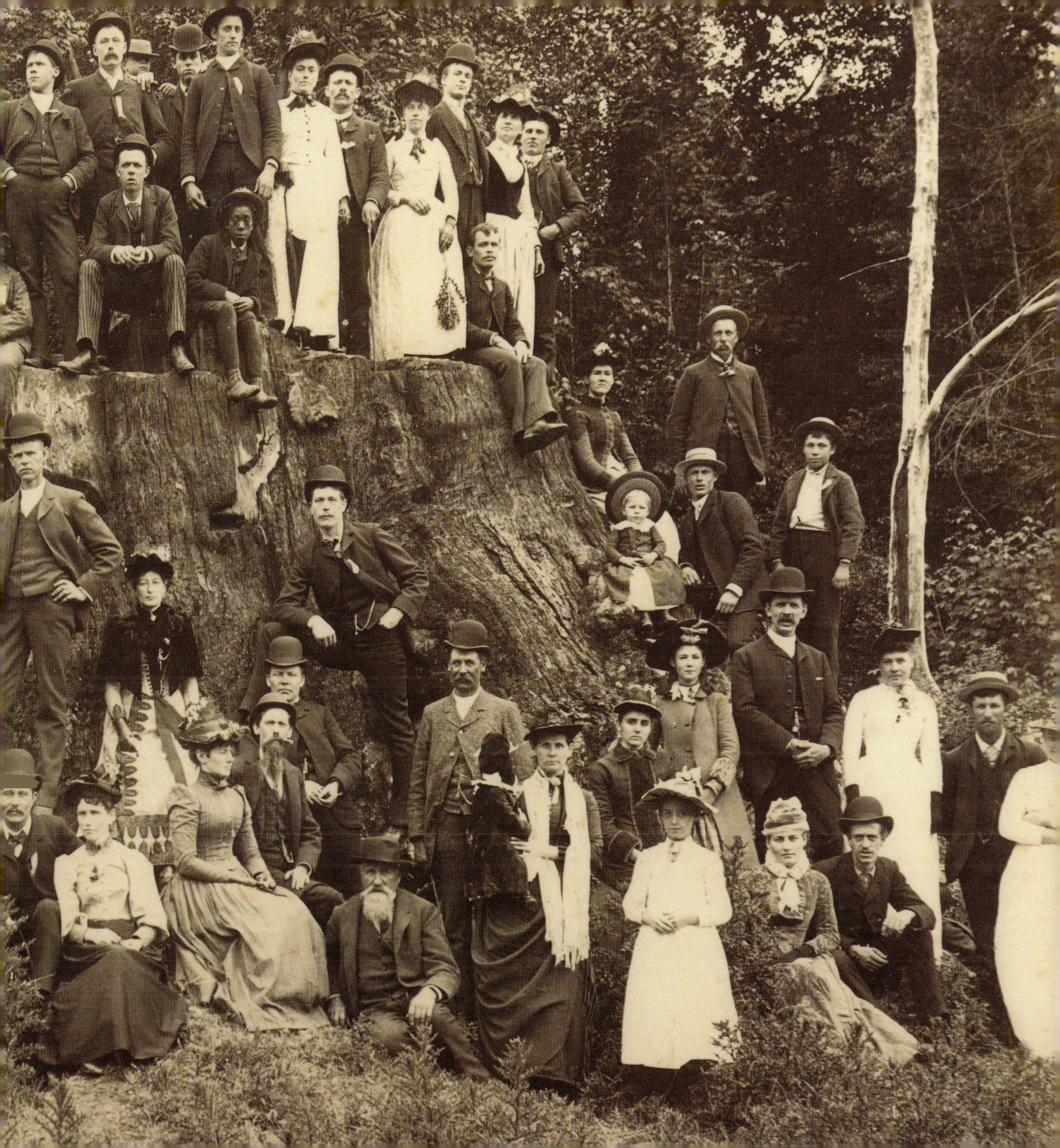

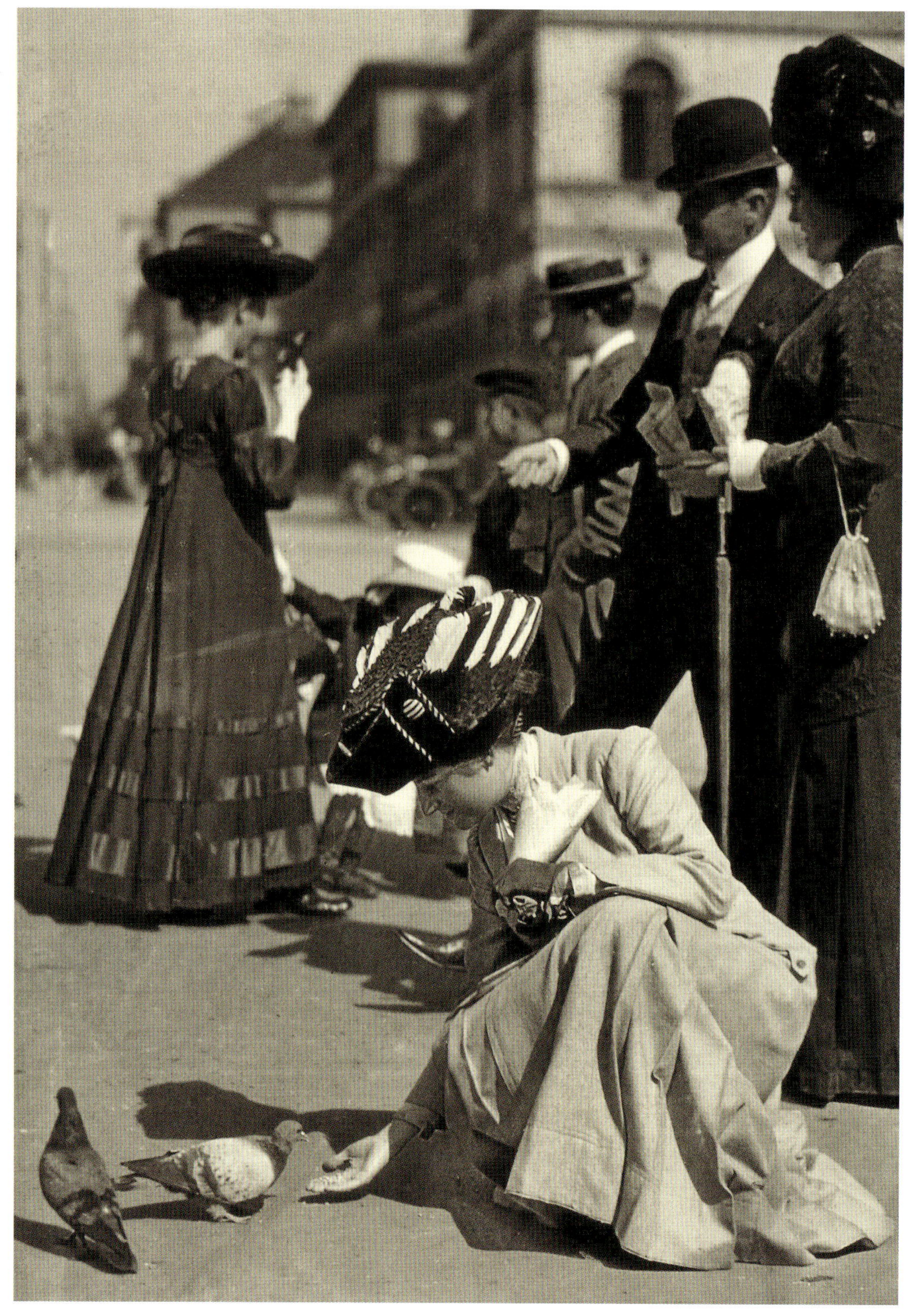

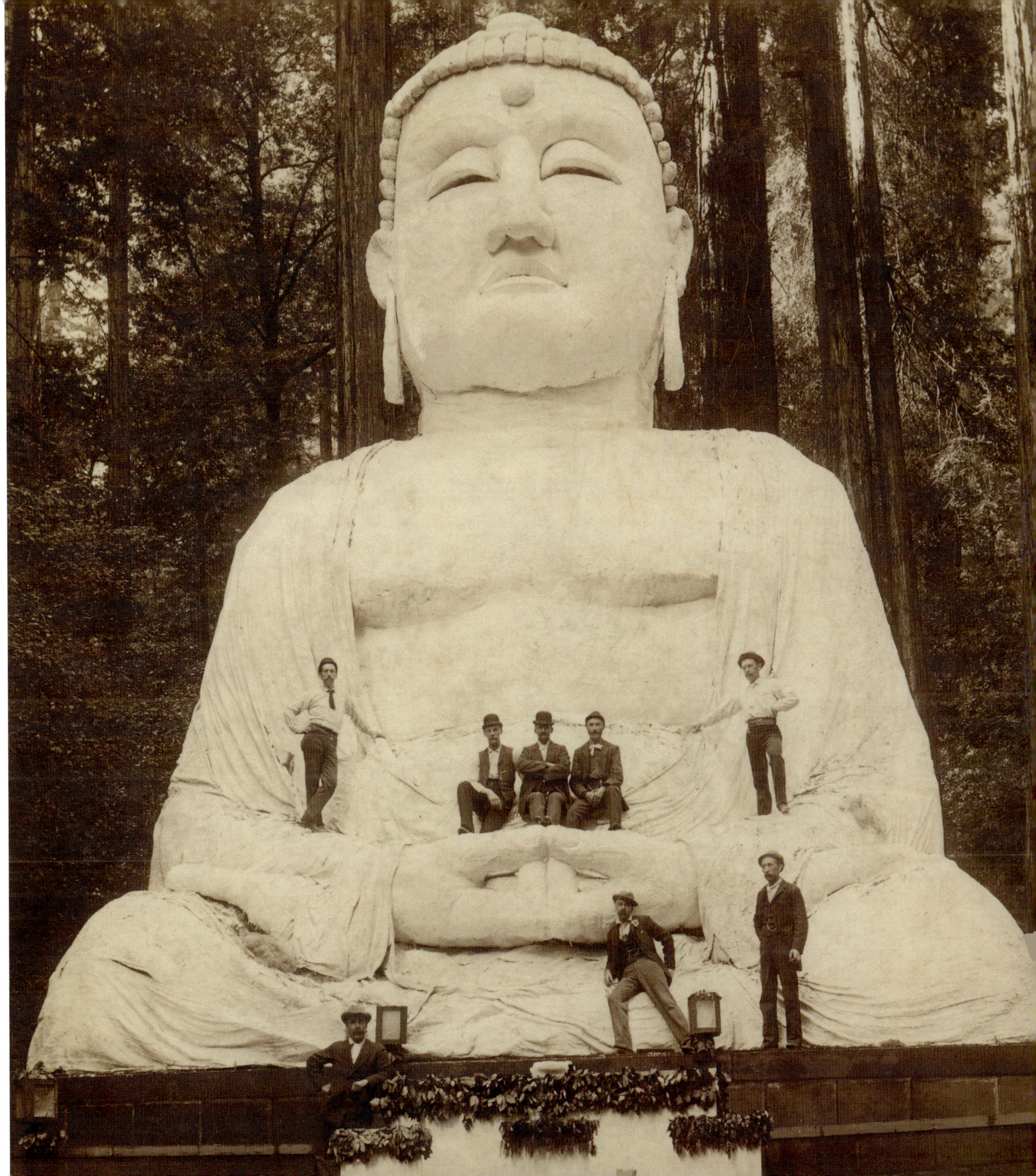

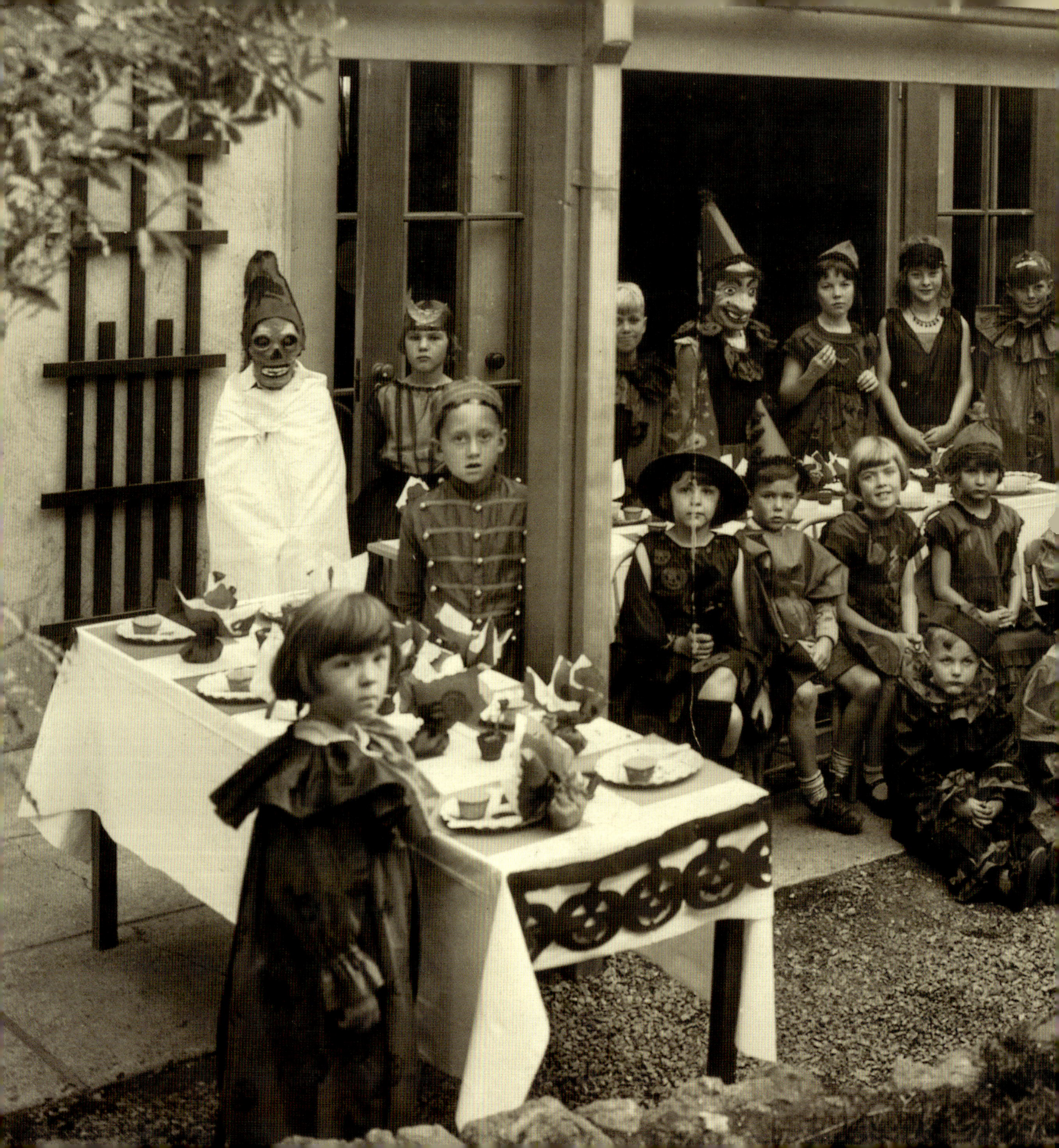

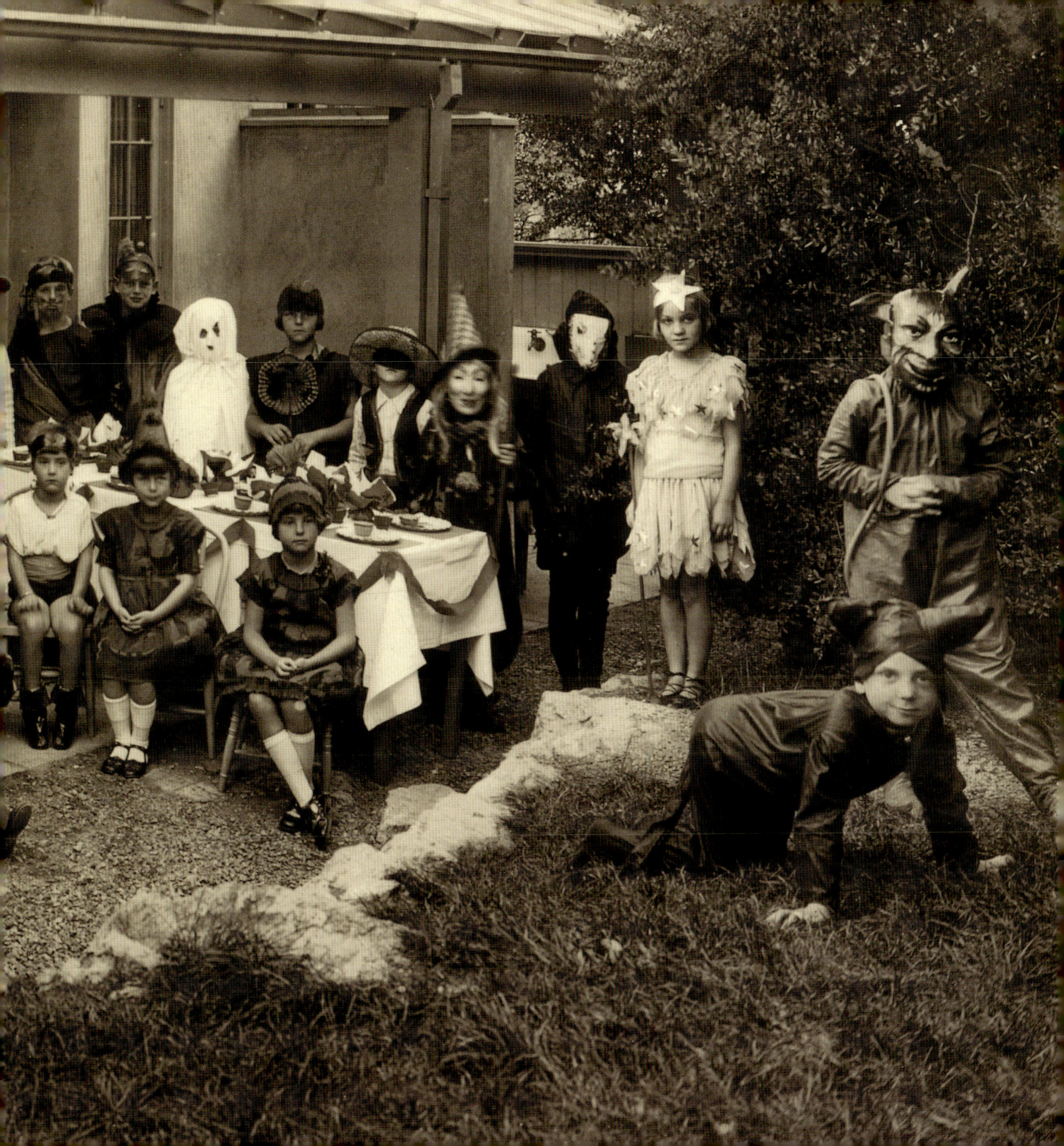

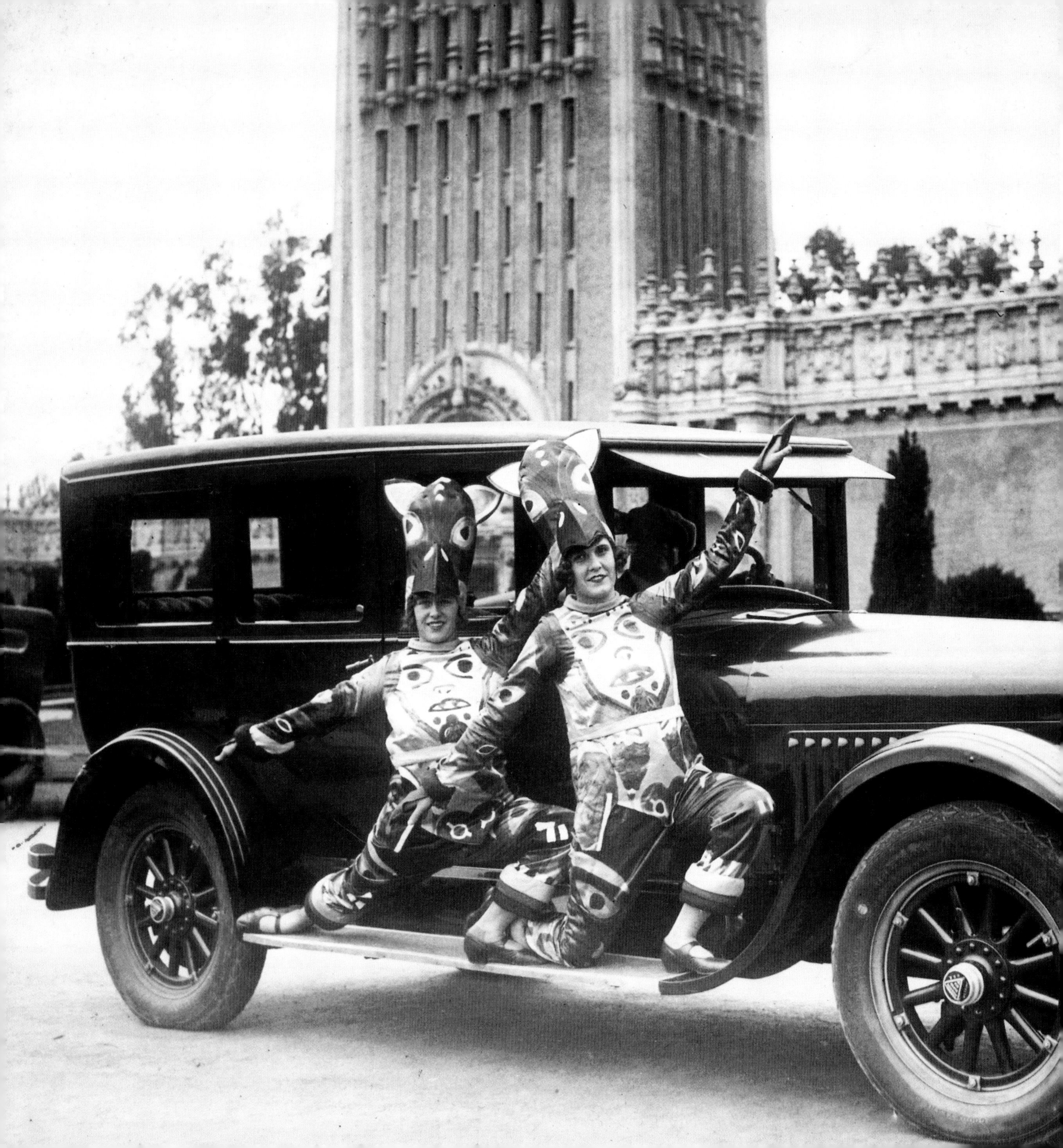

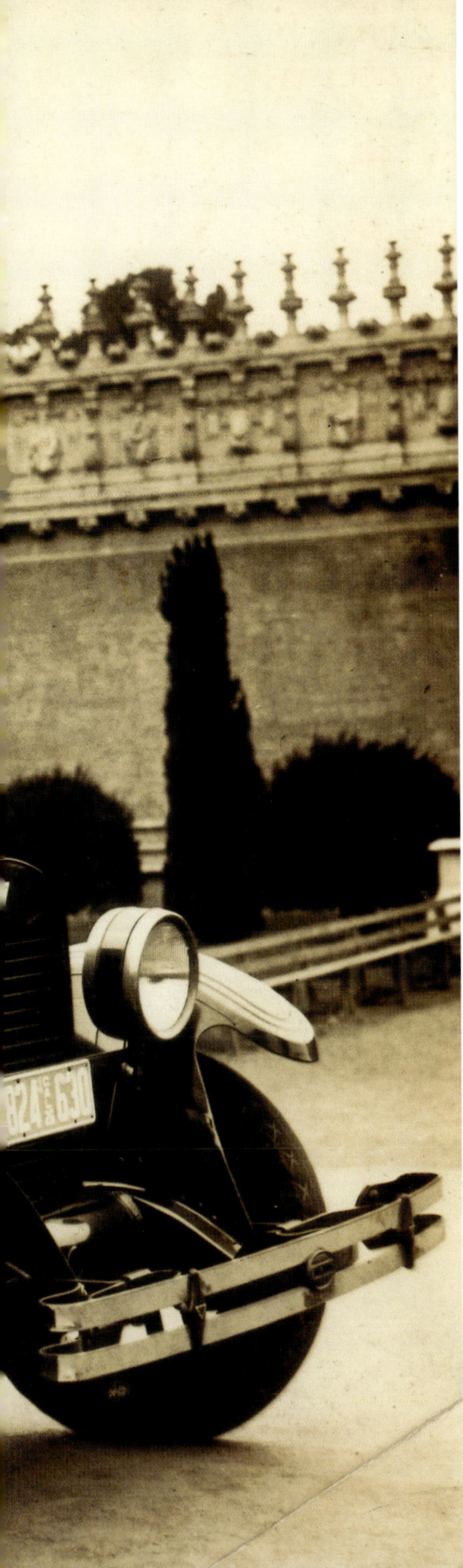
824 630

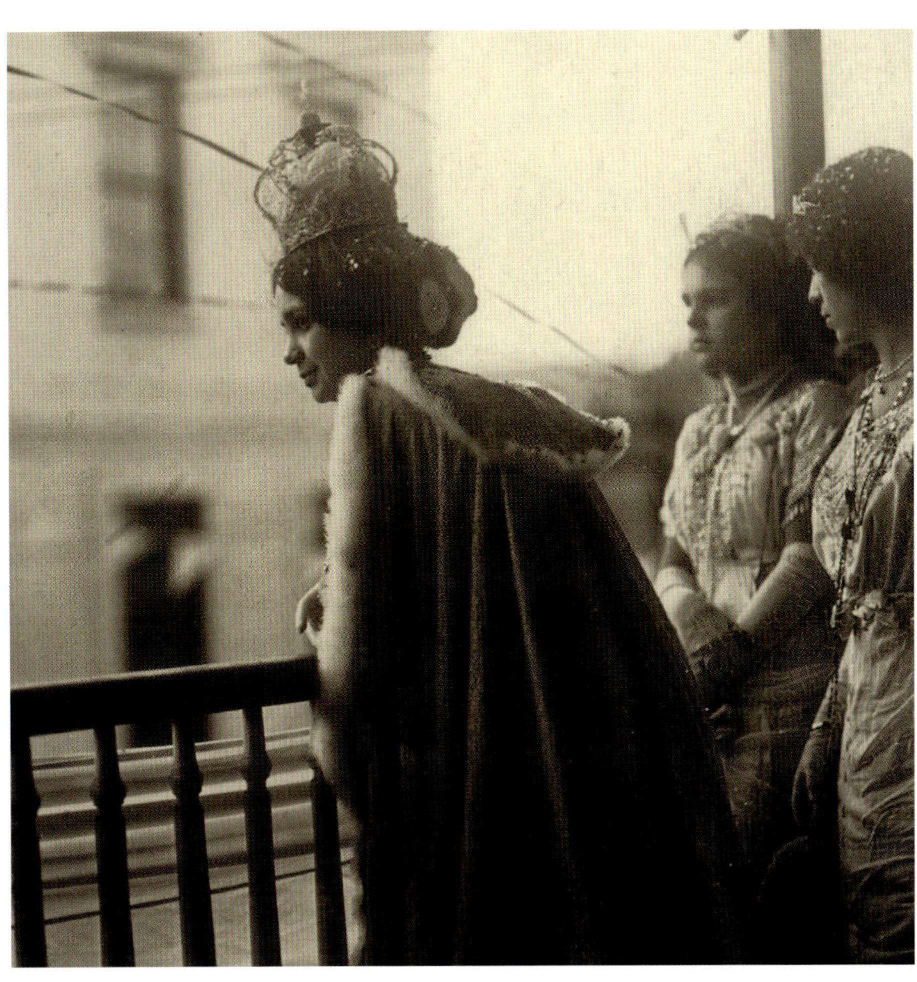

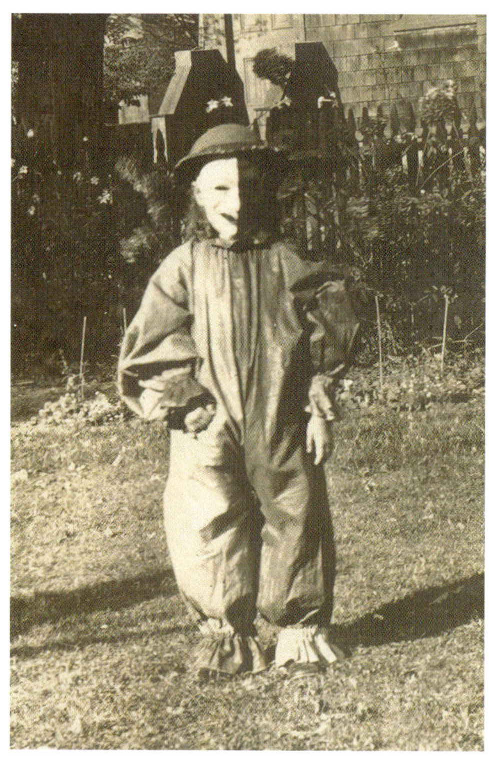
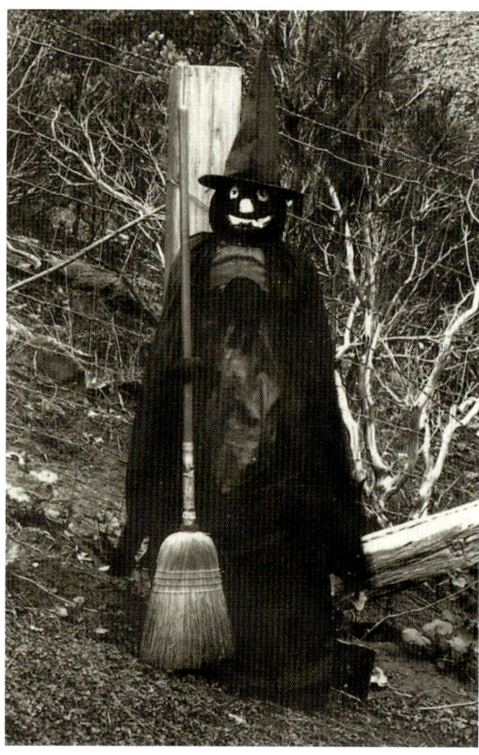
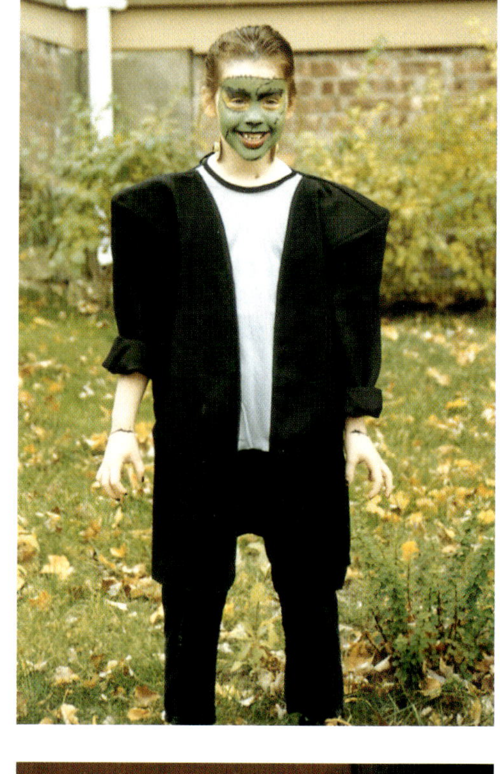
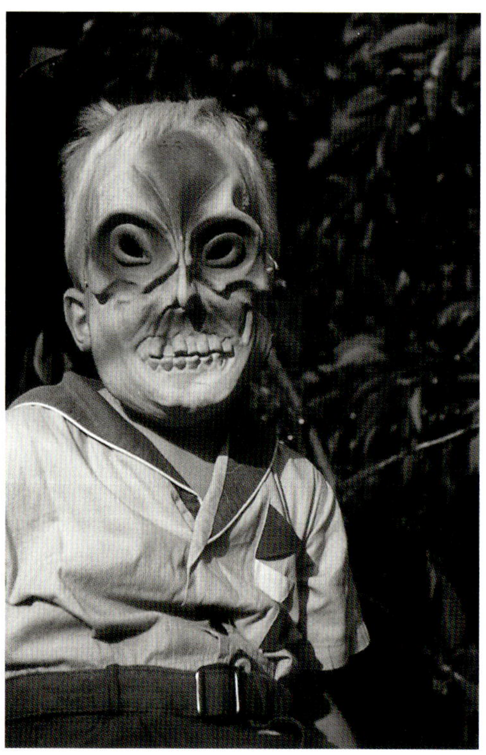
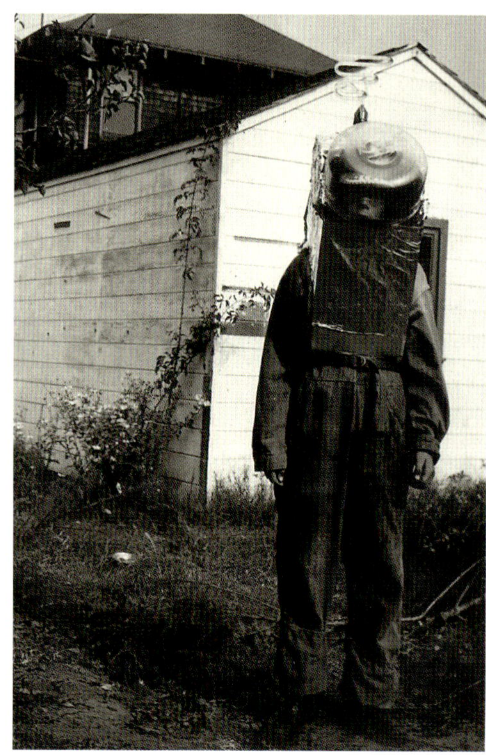
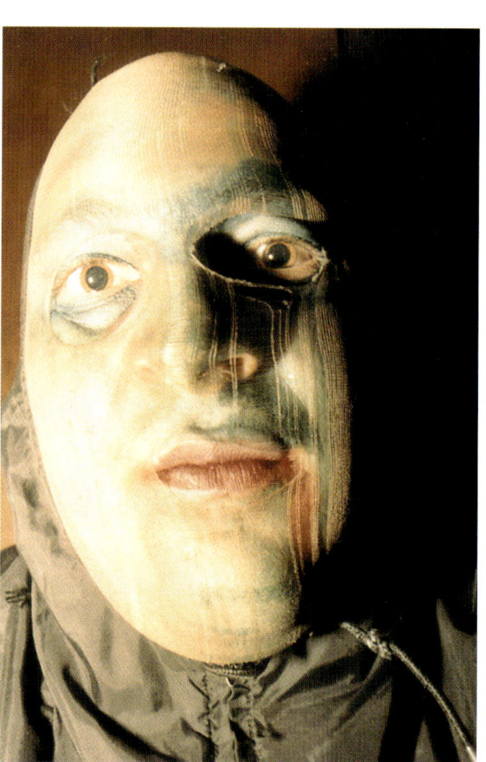

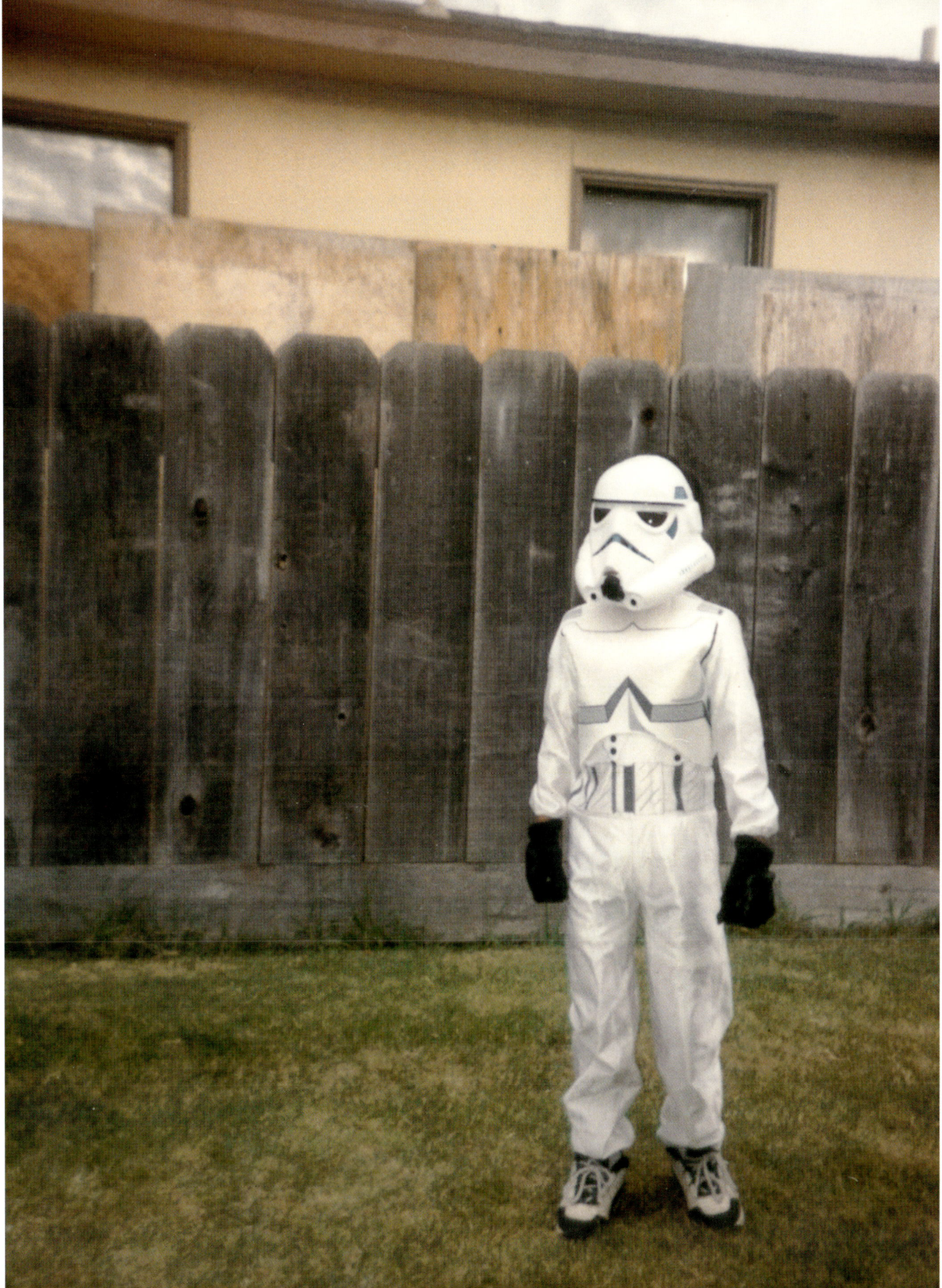

# Adversity

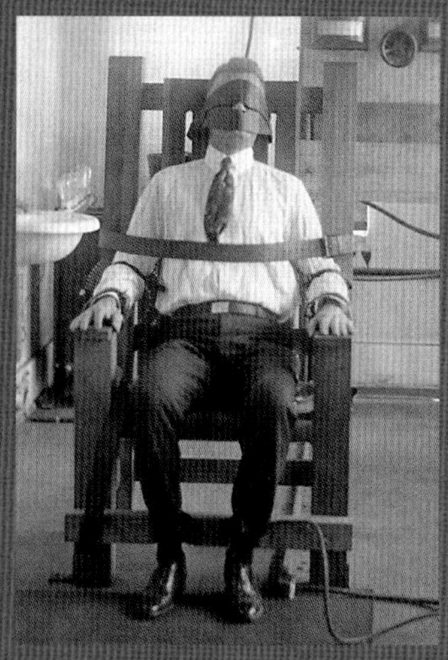

*'You can get much further with a kind word and a gun than with a kind word alone.'*
**Al Capone**

Why is it that the travails and misery of other people hold a greater fascination than their triumphs? This is not a new phenomenon. In the sixteenth century, Pieter Bruegel the Elder's series of graphic images of the seven deadly sins were then – and are now – of far greater interest than his pious renderings of the seven virtues. These days, the success of reality-television competitions is founded less on the triumph of the few eventual winners than on the dashing of the illusions of the many aspiring contestants who very publicly fail before our eyes.

People in unfortunate circumstances, whether dictated by fate or by their own actions, elicit a range of contradictory emotions when seen in photographs. Often these emotions consist in equal part of commiseration with the subject in distress, relief that it is not ourselves in their situation, and, subconsciously, a morbid curiosity in observing the suffering of others.

Criminality and catastrophe are the most common subjects of adversity in photography of people. The mugshot, developed by the American Allan Pinkerton and later refined by the Frenchman Alphonse Bertillon, created a vast pantheon of facial illegality. Scenes of crimes and disaster exert a peculiarly unhealthy hold on our imaginations. Images of illness and disease, when not confined to medical textbooks, can also take on an unintended and unwarranted sensationalism. In the best of circumstances, all these types of photographs should serve as a reminder that there but for the grace of God go we.

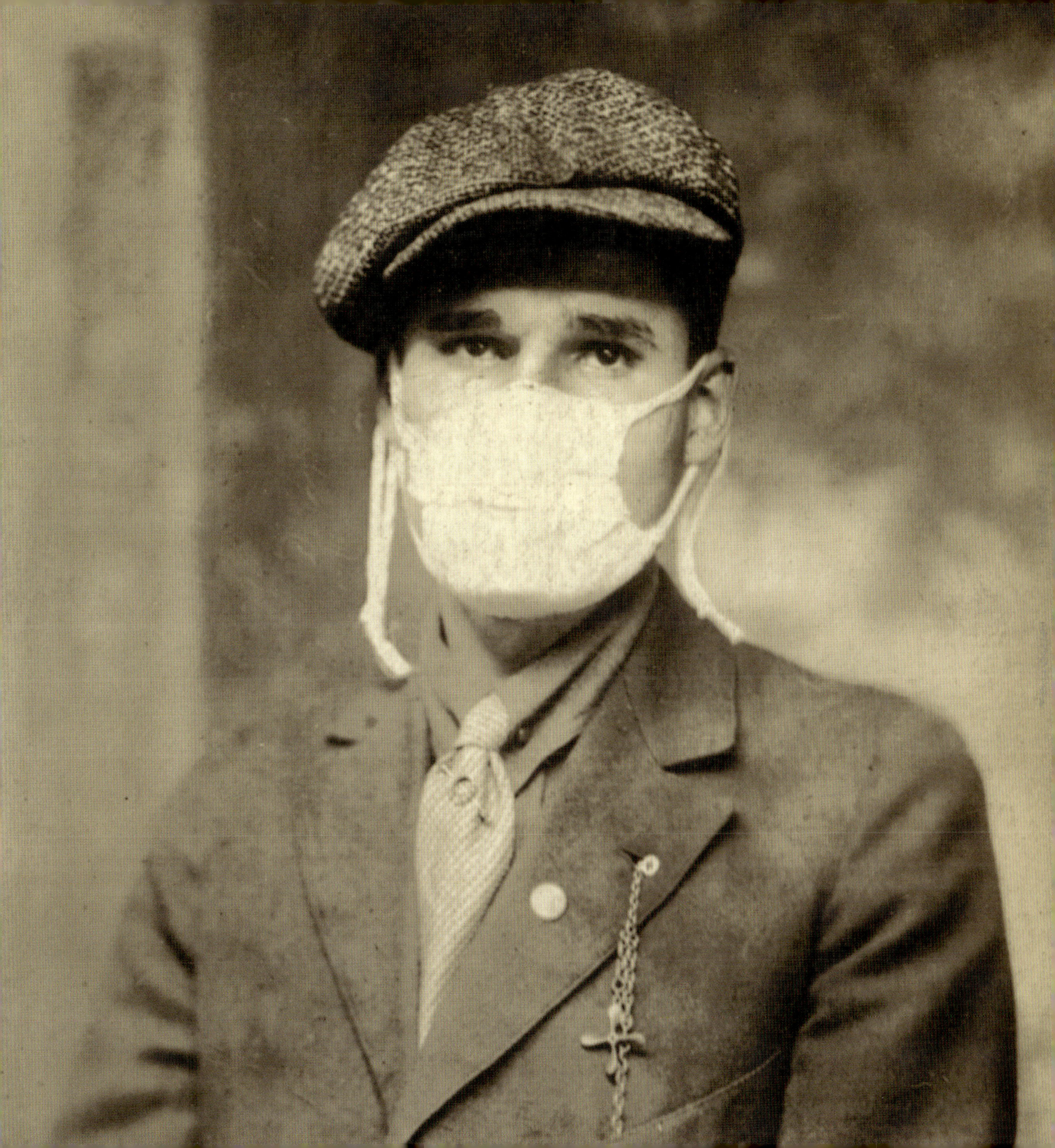

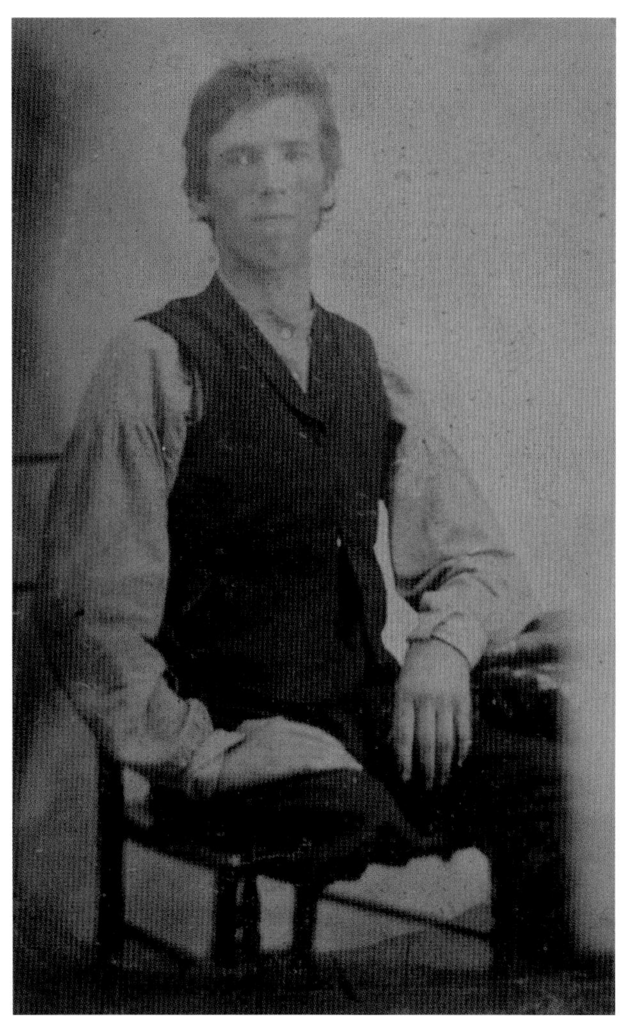

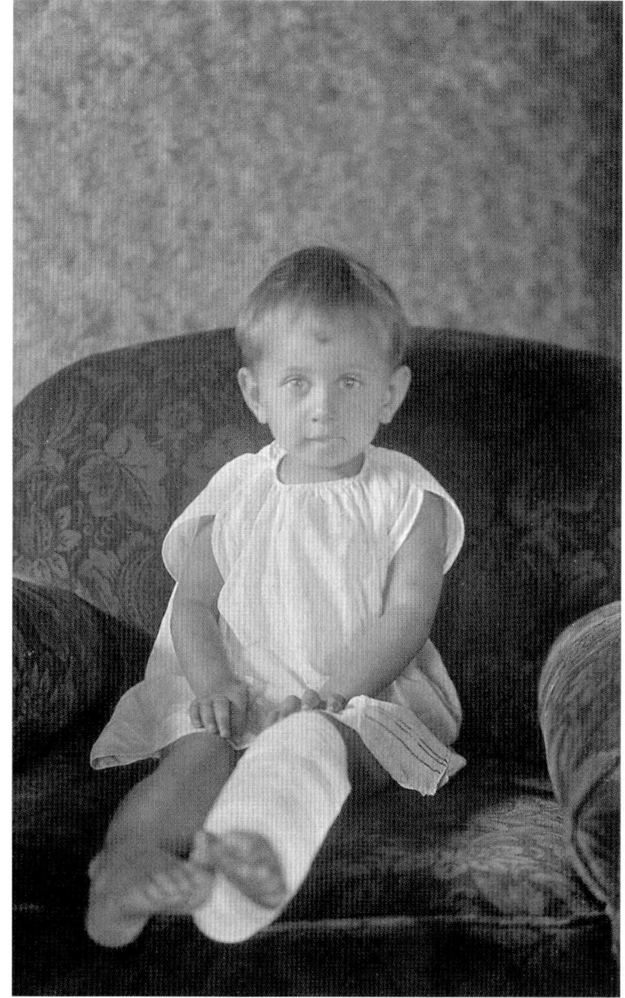

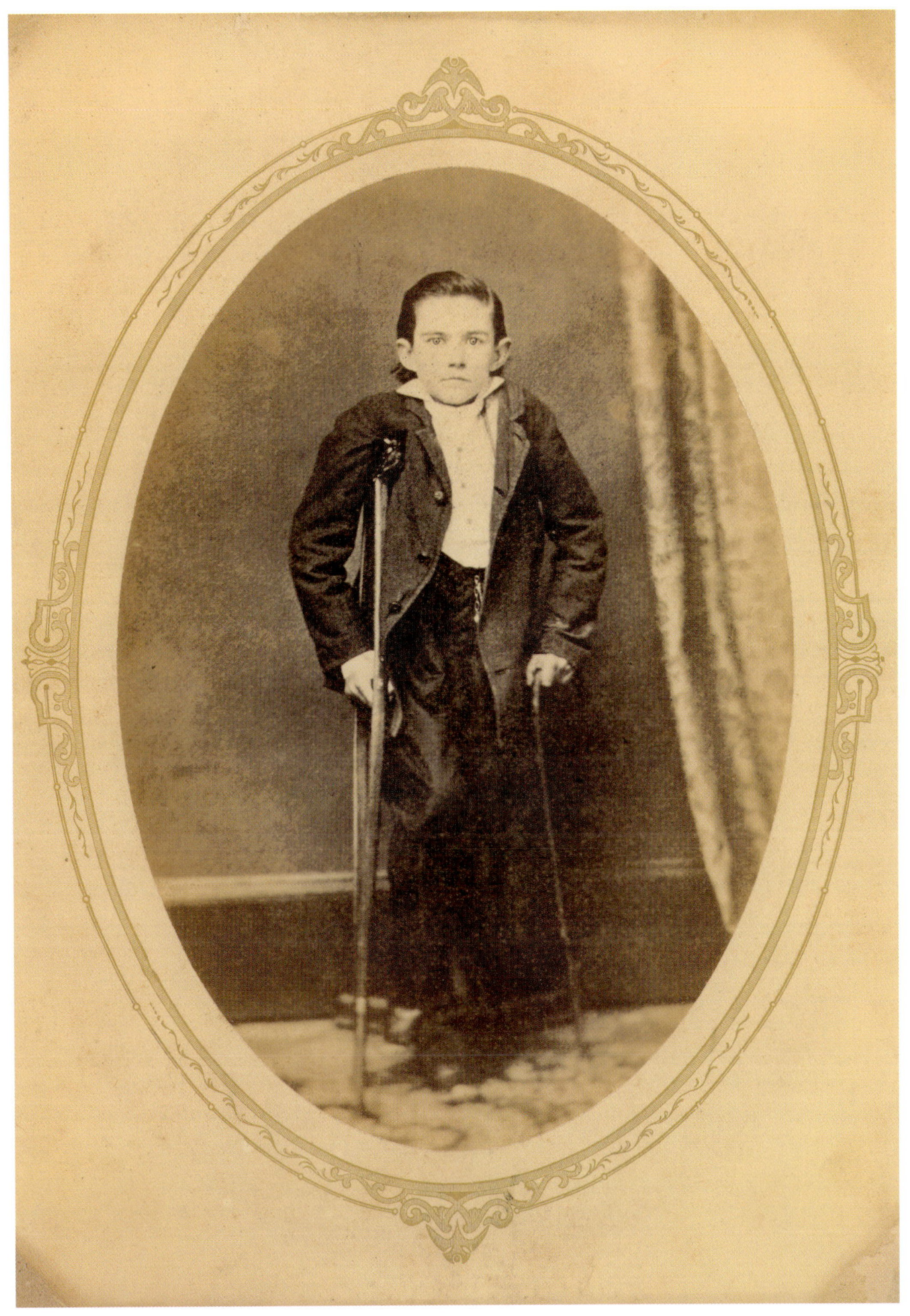

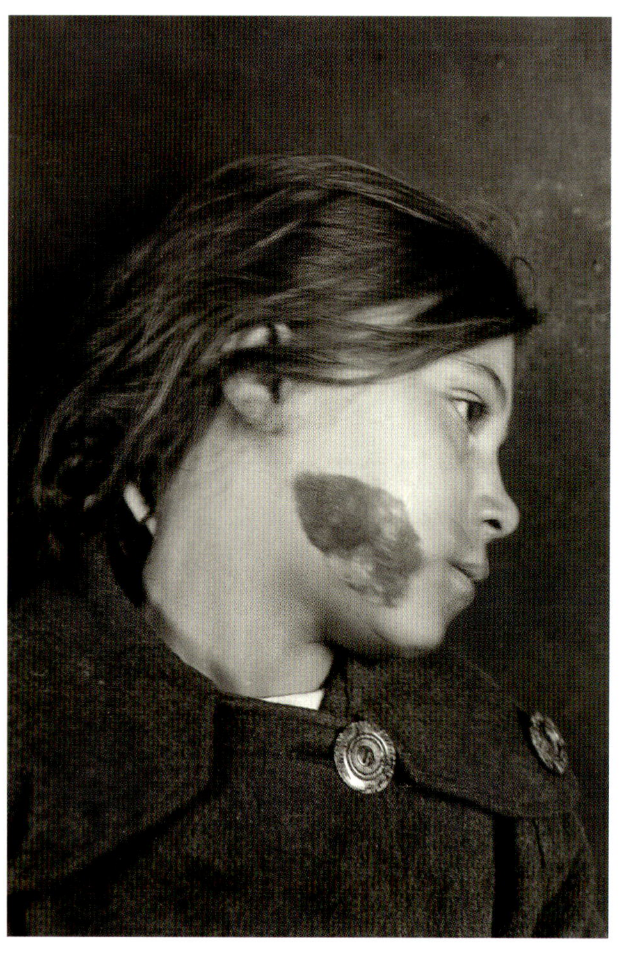

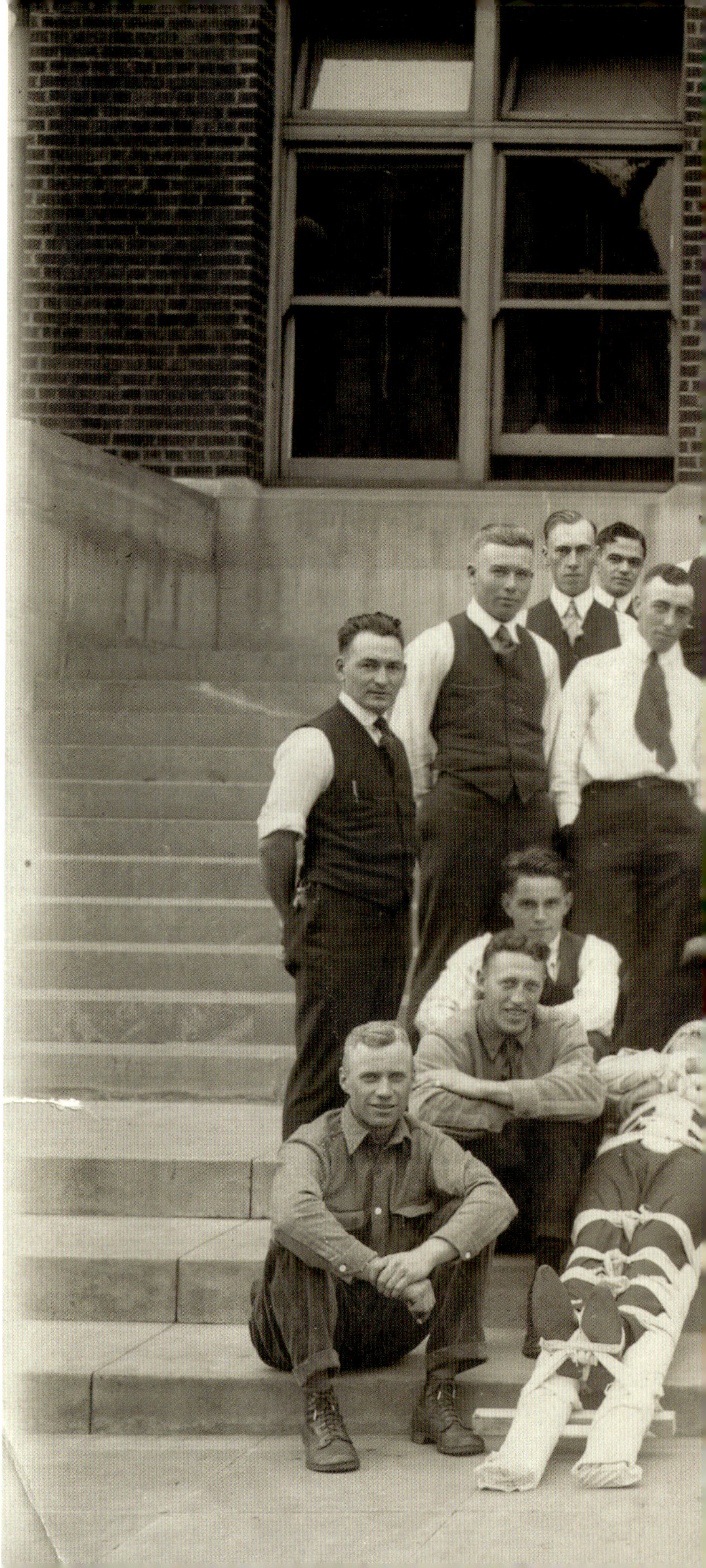

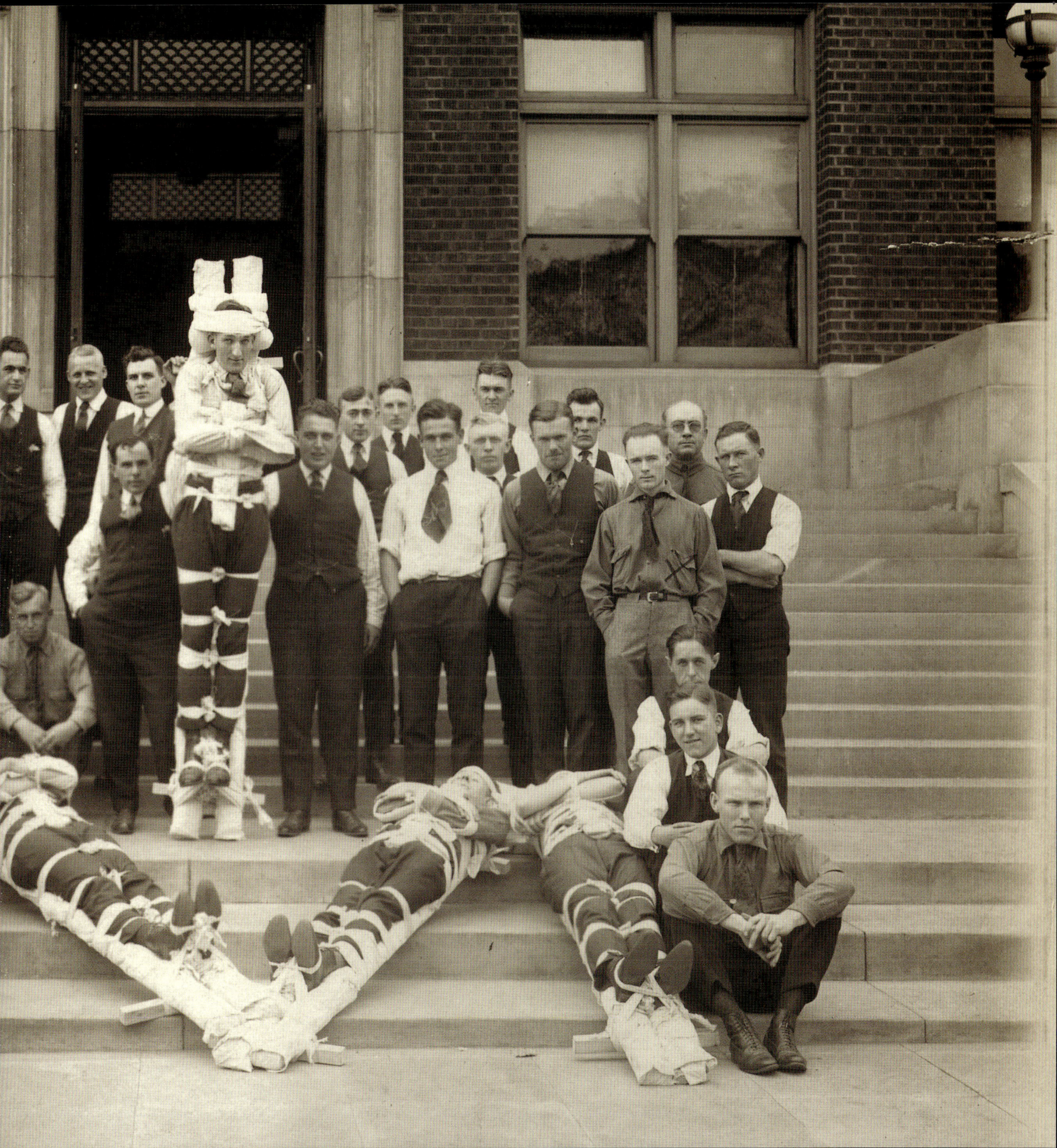

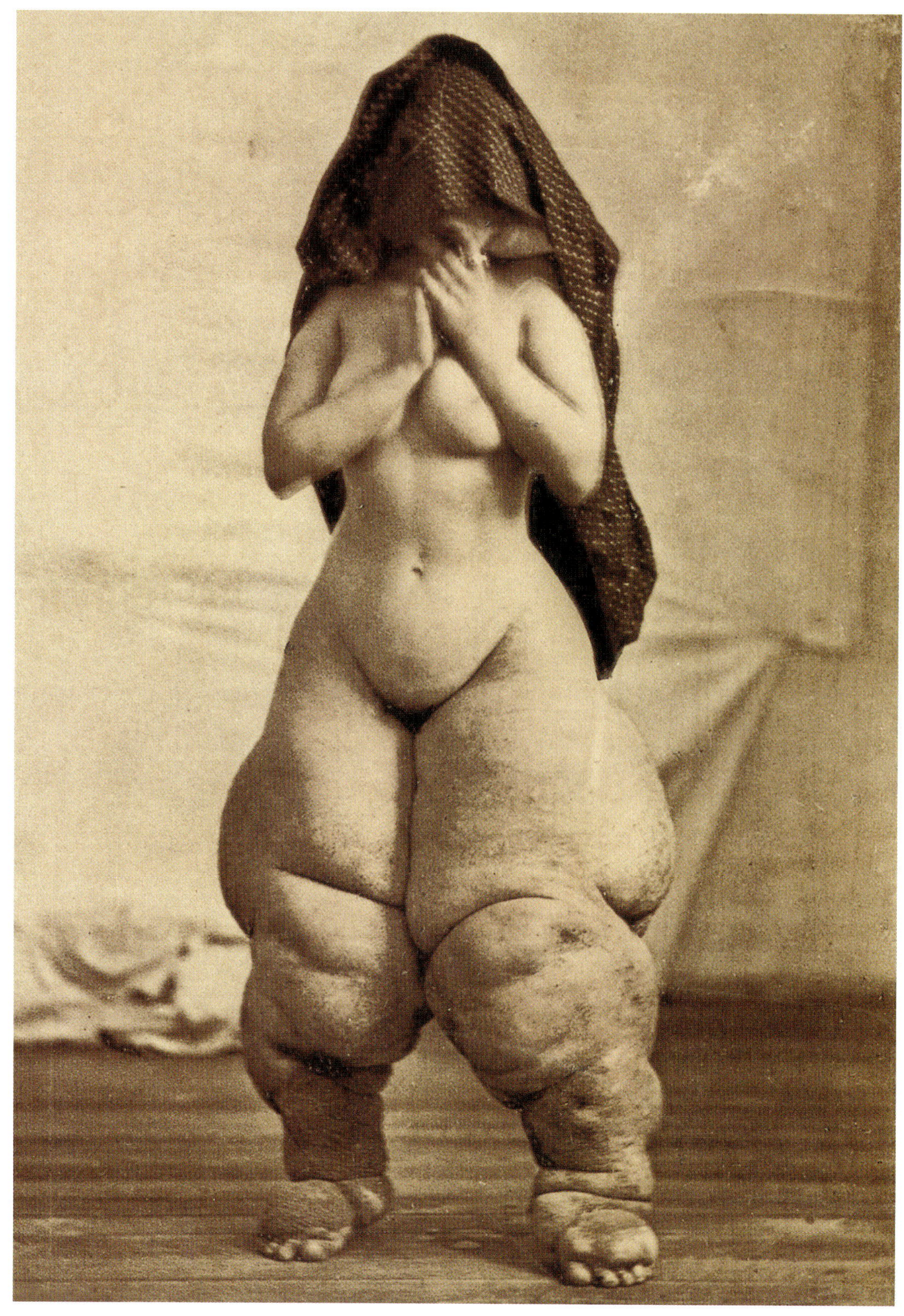

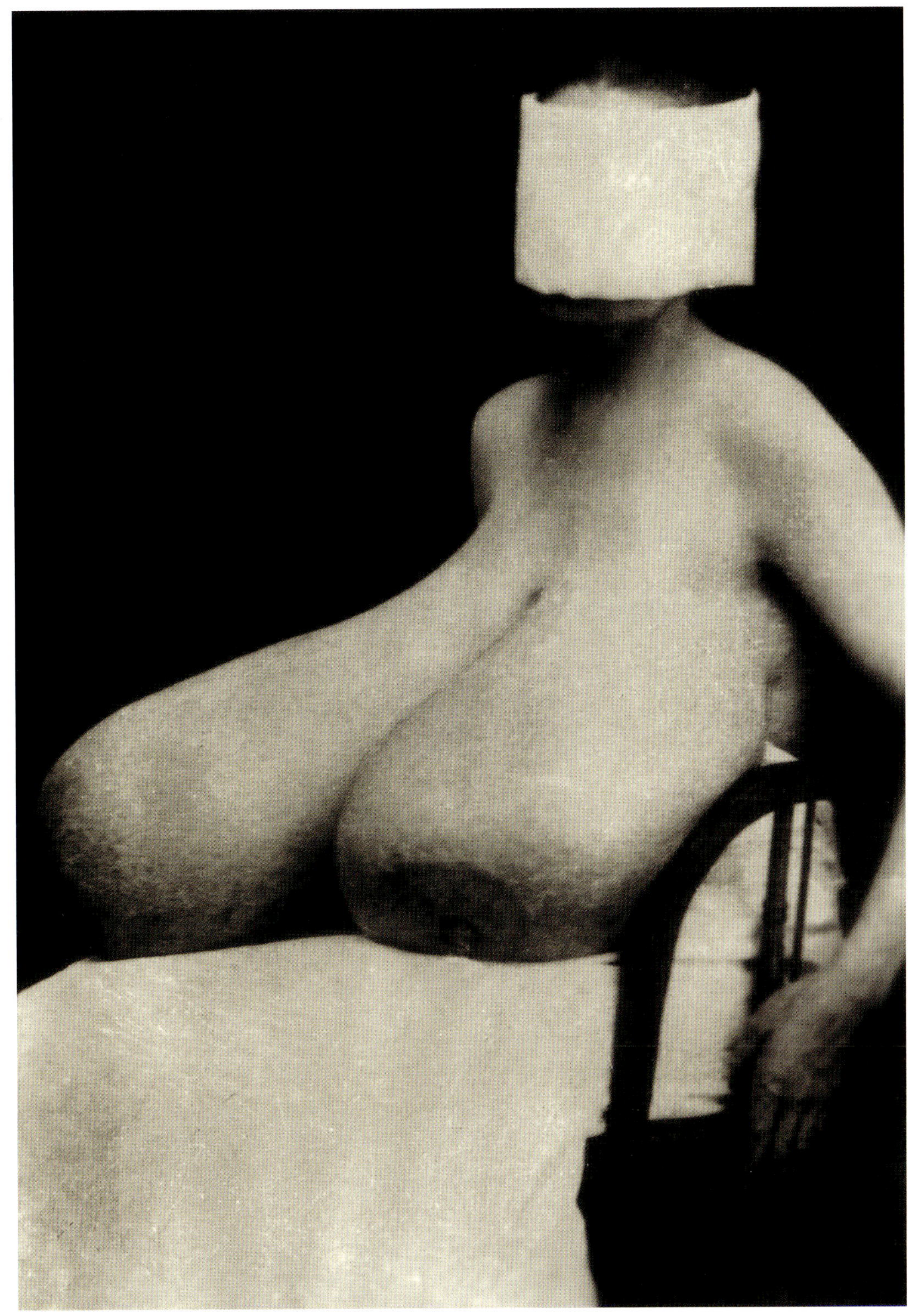

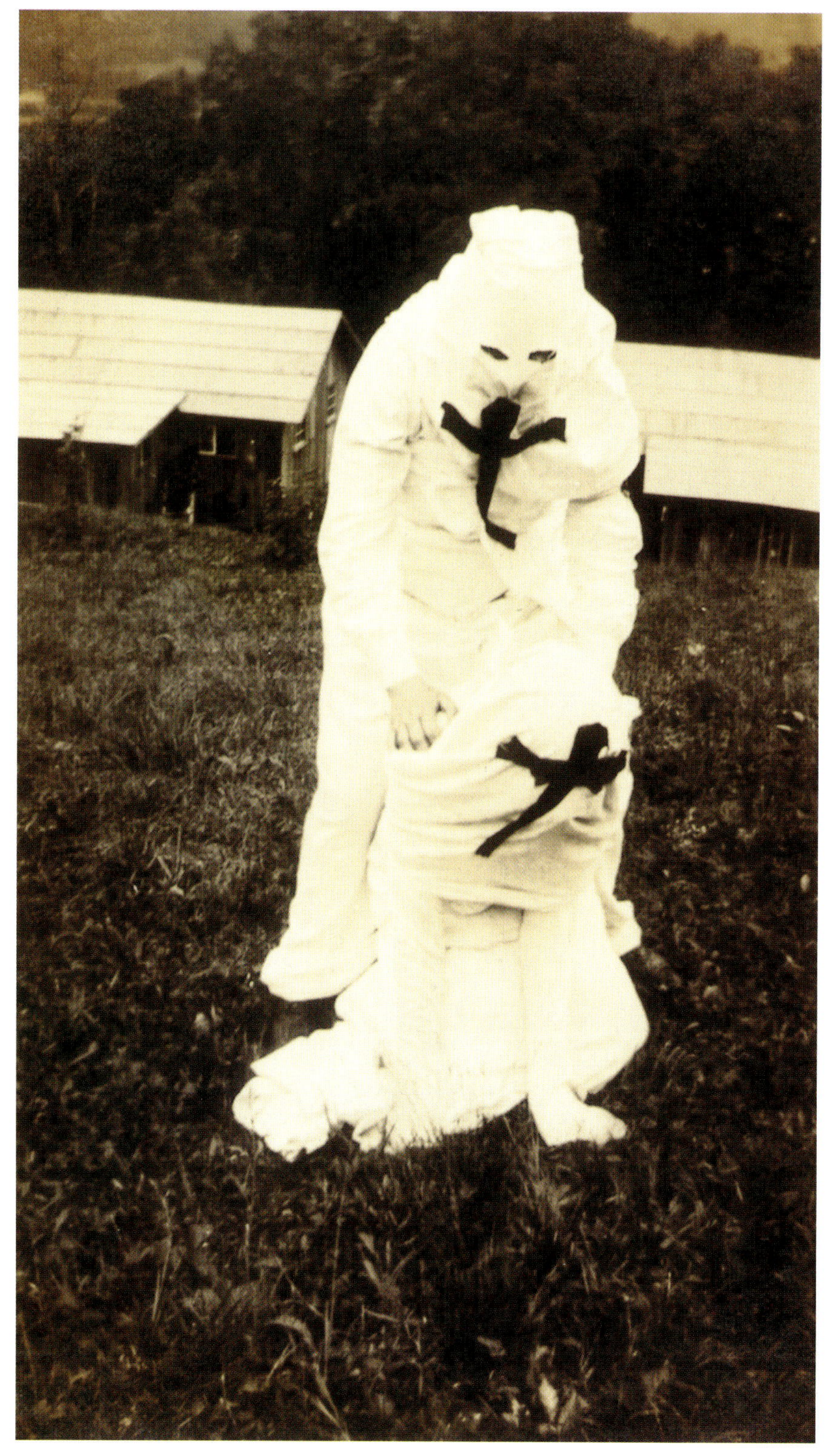

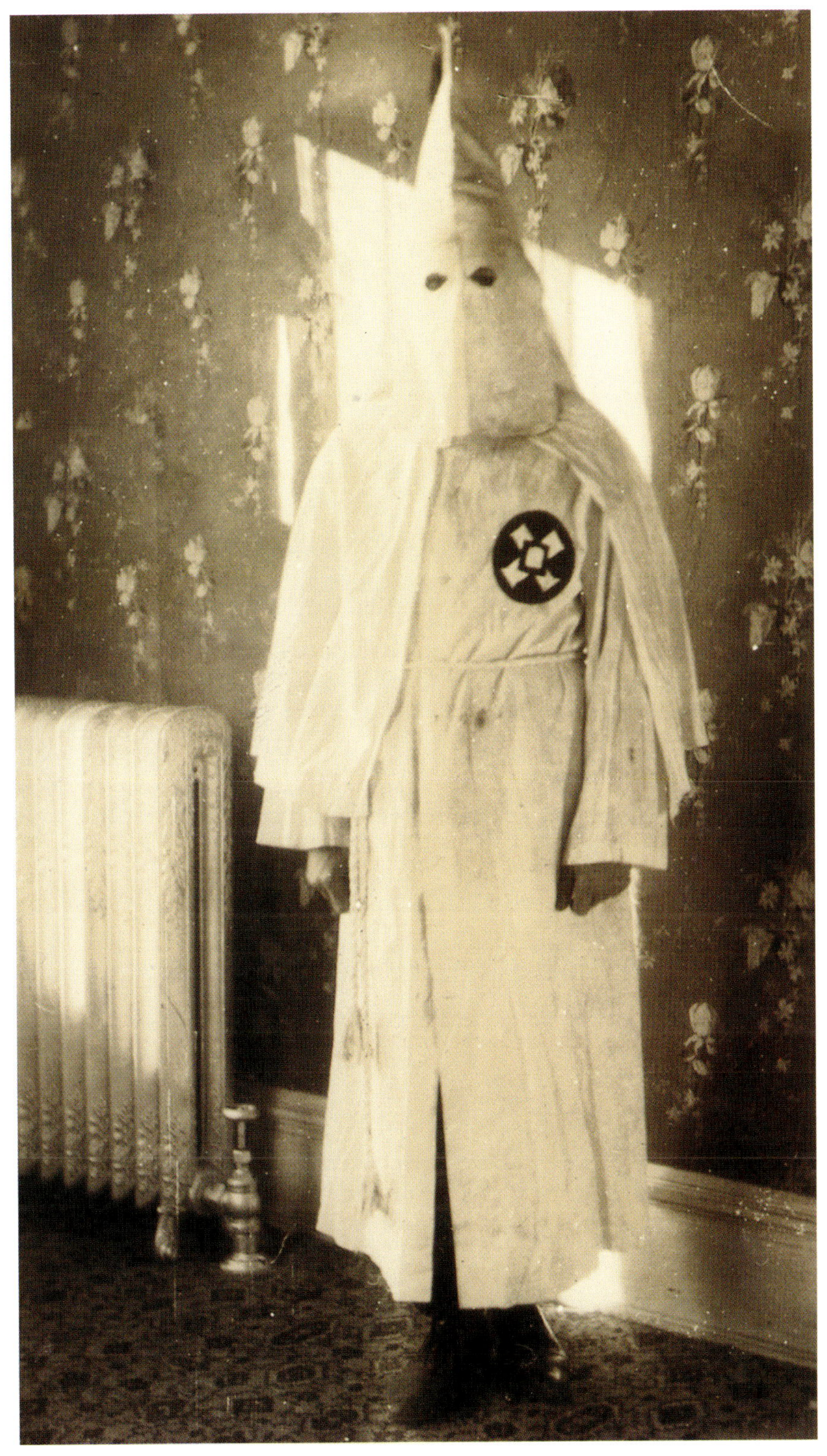

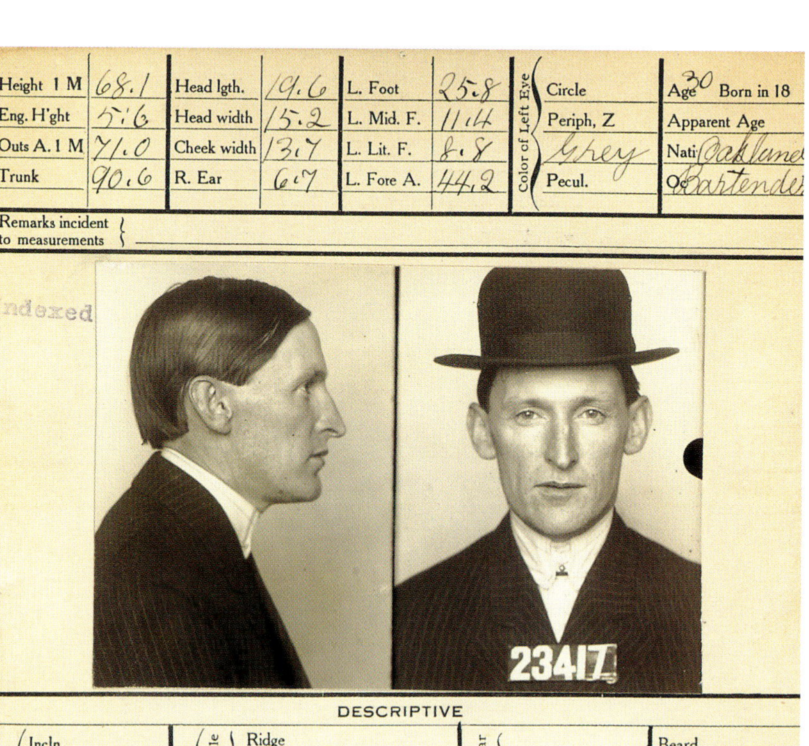

| Height 1 M | 68.1 | Head lgth. | 19.6 | L. Foot | 25.8 | Color of Left Eye | Circle | Age 30 Born in 18 |
|---|---|---|---|---|---|---|---|---|
| Eng. H'ght | 5'6 | Head width | 15.2 | L. Mid. F. | 11.4 | | Periph, Z | Apparent Age |
| Outs A. 1 M | 71.0 | Cheek width | 13.7 | L. Lit. F. | 8.8 | | Grey | Nati Oakland |
| Trunk | 90.6 | R. Ear | 6.7 | L. Fore A. | 44.2 | | Pecul. | Oc Bartender |

Remarks incident to measurements

Indexed

23417

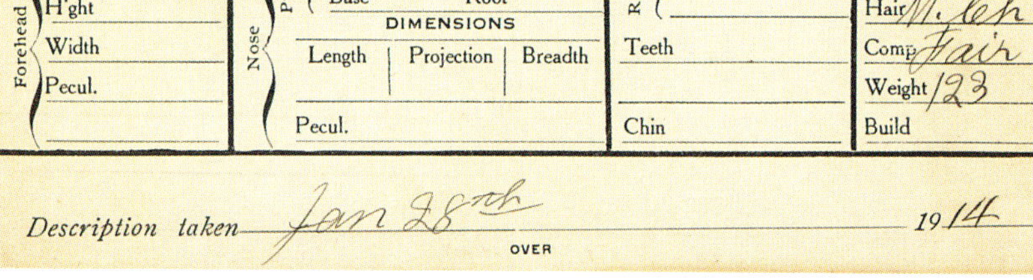

DESCRIPTIVE

| Forehead | | Nose | | R. Ear | | |
|---|---|---|---|---|---|---|
| Incln. | | Profile: Ridge | | | | Beard |
| H'ght | | Base | Root | | | Hair M. Ch |
| Width | | DIMENSIONS: Length / Projection / Breadth | | Teeth | | Comp Fair |
| Pecul. | | | | | | Weight 123 |
| | | Pecul. | | Chin | | Build |

Description taken Jan 28th 1914

OVER

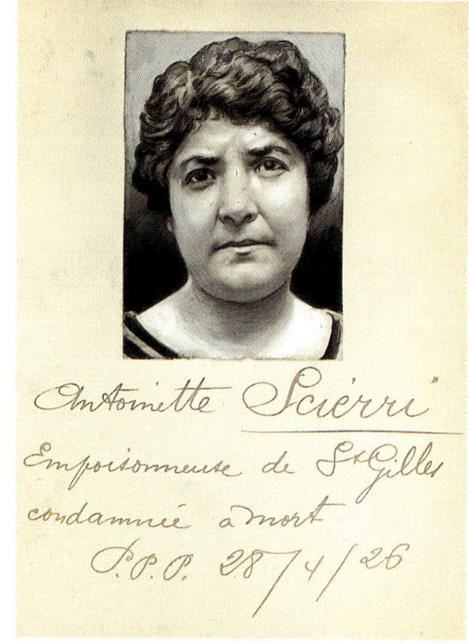

Antoinette Scierri

Empoisonneuse de St Gilles

condamnée à mort

P.P.P. 28/4/26

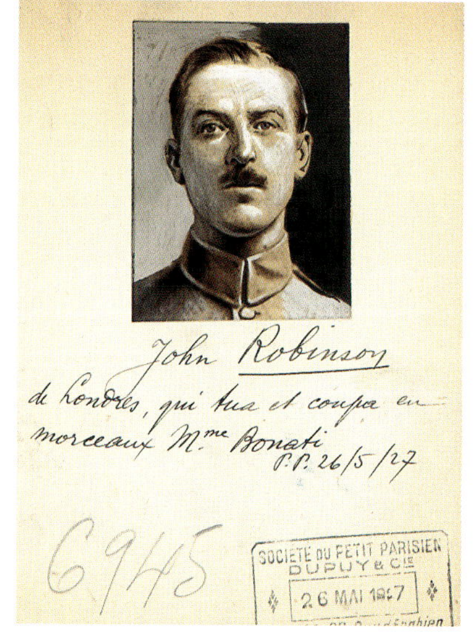

John Robinson

de Londres, qui tua et coupa en morceaux Mme Bonati

P.P. 26/5/27

6945

SOCIÉTÉ DU PETIT PARISIEN

DUPUY & Cie

26 MAI 1927

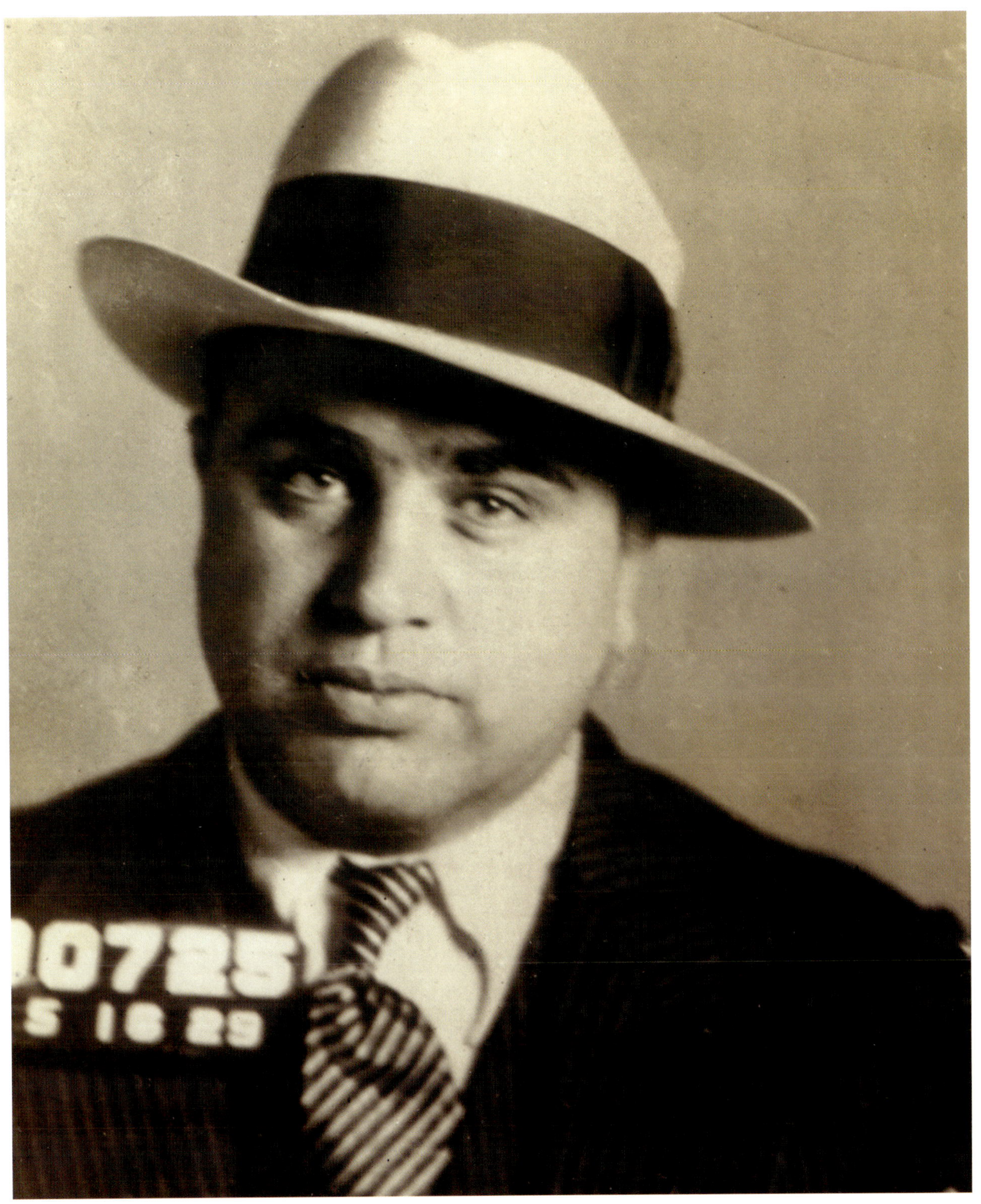
0725
5 16 29

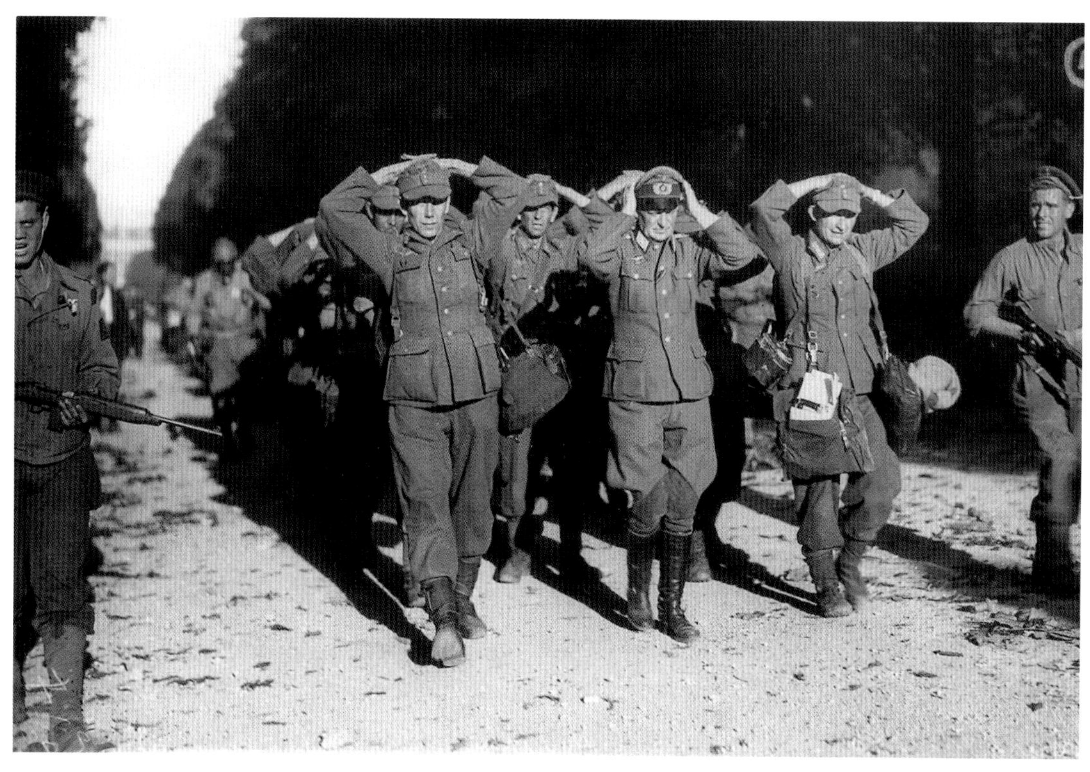

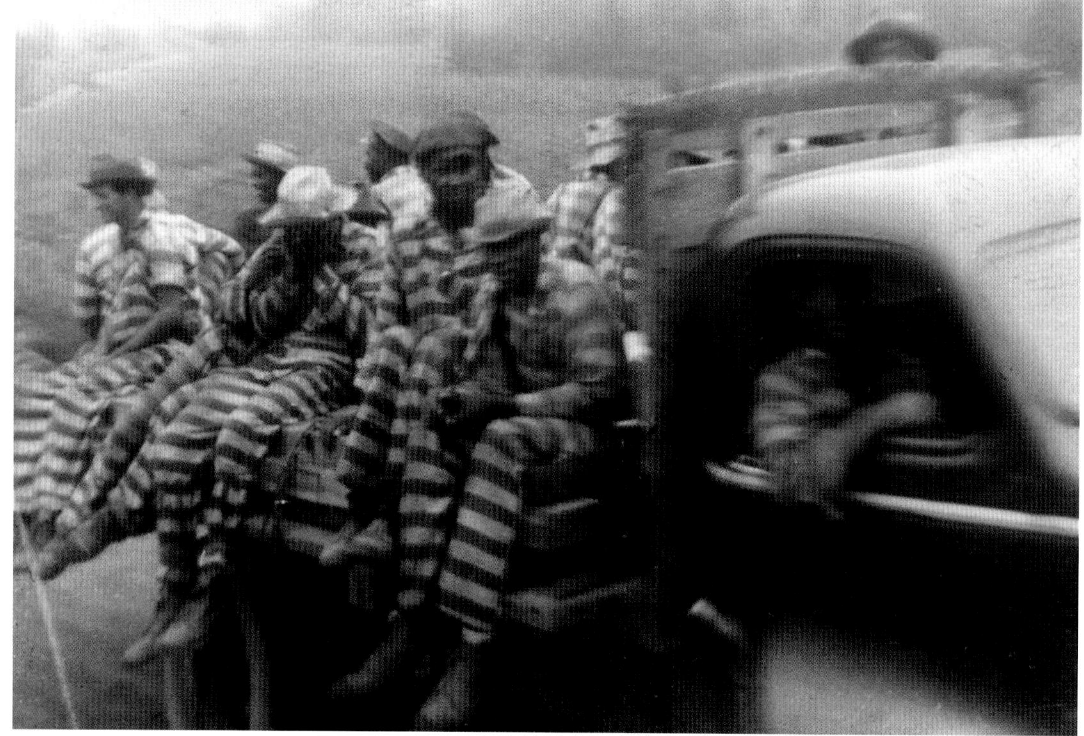

George James Murder case - Oct. 25-1929

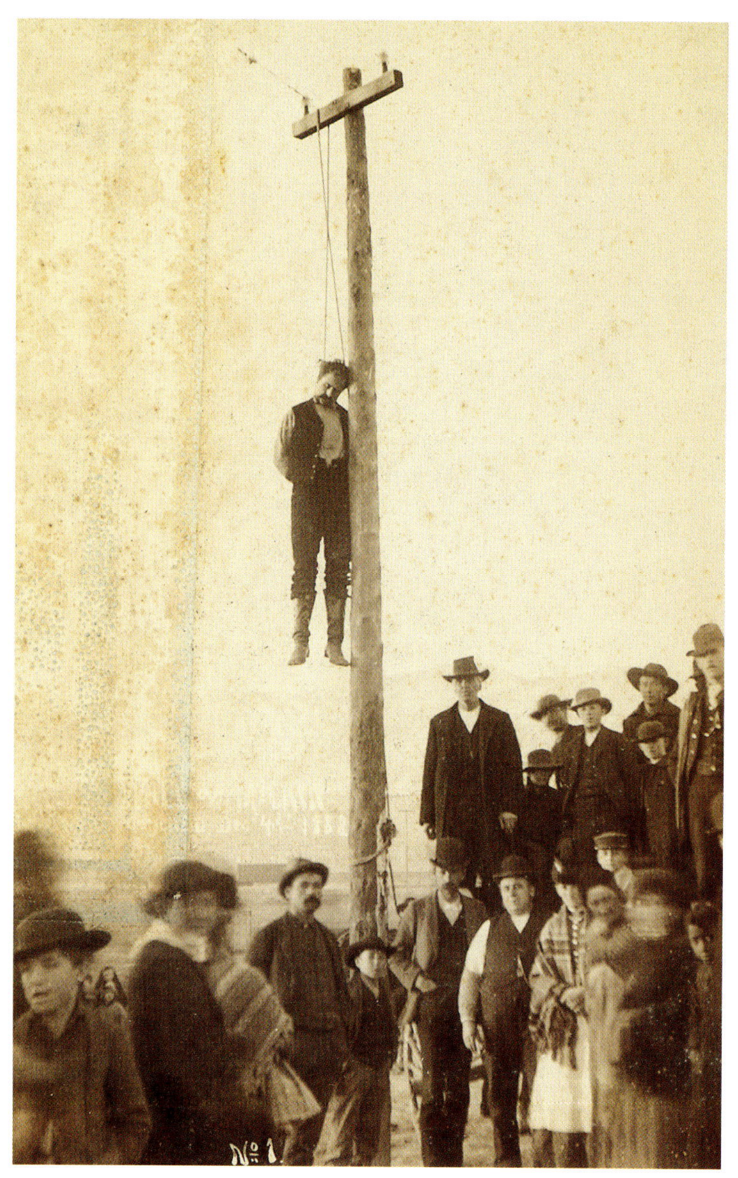
No 1.

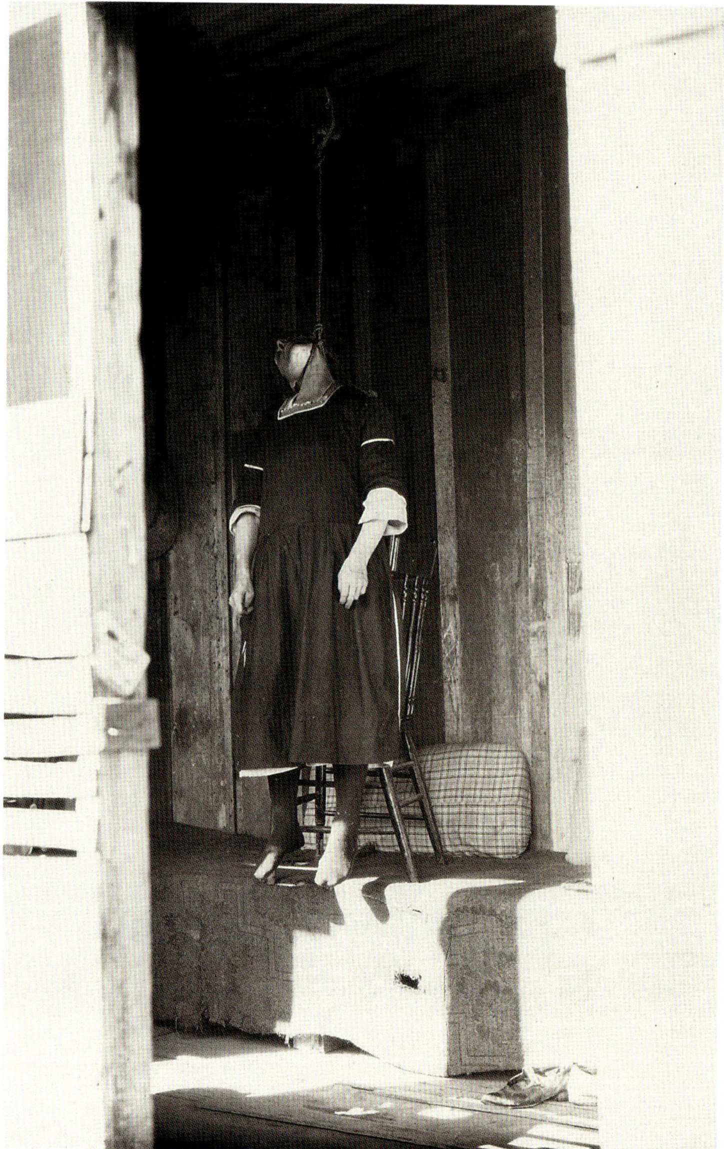

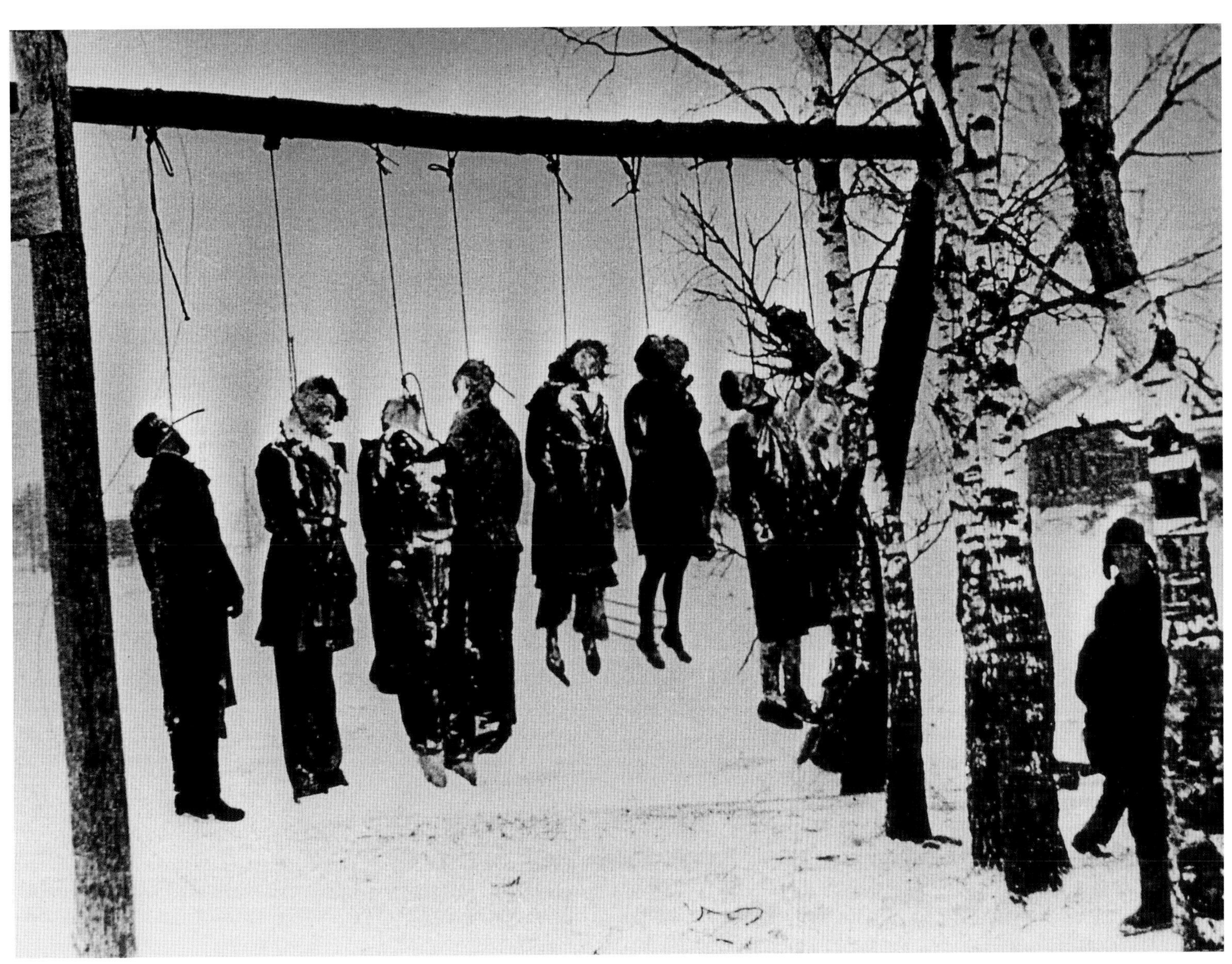

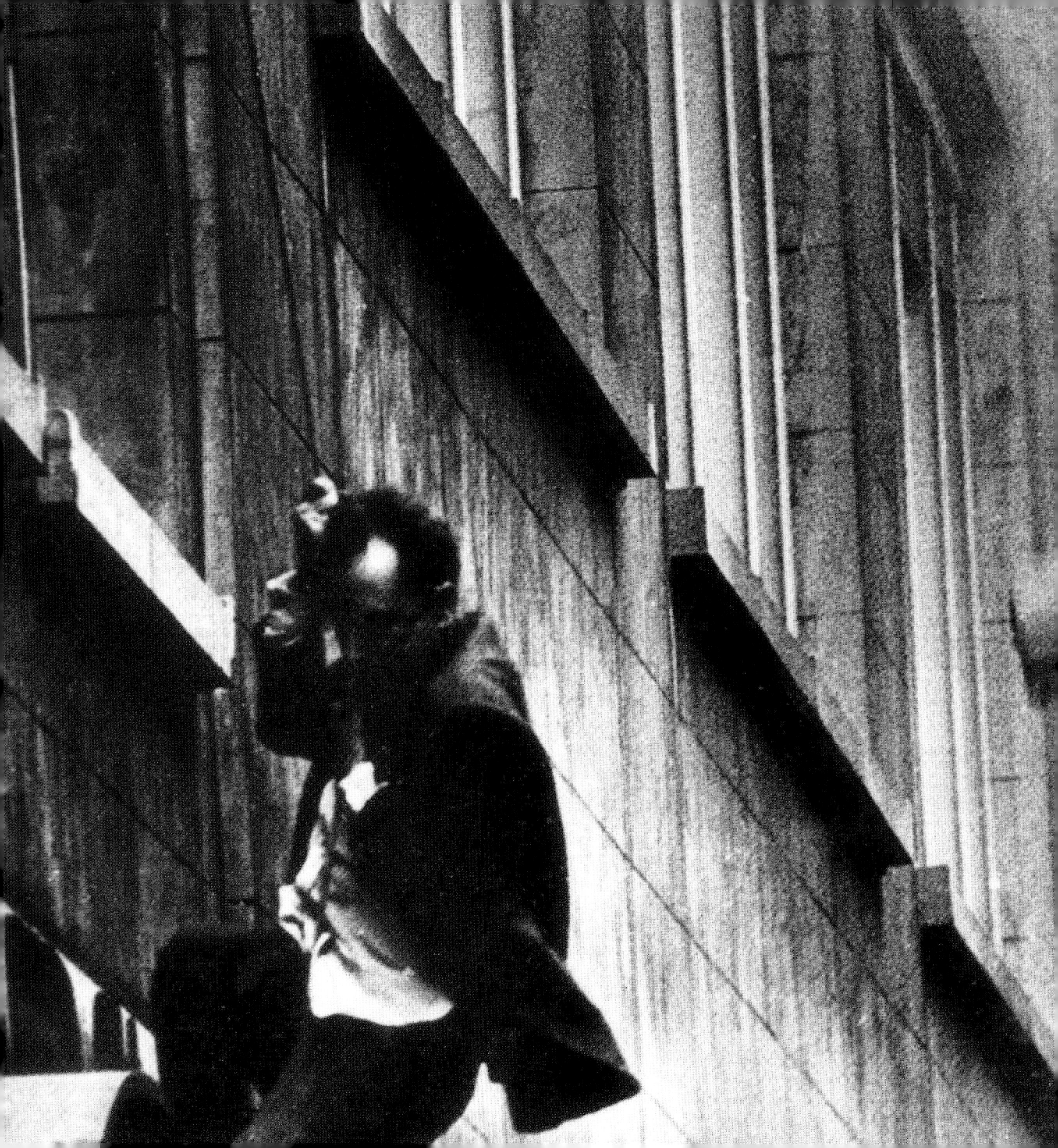

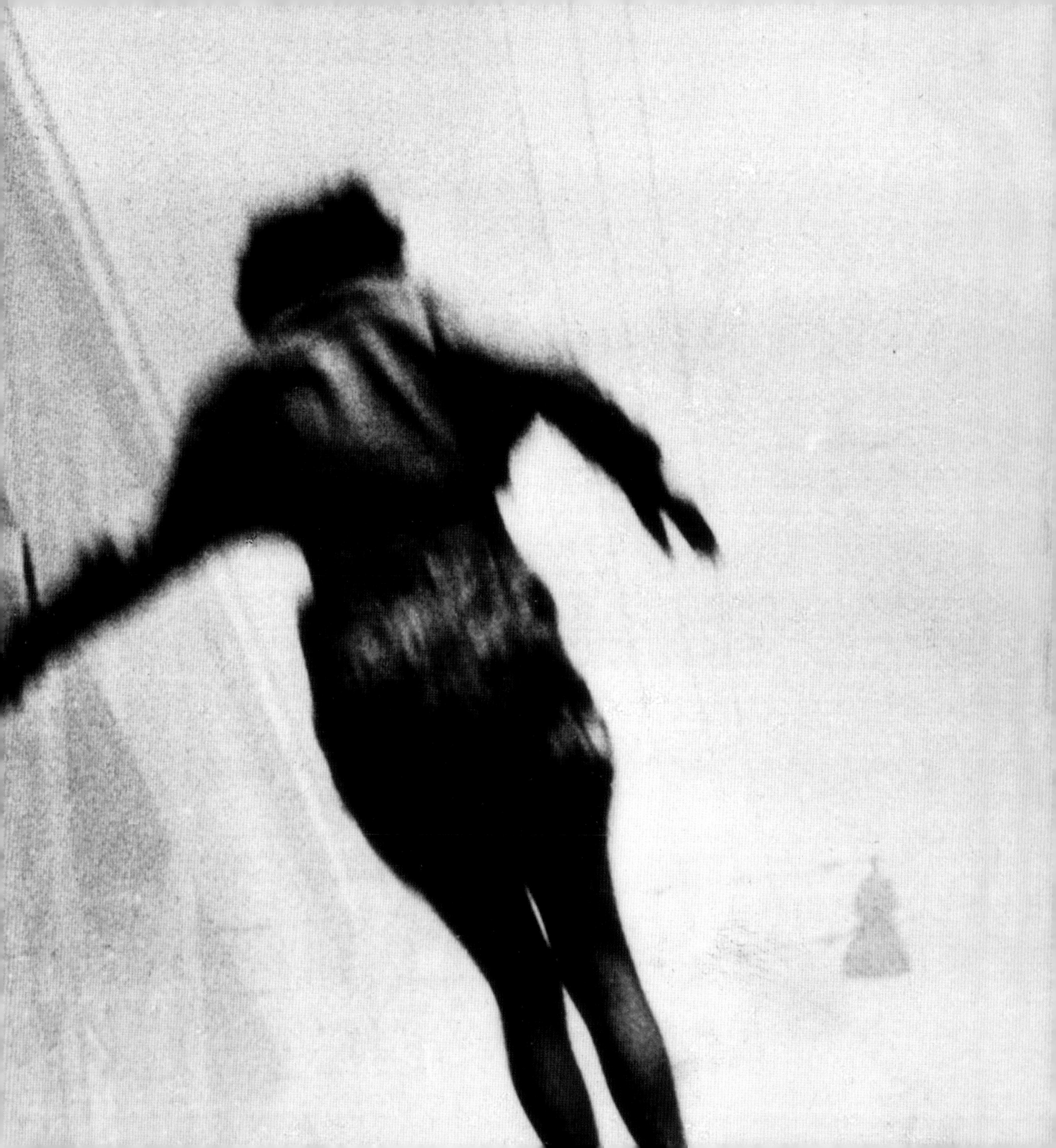

# Inevitability

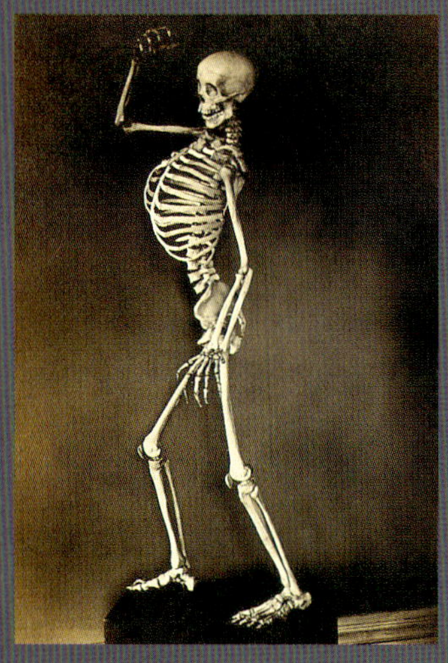

*'Life does not cease to be funny when people die any more than it ceases to be serious when people laugh.'*
George Bernard Shaw

Time spares no one. Photographs often allow our minds to float temporarily on clouds of pleasant nostalgia, but, if we are honest with ourselves, we should realize that they ultimately serve as visible reminders of what we have lost. There is both an anxious and a joyful aspect of photographing children to capture their innocence and youth before they all too soon grow up, but photographs of the elderly are usually of a more thoughtful nature. Many times the photograph is not treated casually as one of many that will be taken now and in the future, but as one that may well be the last such picture to be made of that individual. A photograph of someone tenderly holding their great-granddaughter as an infant will later be shown to that child, now grown, to validate their link to the person holding them, now gone, about whom they have no recollection.

Pictures of the dead exist in greater profusion in photography of the nineteenth and early twentieth centuries than in more recent times. They often display a ritualistic quality in the laying out of the body in its finest clothes for viewing, and the formal posing of the living with the deceased. These gestures appear to be an act of respect for the departed and a comfort to those left behind. Recording these solemn moments provided one final visual memory for the living of someone gone forever. Today, modern society tends to treat death as something inconvenient to be dealt with as efficiently and unemotionally as possible. There is a clear discomfort in the fact that, as John Galsworthy has written, 'the beginnings and endings of all human undertakings are untidy'.

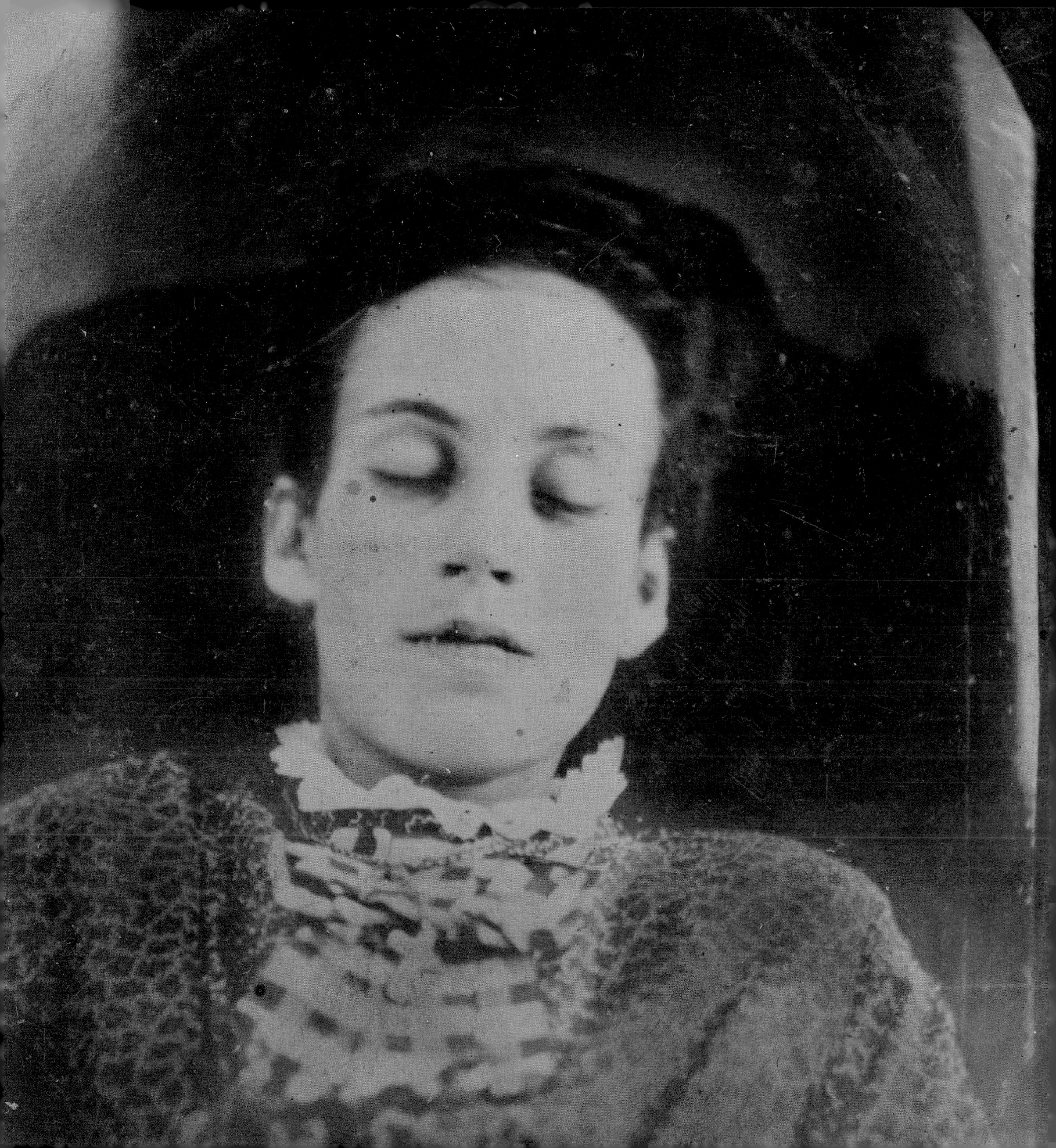

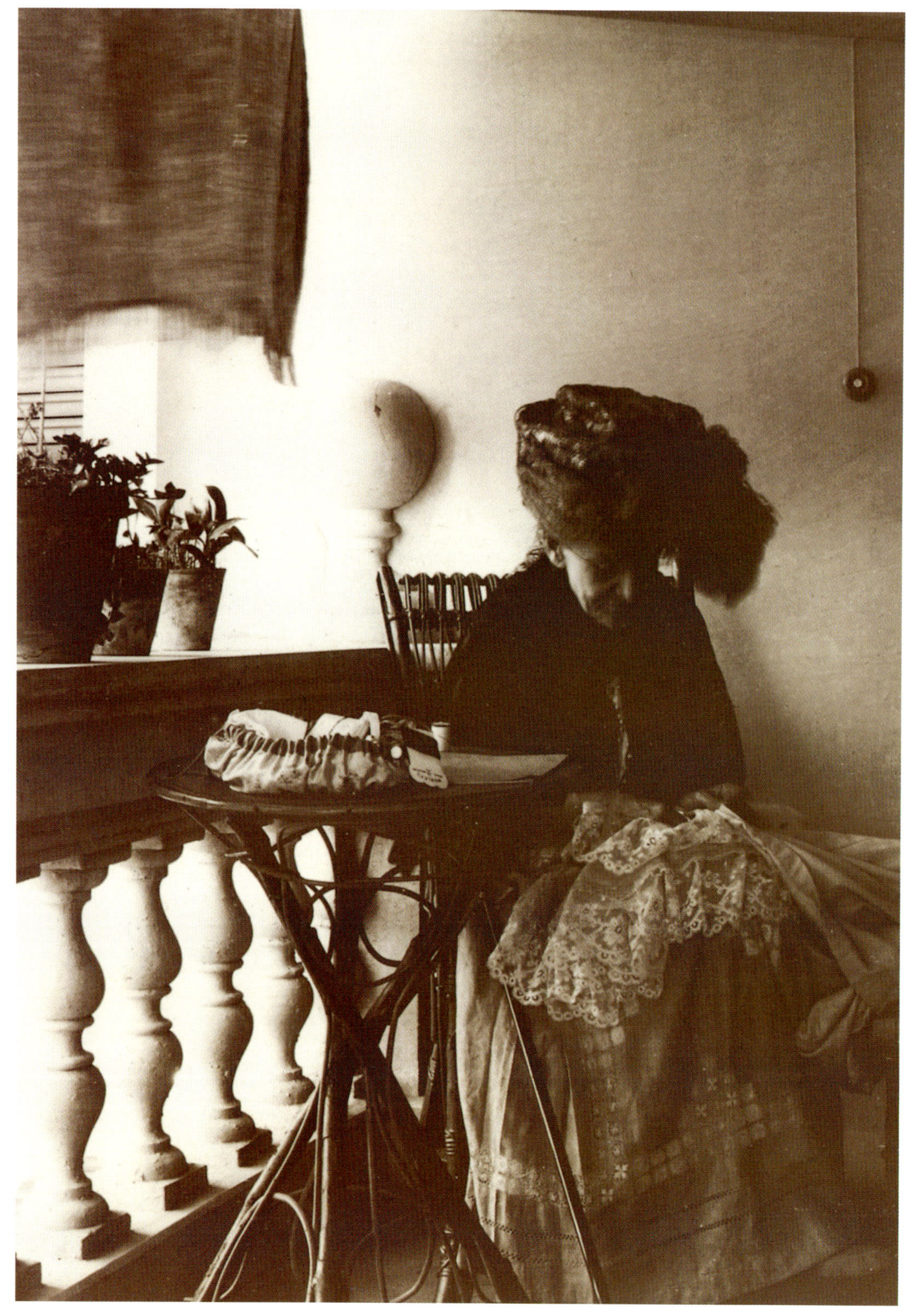

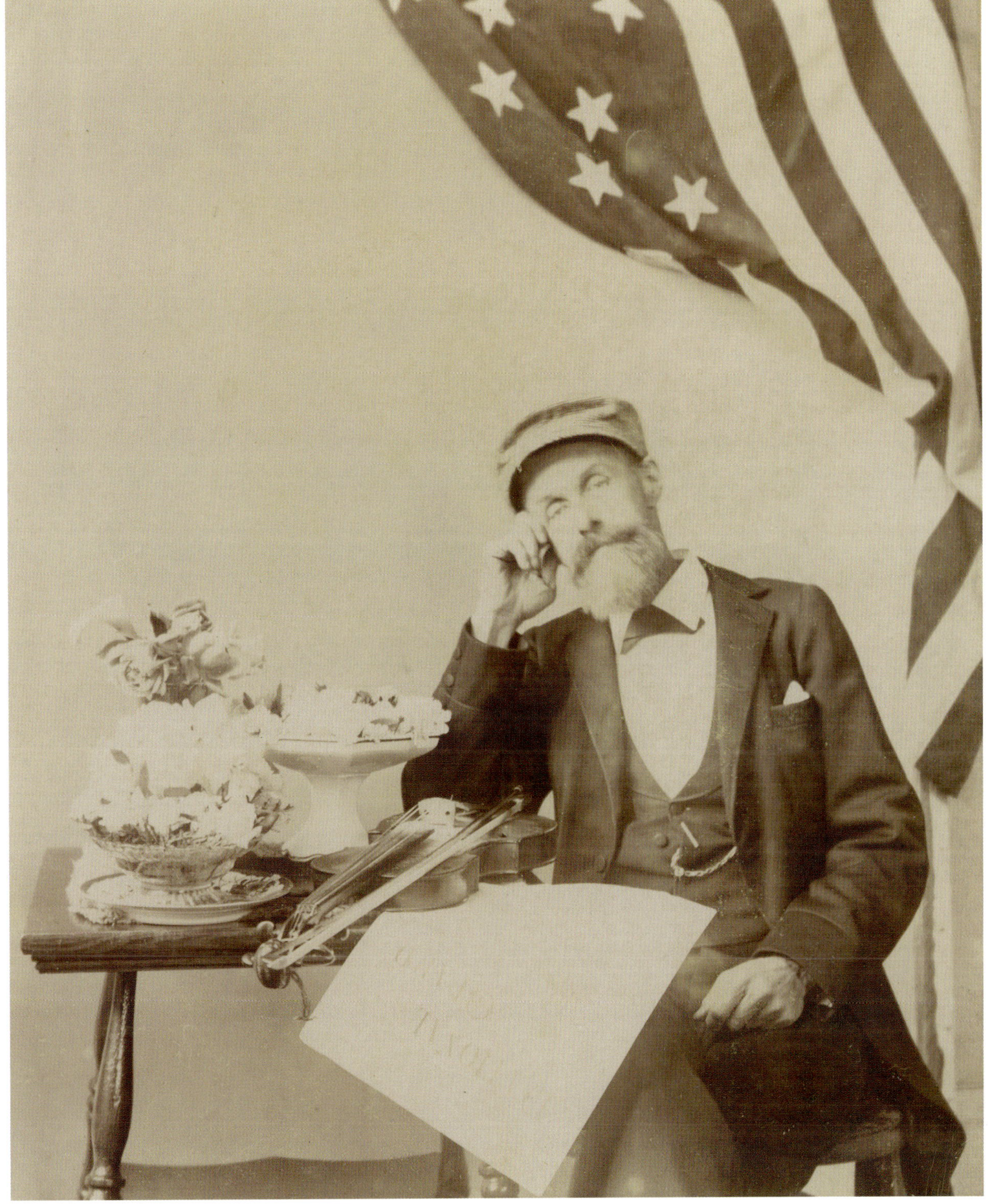

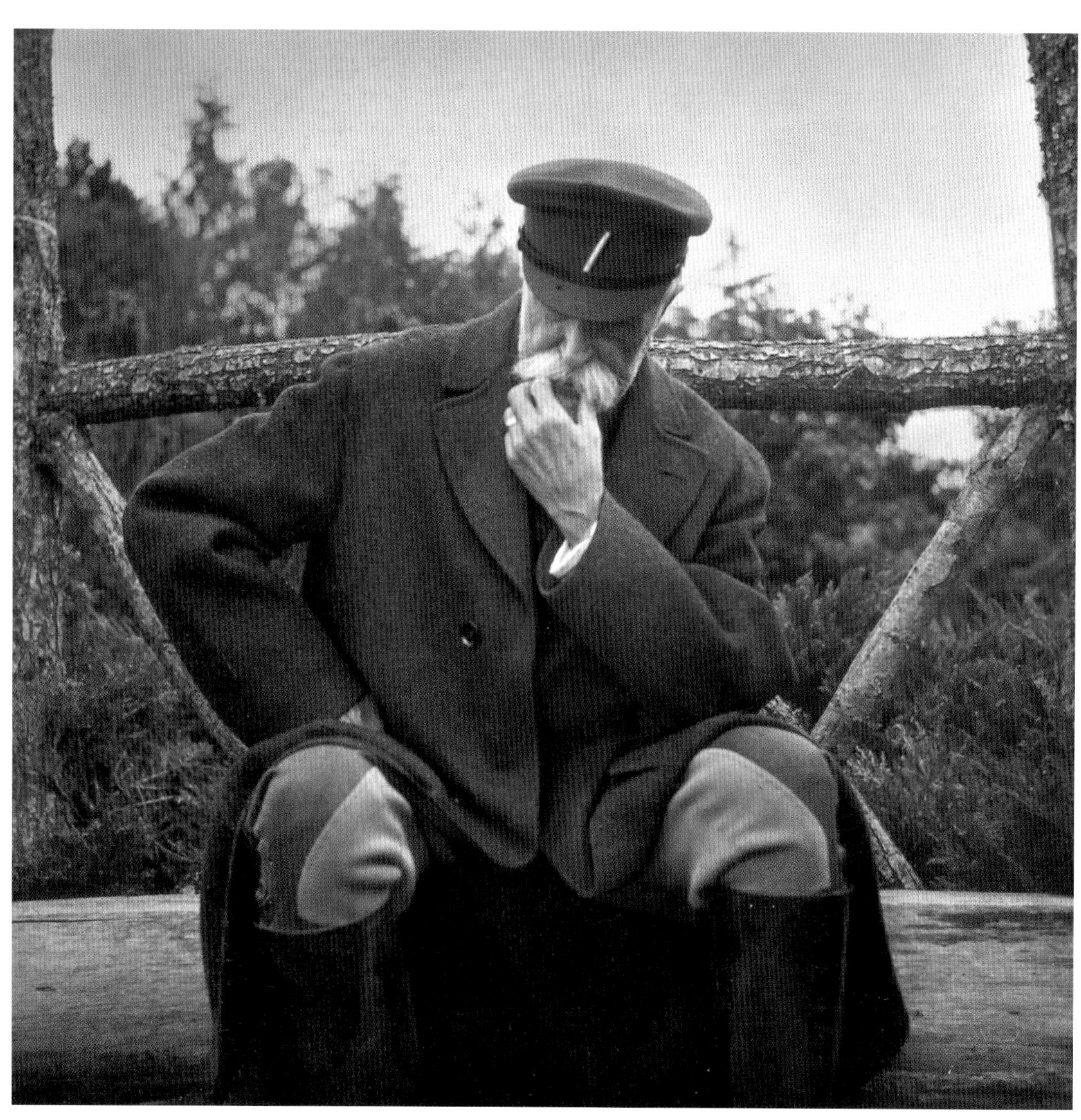

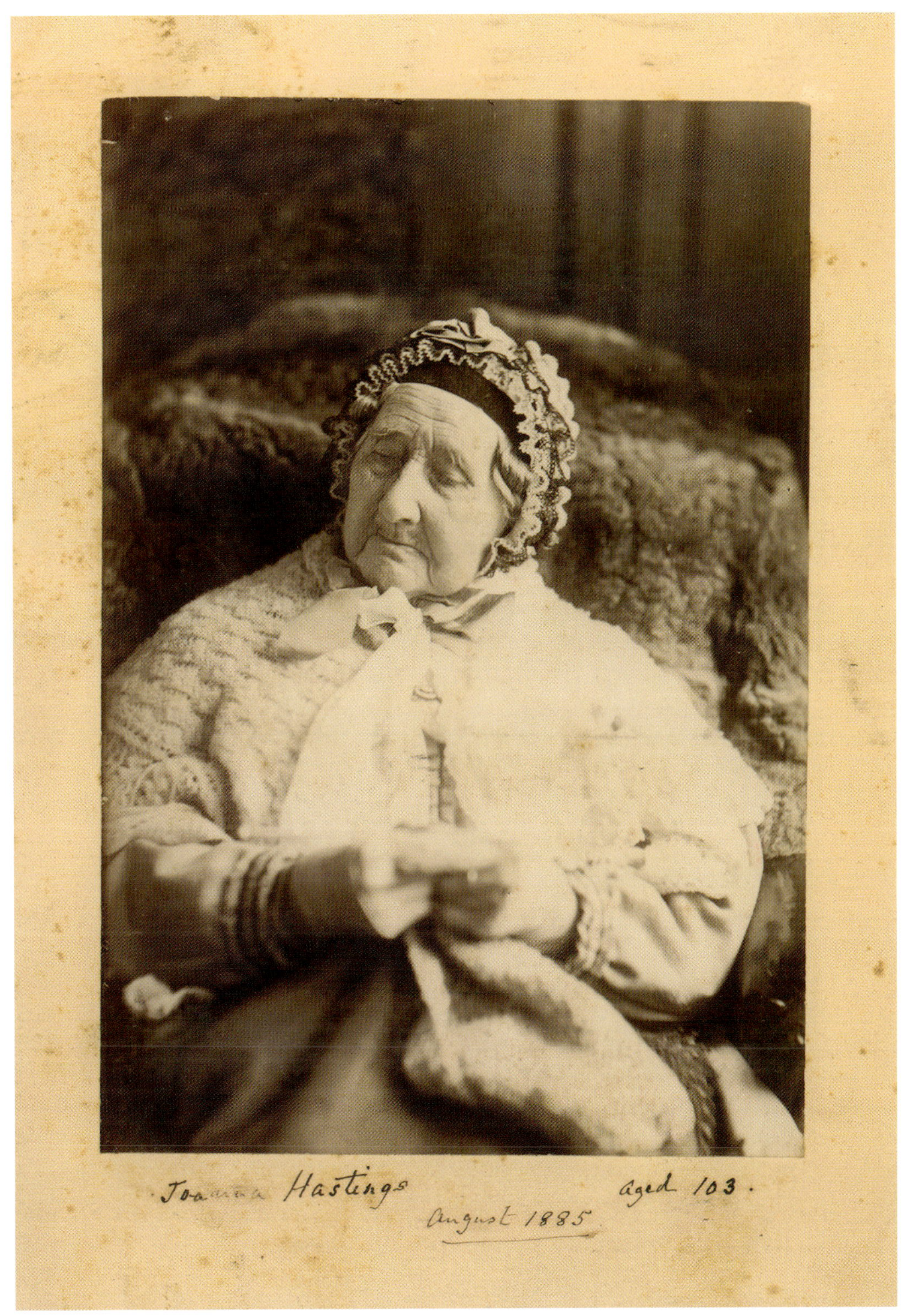
Joanna Hastings
aged 103.
August 1885

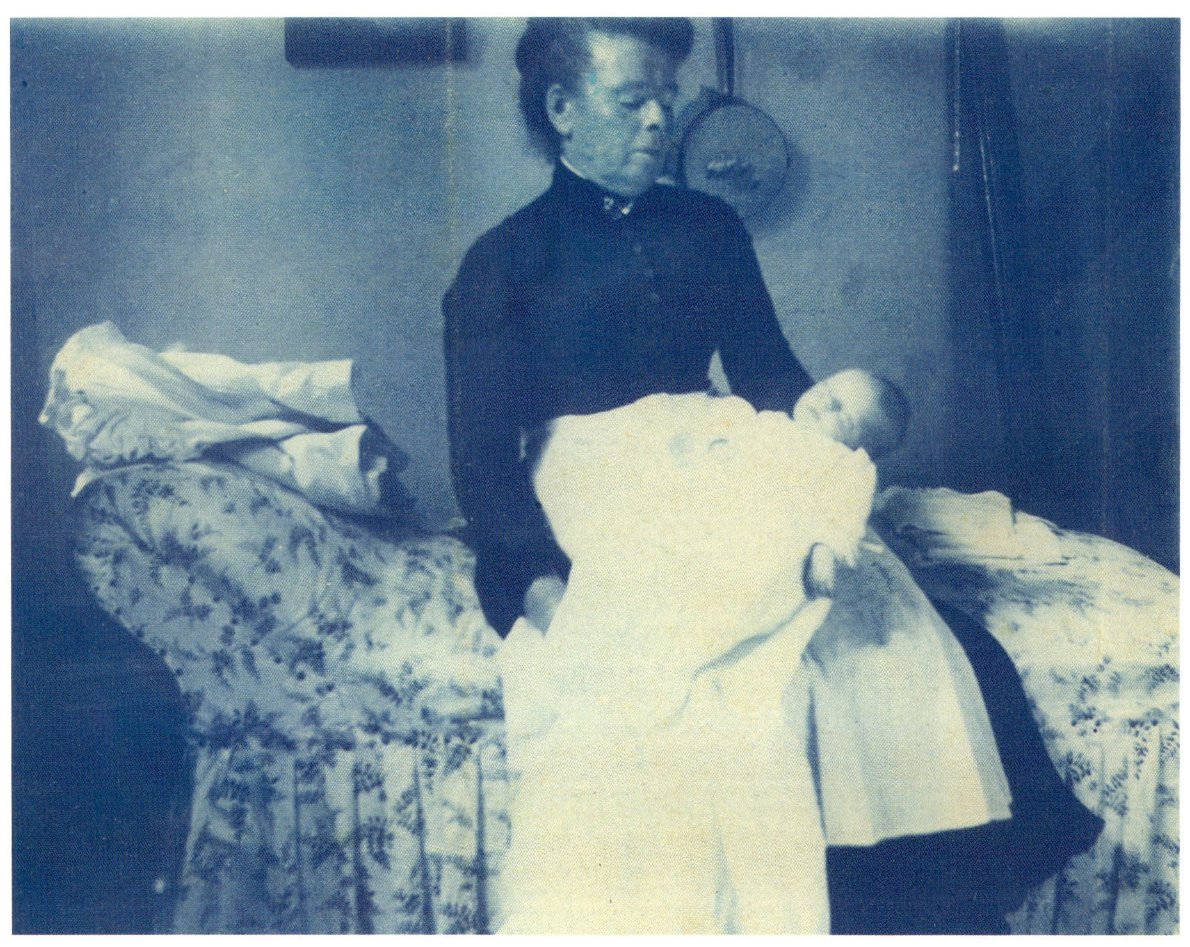

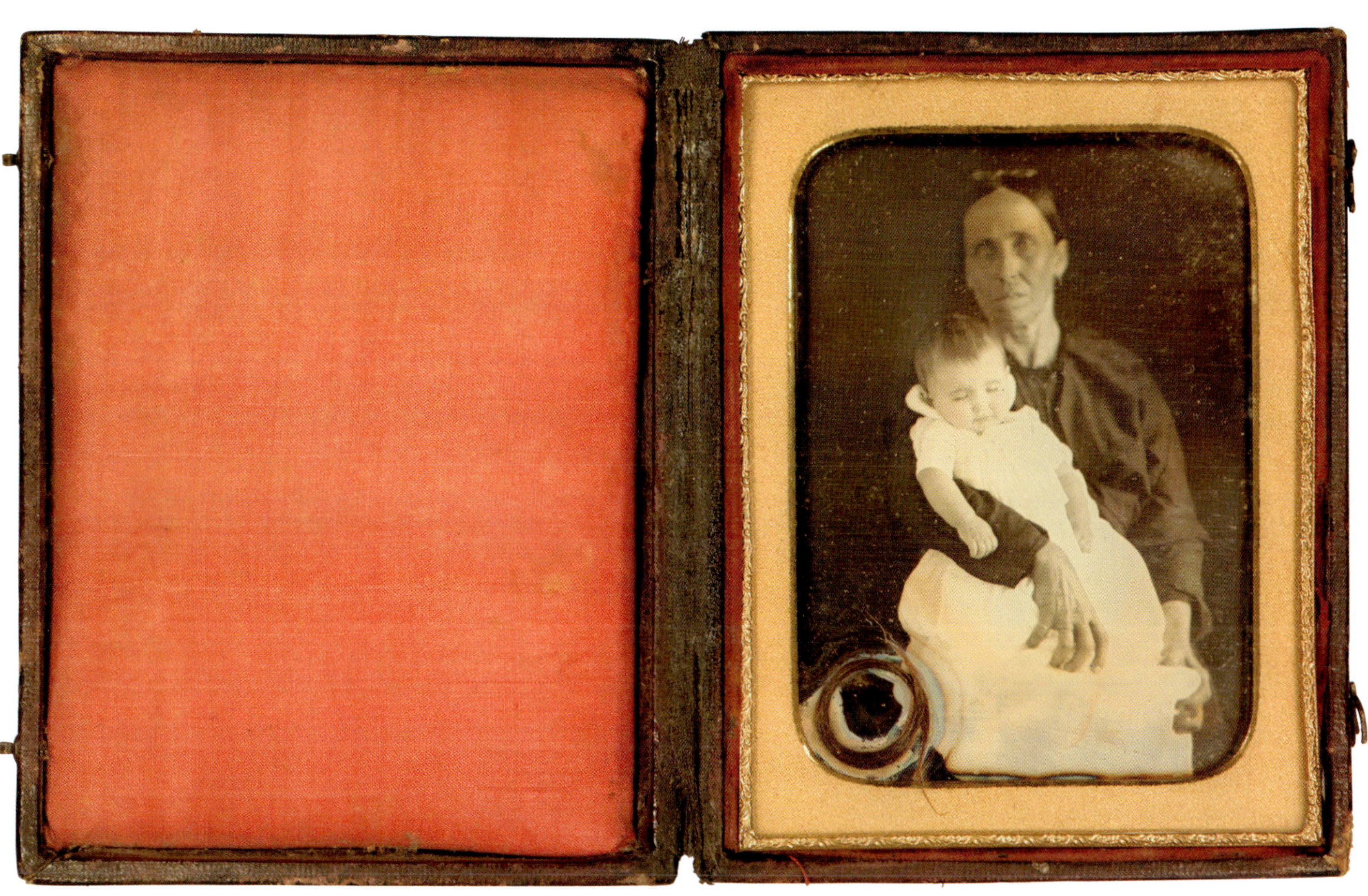

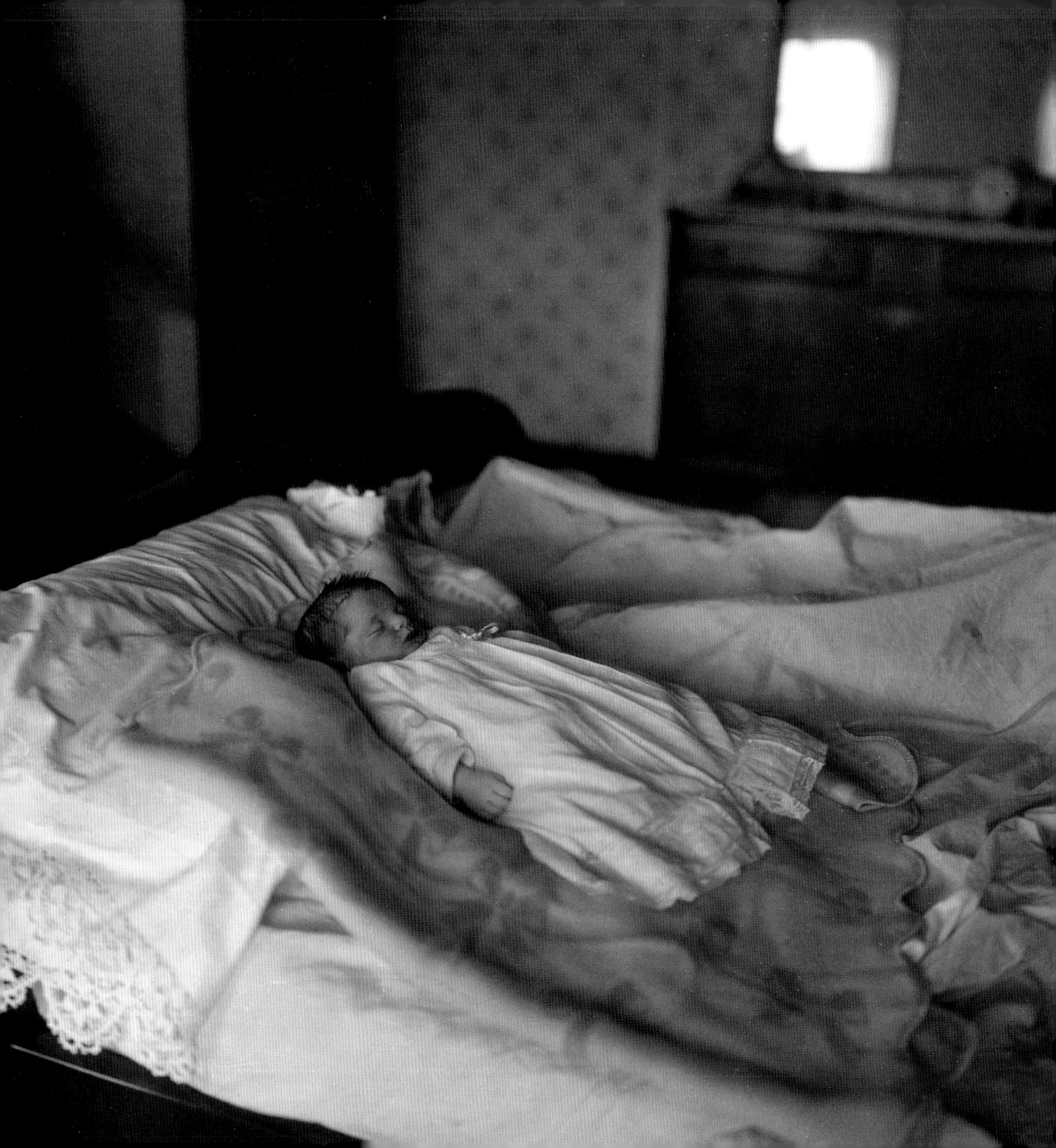

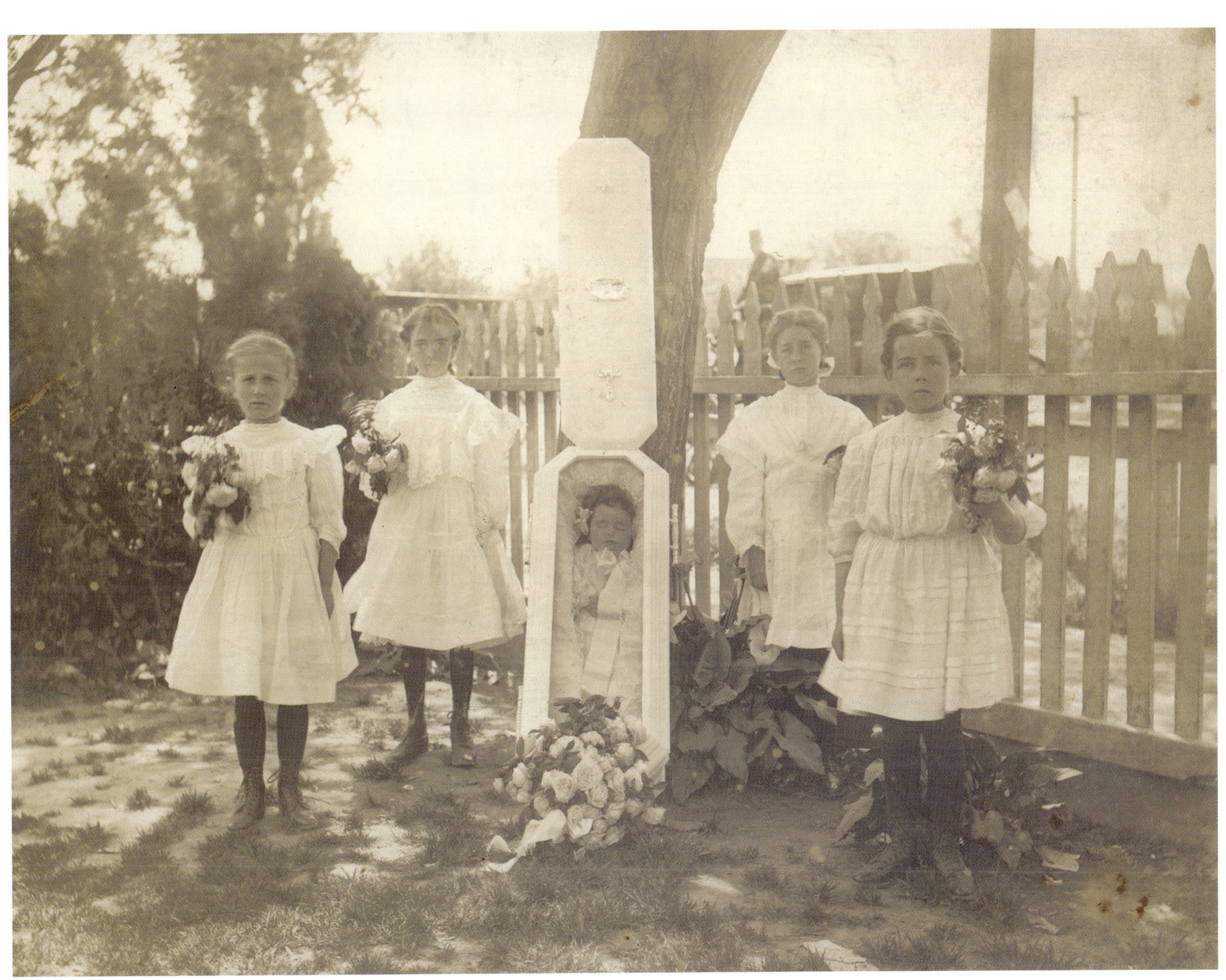

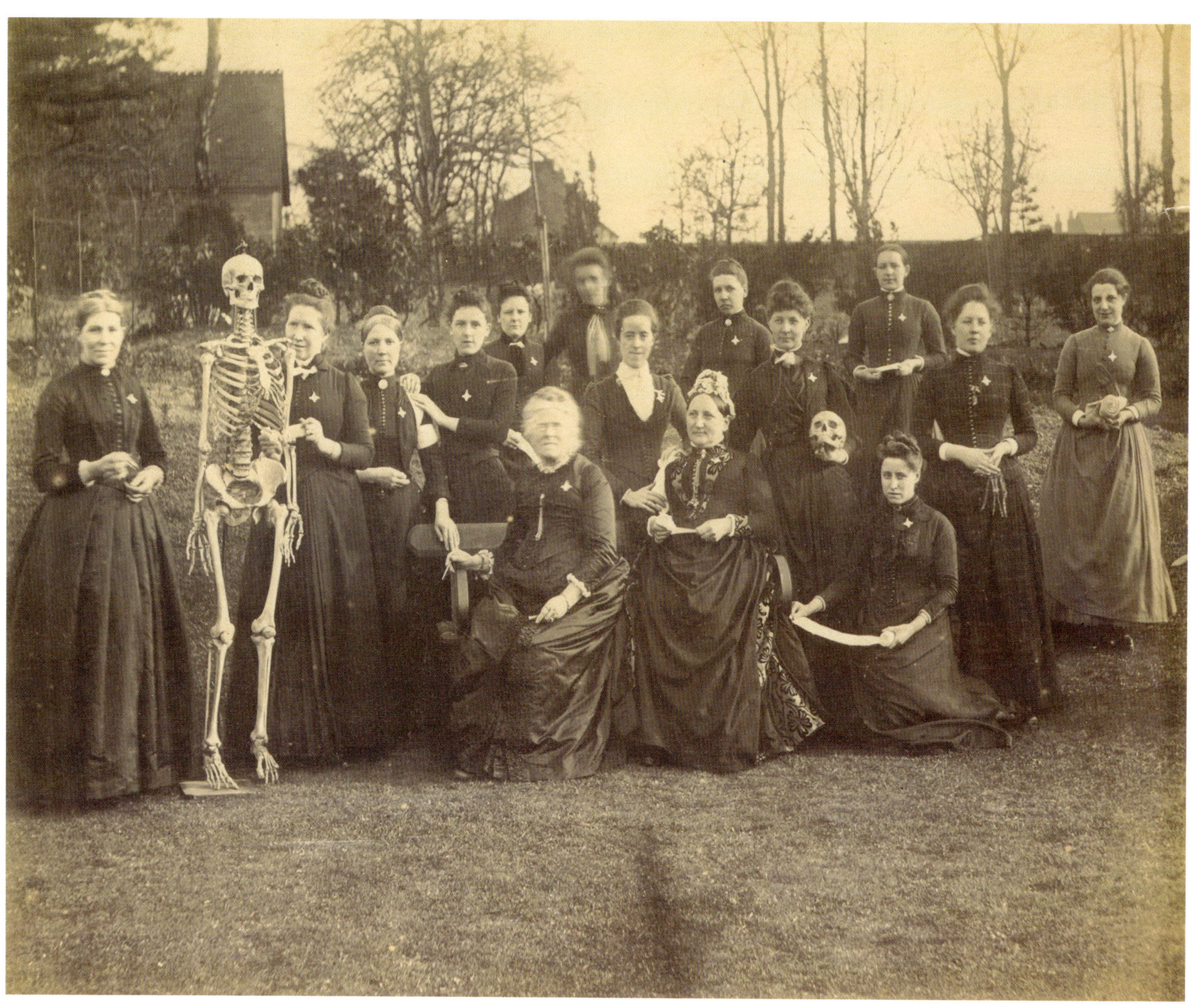

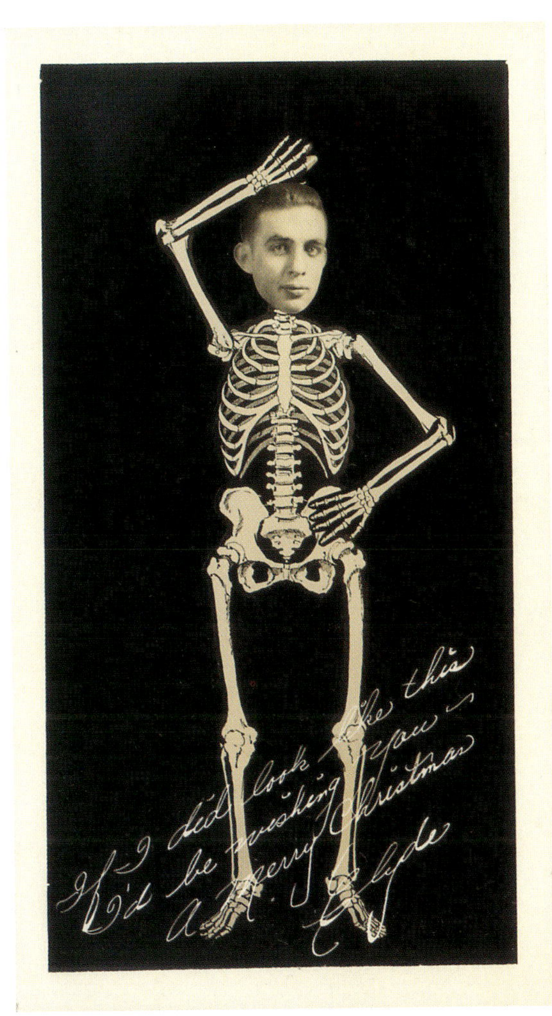
If I did look like this
I'd be wishing you
a Merry Christmas
Clyde

# Notes on the Photographs

Dimensions of works are given in centimetres and inches, height before width. Unless otherwise stated, all photographs are gelatin silver prints.

**a** – above, **b** – below, **c** – centre, **l** – left, **r** – right

1 USA, *c.* 1915. 7 x 7 (2¾ x 2¾)

2–3 France, *c.* 1960. 13 x 18.3 (5⅛ x 7 3/16)

4 USA, *c.* 1910. 13.7 x 8.7 (5⅜ x 3⅜)

6–7 UK, *c.* 1925. 19.3 x 27.8 (7⅝ x 10⅞)

9 USA, *c.* 1925. 8.8 x 14 (3½ x 5½)

10 UK, *c.* 1935. 24 x 19 (9⅜ x 7½)

11l USA, *c.* 1890. Cyanotype. 8.7 x 11.4 (3½ x 4½)

11r USA, *c.* 1940. 16.5 x 11.5 (6⅝ x 4½)

12 'Near Lyon railway station two thieves stole 500,000 Francs from a cashier.' France, *c.* 1950. 18.5 x 24.3 (7¼ x 9½)

13 USA, *c.* 1920. 9.3 x 9.3 (3⅝ x 3⅝)

15 USA, *c.* 1930. 10 x 6.8 (4 x 2 11/16)

17 USA, December 5, 1946. 11.4 x 9.1 (4½ x 3 7/16)

18l 'Judith, Roger, Joseph and Minna Flynn.' USA, *c.* 1917. 17.5 x 22.7 (6 15/16 x 8 15/16)

18r USA, *c.* 1960. 25.3 x 20.3 (10 x 8)

19 Japan, *c.* 1930. 15 x 10.7 (4⅛ x 6)

20 USA, *c.* 1920. 10 x 6.2 (4 x 2⅜)

21 USA, *c.* 1845. Hand-coloured sixth-plate daguerreotype. 7 x 5.7 (2¾ x 2¼)

22l USA, *c.* 1855. Sixth-plate ambrotype. 6.4 x 5 (2½ x 2)

22r USA, *c.* 1855. Sixth-plate ambrotype. 6.4 x 5 (2½ x 2)

23l USA, *c.* 1910. 13.3 x 8.1 (5¼ x 3¼)

23r USA, *c.* 1910. 13.3 x 8.1 (5¼ x 3¼)

24 USA, 1908. Mounted on a hand-embroidered frame with a calendar for 1909. 9.7 x 6.3 (3⅞ x 2½)

25 USA, *c.* 1917. Cyanotype clover collage. 12 x 8.7 (4¾ x 3½)

26 USA, *c.* 1920. 20 x 14.8 (7⅞ x 5 13/16)

27 USA, *c.* 1890. 12 x 9.2 (4⅝ x 3⅝)

28 USA, *c.* 1880. 14 x 10.3 (5½ x 4)

29 France, *c.* 1910. 17.5 x 12.5 (6⅞ x 4 15/16)

30 'Kaffir boys (Queenstown).' South Africa, *c.* 1910. 14.8 x 20.2 (5⅞ x 7⅞)

31 Europe, *c.* 1940. 19 x 12.5 (7½ x 5)

32 USA, *c.* 1910. 11.9 x 8 (4 11/16 x 3 3/16)

33 USA, *c.* 1960. 11.5 x 9.4 (4⅝ x 3⅝)

34 USA, *c.* 1850. Sixth-plate daguerreotype. 6.7 x 5.4 (2⅝ x 2⅛)

35 France, *c.* 1960. 23.7 x 17.5 (9⅜ x 6⅞)

36 'Dominique Aubert, uncle of the artist Paul Cézanne.' France, *c.* 1865. Albumen print. 15.7 x 12.6 (6⅛ x 5)

37 USA, *c.* 1855. Sixth-plate ambrotype. 6.4 x 5.3 (2½ x 2⅛)

38l USA, *c.* 1870. 13.3 x 9.7 (5 3/16 x 3 13/16)

38r USA, *c.* 1930. Hand-coloured print. 14.3 x 9 (5⅝ x 3⅝)

39l USA, *c.* 1910. 17.3 x 12 (6¾ x 4¾)

39r USA, *c.* 1925. 8.2 x 5.5 (3 3/16 x 2 3/16)

40 'After reading the newspaper and finding out how everything was going, Dr Jeremias greeted the Spanish girl.' France, *c.* 1915. 23.5 x 17.8 (9 3/16 x 7)

41 'Cesar, after the flu.' France, *c.* 1915. 22.7 x 18 (9 x 7⅛)

42 USA, *c.* 1917. 9.7 x 7.5 (3 13/16 x 2 15/16)

43 USA, *c.* 1910. 25.3 x 20.2 (9 15/16 x 7 15/16)

44a Postmarked Pulaski, New York, May 24, 1909. USA, *c.* 1909. 9 x 14 (3½ x 5½)

44b Postmarked Parlier, California, April 26, 1912. USA, *c.* 1912. 8.6 x 13.7 (3⅜ x 5⅜)

45a Postmarked Buford, California, June 28, 1907. USA, *c.* 1907. 8.8 x 13.8 (3 7/16 x 5 7/16)

45b Postmarked San Francisco, California, April 6, 1905. USA, *c.* 1905. Photograph with an original drawing dated April 6, 1905. 8.8 x 14 (3½ x 5½)

46l UK, *c.* 1865. Albumen print. 9.7 x 7.5 (3 13/16 x 2 15/16)

46r USA, *c.* 1970. 14.6 x 10.1 (5¾ x 4)

47 San Francisco. USA, *c.* 1960. 24.5 x 19.5 (9 11/16 x 7 11/16)

48a USA, *c.* 1940. 7.5 x 10.5 (3 x 4 3/16)

48b USA, *c.* 1960. 9 x 11.7 (3½ x 4⅝)

49 USA, *c.* 1900. Cyanotype. 12.6 x 9.5 (5 x 3¾)

50 USA, *c.* 1920. 10.3 x 14.6 (4 x 6)

51 France, *c.* 1930. 5.8 x 5.5 (2¼ x 2 3/16)

52 Natal police. South Africa, *c.* 1880. Albumen print. 19 x 14 (7½ x 5½)

53 San Francisco. USA, 1982. 15 x 10.3 (6 x 4)

54 'Rosebud St. George.' USA, *c.* 1920. 11.7 x 8.6 (4⅝ x 3⅝)

55 USA, *c.* 1930. 10.2 x 6 (4 x 2⅜)

56 France, *c.* 1870. Albumen print. 25.9 x 20.4 (10¼ x 8)

57 France, *c.* 1870. Albumen print. 26.6 x 20.3 (10½ x 8)

58 France, *c.* 1880. Albumen print (detail). 16.4 x 21.4 (6½ x 8½)

59 UK, *c.* 1900. Photograph hand-coloured by James Studio. 23 x 17.7 (9⅛ x 7)

60a Postmarked Pocahontas, Iowa, October 24, 1906. USA, *c.* 1906. 9 x 13.8 (3½ x 5½)

60b Postmarked Chicago, Illinois, February 14, 1907. USA, *c.* 1907. 9 x 13.8 (3½ x 5½)

61a Postmarked Rodney, Iowa, December 7, 1908. USA, *c.* 1908. 8.2 x 13.9 (3¼ x 5½)

61b 'Cléo de Mérode.' Postmarked 1908. France, *c.* 1908. 8.3 x 13.1 (3¼ x 5¼)

62–3 USA, *c.* 1925. 19.3 x 24.4 (7⅝ x 9⅝)

64–5 USA, *c.* 1920. 13.6 x 26.9 (5⅜ x 10⅝)

66 France, *c.* 1910. 20.6 x 15.5 (8⅛ x 6⅛)

67 France, *c.* 1900. 17 x 12.7 (6¾ x 5)

68l Germany, *c.* 1925. 11.4 x 8.3 (4½ x 3⅜)

68r France, *c.* 1930. 13.2 x 8.3 (5¼ x 3⅜)

69l USA, *c.* 1940. 10.3 x 9 (4⅛ x 3⅝)

69r Spain, *c.* 1960. 9.9 x 6.7 (3⅞ x 2⅝)

70 USA, *c.* 1930. 25.2 x 20.2 (9⅞ x 8)

71 'Ruby, Elise and Ruth, Pismo Beach.' USA, *c.* 1920. 13.4 x 7.8 (5 5/16 x 3)

72l USA, *c.* 1930. 22.9 x 11.5 (9 x 4½)

72r UK, *c.* 1910. 22.3 x 10.6 (8⅞ x 4¼)

73 USA, *c.* 1900. 13.2 x 7.9 (5¼ x 3⅛)

74a France, *c.* 1930. 8 x 12 (3⅛ x 4¾)

74b France, *c.* 1930. 8.6 x 13.7 (3⅜ x 5⅜)

75 France, *c.* 1930. 23 x 20.5 (9⅛ x 8⅛)

76 France, *c.* 1925. 21.5 x 16 (8½ x 6⅛)

77 USA, *c.* 1940. 24 x 19.5 (9½ x 7¾)

78 USA, *c.* 1940. 10.8 x 8.4 (4¼ x 3⅜)

79 USA, *c.* 1970. 24 x 19 (9½ x 7½)

80 USA, *c.* 1925. 7.9 x 5.4 (3⅛ x 2⅛)

81 France, *c.* 1980. 11.7 x 14.5 (4⅝ x 5¾)

82 USA, *c.* 1930. 7.9 x 5.4 (3⅛ x 2⅛)

83 'Grace R. and Elda Terrell.' USA, *c.* 1900 (detail). 9 x 11.8 (3½ x 4⅝)

84 USA, *c.* 1850. Quarter-plate daguerreotype, with face of woman rubbed out. 6.7 x 9.2 (2⅝ x 3⅝)

85 'Adaline H. Peck and George Henry Hulbison, before marrige Ma did not like her picture and cut it out [*sic*].' USA, *c.* 1880. 9.5 x 6.2 (3¾ x 2⅜)

86 USA, *c.* 1890. 12.2 x 16.5 (4⅞ x 6½)

87 'Where is he? Merry Xmas '98.' USA, 1898. 9.6 x 12.2 (3¾ x 4⅞)

88l UK, *c.* 1890. 15 x 10.2 (5⅞ x 4)

88r France, *c.* 1880. 15 x 10.1 (5⅞ x 4)

89l Germany, *c.* 1925. 13.2 x 8.1 (5¼ x 3¼)

89r France, *c.* 1925. 22.6 x 16.4 (8⅞ x 6½)

90–91 USA, *c.* 1930. 6 x 10.5 (2⅜ x 4⅛)

92 UK, *c.* 1880. 11.3 x 8.6 (4½ x 3⅜)

93l USA, *c.* 1900. 13.8 x 8.2 (5½ x 3¼)

93r USA, 1932. 14 x 8 (5½ x 3⅛)

94 USA, *c.* 1980. 10 x 12.9 (4 x 5⅛)

95 USA, 1966. 7.8 x 7.8 (3 1/16 x 3 1/16)

96 'Wedding in Straupitz 10.8.1935.' Germany, 1935. 8.2 x 5.2 (3¼ x 2 1/16)

97 USA, *c.* 1965. Polaroid print. 7.8 x 7.8 (3 1/16 x 3 1/16)

98 France, *c.* 1920. 11.8 x 16.8 (4⅝ x 6⅝)

98–99 'St. Clair, Michigan, U.S.A.' USA, *c.* 1920. 8.8 x 13.8 (3½ x 5½)

100 USA, *c.* 1970. 9.1 x 13.9 (3⅝ x 5½)

101 USA, *c.* 1980. 8.9 x 11.2 (3½ x 4⅜)

102 Shirley Temple, Honolulu. USA, *c.* 1930. 10.3 x 6 (4 1/16 x 2⅜)

103 Ellery Queen. USA, June 11, 1933. 12.6 x 10 (5 x 4)

104–05 Charlie Chaplin. USA, *c.* 1920. 16.1 x 23.1 (6⅜ x 9 1/16)

106 Cary Grant. USA, *c.* 1935. 11.4 x 7.5 (4½ x 3)

107 Richard Burton, *Look Back in Anger*. UK, *c.* 1950. 11.7 x 9.1 (4⅝ x 3⅝)

108 'D. W. Griffith, Director.' USA, *c.* 1920. 24 x 19.1 (9⅝ x 7½)

109 Arthur Miller. USA, *c.* 1960. 8.1 x 11 (3 3/16 x 4⅜)

110–11 'Howard Carter and Lord Carnarvon posed at the entrance of the tomb of Tutankhamun.' Egypt, 1924. 7.9 x 13.5 ($2\frac{13}{16}$ x $5\frac{5}{16}$)

112–13 'Mata Hari rehearsing outdoors.' France, *c.* 1915. 11.8 x 15.7 ($4\frac{5}{8}$ x $6\frac{3}{16}$)

113 Marlene Dietrich. France, *c.* 1930. 12.2 x 7.4 ($4\frac{13}{16}$ x $2\frac{7}{8}$)

114 'Teddy Roosevelt, and William McKinley on his left.' USA, *c.* 1901. 8.5 x 8.7 ($3\frac{5}{16}$ x $3\frac{7}{16}$)

114–15 Charles Lindbergh after landing in Paris. France, 1927 (detail). 10.8 x 16 ($4\frac{1}{4}$ x $6\frac{1}{4}$)

116 Benito Mussolini. Italy, *c.* 1925. 16.7 x 18.8 ($6\frac{5}{8}$ x $7\frac{3}{8}$)

117 Robert Kennedy at Norrbridge College the day he was shot, June 4, 1968. USA, 1968. 9.2 x 11.7 ($3\frac{5}{8}$ x $4\frac{5}{8}$)

118 'H.R.H. the Prince of Wales, in full dress as "Chief Morning Star", title bestowed on him at a pow-wow of Stony Creek Indians, Alberta, during his Canadian tour of 1919.' Canada, 1919. 20.4 x 15.3 (8 x 6)

119 Princess Elizabeth. UK, *c.* 1940. 17 x 13 ($6\frac{3}{4}$ x $5\frac{1}{8}$)

120 President Bill Clinton. USA, *c.* 1995. 10 x 15 (4 x 6)

121 Prime Minister Margaret Thatcher. USA, *c.* 1980. 25.3 x 20.2 (10 x 8)

122 Man in a false beard. USA, *c.* 1850. Sixth-plate ambrotype. 6.3 x 5 ($2\frac{1}{2}$ x 2)

123 USA, *c.* 1970. Polaroid print. 7.3 x 9 (3 x $3\frac{9}{16}$)

124 'Della, Mother, Ruby, Enid, Loretta, Lora. May 1st, 1913. Fambridge, Idaho.' USA, 1913. 16.3 x 21.9 ($6\frac{1}{2}$ x $8\frac{5}{8}$)

125l USA, *c.* 1910. 12.6 x 7.7 (5 x $3\frac{1}{16}$)

125r 'Beauty.' USA, *c.* 1890. 11.2 x 9.8 ($4\frac{3}{8}$ x $3\frac{7}{8}$)

126l USA, *c.* 1880. 13.7 x 9.8 ($5\frac{7}{16}$ x $3\frac{7}{8}$)

126r 'Schlitzie (right) and friend.' USA, *c.* 1930. 13.7 x 8.7 ($5\frac{7}{16}$ x $3\frac{7}{16}$)

127l Eng and Chang. USA, *c.* 1860. 8.6 x 5.4 ($3\frac{3}{8}$ x $2\frac{1}{8}$)

127r USA, *c.* 1930. 12.5 x 7.6 ($4\frac{15}{16}$ x 3)

128 'Circus star, fattest woman in the world (Alice from Dallas).' USA, *c.* 1930. 16.9 x 10.4 ($6\frac{5}{8}$ x $4\frac{1}{16}$)

129 'Zarkoff and R. C. Heagey, Hollywood.' USA, *c.* 1930. 25 x 20 ($9\frac{7}{8}$ x $7\frac{7}{8}$)

130 France, *c.* 1950. 18 x 17.6 ($7\frac{1}{8}$ x 7)

131 USA, *c.* 1960. 16.6 x 11.1 ($6\frac{9}{16}$ x $4\frac{3}{8}$)

132 USA, *c.* 1965. 21.7 x 16.6 ($8\frac{9}{16}$ x $6\frac{9}{16}$)

133 USA, *c.* 1940. 11.4 x 9.1 ($4\frac{1}{2}$ x $3\frac{1}{2}$)

134 USA, *c.* 1900. 10.1 x 13.2 (4 x $5\frac{1}{4}$)

135 USA, *c.* 1920. 16.7 x 19.6 ($6\frac{9}{16}$ x $7\frac{3}{4}$)

136 USA, *c.* 1920. 19.2 x 24 ($7\frac{9}{16}$ x $9\frac{1}{2}$)

137 'Marvelous Deyoes.' USA, *c.* 1890. 11.8 x 16.8 ($4\frac{5}{8}$ x $6\frac{5}{8}$)

138 Trick photography. USA, *c.* 1860. Sixth-plate ambrotype. 6.3 x 5 ($2\frac{1}{2}$ x 2)

139 France, *c.* 1920. 16.4 x 22.2 ($6\frac{1}{2}$ x $8\frac{3}{4}$)

140 USA, *c.* 1940. 9.2 x 11.9 ($3\frac{5}{8}$ x $4\frac{5}{8}$)

141 France, *c.* 1930. 10.9 x 8.2 ($4\frac{5}{16}$ x $3\frac{1}{4}$)

142 USA, *c.* 1910. 15.2 x 9.8 (6 x 4)

143 Czechoslovakia, *c.* 1930. 8.1 x 10.9 ($3\frac{1}{4}$ x $4\frac{5}{16}$)

144 France, *c.* 1860. Poster with five original albumen prints. 40.7 x 29.5 ($16\frac{1}{16}$ x $11\frac{5}{8}$)

145 'Zardo Trio Presenting Oddities in Jungleland.' USA, *c.* 1920. 18.2 x 23.3 ($7\frac{3}{16}$ x $9\frac{3}{16}$)

146 France, *c.* 1870. Albumen print. 15.4 x 12 ($6\frac{1}{8}$ x $4\frac{3}{4}$)

147 France, *c.* 1930. 23.8 x 17.9 ($9\frac{3}{8}$ x $7\frac{1}{16}$)

148 'Yum, Yum, The Kotton Kandy.' USA, *c.* 1930. 9.4 x 11 ($3\frac{3}{4}$ x $4\frac{3}{8}$)

149 USA, *c.* 1940. 11.5 x 16.4 ($4\frac{1}{2}$ x $6\frac{1}{2}$)

150a 'Tarpon caught at Hours Bluff.' USA, *c.* 1880. 14 x 9.6 ($5\frac{1}{2}$ x $3\frac{3}{4}$)

150b USA, *c.* 1900. 17.3 x 12.4 ($6\frac{13}{16}$ x $4\frac{7}{8}$)

150–51 UK, *c.* 1880. 20.5 x 24.4 ($8\frac{1}{8}$ x $9\frac{5}{8}$)

152 USA, *c.* 1930. 15.4 x 19.8 ($6\frac{1}{16}$ x $7\frac{13}{16}$)

153 UK, *c.* 1920. 16.5 x 11.3 ($6\frac{1}{2}$ x $4\frac{7}{16}$)

154 'A Reading Lesson.' UK, *c.* 1930. 19.2 x 14.1 ($7\frac{9}{16}$ x $5\frac{9}{16}$)

154–55 USA, *c.* 1890. 9.5 x 14.1 ($3\frac{3}{4}$ x $5\frac{9}{16}$)

156 France, *c.* 1930. 16.6 x 12.1 ($6\frac{9}{16}$ x $4\frac{3}{4}$)

157 Soviet Union, *c.* 1930. 23.8 x 15.3 ($9\frac{3}{8}$ x $6\frac{1}{16}$)

158a Running of the bulls, Pamplona. Spain, *c.* 1930. 12 x 8.9 ($4\frac{3}{4}$ x $3\frac{1}{2}$)

158b Running of the bulls, Pamplona. Spain, *c.* 1930. 12 x 8.9 ($4\frac{3}{4}$ x $3\frac{1}{2}$)

159 USA, *c.* 1890. 10.6 x 16.5 ($4\frac{3}{16}$ x $6\frac{1}{2}$)

160–61 USA, *c.* 1930. 6.7 x 19.3 ($2\frac{5}{8}$ x $7\frac{5}{8}$)

162 USA, *c.* 1960. 16.6 x 12.1 ($6\frac{9}{16}$ x $4\frac{3}{4}$)

163 USA, *c.* 1960. 16.3 x 11.3 ($6\frac{7}{16}$ x $4\frac{7}{16}$)

164–65 'Redwood Stump, 22 ft in Diameter, North Fort, Humboldt Co. California.' USA, *c.* 1870. 18.6 x 24 ($7\frac{5}{16}$ x $9\frac{1}{2}$)

166 USA, *c.* 1915. 23.6 x 17.4 ($9\frac{5}{16}$ x $6\frac{13}{16}$)

167 43-foot-tall Daibutsu, replica of the great Buddha of Kamakura, Japan, built in Muir Woods, California. USA, 1892. 19.6 x 14.5 ($7\frac{3}{4}$ x $5\frac{11}{16}$)

168–69 USA, *c.* 1920. 14 x 22.8 ($5\frac{1}{2}$ x 9)

170–71 De Young Museum, San Francisco. USA, *c.* 1930. 24.1 x 29.4 ($9\frac{1}{2}$ x $11\frac{9}{16}$)

171 USA, *c.* 1910. 11.2 x 8.6 ($4\frac{3}{8}$ x $3\frac{5}{8}$)

172al 'Halloween, 1908, Mildred.' USA, 1908. 11.2 x 8.7 ($4\frac{3}{8}$ x $3\frac{3}{8}$)

172ac USA, *c.* 1910. 13.8 x 8.1 ($5\frac{3}{8}$ x $3\frac{1}{4}$)

172ar USA, *c.* 1980. 15.1 x 10 (6 x 4)

172bl USA, 1951. 11.1 x 8.6 ($4\frac{3}{8}$ x $3\frac{3}{8}$)

172bc USA, *c.* 1955. 16.6 x 11.4 ($6\frac{1}{2}$ x $4\frac{1}{2}$)

172br USA, May 1988. 14.8 x 10 ($5\frac{7}{8}$ x 4)

173 USA, *c.* 1985. 12.3 x 8.9 ($4\frac{7}{8}$ x $3\frac{1}{2}$)

174 Lincoln Penitentiary, Lincoln, Nebraska. USA, *c.* 1910. 12.6 x 7.4 (5 x $2\frac{7}{8}$)

175 Influenza epidemic. USA, *c.* 1918. 9.6 x 7.4 ($3\frac{3}{4}$ x 3)

176l One-legged man. USA, *c.* 1880. Tintype. 6.7 x 3.9 ($2\frac{5}{8}$ x $1\frac{9}{16}$)

176r USA, *c.* 1900. 12.3 x 8.9 ($4\frac{7}{8}$ x $3\frac{1}{2}$)

177 USA, *c.* 1870. Albumen print. 18.9 x 13.3 ($7\frac{7}{16}$ x $5\frac{1}{4}$)

178 'Pigmented narvus.' USA, *c.* 1930. 16 x 11.5 ($6\frac{5}{16}$ x $4\frac{1}{2}$)

178–79 USA, *c.* 1925. 20 x 25 ($7\frac{7}{8}$ x $9\frac{7}{8}$)

180 'Young woman with elephantiasis.' USA, 1878. Artotype. 14 x 9.6 ($5\frac{1}{2}$ x $3\frac{3}{4}$)

181 'Bilateral hypertropy of both breasts, patient of Charles B. Porter M.D., Massachusetts General Hospital.' USA, *c.* 1893. Gelatin silver print, printed later from original negative. 15.9 x 11.6 ($6\frac{1}{4}$ x $4\frac{9}{16}$)

182 Ku Klux Klan members with their dog in a Ku Klux Klan outfit, inscribed 'Ku Klux Klan Honorary Member'. USA, *c.* 1920. 10.1 x 5.8 (4 x $2\frac{1}{4}$)

183 USA, *c.* 1920. 12.8 x 7.4 (5 x $2\frac{15}{16}$)

184a USA, 1914. 15 x 14 ($5\frac{7}{8}$ x $5\frac{1}{2}$)

184bl 'Antoinette Scierri, poisoner of St Gilles, condemned to death, P.P.P. 28/4/26.' France, 1926. 15.9 x 12 ($6\frac{1}{4}$ x $4\frac{3}{4}$)

184br 'John Robinson of London, who murdered Madame Bonati and cut her into pieces, P.P. 26/5/27.' France, 1927. 15.7 x 11.9 ($6\frac{3}{16}$ x $4\frac{11}{16}$)

185 Al Capone. USA, 1929. 21.9 x 10 ($8\frac{5}{8}$ x $4\frac{1}{16}$)

186a German prisoners. France, 1944. 11 x 17 ($4\frac{3}{8}$ x $6\frac{3}{4}$)

186b USA, *c.* 1930. 5.4 x 8.4 ($2\frac{1}{8}$ x $3\frac{5}{16}$)

187 USA, 1929. 18.4 x 23.7 ($7\frac{1}{4}$ x $9\frac{5}{16}$)

188l USA, *c.* 1880. 18.1 x 11.5 ($7\frac{1}{8}$ x $4\frac{1}{2}$)

188r 'Suicide from Police Pictures.' USA, 1932. 24.4 x 15.5 ($9\frac{5}{8}$ x $6\frac{1}{8}$)

189 Soviet Union, 1941. 15.4 x 22.7 ($6\frac{1}{16}$ x $8\frac{15}{16}$)

190–91 Brussels fire. Belgium, February 4, 1976. 16.4 x 23.8 ($6\frac{7}{16}$ x $9\frac{3}{8}$)

192 France, *c.* 1890. 15.2 x 10.6 (6 x $4\frac{3}{16}$)

193 USA, *c.* 1880. Tintype. 17.5 x 12.5 ($6\frac{7}{8}$ x $4\frac{15}{16}$)

194 Spain, *c.* 1890. 10.8 x 8.2 ($4\frac{1}{4}$ x $3\frac{1}{4}$)

195 USA, *c.* 1880. 11.4 x 9.3 ($4\frac{7}{16}$ x $3\frac{11}{16}$)

196 Czechoslovakia, *c.* 1920. 12.4 x 12.9 ($4\frac{7}{8}$ x $5\frac{1}{16}$)

197 USA, August 1885. 14.6 x 10.1 ($5\frac{3}{4}$ x 4)

198 USA, *c.* 1890. Cyanotype. 8.7 x 11.3 ($3\frac{7}{16}$ x $4\frac{7}{16}$)

199 USA, *c.* 1850. Quarter-plate daguerreotype. 8.8 x 6.3 ($3\frac{7}{16}$ x $2\frac{1}{2}$)

200 USA, *c.* 1910. 19 x 24 ($7\frac{1}{2}$ x $9\frac{1}{2}$)

201 USA, *c.* 1880. 15.8 x 20.6 ($6\frac{1}{4}$ x $8\frac{1}{8}$)

202 UK, *c.* 1900. 15.1 x 18.8 (6 x $7\frac{3}{8}$)

203 USA, *c.* 1910. 13.6 x 7.3 ($5\frac{3}{8}$ x $2\frac{7}{8}$)

208 USA, *c.* 1970. 8.8 x 8.6 ($3\frac{7}{16}$ x $3\frac{3}{8}$)

Endpapers 'Butte, Montana.' USA, *c.* 1920 (detail). 20.5 x 25.4 ($8\frac{1}{16}$ x 10)

## Collecting Anonymous Photographs

*'... acquire only what you yourself love. This is the basic law of wise collecting. Have faith in your own predilections. Back your own judgment. Blessed are they who say, "I don't know anything about art, but I know what I like," for they may inherit taste. Blighted are those who know all about art but don't like anything, for they will never collect at all.'*
**John Walker, *Self-Portrait with Donors*, 1974**

Both much has occurred and nothing has changed since my book *Anonymous* was published in 2004. There has been an ever-growing recognition of the aesthetic, historical and sociological implications of anonymous or found photography by the media, academia and the general public. Numerous books and articles have been published on this phenomenon. Several influential exhibitions on the subject have also taken place at such prestigious institutions as the International Center of Photography, New York, the J. Paul Getty Museum, Los Angeles, and the National Gallery of Art, Washington D.C. For the collector, this recognition is both a validation as to the worth of their collecting efforts in the past and a warning that the increased profile and prestige of this area of collecting may in the future encourage unreasonable expectations by others as to the worth of the images they possess. And yet, ultimately, the challenges and satisfactions attendant to collecting in this unorthodox field have not changed. It still only takes time, persistence, taste, sunblock and a little money to collect this type of photography.

How does one develop an 'eye' for collecting anonymous photographs, you may ask? The question recalls the words of Jeanette Winterson in her book *Art Objects*: 'Years ago, when I was living very briefly with a stockbroker who had a good cellar, I asked him how I could learn about wine. "Drink it," he said.' Because there are no names, only images, you must just plunge in and, through acquiring, create meaning in your collection one photograph at a time.

In an article in *Art and Auction Magazine*, John Dorfman wrote, 'There are few corners of the collecting world left where pure connoisseurship – and not wallet size – is what counts.... The future value of anonymous photographs will likely depend on provenance ... the eye that chooses the image today may well validate it for tomorrow's collectors.' Because anonymous photographs have no context and are essentially unique, the taste of the collector becomes a paramount factor in the forming of any collection. Years ago in San Francisco, a radio station had a tag line that said, 'If you don't like the news, go out and make some yourself.' In this fascinating yet chaotic area of the art market, opportunity awaits those who wish to define themselves and, in turn, their collection, by the individuality of their selections.

## Acknowledgments

Orson Welles used to tell the story that Billy Rose, the theatrical entrepreneur, saw *Citizen Kane* (1941), and on seeing Orson afterwards said, 'Quit, kid. You'll never top it. Quit while you're ahead.' And Orson later said, 'You know, maybe he was right.' I have often thought of that story while working on this present volume. The enthusiastic response to my earlier publication *Anonymous* (2004) by both critics and public has been gratifying. I had no desire to simply follow up that book with *Anonymous II*, but also realized that I had recently acquired many other amazing photographic images which were unknown to the world that merited being published. It seemed logical, since *Anonymous* was broadly themed, to have a greater focus in its sequel. As so many of the most intriguing photographs of this genre consist of people photographing each other, the idea for this volume was born.

Acknowledgment should be made to those collectors and curators who in recent years have shared my enthusiasm and had the courage to publish similar books under the broad theme that is increasingly known as vernacular photography. Although I am sure I have inadvertently overlooked some, they include Jason Bitner, Jeffrey Fraenkel, Michel Frizot, Nakki Goranin, Sarah Greenough, Marvin Heiferman, Babette Hines, Robert Jackson, Kirsten Jensen, Sarah Kennel, Barbara Levine, Tod Lippy, Frank Maresca, Charles Phoenix, Christian Skrein, Stephanie Snyder, Guy Strichery, Diane Waggoner, Thomas Walther and Mathew S. Witkovsky.

I will refrain from repeating the extensive list of friends, collectors, dealers, curators and scholars that were acknowledged in *Anonymous* except to say that their continued support, advice, encouragement and friendship is deeply appreciated.

In the autumn of 2004, an editor at the *Herald Magazine* in Glasgow hit upon the brilliant idea of sending copies of the newly published *Anonymous* to four distinguished Scottish novelists in order that they should each choose a photograph from the volume as the basis for a short story. The resulting stories were *The Ball* by Bernard MacLaverty, *The Important Thing is To Keep Smiling* by Alexander McCall Smith, *Empty Shoes* by Val McDermid and *The Ascension of Bartholomew Greathead* by Hannah McGill. Because the anonymous photographs they chose had no context, these authors seized upon images that came to life through the inventiveness and originality of their prose.

The present volume has the good fortune to have one of those authors, Alexander McCall Smith, write the introduction. The storytelling, insight and humour that McCall Smith brings to his scrutiny of these images is memorable. Under his influence, you may soon find yourself inventing dramatic scenarios for photographs you encounter in your own lives!

A sequel is an often-dangerous proposition in publishing and is usually to be avoided. I must thank my editor Jamie Camplin for realizing the potential of this present work and steadfastly supporting its publication. His admonition was that it wasn't worth doing if we did not aspire to make it an even better book than *Anonymous*. That task was put in the capable hands of Constance Kaine, who also worked her organizational and design magic on the earlier volume. She and the talented designer Jesse Holborn of Design Holborn have woven the many powerful and poignant images of humanity into a composite portrait representative of both the good and the bad in ourselves. Additionally, they put up with my suggestions and constant refining of the layout with endless good cheer. Acknowledgment should also be made to Mr Camplin's assistant, Helen Farr, for her always helpful assurance, and to Jenny Wilson for her professional editing of my manuscript. My assistant, Jamie O'Keefe, worked closely with me in the preparation of the manuscript, and I thank her for making a difficult task easier.

I dedicate this book to the memory of my parents who understood and encouraged my life in art, and to my family whose photographs keep us close when we are apart. May the photographs of your life always be treasured and passed down to people who care for them.

Robert Flynn Johnson

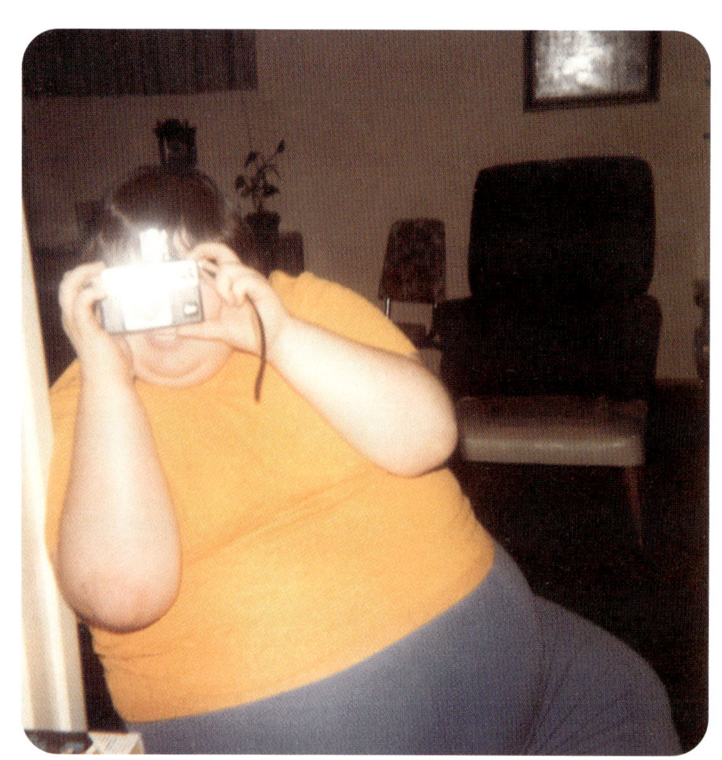

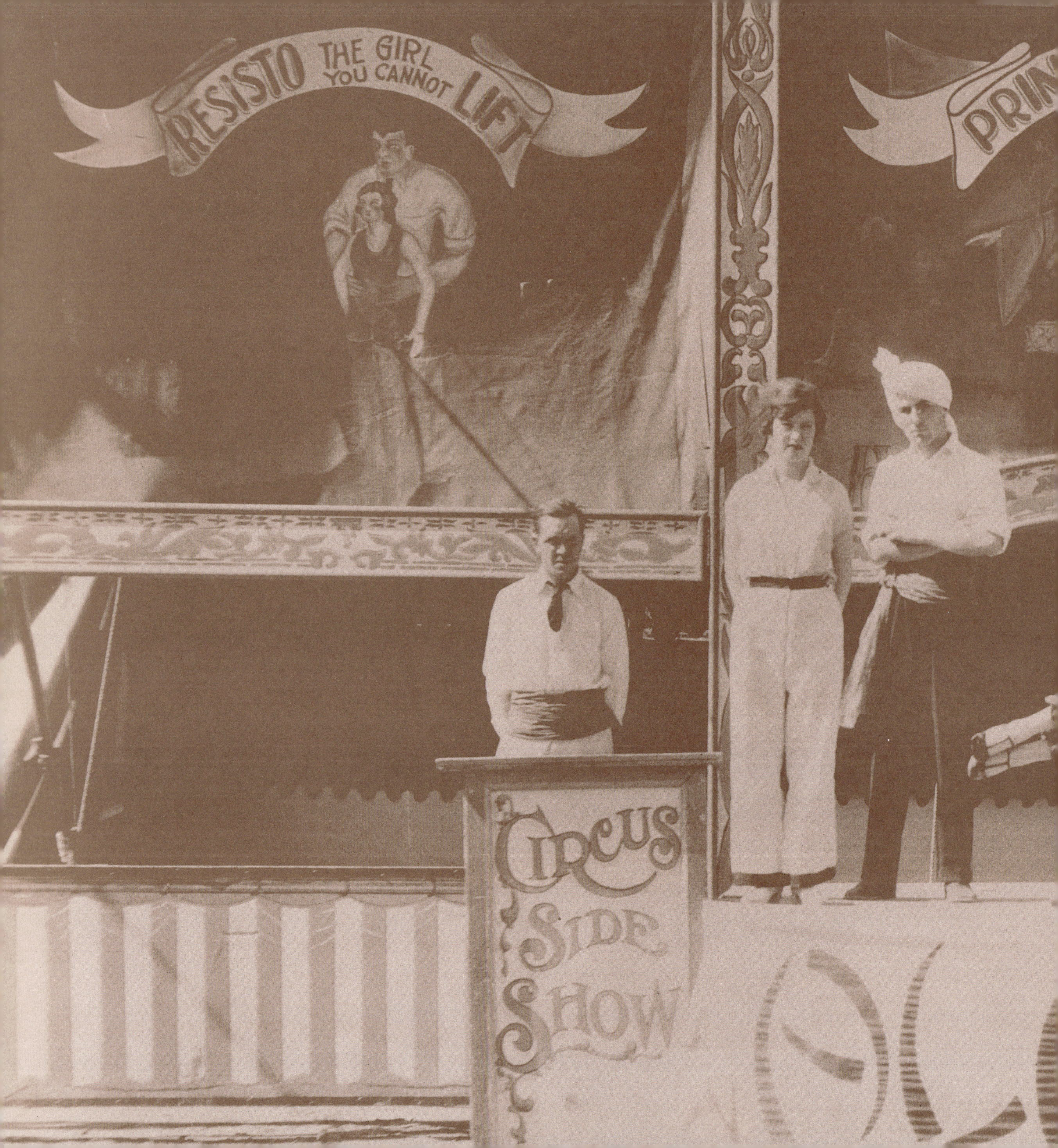
RESISTO THE GIRL YOU CANNOT LIFT
CIRCUS SIDE SHOW